Evolving Work

The idea of Self and the authenticity of particular identities have been rapidly dissolving in the acids of post-modern globalising capitalism. The hegemony of patterns of work, wage-labor and the operation of labour markets in the American West (and European North) has ridden rough-shod over distinctive ways of enabling communities to flourish in many parts of the Southern and Eastern worlds (Global South). But, this is not inevitable. Indeed, as this book indicates, there are many practical examples across the globe – that connect with some of the most significant theoretical challenges to the operation of dehumanising work – which reveal that a profound reversal is taking place. As such, the core theme of this book is to show that a movement is occurring whereby self-employment can be transformed into communal work that employs the Self in ways that release the authentic vocations of people, individually and collectively.

The approach taken in these chapters traverses the globe, utilising the original 'integral worlds' model that will be familiar to students of the Trans4M/Routledge Transformation and Innovation series, developed over more than a decade. Such a standpoint points the way to the release of particular social and economic cultures in each of what we term the four "realities" or "worldviews" of South, East, North and Western worlds. In this book we use the methodology of GENEalogy – identifying the realms associated with each world – to show how the rhythms, that is Grounding, Emergence, Navigation and Effect, of each is leading to greater economic, social and spiritual freedom for individuals, organisations, communities and, indeed, entire societies.

Ronnie Lessem is a co-founder of Trans4m. He has been a management educator and consultant in Africa, Asia, Europe and America and is the author of over 30 books on the development of self, business and society.

Tony Bradley is Tutor in Social Economy and a member of the research team within the SEARCH Centre of Liverpool Hope Business School. He has published a number of books and journal articles on green sociology, political economy and pastoral theology.

Transformation and Innovation
Series editors: Ronnie Lessem, Alexander Schieffer

This series on enterprise transformation and social innovation comprises a range of books informing practitioners, consultants, organisation developers, development agents and academics how businesses and other organisations, as well as the discipline of economics itself, can and will have to be transformed. The series prepares the ground for viable twenty-first-century enterprises and a sustainable macroeconomic system. A new kind of R & D, involving social, as well as technological innovation, needs to be supported by integrated and participative action research in the social sciences. Focusing on new, emerging kinds of public, social and sustainable entrepreneurship originating from all corners of the world and from different cultures, books in this series will help those operating at the interface between enterprise and society to mediate between the two and will help schools teaching management and economics to re-engage with their founding principles.

Finance at the Threshold
Rethinking the Real and Financial Economies
Christopher Houghton Budd

Culture and Economics in the Global Community
A Framework for Socioeconomic Development
Kensei Hiwaki

CARE-ing for Integral Development Series

Volume 4

Embodying Integral Development
A Holistic Approach
Ronnie Lessem

For more information about this series, please visit www.routledge.com/business/series/TANDI

Evolving Work
Employing Self and Community

Ronnie Lessem and Tony Bradley

LONDON AND NEW YORK

First published 2019 by Routledge

2 Park Square, Milton Park, Abingdon, Oxfordshire OX14 4RN
52 Vanderbilt Avenue, New York, NY 10017

Routledge is an imprint of the Taylor & Francis Group, an informa business

First issued in paperback 2020

British Library Cataloguing-in-Publication Data
A catalogue record for this book is available from the British Library

Library of Congress Cataloging-in-Publication Data
A catalog record for this book has been requested

ISBN: 978-0-8153-5607-3 (hbk)
ISBN: 978-0-367-51727-4 (pbk)

Typeset in Sabon
by Apex CoVantage, LLC

We dedicate this book to our respective three new grand-children, Saana, Ben and Tom, trusting that their experience of evolving work will be one through which they discover the fullness of well-being and life.

Contents

Figures

Tables

Part I

Introducing evolving work

Employing self and community

1 Centring

Releasing GENE-IUS: integrity at work

Preamble

Why write this book? It arises from personal experience, connected to what we see emerging in the rapidly changing world of work, across the globe. Personally speaking and firstly, each of us have been overwhelmed by the care we received from doctors, nurses and other healthcare professionals and teams. Ronnie (Samanyanga) had a recent stay in hospital, undergoing heart surgery. Tony had a major spinal health issue and temporary paralysis in 2004. In both circumstances we discovered that those who cared for us were not people simply working on a job. Each one had a vocation, which lay at the core of their professionalism and their employment – some paid, others volunteers – as selves-within-community.

A second, more longstanding, source of inspiration, for Ronnie, was his experience of *Chinyika*, in rural Zimbabwe, a decade ago. Through our *Trans4m Centre for Integral Development* (www.trans4m.com) based in Hotonnes, France – together with *Samanyanga*'s[1] partner, Alexander Schiffer (alias *Mukanya*) – we were engaged with our Zimbabwean colleagues (see Chapter 2), Dr Paul Muchineripi and Dr Steve Kada, in a program to promote food security. In short, the people in the village had been starving, and, three years later all 5,000 were food secure. In seven years the numbers of villagers who had become self-sufficient had grown from 5,000 to 300,000. And none of them had jobs. Equally, very few were self-employed, in any formal sense.

Yet they all now had *livelihoods*. As such they were employing themselves and their communities. What was happening and how did this connect to the vocation-led professionalism of so many in other worlds across the planet?

Thirdly then, through the work with which Trans4m has been engaged, in the four global corners, we discovered something fascinating. "Our shared business", as agents of transformation, was to enable the individual and institutional participants on our individual PhD and communal PHD (Process of Holistic Development) programmes to engage in both fundamental research and, also, transformative action. Now what we found, was that such fundamental research came relatively easily to those from the "developed" world – the US, UK, Germany and Switzerland, in our case. And transformative action came relatively easily to those in the "developing" world – Zimbabwe, South Africa, Nigeria, Egypt, Jordan, India, Sri Lanka and Brazil. But, hardly ever did the twain meet, research-and-transformation wise. Those two worlds, which are really four, as we shall see, virtually never got their act together, in concert.

Recolonised mental landscapes

So what had happened here? Pretty much all the "work in progress", with which we were concerned, as per "economic growth", "sustainable development", and "entrepreneurship" was at least conceptually – though not practically – rooted outside the global South. Furthermore, "empirical research" and "scientific socialism", "employment" as well as "self employment", were shamelessly borrowed by (or imposed on) the "south" and "east" from the "north" and "west". In Zimbabwe or Zambia, Nigeria or Nicaragua, "development agencies" and governments alike sought to "create jobs", to "develop entrepreneurs", or to "grow the economy". Yet go back a couple of hundred years, in the rural villages in these very same countries, and in Chinyika in Zimbabwe today, none of such existed. People had livelihoods but they did not have "jobs". People in Africa drew on "vital forces" (ntu), but did not pursue "enterprise".

And, now, in the developed world, as we turn from Greece to Portugal, from Spain to Italy, from Estonia to Slovenia, not to mention America's rustbelt, people are looking for employment, or increasingly seeking self-employment, and in many cases they will never find either! But, as we write, new figures are released to show UK employment at a 45-year high, but that half of all new jobs, since the end of the Western financial crisis of 2008–09, are in self-employment. To current minds, something strange is taking place.

So we started to read further. Standing out in our memories was the work of Clifford Douglas. He was a genius cost accountant and mechanical engineer (who you will meet in Chapter 15). In the 1920s Douglas maintained that in Britain, as things stood at the time, the state of technology was such that, if everyone worked just a few hours a week, there would be enough food and shelter, and other basic requisites of life, for everyone, worldwide. And, then, we discovered that John Maynard Keynes last century, and John Stuart Mill in the nineteenth century, had said almost the same. So what overall was going on?

Firstly, we invariably found that where there were these great insights, such as those of Douglas and Keynes, they invariably came from the "developed" world, in this case from the UK, and, then, generalised for the world at large. That hurt, because one of us is originally Zimbabwean, and proud of it, and have resisted the prospect of being once more colonised, at least this time mentally, if not physically, once again in this case by the British! The Brit in our pairing is, also, from Polish Jewish stock. Scratch under the surface of many British identities and you find an immigrant's history.

Missing the cultural release of economic genius

Secondly, as we shall see, the approach we have adopted – to recognising and releasing economic and cultural GENE-ius; that is Grounding, *Emergence*, *Navigation* and *Effect* – is invariably by-passed. That is because each one of these genetic elements is concentrated in one world or another, rather than incorporated together within one world, be it, for example, in Zimbabwe or Zanzibar, or, indeed, in the UK or US.

So, to begin, we turn to the overall Trans4m integral approach. Our concern in this book is to find ways and means of breaking out of the self/employment stranglehold of the "west" and "north" to, thereby, co-evolve the employment of Self and Community, more attuned to the "east" and "south". In this respect, we are questioning and redefining ancient wisdom on work, within a newly contemporary economy, for the emergent 21st century world.

As such, at each stage of our analysis, we identify where this communitarian wisdom emerges out of the spiritual narrative and (theological) principles of the major world traditions. Although we predominately focus on those from the Judaeo-Christian scriptures and the traditions associated with them, as they are most familiar to us, we also include chapters focused in Buddhist (Chapter 9) and Islamic (Chapter 17) traditions. At all points we identify with the *Ahl al Kitab*, or "People of the Book", aligned with the worldviews of other Faith communities, those of humanistic spirituality, and our contemporary integral worlds.

In each chapter we ask and seek to answer key questions about the nature of work, in seeing the shift from self/employment to the employment of Self and Communities. At the same time, we follow this theme utilising the transformative integral model, which roots each of the texts in this Routledge *Innovation and Transformation* series of books. The flow of the book, its Parts and chapters reflects this integral approach and pattern.

Integral realities and realms

Our (1, 2) approach to uncovering integral realities, or worldviews, both in ourselves and simultaneously and interactively, in our community/society, takes account of:

- *"Southern" Humanistic Reality:* we *experience* the world primarily through relationships: relationship to nature (including our inner nature) and to other human beings and to the community we belong to, and are enfolded within.

- *"Eastern" Holistic Reality:* we *imagine* the world primarily through an inner-directed cultural and spiritual perspective, seeking to understand the meaning of human existence, how life and the universe unfold within our particular community/society.
- *"Northern" Rational Reality:* we *interpret* the world primarily from a scientific, rational and systemic perspective, seeking to distinguish structures and processes within reality and to translate them into viable concepts and systems.
- *"Western" Pragmatic Reality (The Point of It (the West builds on the rest)):* we *act* on the world primarily through experimentation and practical treatment of things, emphasising the application of ideas through action, with a pre-emphasis on enterprise, in the realm of economics and finance.

We put the four worlds terms "southern", "eastern" and the like consistently in quotation marks. We do that to highlight their metaphorical meaning and to avoid an overly simplistic, singularly geographic association. What matters most is that we are able to recognise that each one of us, and to a degree each particular organisation, community and society, is engaged with one or other world, inwardly and outwardly (inevitably we are each a mix of worlds, but with one dominant).

Moreover, and overall, the humanistic (S), holistic (E), rational (N) and pragmatic (W) perspectives make up an integral totality. That said, from our standpoint, we identify that the first two – natural and cultural – should lead and the second two follow, rather than vice versa, as is the conventional wisdom of social and political economy. The four Parts of the book follow this logic, from "South" to "West", via "East" and "North".

We encourage each of us, as individuals, organisations and communities, if not as whole societies as well, to be aware of our particular reality (or combinations thereof). Equally, we acknowledge that each, personally or institutionally, holds only a part of the understanding of the totality. To understand the integral whole, we are also required to explore the worldviews (Realities) of others, be they individual human beings, private corporations, local communities or entire societies.

Being aware of, able to engage with, and to accommodate the rich diversity of alternative (pragmatic, rational, holistic and humanistic) worldviews is a crucial component of an integral approach to reality(ies). To do so provides a major developmental challenge, in a world in which the "west", together with the "north" has been so dominant, economically and intellectually. Through our integral perspective, we seek to counterbalance an undifferentiated globalisation, which is a rather tragic reduction to one monocultural (primarily "western") pragmatic Reality.

Engaging with each of these multiple Realities is key to knowing ourselves and the immediate organisation or community that we need to activate. These "four worlds" also provide the overall scaffolding for our book, thereby serving to ensure that the "south-east", where the employment of the Community and of the Self takes precedence, counteracts the dominance of the "north-west" experience and understanding of (self) employment, from whence respectively "entrepreneurship" (self-employment) and "jobs" (employment) duly hail.

Integral Rhythm and GENE

While firstly our integral *realities* (worldviews) and second *realms* (knowledge domains) provide what we call our static or stabilising elements, the dynamic is provided most especially, and thirdly, by what we term our integral *rhythm – grounding to effect*, combined with, fourthly, our integral *rounds – self to societal development*. Such a "rhythm", then, underlies the recognition and release of particular individual (self) and collective (community, organisation, society) GENE-ius, which is reflected in the flow of each of the following chapters.

Indeed, such an integral rhythm is our core social "system". In other words, such *G*rounding (origination), *E*mergence (foundation), *N*avigation (emancipation) and *E*ffect (transformation) constitutes our integral rhythm, or trajectory, as a whole, both individually and collectively. We now elaborate on such, bearing in mind that for each of the worldviews, we will be following the GENE rhythm (3), recognising that such does not come naturally to a society. Because of that, development remains inhibited, as a result.

- *G = Grounding and Origination: Cyclical – Experiential:* Community *activation:*

  Individually and collectively, we are *grounded* in a particular nature and community, which needs to be engaged with, if not also *activated*. For any living system, its grounds represent its *local identity* and its *source of origin*. Grounding is about *being in*, feeling and *experiencing*, as well as *describing* a particular world. Thereafter it continually cycles through, and indeed is recycled in *narrating* the stories we are. As such, and overall, we not only respond to a *call* (vocation), individually and collectively, but also begin to *activate* a Community.

- *E = Emergent Foundation: Spiralling – Imaginative:* Awakening *of consciousness*

  Moving to local-global emergence locates us and our community in a developing organisational and societal *context*, co-engaging with a *life world*, duly *interpreting* the imbalances therein, with a view to alleviating them. Here, we envisage dialectic interaction between "local and global", thereby coming to a newly imagined understanding, with a view to *awakening integral consciousness*. Such an emergent, spiralling process always includes a "stepping into the unknown" and "letting go" – thereby becoming as it were a *local-global non-entity* – of some of the previous assumptions. New insights emerge, from out of the blue, which provide clues for the transformative process. Emergence is therefore essentially about *becoming*. It deals with *intuiting* and *imagining* the new *emergent* form, contained in spaces in between one existing form and another. In this respect, what we understand as "spirituality" and "wisdom" each occupies a crucial place in awakening consciousness.

• N = *Emancipatory Navigation: Linear/Conceptual: Innovation driven Research*

The move to navigation requires that the new insights gained are trans-lated into new *concepts*, new systems, new knowledge, new tech-nologies, new institutions, that now assume global, or universal, proportions. Navigation is through *knowing* and about *making explicit* what hitherto had been implicit, through innovation-driven *research* (method and substance). *Navigation* is about activating the *mind*-level, the conceptualising prowess of the human system, through *critical* emancipatory thinking, without losing touch with the emotional and spiritual levels that came before. At this point we conceive a newly *global entity*, as a new concept or even institution, such as "employment of the Self and community", forming the basis for a universalising line of argument, or activity, between science and society, through *innovation-driven institutionalised* Research.

• E = *Transformative Effect: Point – Practical:* Embodying *integral development:*

Moving to effect, finally, requires us to put all prior three levels into integrated, *practical* and now *global-local* action. It is about prag-matically applying the new knowledge that has been developed, thereby actualising the research and innovation that it contains, in order to make a *contribution* to our *education*, organisation and/or society. Such effecting is about *doing* and about *making it happen*, thereby "to the point". This is the ultimate *transformative* level of the GENE-process, activating, metaphorically, the *body* or *hand*. This is the time where the newly global is actualised at a local level, through Embodying integral development, to realise ultimate *inte-grality*, what we term *embodying integral development*.

Core themes

The transformation of work

We now turn from the integral world structure of the book to its core themes. The idea of Self and the authenticity of particular identities have been rapidly dissolving in the acids of post-modern globalising capitalism. The hegemony of patterns of work, wage-labour and the operation of labour markets in the American West (and European North) has ridden rough-shod over distinctive ways of enabling communities to flourish, in many parts of the Southern and Eastern worlds (Global South).

For some time the demise of the conventional labour market and employment – as understood throughout the 20th century – has been predicted, as organisations move from jobs to roles and become 'more agile'. And, other patterns of work and employment are changing in the second and third decades of the 21st century. A recent report on changing employment legalities in the UK (4) concludes that labour market restructuring is still at the margins, but the pace of change is increasing rapidly.

Around 85% of UK workers remain in traditional employment, with 15% either in self-employment or as company directors. But, as commented previously, one-half of new jobs since the 2008–09 crash have been self-employed, with part-time work significantly increasing. Furthermore, the rapid growth of the so-called 'sharing' or 'gig economy' is disrupting many conventional work patterns, as is the growth in short-term consultancies and contracts. Additionally, the explosion of 'intelligent machines' threatens many industrial employment sectors, such that swathes of jobs are disappearing or being augmented.

These changes, alongside those of globalisation, the fiscal crisis of many nation states and the consolidation of Capital in fewer hands and corporations – with consequent eye-watering rises in levels of inequality globally – have all threatened labour markets and ripped the heart out of thousands of localities, threatening the very meanings of employment and the Self. But, this is neither inevitable nor necessarily an existential threat to people and their communities.

Indeed, as we indicate in each chapter – through our *Illustrative Cases*, as well as many other practical examples from across the globe, that connect with some of the most significant theoretical challenges to the operation of dehumanising work – a profound reversal is taking place. As such, a core theme of the book is to show that a movement is occurring whereby self-employment can, and is being, transformed into communal work that employs the Self in ways that release the authentic vocations of people, individually and collectively.

A storyline of work evolving in four integral parts

Employ community: South: communal up-skilling
to intentional community

As such, we begin in the Southern World/Reality of employing the community (Part II), looking at how identity, reciprocity, relationality and communalism are shaping the ways in which entire people groups are employed, beyond the atomising structures of Western labour markets. We begin

Table 1.1 The evolution of work – ultimate effects

	Grounding	Emergence	Navigation	Effect
EMPLOY COMMUNITY (S)	Confederal Association	Common Ownership	Commun-italism	Intentional Community
EMPLOYING THE SELF (E)	Dignified Livelihood	Blessed Work	Awakening of All	Cultural Capital
WORK AS RECREATION (N)	Immaterial Labour	Loving Work	Open Source	Socio-Technical Networking
INTEGRALLY (W) TOGETHER	Common Good	Godly Purpose	Co-operative Action	Communi-Preneurship

with grounding in community, through the Southern African example of Chinyika, Zimbabwe.

The ultimate outcomes (see Chapter 18) of our Evolving Work from this "Southern" worldly perspective – *Employing the Community* – follows the GENE work trajectory from CONFEDERAL ASSOCIATION (G), through COMMON OWNERSHIP (E) onto COMMUNITALISM (N) to INTENTIONAL COMMUNITIES (*E*). The introductory theme indicates that 'community' grounds the fundamental meaning of employment, albeit recognising that the idea of community needs reconstituting in the 21st century. In those situations, where community becomes the heart and framework for employment, local societies develop a livelihood beyond the atomised Self (see Table 1.1).

Employing the self: East: divine trade to cultural capital

From there we examine how employing the Self is a vital aspect of emerging a new world of work (Part III), based in Eastern values, culture and spirituality. Discovering true vocation, balancing life, recognising our common wealth and awakening to the needs of the Earth, others (especially indigenous peoples), and the purposes of life, each enable us to look outside our Self, to perceive a wider meaning to work. We begin our exploration of emerging an awakened Self-hood through the eyes of 13th-century Sufi Islamic mystic Ibn al Arabi.

In this eastern approach – *Employing the Self* – to Evolving Work we follow the GENE trajectory from DIGNIFIED LIVELIHOOD (G), to BLESSED WORK (E), onto AWAKENING OF ALL (N) contributing to and through CULTURAL CAPITAL (*E*). The introductory theme considers how realisation of true calling becomes the grounding for the employment of the Self. Turning towards a greater purpose reverses patterns of private ownership, stimulating fairer relationships in the world of employment, business and trade.

Beyond employment: North: rehoming work
to socio-technical networking

Navigating via the Northern world of technology and systems, we explore how the contemporary world is already beginning to turn from employment, towards an otium of the people, whereby work and recreation become interpenetrated (Part IV). Love can be expressed, further than our natural families, friendships and partnerships, to include the entire ecology, the ways in which we regard the time of our lives and where we place our priorities. At the same *time*, the rapidity of technological change is reconfiguring our relationships to machines, industry and the very meaning of work, such that how we plan for evolving work is becoming as vital a question in our day as was the organisation and management of factories a century ago.

In this northern approach – *Beyond Employment* – to Evolving Work follows the GENE trajectory from IMMATERIAL LABOUR (G), to LOVING WORK (E) to OPEN SOURCE (N) to SOCIO-TECHNICAL NETWORKING (E). The introductory theme examines how 'agape economics' offers a gritty response to the inequalities created by exploitative debt-based employment, both in the two-thirds world and left-behind regions of the 'developed' world. Turning towards recreative work has the result of increasing local economic solidarity and the rehoming of jobs.

Transform employment: West: blockchain distribution to
communipreneurship

Finally, we looked into some of the current and immediately prospective ways and experiments that are taking place to effectively realise and finance new models of employing self and community (Part V). Technological disruption is changing not only the *ways* in which we work but what we understand work *to be about*. Equally, the disruptive capacity of such innovations as distributed information systems and the blockchain are beginning to influence finance, markets and political institutions. Such changes are only at the very beginning of an adoptive cycle, so that it is highly speculative to say what reshaping of institutions will occur as a result. All we can say with any accuracy is that they will be profound.

That said, the degree to which some former economic policy models – such as universal basic income and social credit – are being publicised indicates that public policy-makers are preparing for an era when work, as we have known it for a century or more, will become a feature of life for only an increasingly smaller majority. Automation will probably take away one-third of the jobs that we currently regard as functional over the next two to three decades. Of course, these will be replaced by many new patterns of work and labour markets. But, for an increasing number of people, for longer periods of life, the idea of 'going to work' will become a marginal experience.

As such, we look at questions of revaluing our identities and digital footprints, the political economy of fiscal policies and redistributive systems, as banking and finance alter, and how integral financial institutions are enabling the employment of self and community, in radically new ways.

The effective Evolution of Work – *Transforming Employment* – in this final western part follows the GENE trajectory from COMMON GOOD (G), onto GODLY PURPOSE (E) into COOPERATIVE ACTION (N), finally actualised through COMMUNIPRENEURSHIP *(E)*, in the case we present in Nigeria. In that respect, we complete our cycle by returning to Africa, where we began. Equally, whilst we explore how spiritual wisdom and culture is an important aspect of reconceptualising the evolution of work, economies and society, we conclude by moving from the Judaeo-Christian tradition to that of Islam, integrating together our experience, as *Ahl al Kitab*, the People of the Book. The Ultimate Effects for the evolution of work, through the four Parts of this book, are summarised in Table 1.1.

Integrating scientia and sapientia

From the preceding account it will have become obvious that what we present here is not simply the product of contemporary reflections into the dominance and hegemony of Western economics on alternative global cultures. We take a radical turn in this book – in the direction of seeking to incorporate wisdom – because the origins of this approach have far deeper roots, in spiritual and humanistic philosophical worldviews, which have an ancient antecedence. To employ a medieval distinction of increasing relevance today, the book integrates *scientia* (science) with *sapientia* (wisdom) in its critical reflections on new models of work across the four worlds.

But, why have we chosen to incorporate this understanding and approach – taken from ancient spiritual texts – into a book on reshaping work within the economic cultures of the 21st century? Four genetic reasons stand out for us.

1   Community (G): *Indigenous wisdom is liberating for the 21st century mind and heart.* Many who feel held back or even imprisoned by the monocultural enterprise economics of the West and North often find ancient and indigenous wisdom liberating.
2   Consciousness (E): *In the 'age of integrality' people are looking back in order to move forward.* Second, it is possible to identify that much of the world is tired of post-modern scepticism. So, in order to grasp the dynamics of the integral we need to look back and deeper, if we are to move forward and further, especially in the area of reworking the sphere of employment into releasing Selfhood.

3   Science (N): *Indigenous (Eastern) wisdom emerges out of its grounding in the South, to influence contemporary scientific developments.* The inspiration of spirituality reinforces the cogency of the Four Worlds approach as a scientific model, which preferences the worldviews of the South and East over the West and North. The latter are needed, but only once the former are integrated.

4   Enterprise (E): *Ancient Scriptures have something to say to the post-postmodern world.* It is worth our looking at the worlds of work, employment and the changing economy and society through these wisdom lenses because they actually have something to say which is worth listening to. From the perspective of the revolving door of human philosophy, the Scriptures are both where we came in and, equally, the way out towards the new world of employing Self-in-Community.

How to read this book

There is a further structure to each of the chapters, which picks-up on the GENE dynamic. Each element of the GENE is reflected in a separate section of each chapter, developing the dialectic movement between scientia and sapientia.

Chapter sections – the smaller GENE

This means that alongside reading each chapter – for its position within the overall narrative of Realms and GENEalogical Rhythm – you may wish to read the smaller GENEalogy – from chapter to chapter – by moving between the sections that reflect each element:

• *The Burning Question* – focus on *Grounding (S)*
• *Window into Wisdom* box – focus on *Emergence (E)*
• *Social Theory* exploration – focus on *Navigation (N)*
• *Illustrative Case* box – focus on *Effect (W)*.

The pattern of each chapter follows this sequence of sections. From *The Burning Question* you move to a *Window into Wisdom*. Then, from the *Social Theory*, finally, to an *Illustrative Case*. This offers you, the reader, a range of different ways in which to interpret how the four worlds are brought together. It enables the development of a holistic and integral view of the movement of *Evolving Work* from self-employment to the *Employment of Self and Community*.

You may choose to read the book in a linear fashion. Equally, you may wish to follow the pattern of each element of the GENE, to pursue grounding themes, emergent wisdom, social theory or illustrative cases, from South, to East, to North and, thence, to West.

The overall work GENEalogies – the larger GENE

Table 1.2 offers a map covering the entire structure and pattern of content for the whole book. Again, it is offered as a way into seeing the complete development of the *GENEalogical work* analysis, for each of the four worlds.

Table 1.2 Work GENEalogies

G Employment of Community	Realm of Nature/ Community GROUNDING	Realm of Culture/Spiritual Consciousness EMERGING	Realm of Systems/ Science & Technology NAVIGATING	Realm of Politics/ Markets & Enterprise EFFECTING
Southern Grounding	Communal Identity	Pooling Vocations	Reproductive Economy	Communal Up-Skilling
Eastern Emergence	Gift Relationship	Emerging Reciprocity	Civil Economy	Emancipatory Work
Northern Navigation	Collaborative Platforms	Mutual Submission	Relational Paradigm	Humane Working
Western Effect	Confederal Association	Common Ownership	Communit-alism	Intentional Community
E Employing Self	Realm of Nature/ Community GROUNDING	Realm of Culture/Spiritual Consciousness EMERGING	Realm of Systems/ Science & Technology NAVIGATING	Realm of Politics/ Markets & Enterprise EFFECTING
Southern Grounding	Self-Realisation	True-Calling	Heart's Face	Divine Trade
Eastern Emergence	Home-Working	Spiritual House	Household Economy	Partner with Others
Northern Navigation	Ethical Egoism	Common Wealth	Associative Enterprise	Sustainable Livelihood
Western Effect	Dignified Livelihood	Blessed Work	Awakening of All	Cultural Capital
N Beyond Employment	Realm of Nature/ Community GROUNDING	Realm of Culture/ Spiritual Consciousness EMERGING	Realm of Systems/ Science & Technology NAVIGATING	Realm of Markets/ Politics & Enterprise EFFECTING
Southern Grounding	Agape Economics	Embodying Love	Living in Truth	Rehoming Work
Eastern Emergence	Sustainable Employment	Circular Working	Energetic Recreation	Regenerative Work
Northern Navigation	Automated Work	Connected Society	Redistributed Time	Work as Recreation
EFFECTING	Immaterial Labour	Loving Work	Open Source	Socio-Technical Networking

W Transforming Employment	*Realm of* Nature/ Community GROUNDING	*Realm of* Culture/Spiritual Consciousness EMERGING	*Realm of* Systems/ Science & Technology NAVIGATING	*Realm of* Politics/ Markets & Enterprise EFFECTING
Southern Grounding Eastern Emergence Northern Navigation Western Effect	Transformed Workplaces Valuing Identity National Balance Common Good	Service Values Universal Welfare Income Equality Godly Purpose	Moral Economy Basic Income Social Credit Cooperative Action	Blockchain Distribution People's Fund Citizen's Dividend Communi- Preneurship

Herein, we can see the GENE in operation, both within each world and across worlds. For example, vertically, where the Southern World (Employ Community), as its work-a-day world turns in the Realm of Nature/Community from *Grounding* to *Effect*, so *communal identity*, emerging spiritually through a *gift relationship*, navigating via *collaborative platforms*, builds effectively up towards a *confederal association*. At the same time, now moving horizontally across Realms, from *Nature/Southern Grounding* to *Market/Western Effecting*, we can see that a grounding in *communal identity* emerges through a *pooling of vocations*, navigated via a *reproductive economy*, ultimately rendered effective through *communal up-skilling*.

The same vertical and horizontal process is required for and across each world-of-work for the full evolution of work to materialise. That is the task we have set ourselves in this book, considering how *you* connect to *Evolving Work* and the transformation of *Employment* in the 21st century.

Note

1 This is Ronnie's Zimbabwean 'totem name'. These are not ascribed throughout sub-Saharan Africa. But, as a Zimbabwean by birth Ronnie fully merits his name, which means 'elephant'.

Bibliography

1 Lessem, R. and Schieffer, A. (2009) *Transformation Management: Toward the Integral Enterprise*. Abingdon: Routledge.
2 Schieffer, A. and Lessem, R. (2014) *Integral Development: Transforming the Potential of Individuals, Organizations and Societies*. Abingdon: Routledge.
3 Lessem, R. and Schieffer, A. (2015) *Integral Renewal: A Relational and Renewal Perspective*. Abingdon: Routledge.
4 Adam, S., Miller, H. and Pope, T. (2017) *Tax, Legal Form and the 'Gig Economy'*. London: Institute for Fiscal Studies. [Available at: www.ifs.org.uk/uploads/publications/budgets/gb2017/gb2017ch7.pdf].

Part II

South

Employing the community

2 Chinyika

Grounding local people: communal identity to communal upskilling

GROUNDING COMMUNITY
EMERGENT RECIPROCITY
NAVIGATING RELATIONSHIPS
MUTUAL EFFECT

Introduction: employing the community

Community activation

We start out by *grounding* ourselves in "Southern" Africa. But, not through proverbial self-employment and the flavour of today's western world, which promotes individual (social or economic) "entrepreneurship". Rather, we consider the *employment of the community*, creating livelihoods, not simply cycles of mass (un)employment. In order to do so we begin by asking the Burning Question: what does community mean in today's world? This is a vital theme running through the entire book, as we explore alternatives to the Western world's dominating understanding of work, as contractual employment, in which the Self is diminished and entire cultures are over-ridden.

We also turn in our opening Window into Wisdom to the Gospel of Luke (BQA South) and his particular emphasis on community and 'table ministry'. *The Parable of the Great Feast* invites a radical transformation of sharing in a common interest. Moreover, our initial Social Theory is the story – as narratives are vital in the South – of the practical feeding miracle of *Chinyika*. In this, we move from the "methodological individualism" of so much economics to the "ethnomethodology" of African sociology and society.

It is the story of how the Zimbabwean phoenix, or fish eagle, is rising from the ground of communal identity, through the creation of communal livelihoods, and evolving towards a global social integrity. Following from *Chinyika*, we conclude with our Illustrative Case of creating community through the projects of *Habitat for Humanity*. In the subsequent chapters (2–5) of this first Part, the rhythm of the GENE (see Introduction) takes us from Grounding (Employing Community) to: *Emergence* (Public Happiness); Navigation (the Relational Paradigm): and to the ultimate *Effect* (of Communitalism).

Burning Question: what is the contemporary meaning of 'community'?

Whilst we communicate the theme of 'community' in this chapter, this is not a term that is universally respected. Indeed, many social scientists are, generally, very suspicious of the ideological and mythological idyll connotations of the word. In 1955 Hillery (1) famously identified more than 90 meanings applied to the concept. 'Community', it is argued, is very frequently used as a theme to mask deep divisions, conflicts and inequalities within society, usually by those who control money, wealth and power. It may be used to reinforce paternalism and exploitation. At the same time, its 'lay' rather than academic usage in everyday discourse is undiminished. So, what do we mean by using the term, especially in relation to the "employment of community"?

Community as place

David Kirp (2) characterises the word as a "Rorschach blot upon which myriad hopes and fears are projected". Yet the concept was hardly used in social science until 1915, when C J Gilpin deployed it in relation to central-place theory, as the trade and services hinterland of a village or small town. After that its usage in rural sociology became ubiquitous, as we critically noted more than 30 years ago (3) in seeking to add to the growing disquiet with 'community studies' (cf 4, in their classic critique).

In tracing the historical roots of the idea Raymond Williams (5) saw that community was contrasted against society, to establish a sense of locality, immediacy, identity and personal meaning. But sociologists have generally outlined three sets of inter-connected understandings: place, interest and communion. The weakest of these, as we identified, is connected to place. Community was superseded by Stacey (6) and many political economists as 'local social system' or, 'space-as-place', as in Lefebvre's (7) triad. As such, urban political economy has developed a range of conceptions that have rendered 'community' redundant.

Community as interest

A middle-weight usage connects to the interests and networks that people have. We may talk about the 'gay community', the 'railway-enthusiasts community' or 'the Muslim community'. Often, this is a way of referring to others, to establish a social observatory. But, as Anthony Cohen (8) recognised, when people self-identify they may use community to establish belonging and attachment. Anthropologists have often noted that such attachments – especially when connected to place – may be less deep-rooted than the subjects submit (9). As Cohen comments, interest and identity reflect the fact that "people construct community symbolically, making it a resource and repository of meaning, and a referent of their identity" (op cit, 118).

In this acceptance community is connected to the vitality of a network, institution or place, but also to its capacity for generating social capital (10). Such a sense of community (SOC) relates to ethos and social values, such as integrity, honesty, reciprocity, trust, tolerance and, crucially, cooperation. The classic study by McMillan & Chavis (11) offered a fourfold interpretation of SOC, which directly aligns with the four worlds (see Chapter 1): membership identity (Southern), shared emotional or spiritual connection (Eastern), influence (Northern) and fulfilment of needs (Western). Whilst this model has sustained serious criticism for being far too restrictive (back to Hillery's 90+ meanings) it indicates that whilst Southern grounding if foundational, community has, itself, a developmental GENEalogy, which is represented throughout this book, as we will, once again, identify in Part V, on *Self, Enterprise and New Community*.

Community in communion

This leads to the third and strongest SOC, which is 'communion'. Zygmunt Bauman (12) has credibly indicated that SOC has become directly connected to the macro-level processes associated with globalisation. As my connections to the world enlarge (global village), they spread its productive and consumptive tentacles towards me and flatten differences, as in the homogeneity of so many shopping malls, so I seek to protect my community, its identity and solidarity. This returns us to another aspect of Cohen's insight, which is that the depth of community connections, equally, establishes liminality, boundary and separation from others.

Communion has obvious spiritual connotations in the Eucharistic meal. We will recognise this later, within *Chinyika* and *Habitat*, and their focus on hospitality.

Nor was the naming of *Koinonia Farm*, out of which *Habitat* grew, a superficial act. In the early Acts, Luke uses the GK word κοινωνια – usually translated as 'fellowship' – as a description of the new 'post-resurrection community'. It is noticeable that the fourfold Eucharistic action – taking, blessing, breaking, giving – actually indicates the GENE sequence in order (S-E-N-W), suggesting that this process is far more deeply rooted in spiritual community and communion than our current theoretical models might suggest. They have a deep and ancient ancestry in the human collective unconscious, which gives a fundamental meaning to community, as the seat of *reciprocity*, which is the economic foundation of the South.

As the Jewish theologian and philosopher Martin Buber (13) put it 'all real living is meeting'. He was expressing the view that in situations of real encounter (begegnung) then genuine relations (beziehung) are created. In this sense community is transcendent and transformational. Where there is real meeting between peoples who express a common identity, in situations that are profoundly shared, then, in such places that Buber calls 'the between' (spaces of liminality) the eternal is glimpsed. All indigenous traditions have words for this. Within the Celtic tradition we refer to 'thin places', where the boundary of heaven and earth is permeable. It places community in communion.

Community as solidarity

Such interpretations of community are increasingly evident in contemporary political economy. In many thousands of localities, cities and regions around the world there are movements to establish 'social and solidarity economies' (SSEs) (14). These exist to directly counter the impact of globalisation and the flight of capital between places, where the employment of labour is based simply in wage rates and levels of technical skill, for particular productive processes and industries. By contrast, in the solidarity economies there is an employment of community, as we see in *Chinyika* and *Habitat*, wherein the community of employment enables the Self to become surrendered within a more communitarian (communion) system of social and economic relations.

Nor are these isolated cases. As we will discover throughout this volume such situations of the "employment of self and community" are widespread. More than 2 million social and solidarity economy (SSE) organisations in Europe employ about 10% of the workforce. We examine several of these in later chapters, in Nepal, the Basque Region, Europe and North America, as well as in the South. These are economic and social drivers that are founded in community. As such, beyond whatever ideological and mythological idylls are connected to the term the reality is that the employment of self and community within real SSEs is releasing the economic genius of particular cultures across the globe.

Window into Wisdom: Lukan vocation – a table setting for all people

Both the *Chinyika* and *Habitat for Humanity* stories hold a common thread, which is to offer a place 'at the table' for everyone. This is a dominant theme within the theology and spirituality of St Luke's Gospel and the Acts of the Apostles.

The great procession

Throughout Luke's (Southern) Gospel we are presented with a universal hospitality. At key points in the opening chapters of the Gospel, the theme of 'all are called' is emphasised by Luke. Jew, Gentile, Roman or Greek, everyone is welcome at the table.

When Jesus is presented in the Temple shortly after his birth, the prophet Simeon proclaims Him as a 'light to lighten the Gentiles', not simply for the Jews (2:32). When John the Baptist announces the ministry of Jesus (as in each of the Synoptics) it is only Luke who adds "and all flesh will see the salvation of our God" (3:6). In the "Nazareth Manifesto", with which Luke, uniquely, indicates Jesus' self-declaration (4:14–30), He refers to Elijah raising the son of the Gentile widow of Zarapheth and Elisha healing Naaman the Syrian, while many Jewish lepers were left unclean.

Luke's Jesus associates with Gentiles, the poor, outcasts, those of low status and, most noticeably, women. The journey to Jerusalem is a procession of picking up the castoffs of society (the broken pieces) until the crowd of misfits disperses prior to the crucifixion, but, then, reassembles after the resurrection. Furthermore, the central section (Chapters 5–19) of the gospel contains a repeating series of encounters between Jesus and 'sinners'. This is framed by two specific references to offering new vocations, to Levi (Matthew) the tax collector (5:27–32) and Zacchaeus, another tax collector (19:1–10). Levi is 'called' as a sinner; Zacchaeus is called, in order for Jesus to visit his house. Throughout the gospel Jesus has meals, shares tables with and 'eats with sinners'. The gathering of all the marginalised is very frequently linked with hospitality.

The great banquet

Luke has many more meal scenes in his gospel than each of the other Synoptics. In other words, the economy of the kingdom, for Luke, is built around table fellowship with people who are called from the world of money, not to renounce it, but to see it in perspective, as Jesus breaks bread with them. God's economy is within a real, human economy, where self-employed economics is importantly challenged and is transformed into the employment of community. Luke presents several encounters where the (Western) money-men, like Levi and Zacchaeus, are brought into the (Southern) community, turned (Eastwards) to God and develop a new (Northern) framework for living.

The gospel is full of meals, hospitality and table-talk, where those who are close-to-death find life. But, the meals in Luke also function as metaphors for and reminders of the eschatological banquet in the fully realised kingdom of God. Apart from Luke's account of The Last Supper, the most significant meal scene takes place in Chapter 14, when Jesus attends a banquet of one of the leading Pharisees and, during the course of the meal, tells the *Parable of the Great Banquet.*

A rich and powerful man was preparing to hold a magnificent banquet and tells his servants to send out a message to say that the meal was prepared. Clearly, this was an important preplanned event. But, when all the important guests received their invitations they made excuses – they had self-employed work to do on the farm; they needed to check their possessions; they were recently married and had other things to attend to.

So, the rich man, in his rage, orders the servants to go out and bring 'the poor, crippled, blind and lame' to the great meal. But, even after they do, they report to their master that there is plenty of room left. At which point he commands them to go into the highways and by-ways, round up all who are on the streets and compel them, forcibly, to attend the banquet. None of those important people who had received a prior invitation would ever taste his banqueting food. The implication of the story was clear: those who expected to come to the heavenly feast would not make it; instead God's eschatological banquet was to be populated by the marginal, the outcasts, sinners and the homeless, starving poor.

In this Southern (BQA) Gospel Luke presents Jesus as calling all those who have no (positive) identity in the society in which they lived to share at his table. It was a feeding miracle for those who had lost their identity and needed to find it, rather as those in *Chinyika*, as we shall see, were both fed and had their ancient identity restored through the recovery of the lost ark. In so doing, vocation shifts from being about a specific self-identity to one in which each person's identity is subsumed within the community. But, this is not in the way of Maoist Communism or the Soviet Gulags. The surrender of Self (employment) is through incorporation into a sharing body, where the community is welcomed and employed together. Most profoundly this is reflected in the 'primitive communalism' of the early Church, recorded by Like (Acts 4:32–35). The fourfold quaternity of the transformed Self-in-Community is, once again, evident. They were together in *heart* and *mind*; God's grace connects their *souls*, releasing the *strength*ening effect of sharing food, possessions, land and housing, just as in *Chinyika* and *Habitat for Humanity.*

Chinyika – activating community livelihood

After the west dominates the rest – picking-up the broken pieces

The Shona, in Zimbabwe, think of their great, founding heroes and ancestral sprits, the *mhondoro, who* taught them to smelt iron from the rocks and how to grow millet and sorghum. The ancestors gave them identity, ancestral wisdom and 'a torch' to hand from generation-to-generation (15), guaranteeing the onward movement of life, just as Moses had done for the Israelites, seeking the Promised Land.

Spiritual belief systems equally lay at the heart of Chinyika's evolution in rural Zimbabwe (16). Both Muchineripi, based in Karanga, and Kada, based in Baremba, saw themselves as connected with those ancestors to whom super-sensible power had revealed the land and how to prosper. Whether 'God' or the 'ancestral channel of the life force', each is intrinsic to the African commons and grounded the work of the two 'good doctors'.

The 'Shona' represents a much broader region of precolonial southern Africa than Zimbabwe, according to Raftopoulos (17), with a multiplicity of self-identifications. Zimbabwe is a late 19th-century invention, superimposed on peoples of the Hole, vaNyai or, most commonly, Karanga. The latter, together with the Baremba, feature centrally in the Chinyika story, in terms of their psychic and collective individuation.

The Baremba share a common identity as inheritors of a proud empire and as a pilgrim people, who trace their origins back to Judea, and to Sanna in Yemen. Raftopoulos sees precolonial Zimbabwe as bringing together the broken fragments, into new identities. But, importantly, there was then no recognition, over that extensive historical period, of people seeking "employment" or "jobs". Rather, they were communities on the move.

As such, the Chinyika story, as told by Muchineripi and Kada, takes on from where this overall situation, as per Raftopoulos and for Davidson, leave off. Elsewhere (16) we have told the story of (individual) Paul Chidara (communal) Muchineripi's Royal Chieftainship and Steve Kada's family and early personal history and how their collective work was catalysed by the intervention of Geneva-based NGO, Trans4m. Their studies together and the connection of Muchineripi's communal homeland with their work for Cairns Foods proved truly transformative, in replaying the ancestral history and agronomy of Muchineripi's heritage, through the traditional crops of finger millet (*'zviyo'*), and pearl millet (*'mhunga'*).

Now, we pick up the pieces of this story as it further connects to the movement from self-employment to communal livelihood amongst the 'black Jews', the Baremba people of Chinyika. The structure underlying the Chinyika story, in Trans4mative terms, as we shall see, is that of recognising, and releasing, "southern" GENE-ius, by employing the whole community. In the process we serve to create livelihoods, not jobs, by drawing upon the social commons. Muchineripi and Kada *saw two worlds coming together*. What followed this coming together was a longstanding relationship between Cairns Foods and the Chinyika people.

When black meets white: emergent revelations and the lost ark

It is important to recognise the place of revelation, pilgrimage and the incorporation of identities into a community that is at the heart of the Chinyika story. Chidara and Steve had been spending many hours together, during their studies, travelling together to South Africa and lodging in a small hotel room – back to their 1980 college days. History was repeating itself, from young men to old, replaying their lives.

Furthermore, it was revealed to Steve that Chidara's wife's totem was 'hwesa/mbeva' or mouse, which was also his African totem. They began to review their relational status. Chidara became Steve's 'mukuwasha' brother-in-law because his wife is Steve's sister in terms of their culture. It made him happy that his "sister" was married into the Karanga royal family since Chidara is Gutu Chief designate. What became of even greater significance was that the totem 'mbeva' – the mouse – is that of the Lemba (or Baremba) people. Therefore, Chidara's wife Nakirai is Lemba and her whole tribe is now living in Gutu, where Chinyika is based.

Steve's further revelation was that he had been walking on the road to his ancestral linkages. Steve's home is in Mutasa on the eastern side of Zimbabwe where his original birthplace is in Katerere, the land of the Hwesa Mbeva who are a group of Lemba descendants. In December 2009, Ronnie visited Zimbabwe, together with Trans4m's co-founder Alexander Schieffer, to come and meet the Chinyika community.

While they were interacting with the Chinyika people, the MP for the local Gutu area visited the gathering, introduced himself and addressed the people. He however later said that his main mission was to meet his brother, the white Jew who was present, Ronnie (Samanyanga) Lessem. After this, further investigations by Steve led to more findings regarding the assertion by the Wa-Remba MP that his people were black Jews. They realised that Professor Tudor Parfitt (18), from the School of African and Oriental Studies in London, had carried out extensive research and written a book – *The Lost Ark of the Covenant* – about the Wa-Remba in Zimbabwe, especially those in Gutu, Shurugwi and Limpopo.

Professor Parfitt's lengthy research was based on the search for the lost ark of the covenant of the Jews. As such he researched into the history of the Wa-Remba or Baremba and their ark – the *Ngoma Lungundu*. This was said to have been brought into Zimbabwe and hidden in a mountain cave in the southern part of the country. Parfitt ultimately stumbled upon the 'Ngoma Lungundu' stored in the archives of the Harare museum and announced his findings. What followed was a political, theological and academic commotion over the alleged authenticity of the discovery. The significance for Steve is that he now finds himself having the right to assert who he is locally, as an African in the Zimbabwean nation, and now also as a Jew in a global context.

In relation to Chinyika, as we shall see moreover, the Ngoma Lungundu besides being an artefact, has a spiritual power of renewal for the Lemba and Chinyika community in Gutu. This is an opportunity for the local community to look outside and connect with a global platform. While the Ngoma Lungundu 'drum' (ark of the covenant) lies in peace and serenity in the museum, in Harare, it is calling out loudly for the Lemba and the world, via Kada, to be reawakened to the values of personhood and to the integration of communal indigenous and individual exogenous knowledge. It is providing Southern African knowledge-creating communities with a challenge to revisit their history, religion and intellectual values for purposes of creating an integrated local and global community.

From a Christian perspective, the ark of the convent with its inscribed commandments is lodged in the hearts of mankind, including here in Zimbabwe. The first inscription is taken from the Shema, the Jewish prayer of the Great Commandment, used every morning and evening (Deuteronomy 6:4–9; 11: 13–21; Numbers 15:37–41). It is summarised by Luke 10:25–27, as *'Hear, O Israel, the Lord your God is one Lord, and you must love the Lord your God with your whole heart and with your whole soul and with your whole mind and with your whole strength.'* The second is this, *'You must love your neighbour as yourself.'* (Leviticus 19:18) *There is no other commandment greater than these.'*

This is, for Kada, what all individuals, organisations, and nations should be concerned with, acknowledging the universal sovereignty of the Creator and the practical humaneness and value sharing of southern African 'ubuntu' (I am because you are). *Africa, from its heart then, was privileged with the quality of brotherhood and human passion which it must share with the rest of the world: Steve's mother's plea – 'Uri munhu here?'* We now turn more specifically to the actuality of the Chinyika project.

The actor network: rapoko/Chinyika/Cairns Food/ Zimbabwean government/Trans4m

A wake-up call

Out of the Chinyika community, then, in Steve Kada's words, *a son was raised from the house of the Gutu chieftainship, and was moved by the suffering of his own Chinyika community. He woke up to the call of his ancestors to save his people from the scourge of hunger and poverty.* Chidara then, who, from an urban and exogenous perspective, had become a successfully "self-employed" business person and management educator.

But, he had a wake-up call from his slumber of individual success, prompted by his studies in social and economic transformation, and offering him a vocation to respond to his 'father's communal voice'. More importantly, awareness gripped him and reminded him of his communal responsibility to his people as the son of a chief. Emotively aroused, he initially decided to feed the people who were starving in Chinyika by buying bags of mealie meal (corn) and grain, and distributing these to them.

While in the process of facing this challenge and responding to his 'father's voice' to take care of his people, Chidara had enrolled on the Trans4m masters (MSET), unknowingly together with Steve, in 2005. That was the beginning of the establishment of the Chinyika Community Development Project. *Chidara then reconnected with the voice and vocation that called his people to revisit the source of their food security in the past, the nutritious food and meals that came out of the sweat of their labour. They had been a community that never starved.*

Transformation journey: (self) employed/employing self-community

The voice of the Chinyika community echoed through poems and drama. One villager, at a field day function inspiringly recited the poem:

> 'The grass that turns into gold
> The grass that gives people their livelihood
> The grass that is fed to people and their livestock
> The grass that connects the Chinyika people with the ancestral spirits
> The grass that makes and gives life to people, the grass that turns to gold
>   the magical grass.'

The poem summarises the value and the importance of finger millet, one of the 'key actors', as it were, for the Chinyika community. The golden grain, rapoko, was going to play a critical role in their transformation journey. It would be at the centre of all their activities in developing food security in the Chinyika households. Through this revisitation of the past, Chidara reconnected with the tradition and culture of growing indigenous small grains. For him, the voice of his father had always echoed as a vocation – to serve the community – throughout his lifetime. At the same time, his mother, while she was alive, had not abandoned the clan's adopted exogenously based cultural farming norms, and she remained an indigenous custodian and implementer of the traditional grain growing and food preparation. She was a typical African mother of her community.

Chidara's father, as a chief, had passed on the oral tradition of a true African to his family and subjects. "A true African does not completely abandon his culture despite getting a western education. Western individual education had its virtues but the communal African has to maintain his humane nature".

It is considered immoral, as such, to watch and let a poor person or family perish of hunger when the other person has more than enough. As in the *Parable of the Good Samaritan*, it is a moral crime to pass-by on the other side. Chief Chitsa of Chinyika, in addressing people on one of the field days said, '*Munhu ega ega, mwana ega ega anofanira kuziva kwaakabva*' translated as: "*Each person, each child must look back and know where they came from and be responsible to himself* (employ himself) *and his community* (employ his community) *like what we have witnessed today. Our son Paul has demonstrated that each one of us must be responsible to their people*".

Public–private–civic partnership

Chidara then, representing Chinyika community in his capacity as designate chief and Steve representing the business sector, as HR Director of Cairns Foods, played their respective catalytic roles. As such they created a relationship between the private sector and the rural community, thereby institutionally extending – with the Zimbabwean Department of Agriculture ultimately also playing its governmental part – the *communal actor network*.

On the one hand, Cairns Foods, through their agronomists, provided the Chinyika community with technical advice in growing the traditional and horticultural crops. On the other hand, the Chinyika people provided Cairns Foods with a wealth of knowledge for purposes of product development. Cairns, in its own transformation process, was turning towards foods with a traditional base and flavour in addition to the current western oriented food products on the market.

Cairns in fact, at the time in 2005, produced western products like wines, cornflakes, breakfast jams and tinned vegetables. Thereafter, through its newly constituted research and development team, it evolved a product prepared from small grains, specifically sorghum and rapoko. *The urban African elite was now turning to more traditionally based products like porridges, peanut butter, and organically grown crops.* A market opportunity for traditional small grains like rapoko, peanuts and pumpkins was slowly emerging. Through the private sector, production of these high nutrient content foods, together with communities like Chinyika, resulted. At the same time, the government-sponsored agricultural extension officers had hailed the reintroduction of rapoko on a greater scale than before. Altogether they revisited the traditional knowledge base of growing rapoko and preparation of the delicious meals that the people are now enjoying.

The Karanga people who constitute the majority of the Chinyika people, in fact, are known as people of the soil. Their life depends on the soil, for they till it. They grow their crops on it and draw water from the ground. They bury their dead in the soil. Soil is their natural and communal power. It gives them their identity. It is as if the rock came to life, talked through the people and offered them a communal vocation. The spirit engulfed everyone who sat or stood on the rock.

> *Arise the children of Chinyika*
> *Arise and be who you should be!*

Indeed the people of Chinyika did arise to democratic communal effect.

Towards a democratic village community

Through the reawakening that has been taking place among the Chinyika community, as well as in neighbouring communities today – the feeding miracle has extended from 5,000 people (pace Luke 9:10–17) in 2006 to up to 300,000 in 2017 – individual effort is being channelled, and realised, to ultimately employ the community, thereby creating rural livelihoods. Such practical realisation is encouraged to the extent that it does not create selfish egoistic individuals. *The unifying force between the individual and the community is the focus on fighting the resurgence of food insecurity and the continued battle against poverty. Through meetings and sharing information, facilitated by researchers*, the capacity and strength that the people have in growing enough food and to alleviate poverty has been enhanced, without feeling isolated and 'individualistic'.

In order to coordinate these developments the leadership originally drew from the villages' horizontal structures. *Through a democratic process in the traditional manner, the Chief, headman, counsellors, village development committees, and extension services personnel were all involved*, consulted and contributed to the selection of the project leadership. The leadership, headed by Mai Tembo (Mrs Tembo) has clearly outlined its goals and strategy *specifically to fight hunger through growing rapoko and in the long run eliminate poverty*. They have clearly distanced themselves from the very sensitive, and indeed alien, partisan politics. They do not align the project farming activities with any political groupings. The committees' main purpose has remained that *of building a community consciousness that creates enlightened peoples actions to fight both mind and material poverty; to thereby decolonise the mind*.

The role of women redefined

In the process of putting together the project leadership, the role of a woman has been redefined. The challenge *to take up responsibility has been greatly accepted by the women of the community*. This has been evidenced by the number of women who turn out for the project meetings. In fact, the attending of meetings, the field days involving demonstrations of ploughing, sowing and harvesting have mostly been led by the Chinyika women.

Women's self-expression has manifested itself through recreation, specifically through drama and singing. *The large gatherings provide an opportunity*

*for women to sing and dramatise the social and economic challenges fac-
ing the community.* Their drama illustrates the problems of irresponsible
and lazy fathers and mothers who do not work hard in their fields; about
fathers who spend most of their time drinking and neglecting families. They
also highlight problems created by disease like HIV/Aids. Although men
participate in these dramas it cannot be denied that it is usually a women's
initiative. Mothers are out to educate both the young and old. *Mothers have
awoken to take up their traditional role – the home stands because of the
mother – 'Musha ndimai'.*

Self sufficiency to cash economy: only to a point

The contribution then to a successful rapoko harvest cannot be under-
played. *The active participation of the women has had a profound impact in
the whole farming project.* The village harvest had recorded average yields
of between 1 and 2 tonnes per household unit. Most of the grain has been
retained for consumption by the families. There was however surplus ton-
nage which community members agreed to sell and raise income for themselves. The idea was to ensure better yields for the coming season, so that
families could sell more grains than they sold in 2009.

Muchineripi rock: releasing the GENE-ius of Chinyika: employing self-and-community

In fact Chidara and Steve were introduced, on the masters program mentioned previously, to the GENE cycle of transformation, based on our (19)
"four worlds". First it involved Grounding in and *Community activation* of
indigenous soil, in their case most specifically that of Chinyika. Second, it
involved Emergence and *Awakening integral consciousness*, through a process of co-evolution, in partnership with Cairns Food and its agronomists.
At the same time, Cairns Food itself was awakened to its African heritage,
which led to a culturally more authentic approach to doing business. Third,
a Navigational and Knowledge Creation (*conceptualising*) role was played
by the government's agricultural extension officers, by the agronomists from
Cairns, and, indirectly perhaps, by Trans4M (Geneva), altogether serving to
promote *innovation driven institutionalised Research*, and finally an *actualising E*ffect by the Chinyika people, *Embodying integral development*.
Thereby, and altogether, they CARE.

The enduring communal effect, for 5,000 in the first decade and ultimately for 300,000 villagers in the second decade of the new millennium, was the realisation of food security. This remarkable movement
has served to employ the community through Chidara and Steve, together
with Mai Mlambo, employing their self-actualising selves. But, without
the integration of a Northern worldview the holistic Chinyika is yet to be
effected. Chinyika holds out the vision for a model of food security, for an
entire "southern" approach to creating livelihoods, through employing a

community as a whole, which transcends the "western" approach to (self) employment. *Habitat for Humanity*, as we shall see, is both similar, in employing community, and different, in that it is now spread across our four worlds.

Illustrative Case: Habitat for Humanity

The message of Koinonia

During the height of the Second World War – predating the American countercultural movement by at least twenty years – two couples founded a Christian utopian commune that would, thirty-five years later, spawn one of the most significant *employment-of-the-community* movements of the late 20th century. Clarence Jordan was the leading light of Koinonia Farm, Sumter County, Georgia, in the deep South of the USA. He was a Baptist minister, writer and academic, who was something of an iconoclast amongst the politically and religiously conservative denomination of Southern Baptists.

A vocation beyond violence

Jordan received his vocation to work for racial equality, social justice and empowerment of marginalised people through a particularly vivid and brutal encounter. As a boy, Clarence had attended a Christian revival meeting at a camp for black prisoners. After the meeting he heard one of the prisoners being tortured by the camp warden, a white Southern Baptist, who had earlier been praising God. Out of the inner turmoil this caused he kept his faith but heard a call to dedicate his life to racial equality, social justice and community living.

But, Koinonia Farm was a modest venture when compared with the movement that grew from it. It still operates but is over-shadowed by the world-wide organisation of *Habitat for Humanity*, founded in 1976, by Millard and Linda Fuller, who had learned community in the communal surroundings of Koinonia Farm.

From self-made success to communal hammer

Millard Fuller was a successful upstate Alabama lawyer who had made a fortune from founding a mail-order business. He was a product of and ideologue for the American dream. But, his marriage was failing because his wife, Linda, couldn't reconcile their Christian values with his economic materialism. So, Millard made the decision to choose to keep his marriage together and discard his riches in favour of a life-style that was closer to what he understood Christian community and work to entail.

The Fullers met Clarence Jordan at Koinonia Farm in 1965 and saw what they considered to be a coherent Christian community, with families engaged in their own partnership enterprises, which contributed to the communal venture and supported their social and spiritual sharing. They encouraged the Koinonians to form Koinonia Partners, in the late 1960s, which undertook some small-scale housing projects and, in 1976, founded *Habitat for Humanity*.

The 21st-century website for *Habitat* describes its core principles as: "Treat all human beings with dignity and justice; choose love over violence; share all possessions and live simply; be stewards of the land and its natural resources". Not that its road has always been easy. In the 1950s Koinonia was attacked by the KKK on several occasions and was maligned by Southern Baptists, in the 60s, for its support of Martin Luther King Jr.

Then, in 2005, Millard Fuller stepped-down. He described *Habitat* as having shifted from a "hammering movement" (cf the Chinyika drum of the Ngoma Lungundu) for social change to becoming a corporate organisation (cf the potential South to West turn of the Chinyika cash crop economy). In GENE terms Fuller could see the danger of *Habitat* shifting South to West rather than first Navigating Eastwards.

A movement for employing community

Despite its early difficulties *Habitat* has grown to offer self-build housing options in communities across more than 100 countries and claims to have constructed more than 500,000 homes, during its 40 years of operation. Throughout this period the community enterprise model has remained very much the same. When it is invited to move into a locality – as was the case, in our experience, in Toxteth, Liverpool, UK in the early 2000s – local people and businesses are invited to donate building materials, volunteers are sought and would-be home-owners are up-skilled in self-building techniques.

The financing of home-ownership is through a mix of 'sweat-equity', by which owner-builders invest their labour in the fabric of their property and communal financing. Homeowners pay back the remaining cost of the house through a no-interest, no-profit loan. But, more significant than the financing is the way in which *Habitat* projects seek to engage the whole local population in a scheme to build communal identity.

In the UK this has been particularly evident in Northern Ireland. Since its beginning in 1994 the early focus for Habitat for Humanity Northern Ireland (HFHNI) was on restoring communities that had been blighted by conflicts between Protestant and Catholic communities during 'the troubles'. Cross-community volunteering programmes had involved 5000 young people from both sections working together in its first ten years. By 2004, 43 families had been helped to build their own home. In 2016 the NI group celebrated their 100th self-build house and the involvement of more than 28,000 volunteers drawn from across the sectarian divide.

One of the most remarkable aspects of *Habitat*'s work in NI has been the list of localities in which its mixed volunteer groups have been able to operate. The Lower Falls Road, West Belfast, North Belfast, Downpatrick, Ballymena and Lisburn each have a litany of violence and murderous activity associated with them. But, HFHNI has been welcomed into all these local communities by people who've wanted to put the history of conflict behind them.

It reflects the need for people who have endured years of conflict to work together for a future in which they're in employment of the community. Usually this takes place through volunteering, communal giving and mutual support, in the very physical task of building homes. The Northern Ireland Housing Executive appointed HFHNI as its key social partner in "promoting integrated housing" in 2004. As such, it has been a key player in the post-Good Friday Agreement transformation of The Province, helping to fulfil some of the vocational dreams of those early founders in Koinonia Farm.

Conclusion

The story of Chinyika, in particular, demonstrates the contemporary meaning of community as solidarity, in a way that reveals activated communitalism in the South. The economics of reciprocity extends beyond hospitality to the world of work, wherein employment is revealed to be focused on the entire communal society, rather than isolated, dispossessed individuals.

In the next chapter we turn from the grounding of communal livelihood in the South to the emergence of public happiness in the civil society. We examine what is meant by sacred economics, explore one of the world's largest social and solidarity economy cases and receive further Lukan wisdom from his parable of how to use money.

Bibliography

1 Hillery, G. (1955) Definitions of Community: Areas of Agreement. *Rural Sociology* 20: 111–123.
2 Kirp, D.L. (2001) *Almost Home – America's Love-Hate Relationship with Community*. Princeton, NJ: Princeton University Press.
3 Bradley, T. and Lowe, P. (1984, Eds.) *Locality and Rurality – Economy and Society in Rural Regions*. Norwich: Geo Books.
4 Bell, C. and Newby, H. (1971) *Community Studies – An Introduction to the Sociology of the Local Community*. London: George Allen & Unwin.
5 Williams, R. (1976) *Keywords – A Vocabulary of Culture and Society*. Oxford: Oxford University Press.
6 Stacey, M. (1969) The Myth of Community Studies. *The British Journal of Sociology* 20(2): 134–147.
7 Lefebvre, H. (1991, transl D. Nicholson-Smith) *The Production of Space*. Oxford: Blackwell Publishers Ltd.
8 Cohen, A.P. (1985) *Symbolic Construction of Community (Key Ideas)*. London: Routledge.
9 Strathern, M. (1981) *Kinship at the Core – An Anthropology of Elmdon, a Village in North-West Essex*. Cambridge: Cambridge University Press.
10 Puttnam, R.D. (2001) *Bowling Alone – The Collapse and Revival of American Community*. New York: Simon & Schuster.
11 McMillan, D.W. and Chavis, D.M. (1986). Sense of Community: A Definition and Theory. *Journal of Community Psychology* 14(1): 6–23.
12 Bauman, Z. (2001) *Community – Seeking Safety in an Insecure World*. Cambridge: Polity Press.
13 Buber, M. (1947, transl. R.G. Smith) *Between Man and Man*. London: Routledge & Kegan Paul.
14 Utting, P. (2015, Ed.) *Social and Solidarity Economy – Beyond the Fringe*. London: Zed Books Ltd.
15 Davidson, B. (1969) *The African Genius*. London: James Currey.
16 Lessem, R., Muchineripi, P. and Kada, S. (2012) *Integral Community: Political Economy to Social Commons*. Abingdon: Routledge.
17 Raftopoulos, B. and Mlambo, A. (2012) *Becoming Zimbabwe*. Harare: Weaver Press.
18 Parfitt, T. (2008) *The Lost Ark of the Covenant*. New York: Harper Element.
19 Lessem, R. and Schieffer, A. (2009) *Transformation Management: Toward the Integral Enterprise*. Abingdon: Routledge.

3 Civil economy
Gift relationship to emancipatory work

GROUNDING COMMUNITY
EMERGENT RECIPROCITY
NAVIGATING RELATIONSHIPS
MUTUAL EFFECT

Introduction

We now turn within the "Southern" realm from grounding in communal livelihood to the emergence of public happiness. In so doing, we are moving into the GENEalogical place of community spirituality and culture, as a key to unlocking a path of renewal into understanding the economic. Our Burning Question takes us directly into the relationship between the spirit and the economic, through the Southern focus on reciprocity. In Charles Eisenstein's "Sacred Economics" we are presented with an understanding of the gift economy, both in the terms of anthropology and social psychology, to see that the circulation of gifts is basic to economic life. Then, in our Window into Wisdom we, once again, return to the "Southern" Gospel of Luke, to understand how gifts are to be used, not only in risky service of others but, also, to inaugurate kingdom economics.

Our *Social Theory* looks through the lens of two Roman Catholic, Italian economists, Luigino Bruni and Stefano Zamagni (1). Through them we gain a perspective on a crucial aspect of the economic tradition that has been neglected in the West for more than 300 years, but is re-emerging in our own era. That is the role of the civil economy in distributing welfare and social goods within society. In turn, this takes us to our Illustrative Case of the work of FECOFUN in Nepal. This is a remarkable social movement, which has brought together more than nine million forest workers in 'the roof of the world'.

Burning Question: is a gift economy possible?

In a classic of early UK social policy the eminent Professor Richard Titmuss (2) presented the UK Blood Donation Service as a model example of 'gift economics'. He argued that the civil economy is served best by citizens who are willing to give part of themselves to others, as an act of charitable reciprocity. At the time and since (3), liberal economists such as Kenneth Arrow (4) took an opposite position, arguing that connecting blood donation to voluntarism actually *reduces* choice and diminishes the benefits to society. It is a stark contrast, but one which gets to the heart and soul of the issue. Is it better to rely on the allocative mechanisms of the market to provide the necessities of life or are some things so fundamental to human existence that they are best left to the social policies of the state or, even, the altruism of people in civil society?

An economy of circulating gratitude

More recently Charles Eisenstein (5) has taken-up the challenge of connecting economics and spirituality. He does this through an exploration of money, from early gift relationships to the current world, in which money circulates digitally around the globe faster than the time between two breaths. Eisenstein's basic premise is that 'in the beginning was the gift'. We can understand this as the fact that our parents passed on life to us, or that the sun keeps shining.

There is a moral principle that flows from this – *gratitude*. It is deontological. We have a duty to be grateful. Eisenstein argues that this was the basis of the earliest hunter-gatherer economics. Rather than barter, which was rare, the foundation of an economy lies in giving and receiving. Furthermore, the economic exchange of reciprocal gifting seems to have been less significant than the (integral, as we present it) circulation of gifts. We give to others and, eventually, something even more valuable comes back to us. The problem for our minds, soaked in capitalist market economics, is that this doesn't seem to make any sense. "Why would I give somebody something for nothing?"

Something for "something more"

But, this is to miss the point of indigenous economics. A gift economy isn't an irrational system, it is fundamental to the establishment of a web of obligations, duties, a network of gratitude, in which we recognise that we all owe each other something. Far from "something for nothing" the gift economy is about "something for something more".

It recognises that when we work together we produce more, a surplus, a hedge against the rainy day. There is a sacred basis to the division of labour, if it is based in the employment of self for community, rather than the exploitation of community for selfish gain, which is inconceivable to most indigenous peoples. As such, the nature of this social profit rests on mutual obligations and the recognition that the surplus is to be shared. The employment of self is in order to give something back to the community, to which I owe my existence and from which I receive the gift of economic, cultural and social life.

So, why money?

So, why do we need money and how does this connect to a spiritual 'attitude of gratitude'? It is a matter of scale. Within the family, up to the scale of even the large village, where multiplex role and social relations and regular contacts exist, so that "I am known", there is no real need for money. The giving of useless tokens, like a shell or a bead, as a response to your valuable action in my direction, is simply a matter of recognising my debt to you. Such tokens will circulate around the known world to express this circularity and web of obligations.

But when we get to the scale of mass society, where most of us are unknown to one another we need a sacred token that can represent value but which, also, identifies our mutual debts – this is money, as we think we know it. On most paper notes there is some expression of this: "I or the bank or the king or some other authority promises to pay the bearer", to reflect that we have obligations to one another.

Of course, in the process of moving from one scale to another there are profound fractures and misinterpretations of values and ideology. The slave trade – between 16th and 19th centuries – relied on the exploitation of African and other indigenous peoples being exchanged for 'aggry beads'. The production of these was dominated by Venetian glass-workers, producing hundreds of tonnes of such beads each year. This generated a massive money economy for the Venetian city-state.

Returning to reciprocity

So, are we forced to accept a choice between either a "primitive" gift economy or the objectifying and alienating money economy of late Capitalism? Eisenstein argues that there is a turn taking place in which the sacredness of money, as the means for exchanging gifts and obligations, is returning, as society becomes increasingly unwilling to accept current levels of inequality, based in fiat money. He argues that the innate generosity and sociality of the human species is not willing to accept the status quo or, indeed, the direction of travel of today's money economy much longer. Not because we lust after violent revolution but because we are naturally programmed for gifting, obligations and the circulating of social duties.

But, Eisenstein doesn't advocate "primitivism" and a type of "back to nature" movement that denies the benefits of our incredibly complex civil society. He takes it as a matter of faith that society can and will restore the sacred gift-obligation to money, over time, as we refuse to accept the atomisation of selves and seek to reinvest our generosity in communal living, because that is, fundamentally, what we wish to do. The sacred economy is based in our wishes and desires as, indeed, is all economics. We simply have to choose to make choices based on cooperation rather than competition, reciprocal obligations rather than the pursuit of selfishness, gratitude rather than exploitation. We can choose to restore the sacred to economics as an act of civil society altruism.

Window into Wisdom: the parable of the ten minas – Luke 19:11–27

The flip-side of the coin of choice is risk. So Luke, with his distinctive "Southern" emphasis on the spiritual and literal journey of the 'community of the marginalised', tells the Parable of the Ten Minas (pounds in some translations), which bears a connection to the Parable of the Talents (Matthew 25:14–30).

The parable should be seen within the context of Luke's understanding of the gift-graces (charisms) of God, given through the Holy Spirit. As we see with the extent of the gift of prophecy, through the Spirit, as presented by Luke, we are able to recognise just how empowering God's gifts are. This is the setting for Luke's parable about the operation of a gift economy within the community.

The parable in outline

Luke's Jesus tells the story of a much-hated well-born man – his hearers would have immediately thought of Archelaus, one of King Herod's sons. As so often, this local ruler is to go on a long journey. In this case it is, potentially, to be made king, before he returns to his local seat of power. His parting act is to disperse some of his wealth to ten servants. To each one he gives a single minas (c £30 today). His instruction is to "put the money to work until I get back". Clearly, money and work are connected and it is possible for money to be the source of work.

He was so hated that his local subjects entreat the king-makers not to make him king. But, the powerful man *is* crowned and returns to see how his working money has fared. The first two servants each report that they've increased the original sum by ten-fold and five-fold respectively. They are each rewarded with the ruler-ship of the number of cities equivalent to their growth rate. City-rule would bring a lot of perks with it, as well as much greater risks. This is a tidy reward. The focus of the parable is, however, on the third servant.

All he did was keep the money wrapped in a cloth. He didn't even put it in the bank where it could have gained interest. His reasoning seems rather lacking in diplomacy. He tells the new king "I was afraid of you, because you are a hard man. You take out what you did not put in and reap what you did not sow." He sounds like a socialist accusing his boss of rapacious capitalism!

Understandably, the king is not best-pleased. The 'wicked servant's' minas is taken away, given to the one who has accrued ten. The other servants complain that this is unfair, as the first servant already has more than enough. Then, we get Jesus' punchline: "I tell you that to everyone who has, more will be given, but as for the one who has nothing, even what they have will be taken away. But those enemies of mine who did not want me to be king over them – bring them here and kill them in front of me". Ouch!

A series of gifts

The setting of the parable is a meal at Zacchaeus' house. He has just promised to give away half his fortune and repay all his debts with a massive four hundred percent interest payment. He indicates just how strong his 'attitude of gratitude' is towards Jesus. It is worked out in practical ways, through gifts of money to those who really need it, without expecting to receive anything in return. You can't buy your way into paradise. But, when you receive the gift of paradise the only natural response is to give to others.

The most obvious gifts are the investments that the nobleman makes in his servants. Moreover, the basis of the gifts is interesting. The New Testament (koine) Greek for "put the money to work" is *pragmateuomai* or "trade". From this we get the English "be pragmatic". In other words, be sensible, don't take *excessive* risks. There are boundaries to what you should do with the money.

This makes sense in terms of the gift economy. Being part of the community circle means that we are expected, indeed required, to gift one another. Equally, there are limits on what is expected of us. Duties and responsibilities are within the bounds of reasonable behaviour. But, this is not the full story. Whilst there is no expectation on us to give rashly, those who do so, and make wise investments, are rewarded "even more". That is the nature of faith. It is both a gift and a rich reward, even though we can't earn it.

Finally, there is the wind-up saying, which has all of Jesus' authenticity about it. And it emphasises the primacy of a gift relationship. If we have been given to we will receive more. But, if we haven't been given to, even that which wasn't given will be taken away.

What does this mean? Well, the significance of the 'wicked servant' is made explicit at this point. Although he was technically given one minas he refused to take part in the community of giving and investing in others. Indeed, by not putting the money to work he stole from the community that trusted him. The gift economy of God's kingdom will be good news for all those who properly join it. But, if we actively work against the community we will be excluded from it. And what is true in the kingdom, for Luke, is equally true in everyday life.

Social Theory: the advance of public happiness

Italian political economists Bruni and Zamagni (1) present a straightforward main thesis: *the flourishing of civil society organisations in recent decades is neither a mere accident nor an exception to the normal evolution of the capitalist economy.* They see the surfacing of civil organisations' social and economic roles, both as a symptom that the capitalist economy is undergoing an important crisis and a sign of hope for a new beginning.

Market versus solidarity

For them the civil economy offers a cultural perspective from which we may interpret the entire economic discourse. Consequently, they consider two divergent approaches emerging through a contemporary confrontation of market economics with the social/solidarity spheres. Market efficiency aims at increasing the size of the economic pie. By contrast, social solidarity provides the political criteria for distributing the slices, extending beyond market activities. Clearly, this approach has its antecedents in the writings of Karl Marx and the economic anthropologist Karl Polanyi.

The civil economy turns "eastwards"

Bruni and Zamagni consider that the tradition of civil economy offers a third way (cf Chinyika in the preceding chapter). It is rooted in medieval Christian thought, in seeing human sociability and reciprocity as core elements of normal economic life. This was, until recently, represented in the West through the welfare state's modification of the productive role of the market. Income generation first, followed by redistribution, through statutory instruments and fiscal policy. Such a 'mixed economy' was seen as the post-WW2 settlement.[1]

But, the strict connection between wealth and territory, via GNP, is becoming obsolete under the globalisation of markets. The interests of multinational enterprises do not necessarily coincide with those of national citizens. Consequently, it becomes vital that redistributive mechanisms are applied at the point of production, if increasing inequality is to be avoided, rather than relying on the state to act *ex post facto*. The former settlement recognised that the principle of market efficiency, in income generation, needs to be balanced by redistributive fairness.

But now, the question is being asked, under conditions when inequality seems to be breaking societies apart: what about the ultimate goal of reciprocity? Basically, reciprocity is the principle that allows fraternity to take place. But, this requires, for Bruni and Zamagni, a choice to be made in favour of a 'gift economy', as we saw with Eisenstein, over and against one founded in 'social contract', in terms of regulating human relations.

The invention of Christian economic discourse

The tradition of civil economy has deep roots in the Christian doctrine of the Trinity (divine community-in-selfhood), the Benedictine monastic tradition of prayer and work (ora et labore) and the medieval doctrine of *caritas* within the community.[2] According to Weber this was broken-up by the bureaucratic *zwekrationalitie* (rational rules) of Protestantism, with its 'spirit of capitalism'. But Bruno and Zamagni reject this Protestant historiography, pointing instead to aspects of the pre-Reformation Christian tradition as providing the foundations for the reciprocal, gift economy.

In summary, they argue that the market economy, even as late as the early 19th century, developed from a culture of reciprocity. As a defense of this position they cite the 13th-century Franciscan appeal to voluntary poverty as a distinct "economic school" that connected to early concepts of value, interest, exchange and discount. Out of this tradition arose the 'montes pietatis', which were charitable banks to counter the investment-based banking system that flourished in Italian cities such as Genoa, Venice and Florence. In a real sense they represented the first popular retail banks. Banks such as the *Monte di Recanati*, which rejected the payment of interest, functioned to provide what we would term 'micro-finance', bridal dowries and, also, to offer services of arbitration, conciliation and mediation, in both civil and criminal legal cases.

They see a cultural thread running from ancient Greece though the primitive Christianity of the Middle East (see the Lukan *Window into Wisdom* in this chapter), early and late mediaeval Europe and leading to 18th-century treatises on 'civic humanism', from both Protestant (*The History of Civil Society* by Adam Ferguson in Scotland) and Catholic political economists (*The Lessons of the Civil Economy* by Antonio Genovesi in Naples), each published in 1767.

Onset of authoritarianism and Utopia

The period of 'civil humanism' was swiftly over-shadowed by the political changes that took place in 16th and 17th century pre-Modern Europe, through the Reformation and Enlightenment periods. In particular, the ancient craft guilds with their focus on 'mechanical arts' and popular culture lost status to new industrial inventions and the elitism of a scientific economy. As such, ex-cathedra authoritarianism, divorced from the power of the papal See of Rome, shattered many earlier civic accomplishments, breeding pessimism within Catholicism and an optimistic search for new utopias within the new Reformed intellectual cultures.

Interestingly, Bruni and Zamagni see such utopias as a search for escapism, away from the harsh political realities of hyper-individualistic social thought. Alternatively, others, from a less ideological Catholic background, see these as reflecting a hopeful revolution in the 'rights of Man'. Whichever perspective is adopted there was, certainly, a rift created between Civic Humanism and modernity. Modernist philosophy was taking the path of individualism, adopting the view that sociability is something extrinsic, transitory and accidental. Reciprocity was thereby excluded as an essential dimension of human nature, so that a new anthropology was becoming delineated.

This described the human person as being guided solely by self-interest; a process that Bruni and Zamagni refer to as "Civil Darkness". As such, three 16th- to 18th-century social philosophers – Machiavelli in Italy, Hobbes in England and Mandeville in Holland – epitomise the new dark view of human political economy.

Science of social living: Italian enlightenment and the civil economy

Despite the emphasis placed on Adam Smith as the father of economics and political economy, each of the great capitals of Italian Enlightenment were vital for the creation of economic science, prior to the Scottish Enlightenment. The tradition, for Bruni and Zamagni, must be understood within the context of larger Neapolitan culture, which was one of Europe's most vibrant and important centres in the first decades of the 1700s. Scarlatti and Pergolesi in music, Vico in philosophy – all were at the forefront of European culture. In particular, the role of Antonio Genovesi (1713–1769), from Salerno, who became the leading economist of the Italian School, has often been neglected.

Genovesi used the term "Civil Economy" in his main treatise (*Lezioni di Economia Civile*). As such, he had a vision of commerce in relationship to social well-being. Besides Genovesi, both of his disciples, Filangieri and Bianchini, expressed a strong belief that the process of becoming civilised required an equal distribution of wealth. An ability to transform behaviours of self-interest into factors of common good was needed, following the philosophy of Giambattista Vico, who argued that it is only in civil life that individuals and self-directed passions become social and produce "civil happiness".

*The third sector: between state and market – a
residual non-entity?*

But, there is a third way. In the latter part of the 20th century an economic
sector emerged between that of the private market and the state. As such,
Bruni and Zamagni turn to explaining the nature of the third sector as it is
conventionally construed. The problem is that the definition of its identity
appears entirely negative, as per *non-market* or *not-for-profit* (NPO) in the
Anglo-Saxon world (US and UK) and *non-State* in Europe. It was not until
the 1980s that the term "third sector" actually began to be used in conventional discourse surrounding the culture of the economy.

Moreover, many NPOs in the US began life as initiatives of philanthro-
Capitalists, under the 'virtue ventures' model of "make money any way
you can and, then, give something back". Schools, universities, hospitals,
research and cultural foundations carry the names of their benefactors. So
what ethical anchorage guided their actions? It is rooted in the late 19th
century. As a classical example, Andrew Carnegie writes the following:

> The only point required by the Gospel of wealth is that the surplus
> which accrues from time to time in the hands of a man should be admin-
> istered by him in his own lifetime for the purposes which is seen by him,
> as trustee, for the good of the people.
>
> (from *The Gospel of Wealth*, 1889)

Yet Carnegie was ruthless in opposing worker protest, such as in the Home-
stead Strike of 1892. In the final analysis while the foundation postulates
one-directional philanthropy, associations thrive on reciprocity. This brings
us nto the main theme of this book.

Beyond employment

The notion of a job is a relatively recent social innovation

The notion of a job is a relatively recent social innovation. *Work activity
only became associated with jobs in the second industrial revolution. To
find for each worker his/her best place in the working process was the great
innovation of the Ford-Taylorist system.* What is new in the present, transitional epoch is that we have reached another turning point: de-jobbing. The
fixed job then was alienating but provided security, while the work-activity
portfolio valorises the subject's talents.

Fifty years ago Keynes judged mass employment in a rich society to be a
shameful absurdity. Today we are many times richer! The businesses today
that lay off workers are not so often in a crisis, but rather are healthy businesses that want to increase their margin of competitiveness. In precise
terms, *the problem is that unemployment is no longer a symptom or an*

effect of a situation of crisis, but a competitive strategy. What the civil wel-
fare is aiming at is to ensure the human person's right to live in society.

Welfare society, civil economy and employment

Why is it so difficult today to find a solution to the problem of unemployment or 'bad employment'?[3] For Bruni and Zamagni, it is the consequence of a social organisation that is incapable of adequately valuing human resources. The social time freed-up from the production process by new technologies – under conditions of the third industrial revolution – is transformed into unemployment. In turn, this results from the time used in producing commodities that are not needed, but glitter within the consumption sphere. Instead, we require a restructured post-industrial society, where liberated time – freed by machines from drudgery – is used to expand the liberty of citizens, rather than in creating precarious and illusory jobs.

Unemployment, in fact, is a typical phenomenon of the capitalist mode of production. History, as we saw in the grounding Chinyika case (Chapter 2), has proven that unemployment cannot exist in preindustrial societies. The very notion of unemployment only makes sense in a society in which the remuneration of work is determined by the rules of the labour market.

Demeaning jobs to flourishing work

In a nutshell, Bruni and Zamagni's solution is to dismantle the artificial distinction between fixed jobs and other working (non-contracted) activities, whilst broadening the latter. In our present, transitional, phase something must be done that is analogous to the first Industrial Revolution, when the post-agrarian society emerged. The new technological trajectory underway has to lead us to a new post-industrial model of society. In the past it did not mean historically that agriculture disappeared, but rather it can produce all of an industrialised nation's requirements (alongside international trade) with an employment of 4–5% of its labour force.

Under current private market conditions and rules it is not possible to give work to all those who have been "liberated' by increases in productivity and technical divisions of labour without unleashing problems of sustainability. The proposal is to channel the work "liberated' from the private sector of the economy towards activities that produce goods that the private sector has no interest in producing. These are civil 'relational' goods, such as social care, to which it is impossible to apply the standard logic of exchange.

Self-production to prosumer: the new demand for relationality

By overcoming, then, what they call the "labor atrophy" we can free energy and time and direct these towards activities whose regulating principle is the principle of reciprocity.

The appearance of consumer groups, moreover, and the many new forms of "ethical consumption" are signs of the increasing demand by citizens for their rights as consumers to be recognised. Further to such we see a rapid growth in Fairtrade, farmer's markets, green energy schemes, ethical savings, time banks, alternative currencies. The ever increasing demand for enhanced "quality of life' goes beyond a demand for "well made" products. It is rather a demand for attention, care, service and participation; in other words for relationality. In other terms, the quality refers more to human relationships than to products.

Welfare state to civil welfare model

The civil welfare model, which recognises the organisations of civil society in their capacity to become active partners, indicates that a new category of social-quality markets needs to be created. At the same time, the funding of the 'third sector' needs to change, as it is already doing. Reliance on philanthro-capitalist donations to build "reputational capital" is unsustainable. One alternative is for consumers to receive coupons for third sector organisations when they make enterprise purchases, shifting the transfer from a bi-polar to a triangular model. But equally, many millions of social enterprises are currently emerging – which have multifarious forms of funding and income generation – often related to community work arrangements (see later chapters on social/ solidarity economies). As such, the neo-statist models of welfare-user and consumer-client are giving way to a model of the citizen-pro-sumer, who helps define, and participate in, what is provided.

The basic idea of social-quality markets is that of inserting and strengthening the social dimension inside the market mechanism. The idea rests on the following three pillars:

1   *Establishing rules for determining the effective needs of people.* So that central or local government organises ways of financing those with needs, with the aim of transforming the requirement for services into an effective demand. This may be done through citizen coupons, direct funding of third sector organisations or other transfer payments.

2   *Protection of citizens from risks associated with the pervasive presence of asymmetric information.* Government authorises those suppliers who have real capacity to deliver various types of services.

3   *Need-bearers are able to exercise effective freedom of choice.* Civil society initiates a competition amongst care services, which may take place via intermediary institutions, such as the many 'social enterprise hubs' that are emerging in city-regions and wider territories. The determinant of success should be based on principles of relationality rather than simply ones of market efficiency.

This offers considerable advantages compared to those of the impersonal mediation of the market. In particular, social and civil enterprises enjoy an important reputational advantage that comes from their expressed objective of maximising the well-being of each of the participants in the relationship, with the fundamental advantage that a reciprocal society of welfare is founded in the economic activity of sustainable, profit-making enterprises.

Illustrative Case: forest workers in the FECOFUN cooperatives, Nepal

Nepal, alongside Tibet, is often described as 'the roof of the world'. It is a land of the Himalayas, stunning natural beauty and some of the most remote communities on the planet. But it is also one of the poorest countries in the world. It ranks 140th out of 188 countries in the Human Development Index, 133rd in the Global Competitiveness Index and 95th in the Shadow Economy Index (6). We might ask: how resilient is the roof?' Perhaps surprisingly, to some at least, Nepal has one of the strongest 'gift economies' of any global nation (7), particularly evident in the emergent free school sector (8).

FUN *in the forest*

One example of the enormously high levels of co-operation amongst marginalised groups in Nepal is that of FECOFUN. In 1995 the *Federation of Community Forestry Users Nepal* (FECOFUN) was established with the primary purpose of developing a communal organisation for cooperation amongst marginalised rural forest workers. This formation took place in response to state legislation, initiated from the late 1970s–90s, aimed at transferring ownership of Nepal's massive forest resources to local committees of forest user groups (FUGs). This followed significant violent protests amongst some of the country's poorest communities. Today it numbers about 9 million members, linked together for the purpose of giving voice to one another in the policy-making process (9). Such policies relate to forestry management, rural development, the maintenance of household incomes – especially amongst some of the most marginalised tribal communities – together with reduction of carbon emissions from timber production. They connect social security and green issues together.

The main success of FECOFUN has been in its coverage across this highly dispersed rural nation. There are more than 1,100 local organisations covering seventy-five municipal districts and extending to eighty percent of the almost twenty thousand community forests across Nepal. As a result FECOFUN has become the largest and most influential civil society organisation in the country.

This is all the more remarkable given the history of state repression in Nepal, especially during the Maoist period, despite the level of popular protest movements that have been organised by its central committee. Even so, the movement has only relatively recently begun to achieve its primary objectives. In the early years of the new century it was regarded as relatively unknown by and irrelevant to the needs of marginalised groups, lower castes and women forest workers (10). But, more recent analysis indicates that it not only exerts considerable influence over central government, in accessing rights for indigenous forest workers it is increasingly successful as a 'nested civil society' organisation that meets needs at the most local level (11).

REDDs under the forest bed

FECOFUN has had particular success in enlisting the support of international donor organisations to assist marginalised groups in relation to carbon reduction programmes through the REDD+ initiative (Reducing Emissions from Deforestation and Forest Degradation). Working through the *Forest Carbon Trust Fund* local civil society groups have been able to both establish watershed-level schemes and increase average incomes and community facilities for indigenous groups (12). This movement has seen a reversal of some of the key drivers to deforestation since the 1990s.

Deforestation activity was led by populist politicians in league with large-scale timber conglomerates seeking to appeal to landless rural workers. They did this by converting forest to individual agricultural plots through the distribution of private rights of land tenure, with disastrous environmental and rural wage results. These political movements were particularly evident during the decade-long Maoist-led conflict (1996–2006). But since the People's Movement of 2006 FECOFUN has been one of the leading Nepalese networks capable of working to reverse this trend.

There is substantial evidence that many indigenous groupings who are dependent on Nepalese forests – including forest tribes, landless Dhalits, charcoal workers and wood-fuel collectors – have been substantially excluded from income-generating carbon-reduction schemes. Even so, the impact of FECOFUN has been important, at least on the margins. Together with the *Asia Network for Sustainable Agriculture and Bioresources*, FECOFUN has been able to establish a range of projects, at both national and watershed levels, to advance the REDD+ and rural income enhancement initiatives (13).

Equally, there are a number of examples of how REDD+ projects have led to cases of inter-ethnic conflict, particularly between the Rana Magar and Chepang tribes, in several watershed regions (14). Such conflicts arise because of a lack of attention to the injustices generated by inequitable distributions of carbon reduction income benefits, displacement of families and low-level corruption. More significantly, however, some disputes arise as a result of disruption to what is a remarkable gift economy exercised by the Chepang tribe, Nepal's most venerable indigenous people.

In 2011, Alexander Dill, of the *Basel Institute of Commons & Economics*, mounted a medium-scale (N = 567 households) survey of families within the Chepang tribe, to establish the extent of their sharing and gift economy (7). The results were astounding. Whilst the conventional money economy had a very limited extent within the tribe, levels of gift activity were hugely significant. As Charles Eisenstein indicates in *Sacred Economics* (see previously), in relation to almost all indigenous peoples, there was an almost universal (99.8%) exercise of reciprocal hospitality, in terms of sharing food and water, with other families in the tribe. Similar levels of gifting were expressed in relation to healthcare, agricultural assistance, cleaning and transport.

Even more significantly Dill and his coworker found that levels of *trust* between families were remarkable, enabling this significant level of gift economy to occur.

Dill's conclusions were that the Chepang engaged in a remarkably high – at least by Western standards – level of social capital formation. This wasn't fungible or able to be expressed in terms of any conventional money-based economy. As a result his negative conclusion was that the Chepang would never be able to feature in any table of world comparisons in respect to World Giving Index or Human Development. But, more importantly, the activities of organisations such as FECOFUN were able to function in the way they do because of this gift economy. Their ability to extend participation in benefitting forest workers and mediating conflicts – over such contemporary concerns as the REDD+ process of carbon reduction – can occur because of the remarkably high levels of sharing and hospitality towards strangers displayed by such as the Chepang tribe in Nepal.

Women on top of the world

Some of the most significant impacts of FECOFUN have been at the micro-level, effecting transformative change in respect to civil society-led community employment. In this respect FECOFUN is seen as a role model for rural development organisations. It has a remarkable level of gender balance, although this wasn't the case in its early years. So whilst women have traditionally been excluded from professional engagement in forest management, with low participation rates in governance institutions, there has been a dramatic increase in women's involvement and leadership, as a result of FECOFUN's activities (15), although this perspective is not shared by all commentators (16).

In many respects this presents a mixed picture for women in development. Agricultural employment is falling worldwide, but this trend is less marked for women as for men, meaning that women are often trapped on the farm, when men are able to secure higher income jobs in the cities (17). But, as we saw with the Chinyika experience in the previous chapter, this can often result in the employment of community and enhancement of self-identity, when contrasted against the requirements of working as wage-labourers in an increasingly marketised economy. This appears to be the case for women forest workers in Nepal, who are experiencing much higher levels of community leadership, emancipation and self-determination as a result of mobilisation, through the activities of civil society organisations such as FECOFUN.

Indeed, there is increasing evidence that when women assume leadership for local FUG governance, improvements occur in both household incomes and forest conservation (18). This is because of the greater knowledge that women have of plant species, local ecology, the most efficient collection methods and, crucially, a greater willingness to abide by local community rules, in terms of protection of the forest and its resources (19). Furthermore, as women's participation rose, through the activities of FECOFUN and other integrated FUGs, household incomes increased and the sense of local community self-determination improved (20). None of which should surprise us. As is repeatedly seen, the "Southern" worldview of connection to both community and nature is focused around the activities of women in leadership. Women, often, have a deeper sense of the fragile connections between gift, the sacred nature of life, economy and a desire to see the family and community employed within its own circle, to more directly engender the dignity of the self-in-relation to the hospitality of others.

Conclusion

In the previous chapter, we saw how the "southern" African grounding theme of *uri munhu* (are you human), set within a traditional, local rural Zimbabwean community, set the tone for the communal grounding of employment. What emerges through the work of Bruni and Zamagni is an understanding of the *civil economy, as predating that of the market, even in Western Europe.*

As we have turned from grounding to emergence, so the focus has shifted from the local to the now local-global, and from nature and community, comparatively speaking, to culture and spirituality. Next, we turn to global navigation (Chapter 4), via a newly relational paradigm, recognising that the key to understanding the employment of the community rests in the Southern economic principle of reciprocity.

Notes

1 It has long been argued, for example, that the EU was a creation of Roman Catholic economic apologists, in fundamental conflict with an Anglo-Saxon model, founded in greater economic liberalism. On that basis, the realisation of a British preference for Brexit from the EU was only a matter of time.
2 Pope Benedict XVI (formerly Cardinal Joseph Ratzinger) produced his encyclical *Caritas in Veritate* (2009) to address many of the issues of civil society in response to globalisation and challenges to 'the common good'. Much of Bruno and Zamagni's writing is directly in line with the encyclical.
3 It needs to be remembered that Bruni and Zamagni are writing from the perspective of Italy and Southern Europe where unemployment has become something of a curse, especially for young people. The situation within the Anglo-Saxon and Northern European worlds is less about a crisis of unemployment as one rooted in 'bad' employment, sub-employment and pseudo self-employment.

Bibliography

1 Bruni, L. and Zamagni, S. (2006) *Civil Economy: Efficiency, Equity and Public Happiness.* Bern: Peter Lang.
2 Titmuss, R. (1970/1997, Reissued) *The Gift Relationship – From Human Blood to Social Policy.* London: LSE Books.
3 Shearmur, J.F. (2015) The Gift Relationship Revisited. *HEC Forum* 27(4): 301–17.
4 Arrow, K. (1972) Gifts and Exchanges, in Phelps, E.S. (Ed.) *Altruism, Morality and Economic Theory.* New York: Russel Sage Foundation.
5 Eisenstein, C. (2011) *Sacred Economics – Money, Gift and Society in the Age of Transition.* Berkeley, CA: Evolver Editions.
6 BICE (2010) *Global Index Benchmarks 2010.* Basel: Institute of Commons and Economics.
7 Dill, A. and Club of Rome (2011) *Gift Economy and Trust in Rural Nepal – A Study Among 567 Families of Mountain Farmers.* Basel: Institute of Commons and Economics and One World alc. [Available at: http://commons.de/wp-content/uploads/Gift_economy_and_trust_in_rural_Nepal.pdf. Last accessed: June 11, 2017].
8 Cicero, S. (2013) How a Gift Economy Powers Education in Rural Nepal. *Resilience.* 18 January. [Available at: www.resilience.org/stories/2013-01-18/how-a-gift-economy-powers-education-in-rural-nepal/. Last accessed: June 12, 2017].
9 FECOFUN (n.d.) *Organisation Website.* [Available at: www.fecofun.org.np/index.php. Last accessed: June 12, 2017].

10 Timsina, N. (2003) Viewing FECOFUN from the Perspective of Popular Participation and Representation. *Journal of Forestry & Livelihood* 2(2): 67–71, February.

11 Ojha, H. (2008) *Reframing Governance: Understanding Deliberative Politics in Nepal's Terai Forestry*. New Delhi: Adroit.

12 Khatri, D.B., Paudel, N.S., Bista, R. and Bhandari, K. (2012) *Review of REDD+ Payment Mechanism Under Pilot Project: Implications for Future Carbon Payments in Nepal*. Kathmandu: Forest Action Nepal and Regional Community Forestry Training Centre.

13 Paudel, N.S., Khatri, D.B., Khanal, D.R. and Karki, R. (2013) The Context of REDD+ in Nepal: Drivers, Agents and Institutions. *Occasional Paper 81*. Centre for International Forestry Research. Bogor, Indonesia: CIFR.

14 Uprety, D.R. and Launtel, H. (n.d.) *Study of REDD+ in Relation to Conflict: Case Studies of Two Watersheds of Nepal, Presentation*. Lalitpur: SDC and Forestry Program.

15 Wagle, R., Pillay, S. and Wright, W. (2016) Examining Nepalese Forestry Governance from Gender Perspectives. *International Journal of Public Administration* 40(3): 205–25.

16 Gurung, J., Giri, K., Setyowati, A.B. and Lebow, E. (2011) *Getting REDD+ Right for Women: An Analysis of the Barriers and Opportunities for Women's Participation in the REDD+ Sector in Asia*. New York: Women Organizing for Change in Agriculture and Natural Resource Management/ United States Forest Service.

17 DeSchutter, O. (2013) *Gender Equality and Food Security – Women's Empowerment as a Tool Against Hunger*. Mandaluyong City: Asian Development Bank.

18 Agarwal, B. (2009) Gender and Forest Conservation: The Impact of Women's Participation in Community Forest Governance. *Ecological Economics* 68: 2785–99.

19 Ashur, K. and Shattuck, A. (2017) Forests and Food Security: What's Gender Got to Do with It? *Social Sciences* 6(34): 1–16.

20 McDougall, C., Jiggins, J., Pandit, B.H., Thapa, S.K., Rana, M. and Leeuwis, C. (2013) Does Adaptive Collaborative Forest Governance Affect Poverty? Participatory Action Research in Nepal's Community Forests. *Society & Natural Resources* 26: 1235–51.

4 Relational sociology

Collaborative platforms to humane working

GROUNDING COMMUNITY
EMERGENT RECIPROCITY
NAVIGATING RELATIONSHIPS
MUTUAL EFFECT

Introduction: *we are what we care about*

We now turn further from our prior local grounding in social and cultural context, lodged within the African traditional "south". In the preceding chapter we emerged locally-globally in the "southern" European Christian Catholic community. Now, we move to globally navigating our relational and sociological – as opposed to instrumentally economic – theoretical way.

Our Burning Question opens the chapter by entering the increasingly familiar but weird world of the gig economy. Herein concepts become topsy-turvy, so that what is called 'the sharing economy' loses all sense of social relations. What could become collaborative communities are, in fact, composed of atomising individuals, separated into units of self-employment or client activity. In this labour market, working hours can become zero and workers are completely independent, although defined as totally "dependent contractors". Our Burning Question is: can the sharing economy become ethically developed?

The Window into Wisdom takes us to Luke's account of the Last Supper. This may appear, on the surface, to epitomise what a set of shared social relations should look like. But, from Luke's perspective, we are presented with a clear choice between alternative meanings of 'sharing' and 'leadership'. Our Social Theory lens comes from the work of Italian sociologist Pierpaulo Donati (1), who seeks to recast the sociological understanding of social relations in respect of a caring society. We are who we care for and what we care about.

Finally, our Illustrative Case is that of *Cooperativo Mondragon*, which is the most extensive complex of socially-related cooperatives anywhere on the globe. Through *Mondragon* we see that navigating towards ethical social relations in the world of work is possible. These are questions which require us to consider what are the nature of social relations at work and in society; questions that begin from a consideration of the 'sharing economy', alongside the insights of Pierpaulo Donati.

Burning Question: can the sharing economy be ethically developed?

In the previous chapter we considered some of the principles and wisdom behind the gift economy. Gifting is an essential aspect of all human cultures. But, it has become less significant, in a formal sense, under the conditions of Capitalism, despite a very considerable proportion of all economic activity being undertaken outside the contractual basis of employment, most often by women, in households, through caring and as community support. Various studies place the value of such unpaid work at one-quarter to one-half of national GDP – within Western nations, such as UK, US and Australia – and a considerably higher proportion of national income equivalents in many 'less-developed countries' (2, 3).

Now, as we turn to the ways in which work-in-community can be navigated (through the Northern realm of science, technology and systems), we consider the rapid growth of the so-called 'sharing economy'. It sounds supportive, based in mutuality and an elaboration of community within the sphere of the economic. Indeed, it is one of the most momentous trends in the European economy, disrupting many familiar business models and changing the nature of work for millions of people. And it has many features that point towards navigating from gift to communitalist business.

But, there is a dark side, too. Just because a set of new business models are badged as 'the sharing economy' doesn't make them so. Indeed, when the relational economy becomes subsumed in the worst excesses of the Capitalist market it can produce some monstrous consequences. Our point here is to show, first, what happens when the Southern relational principle turns West, as it seeks to navigate a Northern passage, without emerging an Eastern spirituality. By contrast, when we examine the navigating principles of *Cooperativo Mondragon*, we begin to see signs of a far more coherent Southern, relational model of work being navigated towards the marketplace. But, first, we consider what is, conventionally, meant by the 'sharing economy', within the distorting mirror of contemporary Capitalism.

The rise of collaborative platforms

For most people the sharing economy is about using a collaborative internet platform, which gives producers access to potential users, and consumers easier ways to reach goods and services, utilising tools that enable transactions to take place. According to a recent report (4) for PriceWaterhouseCoopers (PwC) there are five key sectors in which such collaborative platforms are being developed and used to disrupt traditional business models. These are:

- peer-to-peer (P2P) accommodation e.g. *Airbnb*
- P2P transportation e.g. *Uber taxis*
- on-demand household services e.g. *TrustaTrader* or *HungryHouse*
- on-demand professional services e.g. *Quickbooks*
- collaborative finance e.g. *Kickstarter*.

Whilst some of these reflect little more than the capacity of web tools to bring together freelancers into new market hubs, replacing directories such as "Yelp" with the immediacy of connecting providers and users online, others have genuinely disrupted conventional business models. For example, the hospitality and tourist accommodation industry has been severely disturbed by *Airbnb* and its off-shoots. In this case, through platforms such as *Couchsurfing*, genuine shared relationships have been developed globally, as people meet to offer one another hospitality in their homes.

The effect of such collaborative platforms has been to give existing freelancers and small businesses access to new marketplaces. But it has, also enabled the opening-up of possibilities for new patterns of self-employment. In the UK, for example, self-employment increased by 14,000 to 4.8M people, May 2016–17, with 15% of all people in work being self-employed. Recent statistics (July 2017) show that employment in the UK is at 75% of the working age population, which is the highest level since records began in 1971. A very substantial reason for this is the growth of self-employment and a major significant factor in that growth has been the rise of collaborative platforms. In this sense the sharing economy has massively grown the formal economy of employment.

The darker side of sharing

Recent reporting for the EU (5) has indicated the very divergent usage of online collaborative work platforms, according to demography, nationality and frequency of access. The EU-wide survey data indicates that about one-third of all visitors to collaborative platforms have also provided services on them. In that sense, there is strong evidence that such online tools are, genuinely, facilitating a sharing economy.

The problem is that not everyone would agree that such collaborative platforms are properly reflective of a sharing economy. Issues arise in terms of the nature of consumer protection, employment contracts and, fundamentally, the evolution of work. What has become known as the 'gig economy' has generated an embarrassment of opportunities which it is difficult to navigate between. These are represented by online reviews, ratings systems and detailed inventories, all of which are meant to be connected to inventories which precisely match clients with contractors. And, very often they work effectively for consumers.

But, as these markets have matured they have also become more open to unscrupulous practices, dodgy-dealing and outright fraud. More significantly, the gig economy has signposted a series of loopholes in the ways in which employment law operates in many countries, particularly the UK. Indeed, the massive increase in the numbers of registered 'self-employed' can, largely, be attributed to the working and contractual practices of many of the largest collaborative platform companies. A recent report of the UK House of Commons Work and Pensions Parliamentary Committee (6) has highlighted a number of issues surrounding the gig economy, whilst recognising the important contribution to national income and job opportunities that such internet-based business platforms have created. Some of these are:

*   15% of UK work is classified as self-employment, changing the meaning of work and its connection to the welfare state.
*   Self-employed workers contribute far smaller levels of taxes (in the UK, National Insurance Contributions or NICs) than conventional employees, despite equivalence in terms of new pension rights.
*   Minimum rights and protections for employees are often denied to those classified as self-employed, as they are responsible for their own entitlements, such as holiday and sick pay.
*   Many companies in the gig economy are using self-employed workers as cheap labour, overlooking their responsibilities to pay entitlements, and to contribute employer NICs, pension and apprenticeship levies.
*   The indiscriminate use of 'self-employment' often denies workers their rights, leads to exploitation and, effectively, robs the state of crucial revenues which support the payment of welfare benefits.
*   The report's authors summarise by commenting that: "Self-employment is neither inherently good nor bad. It can represent entrepreneurial zeal and a highly desirable culture of self-reliance. It can also be deeply negative, allowing companies to evade responsibility for their workers' wellbeing and increase their profits. It is incumbent on Government to close loopholes that incentivise this behaviour"(3).

The Taylor Review. . .

One of the outcomes of the preceding report was to strengthen the review into new working practices being undertaken by Matthew Taylor, Director of the Royal Society of Arts and advisor to former Prime Minister Tony Blair, which was published in July 2017 (7). The main conclusions of Taylor's review of working practices in the gig economy are:

*   Government is accountable for ensuring "good work for all", meaning working practices that include: fair wages, quality employment,

education and training opportunities, healthy working conditions, a balance between work and life, consultative participation (in decision-making) and collective representation (on boards).

- All workers should have base-line protections and opportunities to progress.
- Platform-based companies (in the gig economy) should classify workers as 'dependent contractors' (DCs) rather than as 'self-employed', with new legislation establishing clear distinctions between DCs and those who are legitimately self-employed.
- The labour market in new working models should allow for the flexibility of those who choose DC status, whilst ensuring 'fairness-at-work'.
- A National Living Wage (above the current UK Minimum Wage) should be rigorously enforced and policed, allowing for progression, so that workers are not stuck in low-pay sectors or jobs.
- At the same time, the costs of employment, such as 'apprenticeship levies' should be minimised, to give employers sufficient freedom to employ large numbers of DCs, whilst Government should ensure enhanced protection for those in the new status.
- Companies should practice good corporate governance, social responsibility, offer good prospects, ensure routes to progression, life-long learning opportunities and more pro-active approaches to healthy workplaces and work-life balance.

. . . and its critiques

As might be understood the Taylor Review was the subject of much immediate criticism. The main critique was that it was overly strong on moral sentiment but weak on practical solutions. In particular, the main proposal to enact legislation to create a new working class of DCs, with all the ramifications this would entail in terms of reforming employment rights and, crucially, financial and fiscal measures, the review looked doomed to begin with. Most criticism was reserved for the supposed failure of Taylor to challenge 'zero hours contracts', arguing that two-thirds of workers on such contracts – where employers/ contractor platforms can choose to not offer any hours to workers in a particular contract period – "enjoy the flexibility".

Taylor's response was to point-out that the review was aimed at a pragmatic solution, to maintain levels of 'new employment' whilst giving DCs the 'right to request guaranteed hours'. Equally, his recommendation that 'workers' (between employees and DCs) should be employed on piece-work rates, enshrined in existing legislation, was meant to maintain flexibility in the gig economy. But, of course, this was seen as shifting the balance further towards the benefit of Capital over and against Labour.

Taylor argued that "While workers were at the forefront of its consideration, the Review also had to be mindful of protecting workers without crushing new business models". It pointed to the enhanced role of Trade

Unions, such as Community, in pressing for more cooperative gig economy platforms. And, in particular, for further tax and fiscal reform to require the employers of DCs to pay some form of employers NICs, in order to not only protect workers but to seek to bridge the spiralling gap in pensions' provision that seeks to engulf Western economies, such as the UK, by the mid-21st century.

Overall, the Taylor Review epitomises some of the challenges of seeking to navigate the evolution of work, from self-employment to mobilising communities, under the conditions of 21st-century emergent business models. As so often, the moral lens used to address these issues, in the systems-based policy-making worlds of the North and West, rests in utilitarianism (act consequentialism), seeking to provide the best solutions for the greatest numbers of individuals. But, it avoids the direct issue of how to effect genuine community-based work.

The current experience of collaborative platforms and the gig economy are hardly an adequate answer to the question of how to provide ethically responsible work for millions. At the same time, they do indicate ways in which these big questions are being answered within current Western policy frameworks. What the preceding account does show is that the Capitalist meaning of a 'sharing economy' is light years away from the relational understanding of work as community mobilisation that is meant here.

Window into Wisdom: the last supper – Luke 22:14–30

Community is, in part, about opening our homes and selves to others. Gifts are openings. They can be given away, with all the risks that entails. Alternatively, we can hold onto them, close off the opportunity, just in case, and find that, like the manna in the wilderness during the Exodus, if it isn't used on the day when it is given, it rots and turns into a stinking mess, filled with worms. Now, we turn from gift to sharing, as we come towards the climax of Luke's Gospel, in the narrative of the Last Supper.

Fresh divisions

In Luke's account of the Last Supper – the Passover meal that Jesus shared with his disciples on the evening before his betrayal, arrest, sentencing and crucifixion – we are presented with two meanings of sharing. These are connected to contrasting meanings of leadership. To make his point Luke offers his own distinctive telling of the story.

At a Jewish Passover there would have been four cups shared around the guests at the feast. These symbolise God's action at the Exodus (6:6–7) of, firstly, fashioning a people (Southern community), secondly, rescuing them from slavery (Eastern awakening), thirdly, removing them by power (Northern process) and, fourthly, acquiring them as a new nation (Western innovation). In Luke's account Jesus takes a cup, which is most likely the first cup – remembering Luke's focus on Jesus' community of the marginalised – gives thanks, and asks the disciples to divide it amongst themselves. This is usually attributed to an act of sharing and distribution, much like offering a collaborative platform. But, the word that Jesus uses for passing the cup around is διαμερίζω or "to divide into parts". Of course, this could simply mean distribute. But, the word is a distinctively Lukan one, used by him in two preceding Gospel passages. In one he uses it in a little parable of a house divided against itself (11:17,18) and in the other about a household divided, father against son (12:52,53).

The implication is clear. As the disciples drink the cup of community they are symbolically showing how they will be divided, scatter and leave Jesus to his lonely trial and execution. This first cup should be about bonding in solidarity. Instead it is about a form of sharing that is more like destructive isolation.

After that, we are presented with the familiar words of institution and the fourfold act of taking, blessing, breaking and sharing the bread, prior to offering the second cup (of renewal). Only after the distribution and the sharing of the cup of renewal does Jesus speak about one of their number being the betrayer. The second cup is described, by Jesus, as that of "the new covenant in my blood". Here is the second meaning of sharing, which is that all receive the gift of solidarity, which establishes a new community, with new rules (covenant), rather as *Cooperativo Mondragon* (see this chapter) has established its extensive Corporate Management Model. But, Jesus doesn't need any such document; it is his body which is the guarantor of the new covenant.

Sharing leadership

Squabbles break out amongst the disciples, after the sharing of bread and wine, in each Gospel. But, whilst in Mark and Matthew these are around who will be the betrayer, in Luke they are about who will be greatest in the Kingdom of God. Jesus' response to this is characteristically both pointed and oblique. He chastised them with the upside-down nature of the kingdom: that the greatest is like the youngest child or the lowest servant. "For, who is greater, the one who is at the table or the one who serves? Is it not the one who is at the table. But I am among you as one who serves" (22:27, NIV).

Another way of looking at the sharing economy is to describe it as the serving economy. For Jesus leadership is about service. Furthermore,

Jesus, through Luke, also uses another fascinating image, which has hugely contemporary relevance. He accuses the Roman rulers of lording it over the ordinary people and calling themselves "benefactors" (ευεργετης) or "do-gooders". Rather, the disciples are to be people who do good through service rather than act as, in modern terms, "philanthro-Capitalists".

Once again, we are presented, as throughout this chapter, with two alternative meanings of sharing. On the one hand, sharing can be about handing-out, which ends up benefitting the provider of patronage. Or, it can be about mutual submission, service, solidarity and, ultimately, making sacrifices for the sake of the new community. The choice is ours to make, between offering others 'the gig' or cooperating in shared servant leadership.

The relational paradigm

Prospects for a relational sociology

Pierpaulo Donati (1) sees scholars from different disciplines frequently referring to "social relations". But the latter are treated as being 'derived from', or as by-products of something else. For most of them (the Weberians) social relations are a projection of individuals. More or less unquestioningly, as 'north-westerners', they assume that the individual is the only reality they confront. For others (Marxists or Durkheimists) social relations are a product of conditioning by social structures and systems. *What really constitutes the "social relationality" of our world*, for Donati, *remains latent, hidden, unspoken, represented in a biassed form, ignored or nullified*. Society, for him though, *is* social relations.

Relational sociology discloses the fact that every human being is relationally constituted as a person. The same holds true for any social institution. Modernity, Donati goes on to say, has tried to immunise human individuals against social relations, and continues to do so. It is precisely for that reason that modernity and "individual employment" (see Chapters 6 and 7) is at an end. *We are ultimately what we care about and if we do not relate to significant others, we are nothing, we become nothing.*

Donati's key point then, whereby he is duly aligned with Bruni's civil economy, is that, common to the classical sociological tradition, *the nature of "social facts" is a relational matter*. All the classics tried to identify and define what a social fact is, from their different perspectives (either social action or social structure or 'the system'), which they usually conceived of as being opposed to, but in fact are complementary to, each other.

Not one of the classic works of sociology and certainly none of the political economists succeeded in grasping what a social relation is (for us because of their overly *northern* if not also *western* orientation). The apex of what Donati has called modern sociological thought can be found in the work of America's 1930s Harvard-based academic, Talcott Parsons (8). His theoretical framework is unbalanced in the direction of 'systematising' social relations to the point of *rigidifying* the relational logic as such.

The underlying issue: when the 'social' is no longer 'human'

Yet today, the feeling is that society is becoming increasingly fragmentary, uncertain, fluctuating, liquid, estranged and manipulated. In other words, it is decreasingly 'human', if not inhuman, in its everyday relationships. Social problems, for Donati, are increasing, while solutions are receding. In brief the epochal change that we are witnessing represents an emerging society characterised by the fact that *the 'social' (our 'south') is no longer seen, heard or acted upon as something immediately human* (see Chapter 2: African grounded interpretation of "are you human?", as *uri munhu* here). So what is the end result?

The social relation as the object of sociological knowledge

To a greater extent than in other periods, our society produces social forms, according to Donati, which, although originating from people, are perceived, lived and presented as in-human or dehumanising. Yet the relational paradigm affirms that: *in the beginning there is the relation!* In traditional (pre-modern) thought, as was intimated via the Chinyika rural community (Chapter 2), the 'social' was largely nonproblematic. What such thought foregrounded were other realities: the primal nature of everything, custom and practice, and the accomplishments of physical ("the grass that turns to gold") and human (Karanga and Baremba with their respective totems) nature.

Insofar as the notion of the social relation is, in some way, present in philosophical as well as social thought, from antiquity onwards, it is also indubitable that it becomes the focus in globalised scientific investigation in the modern era. Sociology was born, in Europe in the 19th century, at exactly the time when the social relation was no longer viewed as something 'given' either by nature or by necessary restrictions of one kind or another, as we have seen, but is something historically constituted and hence variable over time. Indeed historically in classical Greek thought, since there was not a specific concept of the 'social', which was absorbed into that of 'politics', it was impossible to speak of social relations.

The emergence of the relational in the contemporary world

For modernity, in fact, the social relation is, first, the reference of one subject to another, mediated by society (in other words, by culture, lifestyle, interest and identity) to which the subjects who are in relation belong. Since it is a universalised society, not a particular community, which offers what is necessary for mediation (values, symbols, rules, instruments, resources), the relation can assume variable modalities.

Exchange is one such, as a generating mechanism of social relations, which is inclusive of, but above and beyond, *market* exchange. Instead the exchange in question has a complex internal structure articulated in various dimensions, irreducible to each other, such as values, norms, goals and means used. It is usual indeed to present the birth of modern society in terms of *Gesellschaft*, that is a modern society as per German 19th century sociologist Ferdinand Tonnies (9). These are opposed by *Gemeinschaft* (traditional community relations, see the discussion of 'community' in Chapter 2). This is undoubtedly true, for Donati, but the transformation is neither pure nor exclusively economic. In brief, the transition from communitarian to "societarian" is a mixed phenomenon.

Different approaches to the study of social relations

On this basis, Donati seeks to critique each of the major fields of sociological enterprise, from the structuralists, such as Marx and Durkheim, through those who focus on agency, such as Weber and Simmel, to the social interactionism of Husserl, Mead and even hermeneutics advocates, such as Martin Buber.

The Marxist Approach: Karl Marx (10) adopted a supposedly relational approach to society, its actors, structures and processes. Unfortunately for Donati, however, it was a reductive vision. In Marx's opinion man is a purely social being determined by his material social relations in which he himself was historically placed. A primal example of a relational definition of such is given by Marx with reference to "capital", which for him is not merely a material entity but a social relation: precisely the relation of the expropriation of the means of production by the capitalist from the real producers.

The Positivist Approach: Equally, France's Emile Durkheim (11) formulated sociological positivism with a strong focus on social relations. His is the famous argument that the social is all that is configured as a "tie" – from *religio, to tie together* – with religion being the most integrative element for social cohesion.

The Interpretivist Understanding Approach: German sociologist Max Weber (12) thematises social relations in a completely different way. First this is because he highlights their intentional and intersubjective character (instead of their structural, interpersonal and supra-personal nature). For Weber, then, social scientists should not undertake the task of 'explaining' behaviour through causal relations (since every action is contingent, they do not follow predefined causal laws), but of 'understanding' them.

The Formalist Approach: Simmel's (13) fundamental assumption was that *society is reciprocal between individuals* and the social exists via the emergent effect of this reciprocity of "exchange of actions" (see previous chapter). By adopting the formalist idea of this program, general sociology has the aim of discovering the human in himself, for himself, and in that which for him is *inter*-personal. The relational field, as such, is a force-field charged with energies, with cross-crossing social relations, as a network of lines with various points (individuals), which bring them closer together or drive them further apart.

The Phenomenological Approach: In the phenomenology of Moravia's Edmund Husserl (14) analysis focuses on the construction of the social world as a world possessing meaning for subjects who experience it through an intersubjectivity based on the *we-relation*. The central thesis for him is that we cannot understand generalised social relations as abstract and formalised, at a second level, before we can understand, at a first level, inter-subjective actions in the life world, that underlie institutions and social systems.

The Symbolic Interaction Approach: Social relations are considered here as interactions, that is as actions between two agents in which what is central is the symbolic mediation that one exerts on the other, whereby the constitution of the self occurs through the other – America's G.H. Mead (15). Here, social identity is that which permits us to answer the question "who am I?"

The Hermeneutic-Dialogical Approach: Under this heading, for Donati, can be grouped a vast and rather diverse current of thought that treats social relations as a 'dialogue'. By the term *Beziehung* (relation) German-Jewish philosopher Martin Buber (16) refers exclusively to the relation of *you–I* dialogue (of full inter/human understanding) as opposed to *I–it* (which is the objectivising experience). According to Buber, the two paths by which contemporary man has attempted to overcome his "crisis of solitude", that of individualism and collectivism, are both dead ends. The authentic solution is the relation "between man-and-man", including the interpersonal relations and those of community. This, more than all other approaches, advances a general and systematic theory of social relations. This is to say that social relations are the way in which the social system functions. Consequently we can appreciate why both structuralist and agency approaches, both instrumentalist and normative, are unable to clarify the true causal relations in social life.

Observing and thinking relationally

The relational turn

In short, for Donati, relational sociology is predicated on the "relational turn" in society that was reflected by modernity, but goes beyond it. It carries forward that relational vision of society, first stated by Marx, Weber and Simmel, which they only began to explore and interpret, and which has continued today. However, and notably for our purposes, while these sociologists were all German, our Zimbabwean social workers, Muchineripi and Kada, are left out in the cold, not least because the local, Southern, academics, instead of developing a sociology from the indigenous ground up, are exogenously bound to the North and the West.

Overcoming functionalism through relational sociology

If one really wants to enter the relational way of thinking that Donati is proposing here, it is necessary to see it as a critical departure from structuralist and functionalist thought, in particular the versions running from Durkheim to Luhman (17) to Talcott Parsons. Throughout the 20th century, as such, functionalist analysis has been the background, the *leitmotif* and the paradigmatic infrastructure of theory and empirical research, in sociology and other social sciences. To the extent then, in our terms, that we are distanced from the 'south', in practice *and* in theory, this is bound to be the case.

In the first stage of functionalism, it was France's Durkheim, from his own 'northern'perspective, who reduced social relations to "functions". Social entities were defined not according to their full reality, but in terms only of the functions they performed in and for society. These functions, seen as social roles corresponding to the division of labour, became synonymous with social relations. From the beginning, this conception of relationality was characterised in a positivistic manner. In his celebrated *Rules of Sociological Method*, Durkheim (18) opposed the notion of purpose, and replaced it with a notion of function. Finalism had to be banished from sociology. Even if you take the German Frankfurt School of critical theorists today, in spite of their criticism of Parsons for having underestimated the *Lebenswelt* (life world), contemporary critical theorist Jurgen Habermas (19) has ended up re-evaluating a large part of Parsons' work positively.

The passage from modern to postmodern

For there to be social change, it is not sufficient for there to be a new element (for example, new technology) or a new relation in and for itself (for example a novel lifestyle). What is necessary, for Donati, is a complete and differentiated form of relationship between relations and the elements that compose them. This is the new key to understanding social change, he says. The conceptual schemes inherited from modernity, as we have seen, are nearly all nonrelational, and are, predominantly holistic (our 'eastern') or individualistic (our 'western'), the functional 'north' lying in between, with the communal 'south' left out in the cold. This remains the case while contemporary society, ironically according to Donati, is increasingly characterised, as we saw in the previous chapter, by being "relational".

Towards caring

What, then, are the new social forms being generated, overall? They may be conceived as ones where caring about relationships per se predominates. Relations are, thereby, treated reflexively, which makes them flexible, meaning able to differentiate and integrate their internal (human persons) and external (relational networks) components. They respond to the void left by political centrism and instrumental market rationality. A new civil society is therefore being born outside the market and state. The metareflexive, as such, relates to a horizon of values that transcends what is already given, personally and relationally, pushing forward "after-modern" society.

Donati then turns specifically to globalisation and its impact on the evolution of work.

Doing sociology in the age of globalism

The crisis of the lib/lab complex

The present crisis of what Donati terms the *lib/lab* complex (our West/North), that is the rule of society guided by the compromise between market and state or money and power is because both of such serve to alienate people from the relational character of their lives. As such, they colonise civil society without achieving any real success in terms of social cohesion and cultural integration. Indeed this was certainly borne out in colonial Southern Africa. It is, arguably, still the case in postcolonial Africa where market and state vie for power, while local communities get left behind. We would add that such "non-relationality" also gave rise to self-employment (lib) and to wage-labour employment (lab), bypassing the employment of self-and-community.

Linear and limitless progress

Modernity's slogans were "linear and limitless progress", "exploitation of the environment", society as a "dialectic between state and civil society", and politics confined to "constitutionalism within the nation state". Conversely the mottos of post-modernity are "sustainable and limited development", "human ecology", society conceived as a "network of networks", "multicultural society" and "politicisation of the private domain". Simultaneously, for Donati, social relations themselves, previously regulated by generalised symbolic means of exchange, have become transformed by relational dynamics.

What is still left out of account though, further to the above, even by Donati in his overall relational approach, is the implications for, or effect on, work and employment, of these forms of social differentiation. Even so, Donati's analysis points to the implication that the 19th and 20th century notions of work as employment and self-employment need to give way to an increasing cooperativism or communitalism, in the 21st century. We consider the former here and the latter in the following chapter, which concludes our Southern focus on community.

Illustrative Case: *Cooperativo Mondragon*, the Basque Country

The systems of Mondragon

Cooperativo Mondragon (CM) is known worldwide as the globe's largest network of business cooperatives and social enterprise complex. Founded in 1956, as a Roman Catholic experiment in cooperation, social responsibility and worker participation in management and control, it is a remarkable example of what can be achieved when principles and systems of innovation are aligned in the service of a sharing economy.

The scale of Mondragon is vast. It is one of the largest enterprise groups in Spain, dominating the region that is known as the Basque Country. That region has established a measure of independence from the national political economy, by virtue of trade rather than as a result of violence, as with Eta, or through political means, as with 'the crisis in Catalunya'. Equally, unlike the new business models of what is known as the sharing economy, in its 'gig' form (see previously), Mondragon can be seen as one of the boldest global innovation eco-systems for practising the principles of social relationism that Pierpaulo Donati points to.

In 2015 the total revenues of the business complex exceeded €12BN, with the range of 261 cooperatives and associated enterprises employing some 74,000 workers. Its spread is immense, encompassing manufacturing industries, financial services, retail, education and the arts. But, what is less immediately evident is that its navigational powerhouse proceeds from the ways in which its innovation centres, University and new business hubs have been aligned to principles of the sharing economy.

Experimenting with solidarity principles

Mondragon trades on the slogan of "Humanity at work". Of course, this play-on-words evokes the sense that work provides for human dignity. Even so, unless patterns of work are established in a humanistic way, labour ceases to enable creative flourishing, becoming – as with so much of the gig economy – a form of modern-day slavery. As such, the overriding principle of *Mondragon* is that the sole goal of wealth-generation is the welfare of people-in-community, achieved through competitive business and intercooperative solidarity.

It may be surprising to some that CM places such a strong emphasis on competition. That is because, in the terms of this book, they understand that navigating (Northern) from their core principles, which are rooted in Christian spirituality (Eastern), to effective business models, requires a full engagement in the marketplace (Western). CM doesn't seek to overturn Capitalism, but to humanise it. A significant aspect of this navigation arises out of Mondragon's educational centre, established in 1997, as Unibertsitatea Mondragon, today operating on nine campuses spread across the Basque region, serving c5000 students. But, this audacious experiment in integrating science, technology and education into their business complex proceeds from the overarching structures of their organising principles.

Implementing a cooperative-based corporate vision

The Congress (a complex pattern of democratic committees representing each of the enterprises and institutions of CM) agreed a new Corporate Vision in 2011, following the 2008–10 financial crash, in which they saw the way they implemented their cooperative principles – in a new management model – as providing a competitive advantage in the marketplace. The existential threat that the crisis in global Capitalism had posed for CM concentrated their thinking in respect of how they competed in global markets.

On that basis three pillars were adopted, which act as support structures for the managerial oversight of the business complex: intercooperation, innovation-promotion-knowledge, and embracing globalisation. All of this proceeds from a circular, rotating, dynamic model of how the basic cooperative principles are fused together, which was agreed at an earlier stage of the cooperative's life, in 1987.

The central focus is on connecting education with the principle of "the sovereignty of labour". By labour sovereignty they mean:

- Renunciation of the systematic contracting of salaried employees.
- Granting to Labour full rights in the organisation of all cooperative enterprises.
- Implementing ways in which Labour becomes the first and foremost recipient of wealth produced by the enterprise.

- A manifest willingness to extend job opportunities to all sections of society, irrespective of gender, race, religion, politics, ethnicity, class, sexual orientation or other social divisions.

Five further principles flow from this basis:

- Democratic organisation – workers are involved at every tier of decision-making and management control.
- Open admission – participation in Labour is open to all, with two provisos, that any members accept the Basic Principles of the cooperative and, second, that they are professionally and technically able to do the job to which they wish to be admitted.
- Participation in management – rooted in developing self-management and developing channels for participation and transparent communication.
- Wage solidarity – this is stated as "sufficient payment based on solidarity to be a basic principle of its management, based on a permanent vocation for collective social promotion".
- Instrumental and subordinated nature of Capital to Labour, so that wages are based on principle of social relations rather than capital accumulation.

All of which is quite a vision and one which has been implemented in a multiform way through a considerable network of institutional arrangements. But, of course, life is not perfect.

Reorganisation following the crash

Although CM managed to survive the initial phase of the post-2008 financial crash, it suffered a major disruption in 2013, when its flagship manufacturing business, Fagor, which had survived for nearly sixty years, collapsed. It had been caught up in the vertiginous decline in Spain's property prices. So, whilst the principle of intercooperation across CM had meant that it was supported by other enterprises, after €300M had been transferred into the company from 2009–13 the wider Co-operative had to close down Fagor.

Many commentators questioned whether or not the cooperative model could survive. In fact, the institutional resilience of the cooperative complex, which rested on firewalls against contagion that had been established through CM's financial arm, Laboral Kutxa enabled the cooperative model to co-evolve. Despite the very severe indentation to the image of Mondragon, caused by Fagor's collapse, by 2015 CM had invested €247M in new factories, re-employed almost all those who had lost their jobs and returned the business to overall profitability.

How had it managed this? One of the key factors was the availability of capital investment resulting from the principles of solidarity on which the cooperative is based. Whilst the average pay differential in Spanish corporations between the executives and average workers is c100 times, in CM it is six. This releases huge amounts of revenue for reinvestment that is otherwise simply taken in personal remunerations in most businesses. In this sense solidarity is not only a principle worth holding onto, it is shown to be the basis for navigating a business from its organising systems and principles to effecting massive change within the marketplace.

Two years after the collapse of Fagor there were about 200 out of the 1400 workers who had initially lost their jobs who were either without work or who had not taken early retirement, through CM's pension scheme. But, even these workers had been compensated through the cooperative's provident fund, which remunerated those without work at the level of 80% of their former salaries. This episode was a harsh lesson in the competitive pressures that cooperatives like CM face within Capitalist markets. But, what it seems to have done is increase the resolve of the overall business complex to adhere to its fundamental principles of developing community work, without barriers, in both solidarity and through competition.

Conclusion

The alignment we have been establishing, overall, is between the African 'south' and 'southern' Europe, thereby *employing community*. In this chapter we have observed this process in sharp relief, both through the negative image of much of the gig economy and the positive approach adopted within the cooperative movement, exemplified by Mondragon. Throughout, the emphasis has been on navigating towards a new model of employing community, in which social relations predominate over individualised wage-labour employment, as elaborated by Pierpaulo Donati.

This practice of subordinating Capital to Labour in the sphere of work can be seen to develop from the purposive spirituality that St Luke reveals in his account of the Last Supper. Therein is an expression of sharing which reflects participative mutual submission rather than the hierarchical allocative mechanisms of the market. To see how this is worked out within the South, we turn to 'communitalism' and its practical expression, in a more 'Western' way, in Nigeria.

Bibliography

1 Donati, P. (2011) *Relational Sociology: A New Paradigm for the Social Sciences.* Abingdon: Routledge.

2 Eisler, R. (2007) *The Real Wealth of Nations: Creating a Caring Economics.* New York: Berrett-Koehler.

3 Eisler, R. and Otis, K. (2014) Underpaid and Undervalued: Care Work Keeps Women on the Brink. *The Shriver Report Online.* 2 January. [Available at: http://shriver report.org/unpaid-and-undervalued-care-work-keeps-women-on-the-brink/].

4 Lancefield, D. and Vaughan, R. (2016) Shared Benefits: How the Sharing Economy Is Reshaping Business Across Europe. *Price Waterhouse Coopers Policy Reports.* London: PwC. [Available at: www.pwc.co.uk/issues/megatrends/collisions/sharingeconomy/future-of-the-sharing-economy-in-europe-2016.html].

5 Schmid-Druner, M. (2016) The Situation of Workers in the Collaborative Economy. *European Parliament Policy Department A: Economic & Scientific Policy, PE 587.316.* [Available at: www.europarl.europa.eu/RegData/etudes/IDAN/2016/587316/IPOL_IDA(2016)587316_EN.pdf].

6 House of Commons Work and Pensions Committee (2017) Self-Employment and the Gig Economy. Thirteenth Report of Session 2016–17. *House of Commons 847.* May. [Available at: https://publications.parliament.uk/pa/cm201617/cmselect/cmworpen/847/847.pdf].

7 Taylor, M. (2017) *Good Work: The Taylor Review of Modern Working Practices.* London: Royal Society of Arts. [Available at: www.gov.uk/government/uploads/system/uploads/attachment_data/file/627671/good-work-taylor-review-modern-working-practices-rg.pdf].

8 Parsons, T. (2010) *Social Structure and Personality.* New York: Free Press.

9 Tonnies, F. (2001) *Community and Civil Society.* Cambridge: Cambridge University Press.

10 Marx, K. (2015) *The Communist Manifesto.* New York: Penguin Classics.

11 Durkheim, E. (2008) *Elementary Forms of Religious Life.* Oxford: Oxford University Press Classics.

12 Weber, M. (2013) *Economy and Society.* Los Angeles: University of California Press.

13 Simmel, G. (2011) *The Philosophy of Money.* Abingdon: Routledge.

14 Husserl, E. (1970) *The Crisis of European Sciences.* Chicago: Northwestern University Press.

15 Mead, G.H. (1964) *George Herbert Mead on Social Psychology.* Chicago: Chicago University Press.

16 Buber, M. (2013) *I and Thou.* London: Bloomsbury.

17 Luhman, N. (2012) *Introduction to Systems Theory.* Cambridge: Polity Press.

18 Durkheim, E. (2014) *Rules of Sociological Method.* New York: Free Press.

19 Habermas, J. (1985) *Theory of Communicative Action. Volume 1.* New York: Beacon Press.

5 Employing community

Communal confederalism to women's communes

GROUNDING COMMUNITY
EMERGENT RECIPROCITY
NAVIGATING RELATIONSHIPS
MUTUAL EFFECT

Introduction

In this final chapter of the Southern section – grounding the evolution of work in Community and Nature – we turn to the effecting of various aspects of communalism. The Burning Question that we seek to answer asks: Is Commun(it)alism the way forward, in order to transformatively shift work from self-employment to communal working? In this respect we look through the lenses of social philosophers Bernard Stiegler, the late Murray Bookchin and the imprisoned leader of the Kurdish Revolutionary Movement (PKK), Abdullah Öcalan. They are helping to define communal economics in the contemporary world. Together, with Anselm Adodo they present four nuanced versions of commun(it)alism.

Our Window into Wisdom explores the 'primitive communalism' of the Acts of the Apostles. This serves to show that the principles underpinning 21st century communitalism were already being enacted within the first-century Judaeo-Christian community, in Jerusalem. For our Social Theory we visit the pioneering work of Fr Dr Anselm Adodo, an African monk who has instituted one of the most innovative natural healing centres in West Africa. His 'communitalism' demonstrates an integral work of circulating the GENE. It is grounded in a tribal Communis, is effected through a Spiritus, in his monastic sanctuary, navigates its Scientia, in the new *OFIRDI Research Academy*, aligned with the *University of Ibadan Institute of African Studies* and, fourthly, has effected the enterprise of *Pax Herbals*, as a new Economia, within Nigeria.

Finally, for our Illustrative Case, we examine the truly remarkable story of the *Rojavan Women's Communes* in West Kurdistan, inspired by the democratic confederalism of Öcalan and rooted in Bookchin's libertarian municipalism. Fundamentally, Rojava indicates that what appears to be idealistic paradigms can be practically modelled where the conditions demand it and the will of the people is sufficiently aligned.

Burning Question: is commun(it)alism the way forward?

We began this section, on the Southern world GENE circulation, with the image of Muchineripi rock, which was the focus for the Chinyika community gathering and an image of its stability, solidity and permanence. But, how unshakeable is the idea of community as a basis for effecting a new economic model, to challenge the dominance of Western Capitalism, and to release the economic cultural genius of different societies? We briefly consider three conceptions of community-based economic effecting. These come from the work of Bernard Stiegler, Murray Bookchin and Abdullah Öcalan.

Stiegler and effective communitisation

When Bernard Stiegler (1) discusses evolution he doesn't mean it as a metaphor. His work has been to show how the evolution of the modern *homo sapien* has been influenced by the interactions between the fourfold human being (body, mind, soul – the affective centre – and spirit) and the development of technologies (tekhne), throughout history. When it comes to the subordination of human communities, Stiegler sees several processes contributing to the 'symbolic misery' of the individual, seeking individuation (pace Jung), but relatively lost in the modern world.

The process of grammatisation – or the invention of written language and, later, its reproduction through printing and digitisation – has sublimated the power of communal life, as individuals learned how to separate ourselves from one another, through the new power of the written word. Within the advanced machine age we each attach ever newer machines to ourselves (like our smart phones), thus enhancing our capacities, at the same time as further reducing our connectedness to a face-to-face community, despite the artificial linking of social media. Most recently, we have entered a phase of programmatisation and hyperconsumerism, whereby we are not only proletarianised within the sphere of production – selling our labour – but in the sphere of consumption, whereby every moment of time is given over to some activity of consuming. Each of these processes has displaced our energies for collective coindividuation, in community.

But Stiegler is not entirely pessimistic. He sees some processes through which community can be regained. In particular, he recognises the role of the arts and creativity – in what he terms "spiritual labourers", within a political and industrial economy of the spirit – as reversing the degradation of homo sapiens, through communitisation. It is in creative work, by the *frequentation* of art, whereby people are enabled to repeatedly recreate themselves, in *an otium of the people*, through which we rediscover community, rather as preindustrial communities saw art in stained glass at church each week. Or, like Chinyika returning to Muchineripi Rock, community is reclaimed.

The communal organisation of contemporary economic life, for Steigler, rests in the ability of cultures to subordinate the economic to the spiritual labour and time of artistic creation. As such, human flourishing becomes dependent on the power of creatives, scientists, philosophers, social practitioners and legislators to produce social and conceptual practices, which further a political and industrial economy of the spirit. In this way a new communitisation of society occurs, through aesthetic production and consumption, on which to base a culture of temporal cycles and traditions (daily, weekly, monthly, seasonal, annual) – much as former religious calendars – to steer a path away from the demands of 'ever-newness' under monopoly capitalism.

Bookchin and libertarian municipalism

Murray Bookchin has returned to prominence because of contemporary peaceful revolutionary actions in communes and cooperatives, such as those commented upon in this section (cf FECOFUN, Mondragon, Rojava, inter alia). His combination of anarchist philosophy, green consciousness and libertarian politics seems particularly apposite for challenging the state of capitalism and the Capitalist State, in the early 21st century.

Bookchin (2) cites a litany of popular protest movements, in the 16th century Spanish Communeros, the late 18th century American town meetings movement and the Madrid Citizens Movement of the 1960s, as his inspiration. Equally, he could have included the various Occupy and anti-capitalist civic movements from Occupy Wall Street (2011), to the Icelandic 'Pots and Pans Revolution' (2009–11), the Spanish 15-M Indignants (2011–15) and the Iranian Green Movement (2009), amongst many others. The common feature of all these relatively short-lived protest movements is the 'rainbow coalition' of groups, not simply based in proletarian class struggle, but bringing together green, women's movement, student, gay, social housing, middle class, farming, industrial and post-industrial service sector workers and, even, disenchanted senior members of state apparatuses.[1]

An interesting political feature of the new radical libertarian municipal "peoples" movements is that they are attacked as much from the socialist left for 'revisionism', as from the capitalist right for being extremist and "anti-democratic", by which is meant that they seek to circumvent representational Parliamentary democracy and the activities of the state. In this they have their philosophical roots in the classical anarchism of Peter Kropotkin, Bukanin and Proudhon, arguing that genuine radical protest must be grassroots, bottom-up, face-to-face, authentically popular and somewhat Lincolnian: "of the people, by the people and for the people".

But, one of the important questions that Bookchin addresses is whether libertarian municipalism is simply political or, can it embrace economic organisation and the distribution of work? Bookchin argues that the anarcho-syndicalist model of "worker-controlled" enterprises – organised as union-based occupations at a national level and as collectives, at a local level – are always vulnerable to either state nationalisation or the power of Trade Unions to replace worker management with union-man management, as happened in Barcelona in 1937. Furthermore, as he points out, the factory is neither a relevant model for post-industrial society nor does it represent the ideal for worker emancipation, as many workers long for a more artisanal creative type of work, rather than the capacity to "plan their own misery" (cf Bernard Stiegler).

Bookchin's recipe for guaranteeing freedom from material want is to dissolve property and the economy into the civic domain. As he puts it:

> Neither factory nor land appear as separate interests within the communal collective. Nor can workers, farmers, technicians, engineers, professionals, and the like perpetuate their vocational identities as separate interests that exist apart from the citizen body in face-to-face assemblies. "Property" is integrated into the commune as a material constituent of its libertarian institutional framework, indeed as a part of a larger whole that is controlled by the citizen body in assembly as citizen not as vocationally oriented interest groups.
>
> (ibid para 13)

In this respect, vocation, which is where we began this book, becomes a commitment to community, rather than a means of separating individuals from themselves and others. Economic policy is formulated by the entire community, on the basis of face-to-face interactions. As such, the town-country divide becomes further dissolved into 'townships' and 'bioregions', so that the economic is transformed into a more genuine political economy, or communal economy, based in a common vocation.

Equally, it is a romantic and unrealistically false ideology to imagine that any community can become 'self-sufficient', for Bookchin. There needs to be a "Commune of the communes" to enable a shared management of economic resources, but organised as a conferedalist interaction of municipalities, to avoid both the emergence of competing city-states or what he sees as "bourgeois co-operativism" (see previous chapter on *Cooperativo Mondragon*, in the Basque Country). By the second decade of the 21st century it is clearly a practical model that is being implemented, if not in its entirety, in many communitarian situations.

Öcalan and democratic confederalism

Abdullah Öcalan is a man who has divided global opinion. To the Turkish authorities, who have kept him in isolated imprisonment since 1999, he is a terrorist leader, despite calling for the PKK (Kurdish Nationalist Movement) to end the armed struggle, in 2015. By contrast, for many supporters of popular democratic movements, Öcalan is a philosopher-hero, who has inspired the practical grassroots communal experiment in West Kurdistan, of Rojava (see Illustrative Case, this chapter). He has been nominated for both the Nobel and Sydney International Peace Prizes.

Öcalan's principles (3, 4) are enshrined in the model of democratic confederalism, which he has developed from Bookchin's libertarian municipalism. Central to Öcalan's model is that of nonhierarchical politics, to dispense with the structures of the nation state and advance the politicisation of the entire civil society. In a real sense Öcalan's is not a theory but a set of democratic practices, to strengthen participatory democracy for all institutions, groups and intellectual tendencies, as a process of ever-widening grassroots enfranchisement.

The point of Öcalan's conception of democratic confederalism is not to impose a communal solution, as an opposition to the state, which would require an act of violent revolution. Rather, it is to systematically dismantle the state apparatus and economic forms of property ownership, piece-by-piece, in the direction of broadening the participation of every member of the commune, until the community arrives at genuine local decision-making. At the same time, he shares Bookchin's practical understanding that, whilst most everyday decisions can be made locally, the strategy for a political economy needs to be set by a confederation of communes.

As such, Öcalan recognises that, in most cases, the institutions of communes will need to coexist in experimental pockets alongside the nation state. Equally, he is pragmatic enough to recognise that such an approach will only become accepted as it proves to be more effective than the state. Emancipating people – to make practical decisions for their economic prosperity, which solves problems more progressively than those that are developed through the structures of the state – will, inevitably be a gradualist project. Even so, the experience of Rojava (see Illustrative Case) has shown that democratic confederalism is both an acceptable popular solution and can be implemented within a matter of a few years. The extent to which the Rojavan experiment spreads will be a key test of Öcalan's radical populism.

Window into Wisdom: the primitive communism of Acts 2–4

In this section on the Southern realm, involving the grounding of a transformed understanding of work, we have focused on the Gospel of Luke. His Gospel presents discipleship as a journey of the marginalised, collecting up the broken pieces of humanity, and being formed into a potentially new community that disperses in chaos before the events of the crucifixion. All the potential is there. But, the reality of a new community cannot come into being until they receive 'power from on high' – the Holy Spirit.

So, St Luke presents a second volume – the Acts of the Apostles – which narrates the events of that new community, post-Resurrection and the receiving of the Spirit, at the Feast of Pentecost (Acts 2:1–13). But, very early-on Luke reveals that this new community experience affects every aspect of life, including the way in which the economy is organised. In fact, it gives one of the earliest examples in the ancient world of a community, based on Faith (Acts 2:42–47; Acts 4:32–37). Although the 'primitive communalism' of the Acts community doesn't specifically indicate how work is organised, Luke addresses two vital issues that have featured throughout these chapters: how power is exercised and the distribution of possessions.

Exercise of power in the acts community

There is a radical departure from the patronage system on which the Roman Empire was based. That percolated from the Caesar, through provincial Governors, to local officials, citizens and down – in terms of the ability to exercise control, power and violence – to the operation of slavery. The Roman 'gift economy' – with shades of the 'gig economy' – was use to maintain an asymmetrical hierarchy of benefaction and social obligations.

By contrast, the Acts community exhibits the use of gifts as a way of benefitting the entire community. Joseph of Cyprus (Barnabas) sells his property in order for the proceeds to be distributed by the apostles, according to needs. Equally, whilst the apostles can be seen to be exercising leadership within the community, this is clearly in order to organise mutual benefaction. Their powers of distribution operate as acts of service to the community, for the good of all.

The distribution of property and wealth

The most striking feature of the early Acts community is the depth to which there is recognition that all goods are held for the common good, as evidence of the equality that all the people have, under God. The marginalised community of women, the sick, disabled, tax collectors and 'the broken' are all understood to be equally graciously gifted with the holy spirit and, therefore, equally of worth within the community. These are matters of vocation and identity. All are called to serve and give. Each has a right to equal status and to be in receipt of what they need.

Luke tells how "All who believed were together and had all things in common; they would sell their possessions and goods and distribute the proceeds to all, as any had need" (2:44). . . . "No one claimed private ownership of any possessions, but everything they owned was held in common" (4:32). . . . "There was not a needy person among them, for as many as who owned lands or houses sold them, and brought the proceeds from what was sold. They laid it at the apostles' feet, and it was distributed to each as any had need" (4:34–35).

This was a radically different socioeconomic order. It demonstrated communal identity. It enshrined the principles of a gift economy. It was a genuine sharing economy. And, it was worked out in a form of communalism which could be seen as the precursor to each of the models, paradigms and theories presented in this and the preceding chapters. Becoming a fellow believer in the community meant that there was a reorientation to each person's understanding of possessions, power, identity and vocation.

The grounding of communalism

Fundamentally, this meant a reconfiguration of the meaning and practice of work, which was no longer a means of self-employment or material survival, but, rather, a way in which every gift could be used in support of and for the building-up of the community. Furthermore, it was based in an upside-down, nonhierarchical exercise of power (as 'dunamis').

Above all Luke's Gospel writings point to a set of relationships – in the power of Jesus' Spirit – wherein work is a means for service of God and others, connected together in a kingdom community. It is this kingdom that is capable of empowering every form of communalism for the future flourishing of humanity, no longer in employment of the self, but in communal service for the healing of the nations.

Pax Herbals: healing individuals and communities

Father Dr Anselm Adodo, like Dr Paul Muchineripi and Dr Steve Kada (Chapter 2), are all graduates of our Trans4m PhD program in Integral Development. While our overall focus is on both fundamental research and also transformative action in the African cases, pride of place goes to the latter. In comparison, as born out by Bruni, Zamgani and Donati, the European academic environment is more supportive of fundamental research, albeit that there is a Euro-African continuum between the two.

Adodo draws on his natural and communal African local grounding. At the same time, he has emerged through the ranks of the monastic Benedictine global order. Thence, he has navigated – along a relational path – through what he has termed "communitalism". Consequently, he and his enterprise, *Pax Herbals*, are well positioned to effect a "southern" form of communal employment, including, in his case, *nature power*.

Anselm Adodo (6) was born on November 2, 1969, in the serene environment of a modern government hospital in Akure, the capital of Ondo State, western Nigeria. No fuss. No complication. Just the normal birth of an ordinary child on a normal day. A few hundred miles away, war was raging in Eastern Nigeria; the Nigerian civil war, in which one million lives were lost.

The Biafra war lasted from July 1967 to January 1970. It ended three months after Anselm was born. A few hundred miles away, in the eastern part of Nigeria, hundreds of thousands of newborn children were dying of starvation, families displaced, and hopes shattered. It was a sharp contrast to the serenity of the environment from which he emerged. Growing up in a peaceful household, Adodo later read about this war and its atrocities in the history books.

Searching for knowledge and monastic community

Anselm moreover was the son of a father who was a school principal and science teacher, critical of 'unproven, old-fashioned' traditions, and of a mother who was also a school teacher. She was a devout Christian whose Christian faith called some traditional fetish-based practices into question. Meanwhile his grandmother and grandfather were believers in Yoruba tradition, but not to the point of fanaticism.

Anselm's first school was a Catholic boy's college, famed for discipline, high academic standards and excellence in sports. *Anselm* was indeed fascinated by the world of biology, chemistry, mathematics and physics. He *marvelled at the intricate complexity of the amoeba, the sophistication of the human heart and its incessant rhythm, the convoluted complexity of the human brain, and the laws of physics and chemistry*. He also wondered at the audacity with which these laws were stated, as if they were infallible.

Meanwhile, unknown to his father, Anselm had, before being admitted to university, along with two of his friends, paid an exploratory visit to a Catholic Monastery in Edo State, where a group of monks lived, worked and prayed. They interacted with the monks and spent some four days with them. Anselm had read about such monks, and how they were compared with mad people, due to the illogical and strange nature of their way of life. Notwithstanding such, in November 1987, he abandoned his university admission and joined the monastery.

Towards Pax Herbals

What is a monastery?

Perched on a hill one thousand feet above sea level, *St Benedict's monastery was founded by a group of Irish missionary monks, with the aim of spreading the monastic tradition to West Africa. They chose Edo State, geographically located right in the middle of Nigeria, linking the North, East, West and South.* Today, the St Benedict Monastery is of one of the most culturally diverse monastic communities in Africa, representing 15 different ethnic groups in Nigeria.

In 2004, after 17 years of living in a Benedictine Monastery as a monk, Adodo, by now Father Anselm Adodo, had to edit a book that told the story of the St Benedict Monastery, as part of the celebration to mark the silver jubilee of the existence of the monastic community of Ewu. In the book titled, *The Story of Ewu Monastery: Silver Jubilee reflections* (2004), he wrote:

> Monastic life did not start in the desert lands of Egypt, or in the fertile green farms of Canaan, or in the Garden of Eden. Monastic life did not originate in the high mountains of the Himalayas, or on the holy mount of Horeb. Monastic life originated in the human heart. It started the moment God, the almighty and all powerful said: I am one, let me be many.

What sort of man: Monk, Priest, Scholar, Herbalist

Meanwhile Anselm had been busy becoming more than a conventional monk. There was a full-page write-up in the *Guardian* newspaper at the time, one of Nigeria's elite newspaper and arguably the most respected Nigerian daily. The article was titled: "Monk who heals with herbs". The paper featured the picture of a man dressed in traditional and western attire, looking like a traditional native doctor and western physician at the same time. The picture was captioned "what sort of man?"

The article was about a Catholic priest who was also a herbalist, Christian theologian and a social scientist. It was *a tribute to the uniqueness of what Father Adodo was doing: creating synergy, so to speak between 'south' (nature), 'east' (spirit), 'north' (truth) and 'west' (enterprise).* It also hinted at the paradox of a Catholic priest belonging to a highly conservative order who dedicated himself to the promotion of traditional medicine. It was the paradox of a man engaged in fusing indigenous with exogenous knowledge, and the editor of the newspaper must have wondered, like many other observers, what sort of a man this is, combining both the indigenous ('Southern') and the exogenous ('Northern')?

Pax Herbals: communitalism in action

There was a need to harmonise the Southern and the Northern

Pax Herbals had then been established in 1996. It was registered as a private liability company, then, in 2002, it was described as *a Catholic research center for scientific identification, conservation, utilisation and development of African medicinal plants*. Through the utilisation of common plants and weeds, *Pax Herbals Clinic and Research Laboratories*, was then able to develop a natural science-based approach to developing herbal recipes.

By today it has been of help to the local community and to millions of Nigerians. It also has a home-grown business model that puts the interest of the local community as its focal point. Rather than practice capitalist "free enterprise", which encourages the individual to acquire as much for himself as possible, Pax Herbals has developed a model based on what Adodo terms *communitalism*.

At *Pax Herbals*, Dr Fr Anselm and his 150 co-producers, supported by some 1,000 distributors around Nigeria, cultivate their own herbs directly and also through accredited local outgrowers. *Pax Herbals* is the only herbal manufacturing company left in Nigeria that is locally producing its herbal medicines, despite the harsh economic climate which makes it easier and more profitable to be an importer rather than a manufacturer. It is no wonder that the Nigerian market is flooded with herbal products imported from foreign countries.

By so doing, Nigeria is creating wealth abroad and promoting poverty at home. But, through innovation, *Pax Herbals* is determined to continue to champion the preservation of African indigenous knowledge. It seeks to express communitalism (West), of African medicine (North), for the sake of posterity (East) and in order to purposefully and productively employ nature and community (South).

Nature and community to communitalism

The term *communitalism* is functionally different, for Adodo, from communalism or indeed communism. *Communitalism* affirms that some aspects of capitalism, such as individual inventiveness, are worth pursuing and supporting, but such inventiveness must be put at the service of the community, so that both the individual and the community prosper. This, as we shall see, is very much in tune with *the approach of social* credit (Chapter 16).

The key philosophy of *communitalism* is "we are either happy together as a prosperous community or unhappy together" and thereby unprosperous. For *communitalism*, the health and prosperity of the individual cannot be separated from the health and prosperity of the local community. Global health must start from local health, not the other way round. In the process the link between individual, community and enterprise health and whole-making, functionally, is made.

As a flourishing model of health and business enterprise within a particular local community, in Edo State adjacent to Benin City in Nigeria, *Pax Herbals* is activating the local community towards integral ecological and economic, scientific and cultural development. A flourishing agribusiness which allows all families in Ewu local community to engage in profitable cultivation of foodstuffs, medicinal plants and other cash crops will make the village into an economic hub.

When there is an improvement in the material well-being
of the community, the health of the members of the
community will also improve

This is the essence of community medicine. Unlike bio-health, which tends to focus on disease and neglect the root cause of diseases such as financial inequality, unjust wages, unfair working conditions, dysfunctional literacy etc., community medicine – through communitalism – adopts an integral approach to health and well-being.

Communitalism to Pax Afrikana

Turn the clock forward some 20 years; inspired now by his participation in Trans4m's PhD/PHD program, Anselm took a next step, turning Pax Herbals towards his version of Pax Afrikana:

- To serve as a centre for *genuine African holistic healing* that blends the physical and the spiritual aspects of the human person.
- To become a *model comprehensive healthcare centre* where the western (north/west) and traditional (south/east) systems of healing are creatively blended.
- To be an example of how *proper utilisation of traditional medicine* can promote grassroots culturally acceptable, affordable and relevant primary healthcare systems.
- To *disseminate knowledge* of the health benefits of African medicinal plants.
- To carry out researches into ancient African healing systems with a view to modernising them and making them available to the wider world through education.
- To *demystify African traditional medicine* and purge it of elements of occultism, fetishism and superstition and promote its rational use, to make it globally acceptable.
- To be a *truly indigenous/exogenous* herbal phyto-medicine centre that combines respect for Nature and community with wealth creation.

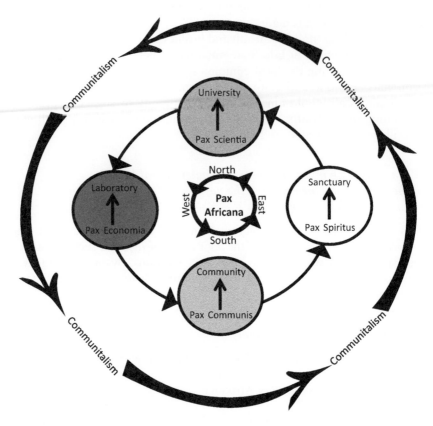

Figure 5.1 Pax Natura, Spiritus, Scientia, Economica

Source: Reproduced with kind permission of Fr Dr Anselm Adodo, Pax Herbals.

Altogether, and integrally as such, Dr Adodo now thereby embraced world-views, or realities, from all four corners of the globe (see Introductory chapter). More specifically, then, Pax Herbals connects to the wider integral model utilised here:

Pax Natura: *South:* identified with AFRICA. Key features are: Indigenous knowledge, community activation, agronomy, connection with the soil, respect and oneness with nature, a communversity of life. Orientation is towards NATURE and COMMUNALISM generally and towards *employing nature and community* specifically.

Pax Spritus: *East:* Identified mainly with ASIA. Key features are: emphasis on inner peace, wholeness, culture, inner security, spirituality, higher consciousness, intuition, feelings and emotions as part of human experience. Orientation is towards HOLISM generally and towards *employing the self* specifically.

Pax Scientia: *North:* Identified mainly with Europe. Fully in control of advances in scientific theories and social theories. Key features are: political systems, institutionalised research, and control of world's economic, political and social systems through colonisation, capitalism, socialism, neo-liberalism, globalisation etc. Orientation is towards RATIONALISM generally and toward *employment* specifically.

Pax Economia: *West:* identified mainly with America. Known for business, enterprise, entrepreneurship, individual quest for profit and competition. Key features are: Practical application of technology for profit, business management and dollarisation of world economy. The orientation is towards PRAGMATISM generally and towards *self employment* specifically.

Pax Natura to Pax Economica

Communitalism is a theory of interconnected knowledge, building further on the cooperative spirit of Africa. It states that knowledge is only complete and liberating when, as indicated previously, it is a combination of *Pax Natura, Pax Spiritus, Pax Scientia, and Pax Economia,* focusing on the Latin word for *peace.*

Pax has over the years become the *motto* of the Catholic Benedictine order of Monks. St Benedict in his rule encouraged his monks to 'listen' daily to the word of God. Listening is an art. It's something we learn to do. It is a skill. Listening requires that I lay aside my opinions and prejudices and *hear* what is being communicated to me.

When we have peace, we see things in the right way and we are able to love God and love our neighbour. The cultivation of peace, then, is the aim of every monk. Peace does not just refer to absence of war or strife. Peace is an attitude of the soul, whereby one firstly accepts one's place in the world, and gives to God the honour and glory that belong to God, and give to others the respect and honour that is due to them.

Peace comes when we transcend our fears by accepting our place in the universe, and accept others as they are. Fear is a source of violence and war. When we have peace, we stop harming others. We begin to relate to others and people with honour and dignity. We stop exploiting and cheating others. This is what *Pax* is all about – communitalism in action – a deeply 'southern' form of relationality. How is this to be promoted through ACIRD?

Harnessing nature power

For Adodo, Africans must embark on a new adventure of knowledge, ultimately involving institutionalised innovation-driven research, leading to indigenous-exogenous knowledge-led sustainable development. This involves *harnessing nature power; fusing prayer (ora) and work (labore);*

*combining nature, spirit, science and economy; culminating in organisa-
tional or societal communitalism, altogether centred in individual and community healing.* Adodo sees his home grown *Communitalism* informed by,
both, Capitalism and Communism.

Illustrative Case: Rojavan women's cooperatives, West Kurdistan

Since the beginning of the Syrian civil wars in 2011 – as part of the so-
called 'Arab Spring' – when a range of groupings began to oppose the
repressive rule of President Bashar al-Assad, the news appears to have
been unremittingly bleak. It has been difficult for most observers to
keep track of the range of interethnic conflicts that have taken place,
whilst recognising the geo-political proxy war taking place between
Islamist factions, apparently supported by Saudi Arabia, on the one
hand, and the Assad regime, backed by Iran, on the other.

Many ethnic groupings have been caught up in the fighting or have
chosen to become associated with one or another bloc. But, alongside
the various other battles, there has been a further development of the
aim of Kurds, in Northern Syria, to establish their own homeland of
Kurdistan. In fact there are four Kurdistans, as with the four worlds.
But, one of the most remarkable stories, amidst the chaos of Syria's
catastrophe, is that of the women's cooperatives movement in West
Kurdistan, otherwise known as Rojava.

A brief history of Rojava

The movement came to prominence in 2012 when some of the Assad
regime strongholds in Northern Syria fell to the terrorism of ISIS (so-
called "Islamic State of Iraq and Syria"). The Bush-Blair promoted
'war on terror', being fought by the US, UK and their allies, was
attracting all the headlines. At the same time, some quite astonishing
local developments were taking place which, in moral terms, shone as
a searchlight on the Western aggressive actions, to protect oil reserves.

The thoughts, writings and peaceful struggle of Abdullah Öcalan, leader of the PKK (which Recep Tayyip Erdogan, in Turkey, has
branded a terrorist movement) inspired the Rojavan experiment.
Öcalan had, in turn, based his philosophy of Democratic Confederalism (see previoulsy) on the writings of the political ecologist, Murray
Bookchin (1921–2006). His theory of Communalism, in turn, had its
roots in Aristotelian and Hegelian philosophy. As we have repeatedly
seen in this Southern section of the book, the source for each of these
streams frequently returns to the same springs of Community, in the
fourfold world of Aristotle. Öcalan, therefore, bases his three pillars

of a democratic and autonomous society, ecological sustainability and gender equality on ancient wisdom for the 21st century.

That said, the Rojavan experiment is a far more practical outworking of the people, seeking simply to survive, let alone thrive, in one of the harshest social environments on the planet, war-torn "Kurdistan". But, it is in the nature of the women-led popular movement that real inspiration is to be found. The women's cooperatives have led the way in building an economic base through which the culture of Kurdistan can be realised, in a territory roughly the size of Belgium.

The women's cooperative movement

The confederation of women's movements in the region is known as *Kongreya Star* (Star Congress), which brings together many Muslim groups, together with the Christian minority, other Arabs, Yazidis, Assyrians and women of no particular faith. It was originally founded in 2005 (as *Yekitiya Star*) as a popular protest movement against the Ba'athist oppression of women and Kurds, under the Syrian Government of Bashar al-Assad. In turn, it took its inspiration from the Kurdish Women's Movement, evolved in the late 1970s, in southern Turkey, northern Iraq and north-western Iran.

Kongreya Star is organised around ten committees, which cover all aspects of women's lives, including education, economy, arts and culture, politics and government, justice, civil defence, ecology, international relations and media communications. But, the cooperatives are based in the principle of women's autonomous solidarity, challenging the patriarchal order and mentality of the prevailing society. In fact, the expression of these principles has been practically worked out in very determined ways.

Their expression of women's liberation and 'self-defence' is based in Öcalan's democratic confederalism, relying on classical anarchist principles of local self-determination, rather than the political structures of an overarching state. *TEV-Dem* (mixed sex communes) communes have been established in the three cantons of Afrin, Kobane and Cizire. In each, assemblies have been formed at village, neighbourhood and locality-levels, in which all local people are enabled to participate. There are some 1,600 communes across the Rojava region, with the single town of Qamishlo creating ninety-eight separate communes, each with its own assembly.

This may seem like a recipe for chaos. In actuality, it brings the most relevant decisions for families right down to street-level, such as the distribution of water, energy and use of open space. Further, decisions that affect wider communities are made at subregional assemblies, in which representatives of all communes participate. But, significantly, these are augmented with any other local people who wish to attend, so that representative democracy is balanced by popular participation, similar to the model developed within the recent *Occupy* movement.

To counter patriarchy, the communes have been divided into those that function for women and men together (*TEV-Dem*) and those that are women-only (*Kongreya Star*, KS). The impact of such emancipation has meant that KS assemblies rarely drop below 50% participation and often reach close to 100%, demonstrating the revitalisation of democratic institutions, in sharp contrast to the democratic deficit often reported in Western nations.

Each of the KS communes has five committees, including an economy committee, which is focused on strengthening communal work, particularly in respect of supporting the cooperative use of common agricultural lands. This is particularly significant for the local culture because of the rich fertility of the Rojava region, which lies within the Tigris-Euphrates basin, often referred to as the cradle of civilisation, in which emmer wheat was first cultivated in excess of five thousand years ago, and from which Abram emerged (the father of Israel!).

Given the international embargo on Syrian produce and importing to the region, the KS communes have focused on recreating a sustainable, ecological form of communal agriculture, remarkably similar, in overall intent and organisation, to that of *Chinyika* (see Chapter 2). Such a model of subsistence production is aimed at transforming unemployment into communal work and reducing poverty and the threat of famine. Equally, the communes recognise the role of women over thousands of years, in both reproductive and productive economic activity, realising the reactivation of a communal economy, in which their culture is based. Their focus on producing home-made and hand-made, seasonally-related produce emphasises sustainability principles-in-action.

The nature of this movement and its place in one of the world's most conflicted regions means that this work is fragile and provisional. By the end of 2016 there were less than one hundred separate women's agricultural communes operating across the region, the smallest with four members and the largest with more than two hundred. As such, this remains an incredibly provisional movement which will be on the verge of survival for several years. That said, within the Cizire canton alone the communes provide more than a thousand women and families with a communal livelihood, and that number is increasing each month.

The values that underpin the women's cooperative movement are uncompromisingly idealistic, including care for the environment, improvement in health outcomes, the removal of exploitation and oppression, mutual respect, friendship, effort and democracy. They see these as the basis for effecting a just, democratic, egalitarian and ethical society, in which basic structures have shifted. Equally, the women's communes have seen a major increase in the willingness of women to taken on leadership roles, to express themselves and grow in self-confidence, within a society that has habitually placed women in an inferior and exploited position.

An alternative economic model

The operation of democratically run cooperatives based in local decision-making communes takes away the power to control and organise markets from the state. In this sense, at least, the Rojavan model represents a modern version of classical Anarchism, as does *Cooperativo Mondragon* (Chapter 4). Jobs are created locally, particularly for unskilled workers, who gain their skills through their practical engagement in productive activity. Equally, as men see women taking a lead in productive work and the organisation of labour, perceptions change, addressing the hegemony of patriarchal and capitalist institutions.

At the same time, the effects of the ongoing wars with ISIS, the Assad regime, bombardments by the US and Russia, the invasion of Northern Syria by Turkey, seeking to annihilate the Kurds, and the economic embargoes, have meant that hundreds of thousands of refugees have flowed into the Rojava region. On that basis there has been a recent attempt to massively increase the scale of the women's and *TEV-Dem* cooperatives. One of the largest, in Dirbesiye, involves 4,000 workers engaged in agricultural and livestock production. Each person invested $100 in the *Kasrek Cooperative Society*, which bought its own agricultural machinery, veterinary clinic and manages the distribution of 37,000 acres of communal land.

There is a longer-term aim, towards industrialisation, again based in communalism and Democratic Confederalism, to unpick decades of underdevelopment, which has been the policy of the Assad regime. Equally, Rojava wants to avoid the dangers inherent in dependence on oil, which was the strategy deployed in south Kurdistan which has, again, become the focus for Western capitalist market penetration. Perhaps most dynamically, the *TEV-Dem* and *Kongreya Star* movements have refused to allow NGO access to the region, in order to circumvent becoming dependent on aid. Through all these strategies, despite being in one of the most fraught and unrecognised regions of the world, the *Rojava Economic Board* continues to mobilise more cooperatives. These are seen as a resistance to Capitalism and, also, a means of self-protection of their society and economic culture, effecting the employment of community.

Conclusion

What has become clear through the series of cases and the paradigms behind them, within this Southern section of the book, is that community mobilisation, for new patterns of working, beyond the employment of isolated selves, is both theoretically coherent and practically feasible. Placing community at the heart of 21st-century work is actually being effected across the globe.

Whether it is through employing the community, as in *Chinyika*, through pan-national cooperative structures, such as *FECOFUN* or *Mondragon*, or the communitalism of Adodo's *Pax Herbals* – drawing together community, spirit, science and reformed capitalist enterprise – community is becoming the rock upon which the future orientation of 21st-century work can be grounded. For, now, we turn from the 'south', where the relational emphasis has been on employing community, and indeed nature, in 'southern' European theory and 'southern' African practice, to the 'east', where we focus on 'employing the self'.

Note

1 The recent BBC Storyville (July, 2017) documentary "Accidental Anarchist", funded by the Sundance Film Festival, told the story of Carne Ross, a former senior British diplomat who has founded *Independent Diplomats*, a company of former senior diplomatic service officers, from the UK, US and Europe, to fight for the rights of local municipal protest groups.

Bibliography

1 Stiegler, B. (2015) *Symbolic Misery Volume 2: The Catastrophe of the Sensible.* Cambridge: Polity Press.
2 Bookchin, M. (1986) *The Modern Crisis.* New York: New Society Publishers.
3 Öcalan, A. (2011) *Democratic Confederalism.* London: Transmedia Publishing Ltd.
4 Öcalan, A. (2017) *The Political Thought of Abdullah Öcalan: Kurdistan, Women's Revolution and Democratic Confederalism.* London: Pluto Press.
5 Adodo, A. (2017) *Communitalism – Towards Pax Afrikana.* Abingdon: Routledge.
6 Adodo, A. (2012) *Nature Power: A Christian Approach to Herbal Medicine.* Ewu-Esan: Benedictine Publications.

Part III

East

Employing the self

6   The noetics of nature
Self realisation to divine trade

GROUNDING HUMAN NATURE
AWAKENING SPIRIT
THREEFOLD NAVIGATION
EFFECT AWAKENING

Introduction

Grounds for employment of the self

As our pre-emphasis shifts from 'south' to 'east' so our orientation changes from the relational to the spiritual, from the communal to the noetic, and, as such, in terms specifically of 'eastern' grounding, nature is conceived of in a different guise. Moreover, and in terms of the overall focus of this book, we now switch to the *employment of the self* psychologically and spiritually (as opposed to employment of the community) over and above the (self) employment.

Of course, in alluding to the 'east', we are spanning an enormous range of humanity, from Eastern Europe to the Middle East, and from the Near to the Far East, not to mention also parts of Western Europe and America which have been significantly influenced by 'eastern' philosophy. However, and that said, there is a common orientation towards "self-transcendence" that all these eastern parts of the world share, spiritually and philosophically.

Yet, by and large, such a spiritual orientation has not been translated into a new approach to work and employment, as per "employment of the self", at least explicitly. This is an imbalance we seek to redress in this second part of our book, as we move through grounding and emergence, onto navigation and ultimate effect, altogether along this 'eastern' path of *renewal*. Our main case incorporates the spirituality of early mediaeval, Eastern Christianity, associated with the Orthodox centre of Constantinople, as seen through the lens of US theology professor Bruce Foltz. He introduces the theme of noetic grounding, in nature, looking from the visible into the hidden depths of what work from a divine perspective can mean.

The Burning Question that we seek to ground this chapter in is: "how important is work in defining 'the self'"? We then turn to our emergent Window into Wisdom, from the 'southern' Gospel of Luke to, now, the 'eastern' Gospel of Mark, again considering identity from a Christian perspective, through the call to the first disciples and the implications that has for our self-understanding of vocation.

Thereafter, we introduce the relevant "social *eastern* theory", in depth, before presenting its effect, in a relevant case study, related to *employment of the self*. From that perspective of identity, thereby related to the employment of "self", we enter our Illustrative Case, through which we consider how the principles and values of the Fairtrade movement have shaped the work of Sophi Tranchell, at *Divine Chocolate*. Her self-identity emanates from the Catholic Christian recognition to "act justly, love mercy and walk humbly with your God" (Micah 6:8).

Burning Question: is my self grounded in work?

Who are you and what do you do?

You are at a party and meet someone new for the first time. Two questions are likely to surface quite rapidly: "who are you?" and "what do you do?" But, how closely connected are these issues of identity? It has become commonplace to recognise that identities are multiplex in advanced societies. We can, at the same time, self-identify according to a range of geographic associations – nation, region, place, even address – aspects of gender, family, demography, race, ethnicity, culture, faith and religious tradition or adherence, economic ties, food and dietary preferences, health situations, political affiliations, musical and leisure pursuits, sporting fan-ships, and many other aspects of life. But for many, it is work, job, employment that takes pride-of-place in the hierarchy of self-identifications.

Recent research on work-based identity suggests that it is a construct that emerges from complex interactions between individuals, groups and social contexts along three dimensions: life spheres, life roles and work facets (1,2). Life spheres describe the situational types listed previously, by which we seek to differentiate ourselves from other persons by our self-identifications. "I'm Tony and I am from Liverpool, but live in the English Lake District; I'm middle-aged, from a white, Jewish background, but am an Anglican Priest and practising Christian, involved in musical theatre, am a vegetarian . . .", and could go on so for many pages, if I chose. In Ronnie's case, interestingly enough, Southern African by birth, he is Samanyanga in Zimbabwe and Gatsheni in South Africa, both of his such identities being place related, though thematically, in each case, he is identified with an "elephant" (samanyanga in shona, gatsheni in zulu) because of his longstanding and thereby scholarly memory. But one of the most significant life spheres, according to most research, is that of 'work interest'.

At the same time, in each of these spheres Tony will operate a number of life roles. For example, in the family, he is husband to Carol, father to Rebecca and Amy, grandfather to Ben and Tom and child of Muriel and Joseph. He has formal roles within his local church and has occupied roles within the local community, in respect of employment generation and economic development. Equally, he could list specific life roles in each sphere. But once again, his most complex set of life roles relates to work, job and employment. In work, his roles relate to teaching and research. His job includes a range of titles, such as Professional Tutor, Academic Adviser, Employability Co-ordinator and several others. His employment is as a University Academic. But he is also the Managing Director of a musical theatre company. And so it goes on. In Ronnie's case, while also being a father and a husband, he identifies himself, overall, as Afro-European, and in that context he sees himself as a social innovator, a business and economic scholar, a conceptual activist, altogether. You might like to complete a similar list – it is illuminating what you include and don't and in what order.

The narrowest range of work-based identification rests on work-related social group and place-of-work. Tony found it easier to describe the first when he was a Christian Minister. Now, the social group of University teachers is far more diffuse and less solid group. But, his place of work, Liverpool Hope University, gives a very precise context and focus because of the singular nature of our institution, being Europe's only ecumenical (by which is meant Roman Catholic and Anglican Christian) University foundation. Ronnie's institutional identification is primarily, as a social innovator, with Trans4m in France, which he cocreated with Alexander Schieffer; and secondarily, as a conceptual activist, with Da Vinci Institute in South Africa, their academic partner. Work facets include attachments to wider grouping, which establish such aspects as 'professionalisation' or 'employment group', whilst local team roles, collegial relationships provide the anchorage to a workplace. Which one assumes the greater significance will determine how frequently, given the choice, which isn't always available, you might move work-places and employments whilst maintaining similar work and jobs.

Such is the complexity of analysing the surface features of work-based identity. But, as we considered in the noetics of nature, derived from Byzantine (and Celtic) understanding, there are far deeper depths below the surface of identity-at-work.

The depths of work-based identity

According to Bothma, Lloyd and Khapova (3) there are three sets of processes which undergird the phenomenon of work-based identity: formation, activation and behaviour. These begin to plumb the depths rather more than maintaining a surface meaning. Different theorists refer to role identities, prototypes or identity standards. Each of these has their origination in conceptualisations of types and archetypes, which date back through personality theorists, such as Carl Jung, to the modalities and humoural theory of ancient Greece and even further to the most ancient civilisations in Sumeria and China. People have always wanted to classify themselves and others, often in accordance with or opposition to the types that they find in sacred texts.

As such, we can see in the ancient Greek world of Socrates, Plato and Aristotle certain work roles accorded to particular archetypal features of the city-state and Republic. Leaders, enforcers, artisans and slave-workers each held a place in the natural functioning community. But, equally, these work-roles proceeded from particular features of the person, most frequently defined according to one of four polarities, in a quaternity of wholeness (and holiness). The point is that there was a wisdom understanding that connected self, characteristics, archetype and work role. In modern divisions of labour and markets this has been lost. The result is the alienation of the self from work. And, equally, this results in a dislocation of the community wherein the noetic of nature, our connection to the divine wisdom and the cord linking nature, self, God and work is broken.

Contemporary theorists (e.g. 4) see the activation of work roles as conditioned by specific events, which guide the choice of different prototypes to meet the requirements of the moment. Furthermore, the behaviours that flow from the activation of specific identity prototypes may result in the pooling of self within a group social identity at work or the verification and legitimation of the person's self within their work role. The result is a very dynamic process of work-based identity formation. But, the resultant loss is of a deep-seated understanding of who I am. My need to change according to the circumstances of the workplace and to select more superficial prototypes from a battery of social and acceptable employment-related identities can cause confusion, depersonalisation and mental illness (see 5).

Recovering a noetic work-place identity

Within most professions the idea of career development has assumed central importance. The principle that a person sees their progression as a worker through various stages, within an upward trajectory, gives a certain meaning to the self. For Thomas and Feldman (6) this is connected to a sense of intrinsic vocational calling, whereas for McCardle et al (7) career is more related to employability and an extrinsic, functional marketability within the pool of labour. The distinction being made concerns the extent to which there is a personal sense of prior selfhood, which is worked out in the labour market. Vocation suggests an awareness of 'calling' and, hence, a 'Caller'; a recognition of the person's place within the natural order of things; even a divine wisdom at work.

We have to say that each of the two authors of this volume have struggled with the achievement of a single career, largely because of its connection to the idea of work hierarchies and the sense of seeking to achieve an end-goal, rather than proceeding in work from an inner starting point. Equally, it is increasingly the case that few people, at least in many Western contexts, work in the same place, job or role for more than a few years. Indeed, we prepare our students for multiple careers, let alone a multiplicity of jobs.

As such, we see in the Eastern model – albeit one that is breaking-down, under the competitive pressures of capitalist labour markets – of employment within the same company-family for life, a closer contact with the noetics of nature. There is in the identification with a particular workplace, role, job-for-life or vocation a greater sense of the heart-knowing, compared to the head-knowing. This is not, in any way, to diminish the sense of professionalism, in terms of adding to the sum of knowledge of a discipline, as a discursive, cognitive activity. This is a vital aspect of the role of work within social and economic development.

But, work that is based in a prior vocation; that serves a greater purpose by engagement in Levy-Bruhl's "participation mystique"; and proceeds from an awareness of the divine connectivity of 'self-emergence' is likely to be more fulfilling. Above and beyond all these understandings of work in the modern world is a sense that the work we are engaged in is a reflection in an outer way of an invisible activity of the cosmos. In that sense work has meaning in itself and, equally, gives meaning to the self that is employed, not through contract but through contact with the world. We now turn to our distinctly Judeo-Christian *Window into Wisdom*, thereby making visible our own respective traditions, for deeper insights into the question we are here addressing, before then turning more systematically to the Social Theory that follows

Window into Wisdom: how does my spiritual self emerge?

The call of the first disciples (Mark 1:16–20, 3:13–19)

As we turn from South to East and, hence, from nature-community to selfhood-spirituality, we also shift Gospels, in our search for windows into wisdom, from Luke to Mark. Most scholars agree that Mark is the basis for the three synoptic gospels of Matthew, Mark and Luke. Matthew (W) and Luke (S) derive many of their pericopes from Mark (E), which they augmented from other sources and moulded according to their own, distinctive, theological emphases, as Gospel redactors. Luke has a distinctively 'Southern' emphasis on the marginalised community, especially of women, who follow Jesus. By contrast, Mark's spirituality focuses on the personal presence of God-the-father in Jesus' ministry, which is represented as one of intense power, action and immediacy. Mark, therefore, is the 'Eastern' Gospel, urging people to a self-resolution, wherein we "decide to believe" in Jesus.

Vocation to self-hood that is centred on Jesus is crucial for Mark. As such, it is useful to begin these reflections on wisdom with Mark's account of the call of the first disciples (1:16–20) and their receiving of Jesus' authority (3:13–19). The experience of receiving a call from God or his prophets and servants is not unusual in the Bible. But, neither is it a common occurrence. No more than one hundred biblical characters are specifically called to a particular vocation or ministry. Consequently, we shouldn't expect to receive a lightning strike from heaven pointing us to a specific job of work. Far more frequent is the spiritual principle that *all people are called* to live a whole life, under God, in which work plays an important part in shaping the self. Equally, our occupations are to be subordinated to the invisible activity of, and relationship with, God; what we have termed a *noetic of nature*, in this chapter, following Bruce Folz.

Submit your job to your faith?

Extreme care needs to be taken in respect to applying the call of the first disciples to our everyday lives. They had a very special place in the history of the people of God. Even so, Jesus calls twelve men to a threefold ministry. They are to be with him, to preach to those they are sent to, and to drive out demons. Mark places a particular emphasis on Jesus as a wonder-worker, engaged in power encounters against the spiritual source of evil in the world.

From other texts we know the occupations of some of the twelve. Those who receive the initial call – Peter and Andrew, James and John – were fishermen. Others who were appointed included Matthew, a tax-collector, Simon the Zealot, who was a politician and Judas Iscariot who was an accountant, in today's parlance. In other words, they were a mixed bunch of artisans, professionals, private individuals and public figures. It is clear that all can be and, indeed, are called.

But, the specifics of the call to Peter and Andrew, James and John are fascinating. They are called by Jesus to "Come, follow me, and I will make you fishers of people" (1:17). Mark describes how they leave their boat and nets (tools of their trade) with their father (family) and the "hired men" (1:18–20). Clearly, they were not wage-labourers but ran their own family business. They were self-employed, in our terms. But, in leaving their means of production, family ties and self-made occupation they are being challenged about their identity.

Settling for insecurity

Later, in Mark, as in the other gospels we see that the disciples retain a place in the community and may, indeed, have spent some time in their everyday work. But, the vital point is that their work was no longer to define them; nor was family; means of production or social status. Their identity was defined in a more invisible way, as followers of Jesus, albeit initially quite visible, at this stage; yet, not for the rest of us.

The fishing industry and fish-salting trades were some of the most stable sources of work in thefirst-century Galil and Judaea. So, again, these disciples were called from stability to a very unstable threefold pattern of life. Relationship with God was their defining vocation. Waiting to be sent out into particular mission fields was their occupation. Engaging in power encounters was to be their work.

Even if we have no specific belief in God, there is an important principle of wisdom here. To become a more fulfilled person and to take on selfhood means leaving behind safety, security and a settled life. Rather, we are to cast off into the depths of an invisible, noetic world, unsure where this will take us. Instead, our vocation is to know that there is a safer security in the 'cloud of unknowing' – as some of the Byzantine mystics described what we might call the 'dark matter' of authentic self-life – than in the secure work that, otherwise, we can let define us. And so, we introduce Bruce Folz and the 'noetics of nature'.

Social Theory: the noetics of nature

For Bruce Foltz (8), Professor of Philosophy at Eckerd College in Florida, with a particular focus on the ancient thought and spirituality of Byzantium – which is still a living tradition in the Orthodox Christian East – important insights and realisations can be found that will shed an indispensable light upon what it would take to sustain a happier, more salutary relation between humanity and earth. For as Husserl (9), the Moravian philosopher and originator of phenomenology, emphasises in his *Crisis of the European Sciences*, the modern natural sciences have failed to maintain the bridges between lived reality and scientific conception. This then has affected our perception of "employment" or "self-employment", as object, as opposed to "employment of the self" as subject. In fact the world *theoria* is rooted *theasthai*, based on the Greek word for theatre. Ancient drama as such involved far more than "looking" at what is "present at hand". *Theoria* was then for the ancient Greeks a special kind of attentive and "experientially engaging" seeing, closely related to wondering. Indeed the Greek word *thea* also means goddess, also related to "theology". It thereby apprehends the rootedness of the visible *in* the invisible that Foltz calls *noetics*.

Indeed in American psychologist William James' (10) *Varieties of Religious Experience*, the noetic suggests "illuminations", or revelations. *This old sense of noetic seeing is rooted then in our sensitive apprehension of the half-hidden, dynamic, inner patterns and orderings in the natural world.* For Karl Marx, on the other hand, this archaic mythic consciousness cannot seriously compete with steam engines and locomotives, whereas Max Weber alluded to the fact that this "disenchantment" of the world was the inevitable consequence of its growing rationalisation. Seeing is replaced by calculation, craft or vocation by self-employment and employment. *The loss of this old way of seeing, then, and along with it the materialisation and flattening and disenchantment of nature – has roots that reach back earlier than the rise of modernity.*

Ousia and Energeia

In the fourth century, the great early ascetics of the Egyptian desert (and later Sinai, Palestine, Syria) articulated a threefold mystical path: *catharsis* or purification of the soul; *theoria* or contemplation of the divine energies; and *theosis*, or union with God.

For *the eternal Logos incarnated in Christ is already expressed, partially but genuinely, in every being that is,* each uniquely mirroring its creator, each grain of sand, each blade of grass, each leaf of a tree, expresses some ineffable meaning. Yet *this noetics of nature never really takes hold in the Latin West,* with the limited exception of Celtic Christianity, and today in our Trump-and-Brexit laden western world we see the material end result.

No wonder, in fact, Trump was voted in, at least in part, because of a lack of "jobs".

The disenchanted nature of modernity

The way then was thus paved in the West for Bacon, Descartes, and all the heralds of the disenchanted nature of modernity. That *the beauty, goodness and order of nature could be windows opening upon divinity was gradually obscured in Western thought, and remains so to this day.* If then the traditional Byzantine understanding of creation is sound, then nature in its very essence would be revelatory of God to those who have eyes to see and hearts to heed. How, then, could this inherently sacred character, of nature and indeed the nature of work, have been entirely effaced through the dominance of modern thought and institutions, as well as the employment practices that go with such?

Gradually modern science moved from seeing the "laws" of nature as insights into a transcendent wisdom and perfection immanent to the world, to a purely operational, "empirical" study of regularities that happen to be as we find them to be, and which we are free to exploit as we please. For Foltz then *technological fixes will not suffice, for we need changes that acknowledge what has actually been lost: not technical mastery, but the noetics of nature.*

Natural beauty and the eclipse of the Holy

We now turn more specifically, conceptually as well as spiritually, to Byzantine Christianity – the understanding of which, for Foltz, has eluded the West for a millennium and a half. For it has always seen salvation as a cosmic event, a redemption of nature and all creation as well as humanity. It sees the Incarnation as a glorification of nature and of matter itself, seeing the final resurrection of the end times as a perfection and transformation of the earthly.

Heidegger's (11) conclusion was that a massive unholiness is enveloping our world today, as a result of the global character of the technological mode

The very element of nature in its holiness (divinely beautiful nature) is undergoing global closure. This is due, in turn, to the localised occlusion, themselves global in their effects, of the salutary, the integral, the wholesome. Meanwhile Russia's Pavel Florensky (12), perhaps the 20th century's most notable polymath, with impressive publications in philosophy, theology, linguistics, art history, mathematics, science and engineering – was silenced by the Stalin regime in mid-career, and his work is now being rediscovered in Russia, in Germany and Italy, and to a lesser extent in the US.

Florensky understood what Heidegger called "the holy" by means of the ancient concept of Sophia or Divine Wisdom, originally revived by the Russian philosopher Solovyov (13), and drawing on the same cosmic spirituality of Eastern Christianity. Thinking nature as "creation", Florensky argues Sophia, as "all-integral creation" is the Great Root. Where Heidegger sees modern technology, Florensky perceives rather disorder, an "encrustation of the heart" (the *en-closure* of the human heart in deranged isolation which has traditionally in Christianity been called "sin"), and an "insane selfhood", as the problem, coupled with the failure of love (might we say "self-centred" employment).

Perhaps it is, above all, the pursuit of depth which is at risk in all assaults upon nature and humanity, as per the traditional buccaneer, or merchant adventurer and the modern oligarch. Perhaps it is this, more than anything, that is ultimately at stake in our environmental/social concerns, and thus cannot be understood through either scientific or ethical categories alone, but only by means of aesthetic-theological considerations, both Judeo-Christian and Islamic in nature and scope.

The notion of Wajh or Tawil

Ibn al Arabi (14) in the 13th century is widely considered to be not just the greatest of Sufi philosophers but arguably the greatest philosopher in Islam. Remarkably similar to the individual *logoi* of Maximos is the notion of the *wajh* or face. Every being possesses its own specific, individual or private "face" that forms its very uniqueness and individuality as the face, or for us *self*, turned or *employed as a* divine face.

He calls this *tawil*. Not surprisingly then, *the locus of knowing is not in the head, but in the vastness of the heart – understood not as a seat of passion or emotion but as the norm in traditional cultures, as the centre of knowing far deeper than discursive rationality.* This then is the locus, in such Sufi terms, for "employment of *the self*".

Layers of nature: physical and human

The phenomenology of givenness

An outside alone then, as per (self) employment, pure exteriority with no depth, is only a surface. It is a plane, a sheer extension. It cannot present a face, for there is no inside "self" to face out. It is mere superficiality. Nature then, for modernity, according to Foltz, becomes an externality (self-employment as opposed to employment of the "self"), with nothing behind it and nothing within it. *Res extensa*, in Descartes terms, stands over and against *res cogitans*. In Hegel, as well as Marx, just as for Descartes, nature is exteriority. *From Bacon to Marx, moreover, physical and human nature is the surface for the "mirror of production", through which communist and capitalist alike find a faithful reflection of human possibilities.*

A face in fact requires an inside. A face is inside out. The America phenomenologist and anthropologist David Abram (15) has articulated this orientation towards, and apprehension of, an inner life of nature. For example (Abram himself is Jewish by birth), in the classical anthology of Hebrew poetry and song is to be found an aesthetic appreciation of the inner life, and inner voice, of nature as a whole that is almost completely lacking in Greek poetry.

Centuries of meditation and Christian ethicks

Thereby in his *Centuries of Meditation* and his *Christian Ethicks* the 17th-century English poet and theologian Thomas Traherne (16) challenged the prevailing view of nature at the time, especially that of Thomas Hobbes. The great mistake in the Leviathan, he said, was to imprison our love to ourselves, as per *self* employment, as opposed to *employment of self/community*. And what is most loveable of all was "the world":

> You never Enjoy the world alright till you see how a Sand Exhibiteth the Wisdom and Power of God . . . You never enjoy the World alright,

till the Sea itself floweth in your Veins, till you are Clothed with the Heavens, and Crowned with the Stars.

Traherne here stands as a link and precursor not only to William Blake (who urges us to cleanse and purify "the doors of perception" that we might see how "everything that lives is holy") but also to transcendentalists Emerson (17) and Thoreau (18) and a whole succession of American nature writers, many of whom (like Muir as we shall see) felt a constant need to purify the spirit through leaving civilisation and inhabiting the wilderness – as did the great prophets and visionaries in earlier times.

The fall as a disorder of the Whole Cosmos: Katharsis

And as Traherne had been to Hobbes, so was Muir to American forester and politician last century Gifford Pinchot, for whom nature needed to be mastered and conserved as a resource and a commodity. *Muir (19), a Scottish-American early environmentalist in the 19th century, on the contrary, looked not to nature as a raw material, but to nature as wilderness meant by the Creator to educate humanity by means of its order and Wisdom, and above all through its beauty.*

Although Traherne's poetic approach to nature had little influence prior to the 20th century, John Muir's view of nature in contrast has been extraordinarily influential as the patriarch of the American environmental movement. Remarkably in fact, both Traherne and Muir – and other writers and naturalists who come after them, to varying degrees – uncover a layer of ancient spirituality, that is preserved much more in the Byzantine tradition than in the West.

For once Christianity had become institutionalised in the great cities of the Roman empire in the fourth century, the almost immediate response for some was to flee the cities and retreat to the desert. There these earliest monastics practiced a purification of the soul that correlated to the purity of the place, a process that they called *Katharsis*. More specifically, this enabled them to practice what came to be called *theorie physike*, natural contemplation or the contemplation of nature.

The glory of God hidden in creation

Dostoevsky and the Eastern views of nature

Distinctive elements in the Byzantine and Russian relations to nature, most specifically in the latter case drawing on the Russian novelist Dostoevsky, are summarised by Foltz in seven points. *First*, like all representative thinkers of the Christian East, Dostoevsky draws heavily on the Byzantine *distinction between divine substance or essence (ousia) and the divine activities or energies (energeia)*, a difference that was not well understood in the Latin

West. *Second*, there is the Eastern teaching of the *logoi* of creation, most clearly stated as we have seen by Maximos the Confessor. *Every being – every blade of grass and cloud and animal – possesses its own individual, unrepeatable Logos.*

Third, Eastern Christianity affirms the iconicity of creation. That is, it emphasises the belief, and the corresponding sensibility, that *creation is itself divine revelation*, God's first revelation of himself presented long before the first scriptures. In his "Sermon on the Mount", and in so many of his parables, *Jesus asks his hearers to look upon the birds of the air, the mustard seed, the lilies of the field, as manifestations of a divine order*, as windows upon the workings of God in the world.

Fourth and *fifth* we may want to list the correlative notions of cosmic fall and redemption. Byzantine theology sees the uniqueness of humanity not in the power of knowledge but in the fact that *human beings alone are dwellers in two worlds, the visible and the invisible*, and it is our task to draw them into unity. *Sixth*, the fallenness of our human condition consists in the malady whereby the *nous (intellectual intuition or consciousness) has departed from its natural seat in the heart*, and got entangled in *dianoia* (discursive rationality), lodged in the head. *Seventh* and finally is the concept of a *three-fold pathway of spiritual growth* that importantly shapes Dostoevsky's thought. It begins with the *purification* or purgation of the soul from desires and passions, proceeds to the next step of *illumination* or "noetic" seeing, and concludes with the *uniting of the soul* with divine energies (*theosis*). Where does that leave us today?

Did Christianity cause global warming?

In 1637, Descartes (20) proclaimed in his *Discourse on Method* that "we can have useful knowledge by which, cognizant of the *force and actions* of fire, water, air, stars, the heavens and all other bodies that surround us . . . we may be able to *apply* them in the same fashion to every use to which they are suited, and thus *make ourselves masters and possessors of nature*". With Ockham, nature had become even more radically autonomous.

The wilful, capricious, despotic God emerging from Ockham through Calvin – antithetical to the loving God of traditional Christianity – became the principle motive for modern atheism, itself springing less from unbelief than from collective self-defence against a deity that had become a metaphysical monster. Far from traditional Christianity being responsible for global warming, according to Foltz, it is its very inversion and perversion into a secular metaphysic – *the onto/theology that displaces and obscures traditional Christianity – that is to blame for these problems that are not just scientific and technological in character, but philosophical and ultimately spiritual.*

Kosmos, Ktisis and Chaos in environmental philosophy

In fact only in the mid 17th century did what has been known as kosmos (world and universe) and *ktisis* (creation ordered and sustained by Sophia or divine logos) enter the English language as "nature". Before that the English word nature had been translated roughly as "essence". In the 17th century then nature begins to designate that great aggregate of what Descartes would term as an *object*.

Slowly and gradually, for Foltz, the more people and things become "nature", the more they lose their own natures, or *selves*. Moreover, in 1632, Locke's (21) definition of "self-consciousness" as "perception of what passes in a man's own mind" appears, and Descartes' newly ensconced dichotomy between *res extensa* (extended) and *res cogitans* (self grounding). Thus the triangular relationship of God, consciousness and nature that is constitutive of modern rationality is generated. *Nature then, rather than designating a mode of being, instead becomes reified and established as an ontic region in itself, the reified realm of all that is not conscious.*

The newly fabricated nature is coordinated solely to *ratio*, to the calculative demands of the rational mind, the calculating risk-taker, or entrepreneur. What then is the alternative approach to employing self and community, to such self-employment?

Illustrative Case – The "Eastern" effect: Fairtrade is Divine

Introducing Sophi Tranchell

For a young, thirty-something film-maker seeing an advert in a national newspaper for someone to take over the reins of a new chocolate company – which had inspiring ethical values but little financial credibility – was an opportunity too good to miss. Sophi Tranchell had been running a small indy film production company, *Metro Tartan Films*, when she saw the advert for a new CEO at a start-up called *The Day Chocolate Company*. The Day in the title was an oblique reference to the need to commit yourself to God, afresh, every day; something that Sophi recognised from her upbringing and life as a Roman Catholic Christian.

That was 1999. In the intervening 18 years Sophi and her team have taken *Divine* into a measureable share of the UK confectionery market, which is one of the most competitive anywhere. *Divine* had a turnover of more than £12M in 2016, operating sales in the UK and US, retailing some 70 product lines – a far cry from the single chocolate bar that Sophi inherited at the turn of the millennium. Of course, the chocolate confectionery industry is dominated by such giants as Swiss-based *Nestle*, who bought out *Rowntree*, US conglomerate *Mars* and *Cadbury's*, which was taken-over by *Kraft Foods*, in 2010, who had earlier bought out and closed the iconic York chocolate factory of *Terry's*, famed for their chocolate orange, with the loss of more than 350 jobs. Against such intense competition *Divine* has a remarkable story, under Sophi's team leadership.

The invisible heart of Divine

But, something that may not be well-known is that many of the most significant confectionery brands in Britain, such as *Rowntree* and *Cadbury*, were founded by Christian Quaker families. They originated their businesses with the express purpose of developing industries that would nourish their workers and consumers in both body and soul. In the 18th and 19th centuries, chocolate was regarded as a major health food, deriving from its medicinal use by ancient Mayan peoples in Central America. It has a spiritual significance that reaches far beyond the supermarket shelf. Indeed, chocolate (cacao) was at the heart of Mayan rituals concerning birth, life, death and sacrifice (22).

It is that tradition that is being carried on by Sophi Tranchell in a way that gives practical expression to the noetics of nature. If you look at the iconography on the wrapper of a bar of *Divine* chocolate it shows contemporary reworkings of faith symbols from across the world, all surrounding a heart-shape, which forms the 'v' at the centre of the "Divine" brand name. Indeed, the wrapper for one of *Divine*'s dark chocolate bars uses the imagery of a fourfold Celtic cross, surrounding a circle, an archetypal icon at the heart of Trans4M's work, pointing to the four worlds emanating from an inner moral core.

Whilst the spiritual significance of *Divine*'s branding may not be widely understood, the use of the Fairtrade Labelling Organisation (FLO) mark is recognised by millions. It points behind the surface of the chocolate bars to the purpose that they embody, which is to personalise the supply chain. Sophi has a deep commitment to radical social justice which began in her teenage years when she was involved in direct action campaigns against UK corporations supporting the apartheid regime in South Africa prior to the release of Nelson Mandela from Robin Island. Now, in her early 50s Sophi regards herself as more radical than ever, but with a radicalism fuelled by a Catholic social conscience.

This has been the inspiration for the main work of *Divine* which is to improve the lives of cocoa growers in northern Ghana. As with almost all Fairtrade companies they provide a premium to primary producers. But, what makes *Divine* different is that they are 45% owned by the cocoa cooperative *Kuapa Kokoo*, based in Kumasi. This means that, effectively, the UK and US staff of *Divine*, including Sophi, are employed by their cocoa farmers. The reality is that they share in a common work, where the notion of employment is subordinated to the principle of collaboration and solidarity along the supply chain.

A recent study by Prof Bob Doherty (23) – at University of York, the UK's most significant chocolate city – in which Sophi was involved, looked at how a range of Fairtrade suppliers sought to implement the nine original principles of the Fairtrade movement. What became clear was that some fair traders are fairer than others. As Fairtrade has 'mainstreamed', with some products being packaged and retailed by corporations that are largely non-fair traders, such as Proctor & Gamble and Cadbury, so the principles of the movement have become diluted. Some companies only adhere to the two most basic requirements of FLO – minimum pricing and the payment of a social premium to farmers, growers and primary producers – whilst others, most substantially represented by Divine are 100% Fairtrade and have gone beyond the nine principles, through selling the company to their farmers.

The extent to which Fairtrade principles have been diluted was most forcibly revealed in the decision of Fairtrade USA to split from Fairtrade International, in 2011. Under the banner of "Fairtrade for all" FTUSA took the controversial decision to source coffee and cocoa from corporate-owned plantations which employed hired labour, rather than solely from small cooperatives of growers. This aspect of 'mainstreaming' was intended to spread the reach of Fairtrade products. But, it revealed the extent to which the principle of retaining the connection between self-sufficient producers, the land, a socially just supply chain and consumers was being broken.

Arguably, this was as much a spiritual issue and, certainly, one about core values, as it was simply about the economic distribution of fairly-traded goods. The crucial link between dignified work and the sustainability of self-hood, in community, was at stake in this decision. As Doherty comments: "There are very few national, branded Fairtrade organisations left in the United States and it would be a very sad thing if that happened here. Fairtrade Organisations in the UK have been heavily socially led and they've led to innovative impacts on producer organisations such as joint ownership in Fairtrade brands" (23, para 12).

Personalising the supply chain

The value of introducing consumers to the real people who are involved in supplying raw materials and products has become evident in the numbers of companies that use this marketing technique. As Sophi comments: "We all relate to individual stories much more than data. It's exciting to watch this becoming more common, and I'm especially pleased to see women cocoa farmers starting to be given the same opportunities as men" (24).

This principle is, equally, reflected in Sophi's own story. She describes the deep impact that Gordon and Anita Roddick, the founders of Body Shop, had on her, when Gordon decided to be one of the first significant investors in Divine. His mentoring of Sophi, transmitting his values about person-to-person working, made a lasting impression, especially given that they completely elided with her spiritual understanding of the importance of one-to-one sharing, derived from her Catholic faith.

As such, personalisation and bringing the self into fair trade supply chains is far more than a marketing ploy. That is why the national secretary of Kuapa Kokoo, Comfort Kumeah, spends several weeks each year travelling in the US, UK and Europe, bringing the slogan of the cooperative "Pa pa paa", "the best of the best" to local groups, often supported by churches. This is the purpose behind Sophi's leadership of Divine and, equally, it undergirds the work of the producers in the cocoa cooperative. When we work together as people who collaborate, on the basis of creating a fairer world, we begin to bring our deepest selves into contact, with each other, nature and the origin of both, within the Godhead.

Conclusion

As we have entered the Eastern realm we have considered the distinctiveness of spirituality to the meaning of work. We began by looking at the nature of vocational identity versus a functional understanding of employment. In the calling of the first disciples we were reminded that vocation implies an external Caller, whether God, the Universe or Nature, itself. But, as we saw, in considering noetics, the increasing objectification of Nature has separated work and employment from the sense of who we are and our place in the world. By contrast, business such as *Divine Chocolate* are seeking to restore that sense of noetics, of place, and to infuse – through the supply chain – people, their land and their markets with a 'sweet taste' of mutual connectedness.

Following from this entry into communal spirituality we turn to the emergence of household economics. We examine the balance between work and life; how work can provide a home for the homeless spirit; what is meant by the household economy; and how the founders of one of Britain's most iconic businesses constituted their entire enterprise around the idea of partnership, akin to the family home.

Bibliography

1 Duke, R.D. and Greenblat, C.S. (1979) *Game-Generating-Games: A Trilogy of Games for Community and Classroom.* Beverly Hills: Sage.
2 Lloyd, S., Roodt, G. and Odendaal, A. (2011) Critical Elements in Defining Work-Based Identity in Post-Apartheid South Africa. *South African Journal of Industrial Psychology* 37: 1.
3 Bothma, F.C., Lloyd, S. and Khapova, S. (2015) Work Identity: Clarifying the Concept. Chapter 2, in Jansen, P. and Roodt, G. (Eds.) *Conceptualising and Measuring Work identity – South African Perspectives and Findings.* Capetown: Springer.
4 Burke, P.J. and Stets, J.E. (2009) *Identity Theory and Social Identity Theory.* [Available at: www.scribd.com/doc/19720726/identity-theory-and-social-identity-theory. Last accessed: August 14, 2017].
5 Brown, A. (2004) Engineering Identities. *Career Development International* 9(3): 245–273.
6 Thomas, W.H. and Feldman, D.C. (2007) The School-to-Work Transition: A Role Identity Perspective. *Journal of Vocational Behaviour* 71(1): 114–134.
7 McArdle, S., Waters, L., Briscoe, J.P. and Hall, D.T. (2007) Employability During Unemployment: Adaptability, Career Identity and Human and Social Capital. *Journal of Vocational Behaviour* 71(1): 247–264.
8 Foltz, B. (2014) *The Noetics of Nature: Environmental Philosophy and the Holy Beauty of the Visible.* New York: Fordham University Press.
9 Husserl, E. (1970) *Crisis in the European Sciences.* Chicago: North-Western University Press.
10 James, W. (2015) *Varieties of Religious Experience.* Edinburgh: Crossreach Publications.
11 Heidegger, M. (2010) *Being and Time.* Albany: State University of New York Press.
12 Florensky, P. (2014) *At the Crossroads of Science and Mysticism.* New York: Semantron Publishing.
13 Solovyov, V. (2009) *The Divine Sophia.* Ithaca: Cornell University Press.
14 Ibn Arabi (2002) *The Meccan Revelations.* Pleasant Hill, CA: Pir Press.
15 Abram, D. (1997) *The Spell of the Sensuous: Perception and Language in a More-Then-Human World.* New York: Vintage Books.
16 Traherne, T. (2016) *Centuries of Meditations.* Bloomington, IN: CreateSpace Independent Publishing Platform.
17 Emerson, R. (2017) *Nature.* Bloomington, IN: CreateSpace Independent Publishing Platform.
18 Thoreau, L. (2004) *Walden.* Princeton, NJ: Princeton University Press.
19 Gisel, B. (2017) *The Wilder Muir.* Yosemite, CA: Yosemite Conservancy.
20 Descartes, R. (2004) *Discourse on Method.* Mineola, NY: Dover Philosophical Classics.

21 Locke, J. (2017) *Two Treatises of Government*. Bloomington, IN: CreateSpace Independent Publishing Platform.
22 Martin, S. (2006) First Fruit from the Maize Tree and Other Tales from the Underworld, in McNeil, C.L. (Ed.) *Chocolate in MesoAmerica: A Cultural History of Cacao*. Florida: University Press.
23 Doherty, B., Davies, I.A. and Tranchell, S. (2012) Where Now for Fair Trade? *Business History* 55(2): 151–69.
24 Harpers Bazaar. (2017) *Work It Out: Sophi Tranchell on Business with a Social Conscience*. 31 May. [Available at: www.harpersbazaar.co.uk/people-parties/ bazaar-at-work/news/a41770/work-it-out-sophi-tranchell-business-social-conscience-divine-chocolate/. Last accessed: August 15, 2017].

7 Economics of the household
Home working to partner with others

GROUNDING HUMAN NATURE
AWAKENING SPIRIT
THREEFOLD NAVIGATION
EFFECT AWAKENING

Introduction

Economics of the Household

Building upon the "noetics of nature" as our "eastern" (Byzantine) spiritual grounding, we focus more overtly in this chapter on a cultural and spiritual approach to economics that emerged from Russia in the early part of last century. To a large extent, this has been ignored ever since. In fact its focus on employing self-and-community bypasses both employment (communism) and self-employment (capitalism), but is yet to be fully developed as such, albeit that it has certainly inspired Bruce Foltz (Chapter 6) in America.

Picking up the theme of household economics we address the Burning Question, by way of grounding: can business provide a home for the homeless? Our Window into Wisdom, in this 'eastern' instance, moreover, draws upon the gospel of Mark. We look, as such, at the failures of the first Christian disciples, through the eyes of Mark, redacting the stories of St Peter, to gain wisdom regarding the true nature of the household economy.

But, we are not looking at those who are, literally, without shelter. We know that, in so many parts of the world, Western economics has created a housing crisis. As such, in our Social Theory, we are more concerned with the way, drawing on social and economic theory developed in Russia at the turn of the last century, in which work is evolving to accommodate the demands of family life, wider goals of being 'at home' and the so-called 'work-life balance', for those who otherwise see themselves and their communities as homeless economic units.

There are past models that have sought to address these challenges, but today's solutions are very different, emphasising the individualism that fragments relationship, even within the Self. Consequently, we introduce the familiar, to many, story of John Spedan Lewis. But, the deeper values that motivated his formation of the *John Lewis Partnership*, address what Spedan Lewis saw as capitalism's perversions, which are less well-known.

The Russian idea

While Russia, stretching uniquely across Eurasia, has the distinctive potential of bridging east and west, more often in its history, one has been opposed to the other, both internally and externally. As such, whereas the somewhat invisible home grown "cosmism" (not communism), as we shall see, is a unique blend of Slavophile (eastern) and westernisers. Yet, the much more visible "western" or "northern" import of Communism – all too often wrongly conceived as "eastern" – decimated the country over six oppressive decades. Instead of a local-global fusion – in this case the Economics of the Household which is the focus of this "eastern" chapter on the path of renewal – the global Marxism triumphed over the local brand of cosmism, with anarchism lodged somewhat awkwardly in between. Today, moreover, Russia is a pale shadow of such a rich cultural heritage, at least politically and economically.

Yet what is altogether remarkable is the strength and vibrancy of what the Russian writer Berdyaev (1), at the turn of the last century, called the "Russian Idea". Even so, that remains invisible to most, without, if not also within, the country, in today's Russia. More specifically for the Russian philosopher Soloviev (2), in whose footsteps Berdyaev followed, in the former's Philosophical Principles of Integral Knowledge:

> Active cultivation of the natural world firstly is an economic activity; its primary elementary form is the family. The second basic form of society, which is inextricably linked with the first, determines the relationship of people not to nature but immediately to each other, and has its direct object not people's labour, but people themselves in interaction as members of a collective whole. Such a political society is engaged with lawfulness or a system of rights. The third form of society is determined by the religious character of the person, not his material existence (economic) or lawful existence (political) but now his absolute existence in sacred society.

What still remains to be achieved is to turn such emergent cultural and spiritually laden social philosophy into an explicitly navigational social science, and thereafter into an effective economic and integral recreational practice. In fact, as we shall continually see, the full recognition and release of GENE-ius, for us the key to "development", in a particular society – Grounding, Emergence, Navigation, Effect – all too seldom takes place. For such, we will later turn to Sergey Bulgakov, after first addressing the Burning Question in this context, and opening the "eastern" Window into Wisdom.

Burning Question: can economies and businesses provide a home for the homeless?

Two sets of stories often dominate in discussions of businesses that have aimed to create a family and household economy for their workers. The first is that of the late 18th- and 19th-century industrial pioneers, who created 'model villages' for their workers, such as New Lanark, near Glasgow, *Cadbury* at Bourneville, Birmingham and *Lever Brothers*', at Port Sunlight, between the Mersey and the Dee. The other story is that of "old Japan" (pre-1980s) and other Asian business, with a tradition of providing both job security and a range of housing and other worker benefits that established many corporations as "family-style" businesses, albeit largely for men, with natural families excluded.

A serpent in paradise

But, both models have been acutely challenged for their exercise of social control. In her recent book, *Dreamstreets*, which is ironically titled, Jacqueline Yallop (3) examines the history of the 'model villages' movement, from Robert Owen onwards. Her conclusion is that, despite the apparent utopian ideals of these early factory community settlements, their primary purpose was to exert authority over workers, to control and inhibit individualism.

This exercise was performed in a variety of ways. Whereas *New Lanark*'s worker houses were almost all identical, Lord Leverhulme's *Port Sunlight* model was rather the opposite. In creating an almost-too-perfect "chocolate box" housing mix the owning family covered over the darker aspects of the settlement, which involved separation of the sexes, enforced religious observance and what Yallop sees as suffocating conformity.

That view is, however, almost certainly a parody of a much richer social history. Many of those who worked and lived in the model villages would have enjoyed an almost paradisiacal existence, when compared with the slums, tenements and street-life of 19th-century Manchester, London, Birmingham or Liverpool. The self-interest of John Cadbury or Joseph Rowntree was, clearly, modified by their deeply-held Quaker beliefs in spiritual freedom and the dignity of the Self.

Equally, the contemporary Western celebration of individualism would have seemed very strange in the urban or rural communities of 19th-century Britain. There, the exchange of deference for paternalism would have been regarded by many, if not some of the more radical reformers, such as Tom Paine, as the 'natural order' of things, akin to the French *ancien regime*. Self-interest by a few industrialists could reflect self-fulfilment, or, at least, self-acceptance, by their many factory workers.

In a rather similar vein the post-War history of Japanese business reflects a common set of concerns, which are largely breaking down. The conventional story of Japanese working practices is that of lifetime employment, the *nenko jeretsu* system of seniority-based salaries, rotation of employees between departments, to build organisational understanding and employee loyalty, and the phenomenon of *hatarakanai ojisan*, unproductive middle-aged male workers, "cruising" towards retirement. Of course, Japan has undergone two decades of flat-lining GDP and a dissolution of its "old Japan" business model of low-cost copying of other, more innovative technologies.

Now, its industrial cost-base is much higher, it has an almost catastrophic demographic transition – whereby annual sales of incontinence pads out-compete those of baby nappies – and a younger generation of workers, especially women, expecting a more Westernised career path. Fewer women are marrying, seeing it as the 'career grave'. Instead, they want more individual freedom, *less* security and a greater ability to move between jobs and enterprises. All-in-all these changes can be viewed as either serpents in paradise or liberation of the personal Self.

Work-based family benefits are basic

Even in the cradle of corporate capitalism things are rapidly changing. It is widely recognised that in order to retain top-quality employees American corporations have to improve their work-family benefits offerings. At the start of 2017 *American Express* (Amex) introduced a 20-week fully paid maternity/paternity policy, with a further eight weeks 'medical recovery' time for birth-mothers. Whilst this would be seen as entirely uncontroversial in Britain or Europe, this feels like a game-changer in the US.

Other US companies offer baby-at-work opportunities for nursing mothers, childcare centres and "baby-bonding bonuses". In Britain, some large corporates, such as *Goldman Sachs* have introduced creches to their expensive office blocks, although *GoldmanS* is unique within the City of London. A small percentage of companies offer concierge services, where employees are helped to juggle their work-life balance by having their grocery shopping, vacation planning or dry cleaning organised for them, whilst at work. Far more regular is the provision of flexible working hours (flexi-time), to accommodate parenting and the care of elderly relatives.

More enlightened companies recognise that helping to culturally-bond employee families together is a worthwhile strategy for seeking to build community. This may be through family outings, holiday celebrations, sporting events or 'spirit days'. At the same time, many large-scale businesses, suffering cost pressures, are closing their in-work childcare facilities. This has happened at a number of UK Universities.

But, one main alternative, especially making-use of the advantages of technology-based working practices, is offering remote working. So, when Marissa Mayer banned this practice at *Yahoo*, in 2013, there was a massive reaction, with many long-term staff leaving for other tech companies. Ironically, Mayer's reason was to encourage a collegial approach to working in the technology giant, in order to encourage face-to-face contact instead of meetings via social media or e-mail.

As such, it is widely recognised that there are both benefits and costs to business of providing flexible working patterns. The UK Department for Business, Innovation & Skills (Biz) set up a review of such practices in 2011, which was conducted by the Policy Review Institute and reported in 2014 (4). Its main findings were that productivity increases, absentee rates reduce and cost-savings in terms of staff-retention were each evidenced. But, there was less indication of flexible working being a major factor in firms recruiting staff. Family-friendly policies had far less impact in the UK, outside London, than in the US, although they did encourage greater levels of entry to the labour market by mothers, reinforcing a trend that has been evident for at least three decades.

Unsurprisingly, the study identified the main costs of work-life balance strategies as those to do with implementation, administrative and procedural processes and those related to accommodating requests from staff. Inevitably, the greatest burden fell on small and medium-sized enterprises (SMEs), for whom the cost of flexible policies frequently out-weighs the benefits of implementation. Perhaps, the most surprising conclusion – from their review of the published evidence and other surveys – was that the provision of work-life balance procedures significantly exceeded the requests for them. The obvious conclusion is that a cultural change is taking place in business, related to social pressures, which is, as yet, not fully reflected in the expectations of workers.

Beyond the homeless worker

As we will see, for Bulgakov, labour is more than productivity and the economy more than the utilisation of factors of production, of which labour is, conventionally, seen as most significant, within both neoclassical and Marxist economics, albeit for very different reasons. Rather, when a political economy of the global household of humanity is introduced what emerges is a new culture, through which the natural is made manifest and the power of labour is seen as recreative rather than simply employed.

It is possible, therefore, to see in some of the changes that are taking place within the labour market, in terms of work-life balance, seeds of a new economic model. Of course, these are not being implemented for the reasons of providing an otium of the people, wherein work is seen as a part of the dignified recreational task of humanity. They are, as yet, simple responses to the perceived needs of the labour market. And yet, such cultural changes may be harbingers of a more thorough-going transformation of work patterns, as we move from 'balance' to sophia – wisdom-at, -in and -through-work.

What is clearly evident is that contemporary workers, at least in some so-called 'advanced' economies are demanding a different social contract in their working lives. Whether this is the requirement of Japanese women to have a career and, therefore, shun conventional relationships, gender divisions and even human and sexual intimacy, in order to fulfil their Self-hood. Or, it may be the requirement of European or American families, to have work organised around the development of a micro-household, rather than, in reverse, the self and household being subservient to their place in the economic system.

In each of the outlined ways the world of work is being restructured in ways that hold, what John Spedan Lewis termed, the seeds of an idea: which is, Selves that are seeking to own work rather than being owned by owners who are using them as mere units of a production function. Still, this remains a long way from the spiritual and wisdom-based household economy of Bulgakov. The current solutions are in danger of reinforcing Western individualism and the further fragmentation of understanding true Self-in-relationship. Even so, there are glimmers within the mist!

We now delve deeper, seeking words of wisdom that draw on our Judeo-Christian heritage, in this case, in particular once more, the "eastern" gospel of Mark.

Window into Wisdom: drawing on God's spiritual household

Works in progress – discipleship failures
(Mark 4:35–41; 6:45–52; 8:14–21)

It is almost certain that Mark is really Peter's Gospel. The John Mark of Acts (12:12, 12:25, 13:5, 15:35–41, inter alia), Colossians (4:10) and 2 Timothy (4:11) is most likely the same young man who flees from the soldiers arresting Jesus, at the time of Peter's denial. The tradition that says that Mark was with Peter in prison, taking down notes of the Apostle's recollections of his experience of Jesus is well-attested. So, we are closer to the historical Jesus when we read Mark than at any point in the New Testament which was, of course, put together after the Resurrection.

In that sense, we can use a phrase from the opening of Peter's First Epistle as a way into a consideration of the disciples' frailty. Peter writes to communities of Jewish Christians who have been dispersed across Asia Minor, during the persecutions of either Roman Emperors Diocletian or Vespasian, as 'resident aliens' who have been called by God. Later on he describes them as "God's spiritual household" (1 Peter 2:4–5). Throughout that Epistle there is the theme of God providing a home for the homeless.

The house of unfinished stones

Similarly, the sense of unfinished business is evident – so far as the work of the disciples is concerned – throughout Mark's Gospel. Mark is the most critical of the disciples, who are often portrayed as foolish, ignorant, uncomprehending and weak. This is further evidence, if such were needed, of Peter's viewpoint behind Mark's authorial hand. Peter knows only-too-well just how lacking he and the other disciples were in their responding to the call of God-in-Jesus Christ. There is a sense that Peter is dictating his story of failure to, in some small way, make amends for his denial of Jesus, even thogh he knows that he is completely forgiven and restored (see John 20).

But, what do these passages of discipleship failure (which you will need to read for your Self) tell us about the Self at work? It is simply that we are frail, weak, get things wrong and, above all, are works in progress. We will often be tempted to portray ourselves as wise, all-knowing, smart, intelligent and skilful. And, you may be those things! Yet, the reality is that we mess up, make mistakes and even seek to cover up when we do so. By contrast, God accepts us. Although Jesus was frequently sharp in pointing out their lack of faith and inability to see the imminent presence of God around them, He doesn't give up on the disciples, even when they give up on Him.

There is a home for the homeless. The resident aliens are accepted into the household economy of God. The failing disciples are repeatedly forgiven and accepted for who they are. When their weaknesses are exposed it is simply to help them learn. And, when they fail to do so they remain accepted. In the world of work there may not be many employers who act in the way that God does to those He has called. But, as works in progress ourselves, we can know the acceptance that goes beyond merit, which is being brought home into God's family and household. Even more so, as Peter puts it, we are the very living stones of that house (1 Peter 2:5). It wouldn't even exist without us. That is the extent of God's acceptance.

Socio-economic theory: economics of the household

Philosophy of economy

Sergey Bulgakov was one of the major figures of the so called Russian Silver Age (early last century). As economist, philosopher, publicist, politician and founder of a Christian Socialist party, during his "second life", when exiled from the Soviet Union in 1922, he became arguably the 20th century's foremost Orthodox theologian. Thus his unique amalgam (5) of philosophy and economics – *Philosophy of Economy* – was an attempt to formulate an alternative philosophy that preserved what he considered Marxism's main insights (liberation from social and economic oppression) yet eliminate its disregard for individual dignity (employment of the self).

The revolt against positivism

Bulgakov's search for a new social philosophy was part of a broader European movement, a prominent member of which was the founder of phenomenology Edmund Husserl. Historians have described this as "the revolt against positivism". At the turn of the 20th century, thinkers throughout Europe questioned the foundations of 19th century attitudes towards science, literature and society. In social thought the questioning of dominant 19th century beliefs frequently involved a reevaluation of Marxism and a dissatisfaction with the application of Darwinian theories to social life. The revolt against positivism took a variety of forms: German neo-Kantism, Sigmund Freud's "discovery" of the unconscious, Husserl's phenomenology, and French post-modernist Saussure's approach to language as structure being leading examples.

Positivism in general, and Marxism in particular, subjugated the needs of individual human beings here and now for the sake of collective humanity in the future. His own response was that of a "philosophy of economy". In this book, as we shall see, Bulgakov replaced Marx's vision of society as a class struggle based on material interests, in which the mode of production determined social forms and ideologies, with a view at whose crux stood the relation between man and man.

Towards a sophic economy

Bulgakov took as his point of departure, in that guise, an imagined original state in which man and nature lived in perfect harmony. To this initial state, analogous to the State of Nature postulated by John Locke or Jean-Jacques Rousseau, Bulgakov gave the name "Edenic economy" – the world before original sin. Yet the world in which we currently live, as pointed out in "the noetics of nature" (see previous chapter) is fatally separated from that harmonious state. Prisoners to our material needs, this is the world that Marx took to be our only one, basing his doctrine of economic materialism on the "fallen" state of humanity.

In this imperfect world Bulgakov then turned to a biblical notion – Sophia – as a way out of mere labour that characterises the fallen world. Sophia is joy, play and wisdom. The economy, even if Eden has been lost, could once again become "sophic". Such a sophic economy was also an ethic – one that prescribed joyful labour "in Sophia", as an antidote to the grim eking out of existence, as per contemporary "employment", that was so prevalent in life and accepted as necessary by Marxism and other economic doctrines. Today, at least in the UK, the equivalent preorientation is with heavily extolled "hard working people".

The central feature of Bulgakov's sophic economy then, and one that complements the rejection of a linear conception of history and emphasis on process rather than ends, is its replacement of social theory – Marx's – that, like most social theories of the 18th and 19th centuries, described society in terms of external forms (institutions, classes, forms of government), by a vision that instead stressed the internal content or "spirit" of society (hence our "employment of the self"), set within the economy as a household.

Basic functions: consumption/production: inhaling/exhaling

Economic life, in the concrete and personalised world conceived as household (as opposed to an abstract economy with its depersonalised factors of production), can ultimately be connected, according to Bulgakov, with a metabolic process of a human being, that is as a circulation or an alternation of inhaling and exhaling. In the language of political economy, production corresponds to exhalation, consumption to inhalation. The economic cycle then consists of these two acts. In that context he asks the general question: how is economy possible? Reduced to two particular questions, of the world household, he asks specifically: how is production possible, and how is consumption possible? We start with consumption.

Consumption involves nourishment. By such nourishment in the broadest sense, he means the most generic metabolic exchange between the living organism and its environment, including not just food but respiration and the effects of the atmosphere, light, electricity, chemistry and other forces on our organism, insofar as they support life, in the context of the world household. The world enters us through all the windows and doors of our senses and, having entered, is apprehended and assimilated ("consumed") by us. In its totality this consumption of the world, this ontological communication with it, this communism of being, lies at the foundation of all our life processes, and of our world household. We now turn from consumption as inhalation to production as exhalation.

Secondly we face the question: how is production, in the world household, possible? Production is the exertion of the subject on the object, or man on nature, such that the subject of the economic process imprints or realises his or her idea, objectivises his or her goals, through the object of his or her economic action. Hence of us, in this "eastern" context, comes the notion of "the employment of the self". In this aspect the product of any finished productive act is like a work of art, or indeed recreation, which is characterised by the mutual penetration of matter and form through the person's idea.

Labour is more than productivity

First of all then such political economy – in theory in the work of Adam Smith (6), in practice in the case of most of his followers – narrowed the concept of labour to "productive" labour, or "employment', resulting in material goods. Consequently attention was focused on this single aspect of labour, the objective, externalised one, which is actually its periphery. As such its significance as a bridge between subject and object, by means of which the 'self' comes into the object and realises its ideas, projects, and models were entirely neglected. But if political economy with its "economic materialism" knows labour only in its products or objects, and misses it in the self-as-subject, then an analogous error repeats itself in the opposite pole – in Kantian subjective idealism. The Kantian self as subject is idle for Bulgakov (7), devoid of any working energy, as per self analysis as opposed to "employing the self".

Labour, however, is usually placed among the factors of production, along with land and capital, in the theory of the production of material goods. In this respect the so called "labour theory of value" is more interesting. Here labour has a unique value as the basis of the value of goods. Yet it is understood by Marx (8), in an extremely narrow sense, merely as applied to explaining the theory of exchange value.

The task of political economy

The sense of economy as an interaction of collective humanity and nature, sophic or indeed anthropoelogical in its foundations and endowed with cosmic meaning, is not of course present in the minds of particular economic actors as they go about their practical lives. Their attention, riveted to the particular, remains ignorant of the whole, the world as household as it were. As a result, at least today, they vote for Donald Trump or for the UK's Brexit.

"Economic man", as such, is a sermon for commercialism, naively exposing political economy's central nerve and revealing the focus of its orientation. The first obstacle we encounter, in relation to it moreover, is the vagueness of its most basic concept, wealth, which is as amorphous and unclear as most "real life" notions. The mercantilists defined wealth as money, the physiocrats as agricultural products, the free traders as industrial products, the socialists as material goods, and John Ruskin as human life – as opposed to pure "illth" – each is right from their own relative point of view.

Man though is spirit incarnate and spiritualised flesh – a spiritual and material being. This is why there is no distinct boundary between the material and the spiritual and why everything has two sides; from this standpoint everything should be included in the science of economy, in the world as household. This is not the way of a conventional 'western' approach to economics, or indeed employment. We now finally turn to a practical case of such a "world as household", albeit, unusually, in retail guise.

Illustrative Case: the case of John Lewis: on being at home

Is poor productivity a mystery?

During a broadcast recorded for the BBC, close to his death in 1963, John Spedan Lewis, founder of the John Lewis Partnership, succinctly defined the origin of his vision. "It was the seed of an idea for a better way of managing business. So, that, instead of the many being exploited by the few, there would be genuine partnership for all; managers and managed alike, all pulling together for their common advantage. General change in this way, would, I believe, give us a vast increase in production, and a much healthier, happier world".

For some decades there has been a conundrum surrounding the operation of the UK economy. Whilst work levels have boomed, hitting record numbers in 2017, productivity rates (as measured by GVA, gross value-added output per hour) have remained some of the lowest amongst the OECD nations, for a period stretching back to the Second World War. But, is this so much of a mystery? Figures produced by the Office for National Statistics (ONS), in July 2017, show that whilst unit labour costs – including wages, bonuses, pension contributions and in-work benefits – have had an upturn in 2016–17, to 2.1%, over the previous 5 years they have grown by only a fraction more than 1%. Not a recipe for a much healthier and happier workforce. Given such poor returns to workers, is it really any surprise that productivity rates are so low?

By contrast, a recent study of employee-owned businesses (EOBs) in Scotland concluded that productivity rates were far higher than in more traditional joint-stock managed companies (9). As the report authors indicate: "EOBs in Scotland strongly resemble EOBs elsewhere by outperforming conventionally based firms with less dispersed ownership structures. While the organisational determinants behind this superior firm performance remain less well understood, our research suggests that the organisational model within these firms engenders greater levels of performance" (ibid p. 8). This has led the Scottish Government to develop policies to foster a culture of employee-ownership, this being replicated by other left-leaning politicians in the UK.

An idea whose time has, at last, come

The transcript of an earlier broadcast by J S Lewis, from 1957, shows that he believed that the idea of worker ownership had already come. He put it like this: "I feel quite certain that the general idea of substituting partnership for exploiting employment is now-a-days in the air and will spread through industry of all kinds. It is already dear to many hearts besides my own, for it makes work something to live for as well as something to live by. Here may be the new source of working energy of which our country is in such grave need" (10).

Although the language is slightly dated the sentiment is up-to-the-minute. Indeed, his conclusion that capitalism had become perverted and was at the point of breakdown could hardly be more contemporary. That he envisaged the future of a police state, if things didn't improve, rather than a world of oligarchs, rampant inequality and perilous globalisation, reflect the concerns of the Cold War, pre-dating current technological and communications changes. But, he had reached these conclusions after a lifetime of working on this "experiment in managing businesses differently".

Even so, as recently as 2012, when Nick Clegg MP – the Deputy Prime Minister and, then, leader of the Liberal Democrats, in the UK Coalition Government – called for the creation of a "John Lewis economy" there were howls of derision from many quarters. Writing in *The Spectator* Martin Vander Weyer (11) questioned why so few businesses had adopted the worker-ownership model, concluding that "each is the creation of a driven individual with a vision – and a willingness to give away or share wealth that he might otherwise have kept to himself. There aren't many of those around". In fact, the *Employee Ownership Association* has more than 240 such UK businesses in its Directory, with the largest being *John Lewis'* and including *Divine Chocolate* (see Chapter 6), *Arup* (see Chapter 8), *Grant Thornton, Santander* and *Wilkin & Sons* (Tiptree jams). But, there is little doubt that the John Lewis' founder was such a visionary.

The gift of trust

Spedan Lewis handed over the business in two settlements. The first, in 1929, after his father, the founder John Lewis, had died in the previous year, involved ceding financial control in exchange for receiving the market value of the business in ordinary shares. But, by the time of his retirement, in 1950, Spedan Lewis had undergone something of a secular conversion, recognising that the only way the business could genuinely become worker-owned was if he gifted his entire stake to an independent Trust, over which he had no final control. He recognised that he was the spearhead of a Self-in-Community, with the business operating as a corporate household. As such, the Trust oversaw the Partnership which has its own written Constitution (cf Mondragon, Chapter 4).

The basis of the Constitution is the well-being of the Partners (workers) and to provide satisfying, worthwhile employment. This rests on

the underlying model of a household economy, as suggested by Bulgakov, to provide ". . . happiness for each and all of its members, as does
every good family and . . . club" (10, ibid). That said, Spedan Lewis
was, also, realistic enough to recognise the inequalities of knowledge,
power and profit that any large-scale business generates.

Consequently, he created an in-house magazine for the business,
into which any Partner could write anonymously, if they wished, to
challenge any aspect of the business. This celebrates its centenary in
2018, being the longest-lived company magazine in the world. To
address disparities in power the Constitution applies a range of organisational structures that democratise decision-making at every level,
with real abilities to hold management to account and voice Partner
concerns. Profit-sharing is the basis of the financial structure so that,
after reinvestment, which is determined by the Partners' Council, all
other profits are shared as a dividend to the worker-owners. In each of
these ways the business continues to operate its model of a household
economy, based on mutuality, trust and the founding vision of John
Spedan Lewis.

Conclusion: East meets West

Entering a European era where Russia must lead

Creative culture (12), for Berdyaev as for Bulgakov, is impossible without
tradition, without one's distinctive character. Only by its indigenous culture,
be it Karanga (Zimbabwe) or Yoruba (Nigeria), Celtic (UK), Neopolitan
(Italy) or Slav (Russia), does each people serve exogenous world culture, in
national flesh and blood. While, for Berdyaev, we must repay our debt to
Western thought, to which we are obligated for much, we are now entering
an epoch, he says, when Russian philosophy can and must lead Western
philosophy out of its dead end.

We need to bear in mind, for Berdyaev moreover, that Russia's Westernising tendency was that of an immature youth, still apparent today. Such a
Russian Westernising consciousness is atheistic and materialistic. Yet the full
consciousness of Western nations is by no means such. They also contain
religious truths. It is not only on the grave of Karl Marx, but also of those
of Hegel and Schelling that Russia stands. Russia stands then, for Berdyaev
as for Bulgakov, at the centre of two currents of world history: Eastern and
Western. Only Russia, he says, can resolve the question of the East for European culture. If Russia has a world mission, this mission is the unification of
the East and the West in one Christian humanity. That is a far cry from the
Russia of Marxism or of today's political and economic Russian oligarchy.

Emergence inhibits navigation

In fact for Norwegian political scientist and social anthropologist Iver Neumann (13), in his Uses of the Other, if in our ongoing representation of Russia we do not allow for more reflection of how the deeply entrenched patterns reviewed here in "the Russian idea" remain a more or less unacknowledged factor, we will add our voices to the chorus that confirms the dominant version of Russia as a learner, at least in a political and economic respect. As such it is forever about to make the transition into, if not attempt to dominate (perhaps out of a sense of inherent inferiority) Europe, if not Asia and the Middle East as well.

In fact Russia's political and economic backwardness, Neumann says – that is, its low degree of functional differentiation of power between politics and economics, between state and society – meant that the country continuously had to face up to the challenge posed by the more highly differentiated and therefore more efficient economic order in Europe. This was particularly the case for the "northern" and "western" European countries, of course, in the 20th century, and even more so, for the United States of America. Of course, though, the possibility always existed that some new idea may emerge and spawn a specifically Russian model for political and economic organisation, but none is explicitly apparent as yet.

The problem then, as matters currently stand, is that such a new Russian economic model, in systematic, navigational guise, is yet to emerge, and Russia is by no means alone in that regard. Pass through the corridors of academe, in the Soviet Union or indeed in China, in the schools of economics and of management (now business schools) and you would in the past (from 1920–1980) have been taught standard Marxist theory, imported from Great Britain where Marx and Engels spent most of their productive lives. Turn the clock forward, to Russia in the new millennium, and it is now the US and the UK who rule the economic and business roost, with standard 'western' theories of economics and business administration pervading these new business and economic academic corridors. Such 'western' conventional wisdom is then passed on, knowingly or otherwise, to practitioners. We may be dismissive of such economic and business tomes, most especially those American long winded ones, but they reflect the very systematic nature and scope that is absent in Russia, or other such emerging nations today. Instead, then, of building on Bulgakov, rendering his Philosophy of Economy more systematic, we have economics 101, and the neoliberal policy makers, and practitioners, to follow!

Further to such, we have "shock therapy" as per the US neoliberal macroeconomist Jeffrey Sachs (14), on the one hand, or the Russian oligarchs on a micro enterprise level, on the other! For if you fail to draw naturally and communally on your own roots, or grounds, and what is emerging beneath your own feet, culturally and spiritually, you will inevitably suffer "shock" as you come out into the 'western' or 'northern' scientific and economic open, from your 'eastern' or 'southern' grounds. Moreover, as you come out of shock, you will resort, as Russia has done, to a lowest common denominator, politically and economically, rather than drawing on the richness of your own nature and culture, to ultimately navigate your way.

This is particularly ironic in the Russian case as the very notion of "integral knowledge" emerged, via Soloviev, on home cultural grounds, but has never been developed for political and economic purposes. At the same time the very inner-directedness to which Bulgakov continually alludes, in the context of a spiritually laden "sophia economy" more akin to "employing your self-community" than either to communist laden employment or capitalist oriented self-employment has sadly passed contemporary Russia by. In fact we (15) have specifically elaborated on the implications of such for pursuing, or indeed not pursuing,

Bibliography

1 Berdyaev, N. (1948) *The Russian Idea*. New York: Palgrave Macmillan.
2 Soloviev, V. (2008) *The Philosophical Principles of Integral Knowledge*. Cambridge: William Eerdmans.
3 Yallop, J. (2015) *Dreamstreets: A Journey Through Britain's Village Utopias*. London: Jonathan Cape.
4 Smeaton, D., Ray, K. and Knight, G. (2014) *Costs and Benefits to Business of Adopting Work Life Balance Working Practices: A Literature Review*. London: Biz.
5 Bulgakov, S. (2000) *Philosophy of Economy: The World as Household*. New Haven: Yale University Press.
6 Smith, A. (2003) *The Wealth of Nations*. New York: Bantam Classics.
7 Bulgakov, S. (1993) *Sophia: The Wisdom of God*. Hudson, NY: Lindisfarne.
8 Marx, K. (1992) *Capital*. New York: Penguin Classics.
9 Brown, R. et al. (2014) The Performance of Employee-Owned Businesses in Scotland: Some Preliminary Empirical Evidence. *Fraser of Allander Institute Economic Commentary* 37: 3. Strathclyde: University of March. [Available at: https://pure.strath.ac.uk/portal/files/31083372/FEC_37_3_March2014_Brown-RMcQuaidRRaesideRCanduelaJ.pdf].
10 Lewis, J.S. (1957/n.d.) *Dear to My Heart*, Transcript of a broadcast on the BBC, in 1957. John Lewis Partnership. [Available at: www.johnlewispartnership.co.uk/content/dam/cws/pdfs/about-us/our-founder/Our_Founder_Dear_to_my_Heart_Speech.pdf].
11 Weyer, M.V. (2012) Any Other Business: Have You Wondered Why There's Only One John Lewis Partnership, Mr Clegg? *The Spectator*, 21 January.
12 Jakim, B. and Bird, R. (1998) *On Spiritual Unity: A Slavophile Reader*. Hodson, NY: Lindisfarne Books.
13 Neumann, I. (1999) *Uses of the Other: The "East" in European Identity Formation*. Minneapolis: University of Minnesota Press.
14 Schwartz, A. (2006) *The Politics of Greed: How Privatization Structured Politics in Central and Easter Europe*. New York: Rowan & Littlefield.
15 Lessem, R. (2016) *op cit*.

8 Commonwealth

Ethical egoism to sustainable livelihood

GROUNDING HUMAN NATURE
AWAKENING SPIRIT
THREEFOLD NAVIGATION
EFFECT AWAKENING

Introduction to the threefold commonwealth

The communal ground of Byzantine Christianity (Chapter 6) and of Orthodox philosophy and spirituality (Chapter 7) have neither been converted into
social science or social or economic policy. As such, Western self-employment
has continued to triumph over self-in-community. But as we see in this chapter, the work of Croatian-born Rudolf Steiner (1) was able to carry the 'eastern flag' into the West and North, through anthroposophy and his principle
of three-folding (liberty, equality, fraternity) a *Commonwealth*.

Interestingly Steiner's principles have been most strongly manifested not
in Europe, but in Egypt, by Sekem (2), acting as a crossroads between the
Middle and *European* East. All too often we find fundamental research is
undertaken in the developed world and transformative action in the developing, though, sadly, all too seldom is there cross-fertilisation between the
two. In this chapter, then, we bring the two together, mediated by Swiss
anthroposophist Rudolf Isler, with a view to navigating the employment of
self-and-community.

We begin by asking the Burning Question: is there a future for developing sustainable livelihoods in economies and enterprises? As we, briefly,
examine the recent history of the environmental movement we see that the
'greening of business' is moving forward rapidly. But, it remains to be seen
whether or not this is fast enough to save a human commonwealth on the
planet. To probe further we open our Window into Wisdom, thereby looking at a Christian response to a rich young man, through Mark's focus on
the Self, prior to investigating Rudolf Steiner's social theory of *Threefold
Commonwealth*.

The problem of wealth was no less a barrier to commonwealth in the
first century CE than it is today. Our two Illustrative Cases then consider

the life and work of social innovator Ibrahim Abouleish in Egypt, founder of Sekem, and of Sir Ove Arup, who is widely regarded as the 20th century's most innovative and aesthetic engineer. The business that he built up – which continues to thrive – was established with the values and vision of a commonwealth at its heart. First, we turn to the Burning Question of the sustainability of our planet.

Burning Question: is there a future for developing sustainable livelihoods?

Pioneering complexes, based in diverse practices that can each come under the umbrella of 'environmental production economics', such as Sekem, Mondregon, Arup Engineering and some of the other cases that we've featured in previous chapters, each emerged from the work of 20th-century innovators. Since then, in more recent years, principles of sustainable livelihood and green business have become common currency.

Far from being at the margins of political debate, concerns regarding how business, production and consumption impact on climate change, environmental destruction, species extinction and, indeed, anxiety about the very air we breathe, inter alia, is front and centre of global politics. And, green action, by businesses or consumers, within civil society, is the epitome of Steiner's ethical egoism. If we do not live, work and act sustainably as individuals we cannot live sustainably as a society.

The road from Rio

How did we get here? Whilst the Rio '92 Earth Summit was widely regarded as an abject failure, its follow-on conference, twenty years later, marked a massive turnabout for the global community of nations. Similarly, the 2016 Paris Accord (from the Conference of the Parties – COP21 – of the UN Framework Convention on Climate Change) represented an enormous shift in the official attitudes of nation states in respect of human intervention causing global warming, compared to the COP-3 Kyoto Protocol of 1996. What a difference 20 years of unremitting data, statistics, research, analysis and scientific papers can make, despite the climate change deniers.

Not, that, official pronouncements will necessarily result in direct action. Steiner was correct in being wary of the state as an arbiter of anything other than legalities. What is of much greater significance is what they say about the place of environmental action and sustainable production within the popular debates of "representative democracies". Equally, we note Steiner's ambivalence towards democracy as a range of political systems. That said, we can see that there is a general acceptance of the need for dramatic, radical and fundamental change in respect of the relationship between economic development, postindustrialism and environmental protection. Sustainable production is, in Isler's terms, an economic need rather than simply a market pursuit.

The green issue-attention cycle

Ecology, production methods and politics were, famously, connected, by the political scientist Anthony Downs (3) to his five stages of 'the issue-attention cycle'. In his original paper, which was remarkably prescient in many respects, he predicted that environmental issues would fade from public gaze, as it ceased to receive the same level of media scrutiny, as in the early 1970s. But, of course, that never happened.

Reports such as Al Gore's film *An Inconvenient Truth* and the Stern Review (4) of the impact of CO_2 emissions on future economic growth, in the early years of the new millennium, energised widespread public disquiet about production methods, levels of consumption and even human survival, in relation to planetary capacity. The backlash of climate change deniers fuelled the arguments of 'ecological economists' to point-out the inherent oxymoron of 'sustainable development'.

There were two substantive reasons why issues to do with sustainable production hadn't faded into obscurity. Firstly, it was because 'green' had become identified as far more than a single issue. The environmental crisis and debates about industrial production methods had outgrown their original clothes as a one-campaign political concern. The societal need for ecological production had become more of a shorthand for many, if not most, concerned with the severe disruptions and negative consequences of advanced Capitalism.

But, we contend, there is a second reason, which is equally significant and, which, in a curious way, confirms Downs' thesis: the post-problem phase of his cycle had turned into "an opportunity phase". Of course, it is a terrible management cliché to say that "there are no such things as problems, only opportunities". But, in this case, that has turned out to be at least part of the story. For example, the proliferation of Green Business or Sustainability Awards, blogs and advocacy groups all point in the same direction: the most recent stage of environmentalism has seen a shift from a consumption sphere-based civil society movement to one that embraces capital, businesses and the production sphere.

The greening of business is official

Recently, the UK Confederation of British Industry (5) produced a report claiming that British business could boost the economy by £20BN per annum by adopting the green production policies they proposed. It was full of bullish pronouncements:

> Implementing the recommendations set out . . . as a package could enable green business to outperform government expectations, significantly boosting UK growth. Creating the right conditions to drive low-carbon markets and stimulate investment, and adopting a more strategic

approach to maximise the economic value of the low carbon transition, could enable UK green business to grow more quickly than the government's figures project.

(ibid p. 30)

John Cridland, the Confederation's Director, claimed that there was no distinction between "going green and going for growth". In the past five years the mood music has become even more conducive to the pursuit of a sustainable production agenda. Following President Trump's announcement to begin withdrawing the US from the Paris Climate Protocol (at the G20, July, 2017), corporate America hit back, recognising the pressure from consumers and board members to commit to a greener business future. As Bloomberg (6) reported:

> "This [green production] work is embedded in our business," Wal-Mart spokesman Kevin Gardner said in an email. It's "good for the business, our shareholders and customers; if ultimately we are able to positively impact the environment in the process, that's a win too". Wal-Mart was one of 81 companies that promised to reduce emissions in the run up to the 2016 Paris global climate negotiations. The company upped its targets last November [2016], saying it would get half its power from renewable sources by 2025.

Whilst *Wal-Mart* or *Nestle* may not be favoured businesses in the eyes of many environmental campaigners, green activists lined-up to praise the stance of so many of the world's leading corporate giants, who opposed and, frankly, ridiculed President Trump's isolation, in a minority of one. The mood of big business was summarised in a statement from the "B Team" (7), of which Richard Branson is cofounder and cochair, published as soon as the Trump White House's "considered decision" was made public:

> In taking this action, President Trump has gone against the thinking of mainstream business in America. More than 1,000 companies have, over the course of the past year, made clear their support for the move to a low carbon economy. He stands opposed to companies which comprise the heart of American commerce . . . He has even gone against the thinking of his own supporters, who overwhelmingly support renewable energy – 84% of Americans who voted for Trump support the further expansion of solar power in the US, and 77% believe public land should be used to generate renewable power. Americans embrace clean energy because they know it is more affordable. It will reduce their bills and create more job opportunities.

Game, set, match, well possibly! As such, we can see that the most recent stage has involved the social movement transitioning from the sphere of consumption and popular protest to the spheres of production and distribution, so that 'green' is now seen as offering an important edge within the marketplace. But, of course, the media pronouncements of business leaders are one thing, the evidence of a shift in business behaviour is quite another. On whether sustainable production methods will 'save the planet', the jury remains out.

Sustainable production and consumption patterns

Whilst recognising Steiner and anthroposophy's understandable reluctance to embrace state action, we live in a world of global compacts. To this end, as the United Nations' Millennium Development Goals, to be achieved by 2015, drew to their close, a new series of Sustainable Development Goals were introduced, with an aim date of 2030. These seventeen goals cover the entire gamut of human activity influencing economic, social and cultural development. The twelfth of these addresses the sphere of sustainable production and consumption.

The purpose of Sustainable Development Goal 12 is to engage in discourse and practical action surrounding issues arising from a burgeoning global middle class, to the mid-century. Equally, the global population is predicted to reach 9.5BN by 2050, requiring three planets worth of resources and output to meet current lifestyles. As such, there are a number of challenges that are being placed at the door of business, in order to achieve the need for sustainable production.

Perhaps the two most significant requirements are for business to consider the social impact of products and services, in order to find sustainable solutions. The second is to identify 'hot spots' within the value chain, where interventions can have the greatest impact for reducing waste of resources. Even so, beyond these laudable aims, unless we find ways to shift the economy from one based on capital use for profit maximisation to one based in meeting basic and holistic human needs, no amount of United Nations goals will effect sustainable production.

**Window into Wisdom: on common wealth
in Mark (10:17–22)**

Mark does not raise economic concerns very often. This makes Jesus' encounter with "a rich man" particularly striking. The man asks "what must I do to inherit eternal life?" This appears to be a soulish question that might result in a wonderful dialogue with the guru about prayer and relationship with God. But, as usual, Jesus cuts straight through to issues of the true spirit within the man's life. Jesus' return question is "why do you call me good? No one is good except God alone". The obvious rhetorical import is to question whether the man recognises that Jesus is God's Son. If so, whatever he says is beyond argument.

Only one thing is required – everything

He reminds the wealthy man of the six most socially directed commands in the 10 Commandments, turning "you shall not covet" (Exodus 20:17; Deuteronomy 5: 21) into "you shall not *defraud*". This appears to be a direct challenge to the man's wealth-generating activity. In business there can always be a temptation to raise one's own financial interests above those of others. But, the man is up to the test. "All these I've kept since I was a boy".

The response of Jesus is, immediately, to invite the man to join his disciples. And, there is only one thing he has to do. "Go, sell everything you have, give it to the poor; and, then, you will have treasure in heaven". The man turns away, sad-faced because he has great wealth. So, Jesus turns to his disciples. "How hard it is for the rich to enter the kingdom of God". This must have baffled them because it was standard Jewish teaching to equate wealth with God's blessing.

Can camels get through needle-eyes?

Then we get the evocative one-liner: "It is easier for a camel to go through the eye of a needle than for one who is rich to enter into the kingdom of God". This is most likely a reference to the narrow entrance of one of Jerusalem's main trading gates, known as 'the eye of the needle'. It may have been here that the man had his business interests, we don't know.

But, the message of Jesus is that personal wealth gets in the way of common wealth. In the melee of trying to make it in business we can tread on others, or, at least, not seek our shared interest. Wealth can be a barrier to real human relationships that force us to get through the gate ahead of everyone else. And, when we're through we often forget about those behind. Even so, it is important to notice the way that Mark indicates Jesus' response to the man who had kept the commandments: "Jesus looked at him and loved him" (vs 21).

It was in the man's own interest to give up his self-wealth and join the common disciples. Jesus knew this was the best action he could possibly take. But, it is unusual for anyone to trade Self for Community or personal wealth for common wealth. That is the problem, which Rudolf Steiner addressed, from a philosophical and theoretical perspective.

The theory of a threefold commonwealth

An earning or needs economy

For Swiss anthropological (anthroposophy was developed by Steiner early last century as a "spiritual science") economist, Rudolf Isler (8), one of the most recent (2013) interpreters of *Steiner's social and economic approach, the Austrian polymath recommended turning economic thinking on its head and transforming the earnings economy into a needs economy.*

This change is so fundamental that we would have to see many economic processes in a different way. Need as orientation and impulse for the economy, for Isler as indeed for Bulgakov, arises from human culture. It must not be induced or created autonomously by economic life in isolation. This means that all commercial companies (not just charitable institutions) require an ideal objective. What then does a need based economy specifically mean for the production process?

Production factors and products

Specifically then, according to Isler, we should undertake our work because humanity needs it. If we suspect or even perceive that this is not the case, our work becomes an inner burden to us. This real economic value of our work, to humanity moreover, cannot be encompassed simply in figures.

The capacity to work, then, is a human attribute, a part of our intrinsic nature. *If people find that others are dictating their labour and can compel them as employees to do something they do not wish to – for instance producing weapons and poisons – then they feel that their rights are being infringed.* An employer moreover, for Isler, ought not to lay off employees without trying to find them another job. An individual employer, however, is not in a position to do this alone and should therefore enter into association with others in order to participate contractually in an organisation involved in the overall economy.

Overcoming the labour market

When Rudolf Steiner therefore energetically proposed abolishing wage dependency that forces us into work, he was not merely concerned about the legal protection of working people but also about *economic performance*. Strict mutuality holds sway in the market economy, as outlined in Chapter 3, in that services are exchanged reciprocally. The market economy connection should not obtain, directly then, between the performance of the individual and his income.

In other words, when we speak of the "labour market", as in every market, we accommodate supply and demand, which is meant to give rise to the price level, or in this case to an employee's wage. These economic structures and procedures prevent us in fact from learning to think and feel socially/sociologically (see Chapter 4). *We are integrated into the "labour market" like a cog in a machine.* This mechanistic paradigm will continue to apply as long as we are limited to a purely egotistical outlook; and prevailing economic theory today relies on this distorted view of the human being.

Changes in accounting

Nowadays then, according to Isler, the formal thing is for salaries and wages to be accounted for, in a profit-and-loss account, as staffing costs. This means that the incomes people live from appear as a cost factor within the company. But in reality human existence, for him as for Steiner, is the *goal* of the company. The aim of the economy, after all, is to meet human needs – that is the generally accepted definition of economics.

In business economics, by contrast, the company's goal is regarded as *profit. Instead of asking* (see Table 8.1) *what the cost of labour is, one would learn to ask, can enough income arise from work to ensure all who contribute can live from it?* Profit distribution is a matter of all workers who have together created the yield, and all of them have a right to decide how to distribute such between:

1   private incomes
2   donations to cultural institutions
3   social payments e.g. help for single mothers
4   reserves for improving the company
5   repayment of debts.

Table 8.1 A transformed P & L account

Expenditure	Income
Overheads	Sale of goods and services
Cost of materials	
Energy	
Administration	
Rent – interest	
Depreciation	
Reserves	
Repayment of loans	
Sundries	
Profit	
Share for staff	
Donations for cultural life	
Donations to social welfare	

We now turn to the heart of the matter, for Isler as for Steiner, whereby, in the latter's *"threefold commonwealth"*, *economic life should be based on fraternity, political life on equality, and cultural life on liberty.*

Political democracy, economic collaboration, cultural freedom

The key idea of Steiner's so-called three-folding is freedom. In the social order, the state is not the highest and ultimate authority. People active and involved in different areas can themselves largely regulate their own affairs and concerns. This applies, above all, to educational, cultural and economic matters. In each system *people are sovereign in different ways: in the state through democratic decisions, in the economy through contractually agreed collaboration and in the cultural sphere through free acknowledgment of individual initiatives.*

There is only one domain, for Steiner, from which the state should not withdraw. It must safeguard the rule of law, and this is its intrinsic task.

Rudolph Steiner (9) then based his *Philosophy of Freedom* on the *potential* autonomy of each individual, and this is his focus in all his works. At the same time, the ideals of equality (political) and fraternity (economic) serve freedom (cultural), each in their own way, because they allow every individual to be a codetermining partner in society. In fact Steiner maintained that egotism is a necessary concomitant of modern, developing consciousness, which will continue to increase as we evolve into self-aware individuals. However, *in the economy, forms of organisation need to be developed which counteract egotism and continually urge us not only to perceive our own interests but also those of people with whom we are connected.*

The economics of association

It is of course right to think of a person's hours of work as part of their life. But nature and capital (including intelligent inventions) play a part in production besides work. So *prices must make it possible to sufficiently sustain cultural and spiritual life, the source of inventiveness. Nature too must be taken into account through care, environmentally friendly usage and recycling of waste.* At the same time, job placement is not the function of government departments. *If people have to be laid off in one company, it is the task of intercompany collaboration to offer them places where they are needed*; and this applies also to cultural and social professions. The case of the Mondragon Cooperatives in the Spanish Basque country, as we have previously cited, is a primary example of such. Economic life, then, must become dependent on, in this case, a cooperatively based legal order that arises from a sense of justice. Law plays its part then in establishing rules according to which income can be fairly allocated, and also work can be fairly distributed.

A living threefold order

The rules for income distribution belong to the political life of rights. Sharing of profit is not a financial act, as such, but an application of justice to the economy, as is evident in the Mondragon case. The application of rules in an individual instance, though, belongs to the cultural and spiritual sphere. The trusted representatives do not hold their position because some higher authority has appointed them, but they are recognised in their roles because they are professionally qualified and have life experience.

Through adjusting production to need, *associative collaboration* between different types of companies creates the basis, in *economic* life, for just income distribution. We now turn to the act of giving in economics.

The importance of gifts in economics

Giving is the fundamental gesture of motherliness, the opposite of the male principle of exchange. When we exchange, we only give something if we receive in return. *Exchange leads to competition, dominance, repression and war. Giving, by contrast, ties people into community, and leads to peace* (see for example the Civic Economy in Chapter 3, indeed the core focus of Part II). In a balance sheet, short-term monies receivable (creditors) and monies payable (debtors) are *liquidity*, in other words *loan money*. In a profit and loss account, expenses and income are presented as *purchase money*. Profit, on the other hand, is neither purchase money nor loan money. It is the net operating result which we can use by free decision. Thus it belongs, believe it or not for Isler, to the category of *gift money*.

Table 8.2 Repositioning gift money

Expenditure	*Income*
Purchase money	Sale of goods and services
Overheads	
Cost of materials	
Energy	
Administration	
Rent – interest	
Depreciation	
Reserves	
Repayment of loans	
Sundries	
Profit	
Gift money	
Income of all staff	
Donations for cultural life	
Social welfare	

If we regard the incomes of all staff in a company as profit distribution rather than "staffing costs", we remove them from the purchase money realm. We give every staff member a share of the profit which they need, and which we wish to give out of our free will.

We now turn from labour to land.

The administration of land by the cultural sphere

An individually formulated assignment of purpose is needed, for Isler, for every place on earth, for every plot of land. However, the formulation itself is not enough – the land must be connected with *living* cultural activity. In other words, people must inwardly sustain this idea by developing and elaborating it for themselves. *They must be people who are not only able to run a farm business, but who also understand how to produce food of real benefit to human beings and how to cultivate the soil and landscape in a living, nurturing way.* Land used for industrial purposes, for Steiner, should also be connected with this idea: it should serve the production of items necessary and beneficial to humankind. At all farms as such, developments have shown how important it is to keep alive the idea which initially inspired the work – when new people join a project and as generations change.

qAdministration of cultural life, for Isler ideally speaking, has nothing centralised about it, but lives from the insights and initiatives of the people involved. This applies equally to schools, colleges, universities, research centres, artistic institutes and to the cultivation of religious life. Land administration must therefore become infused with this living, spiritual life.

Steiner therefore sought after a concept of an economic value for land that could not be expressed in monetary terms. In the course of his life (1861–1925) he integrated land into his concept of the threefold social organism (cultural, economic and political), stating that the land should not be administered in the economic sphere because economics creates a market for everything. Since ownership of land is not a commodity but a right of use, the foundations – as opposed to the everyday running – of land administration, for him, must in fact be created in the rights sphere. *Land principally belongs to all people because they have an equal right to live on the earth.*

But in actually allocating land in each case, individual capacities and needs must be assessed, and this is a task for the cultural sphere. Two preconditions must be made by users of land: the professional, specialist expertise needed in each case, and the will to use these for the good of humanity.

We now turn from land to capital.

Administration of capital by the cultural sphere

It is said, Isler maintains, that the capital market ensures that capital is directed to where it is needed. If the capital yields profit, it is assumed that it has been used in an economically productive way. The market economy therefore declares profit to be a positive force, and denies human beings any further responsibility in the matter. *For Steiner though, responsible capital administration must replace the capital market. For this, structures are needed to be administered by the cultural life, spurred on by individual ideas.*

In addition, to avoid isolation, every enterprise needs a supervisory board composed of professionals who can come from very varied fields of society, and whose task is to be aware of how the company is run, and keep a check on it. First and foremost they need to keep an eye on the company originator's ideals and purpose, and safeguard this against the profit motives of external funders.

Enterprising activity is practically applied cultural life

What has been described shows that a principle characteristic of cultural life applies to the forming of company capital. This principle for Steiner is as follows: deploy individual initiative and collegiate connection with others who understand the initiative. In other words, *enterprising activity in the economy is practically applied spiritual life, and the forming of company capital is therefore a matter for this cultural sphere.* At the same time, the skilled manual worker participates not only in the economic, but also in the cultural and spiritual spheres.

In contrast, and according to modern business textbooks, as per Economics 101 in conventional business studies, the overarching aim of a company is to maximise profit – defined as the excess of income over costs. In future this overriding aim should for Isler instead be formulated as the production or provision of something that supports the common good of humanity. The second aim will be to enable the people working in the company to live well from the income, and not to be simply treated as a cost factor. A third objective will be for the company's product and services to be offered at a fair price. Commercial businesses, overall then, while active in economic production must also develop their cultural sphere and their legal structures. It is in so doing, through sharing the rewards from each of these factors, that a true common wealth, based in liberty, is produced.

Illustrative Cases of sustaining livelihoods: Sekem and Ove Arup

Sekem: seeding development: marriage of the occident and the orient

Ibrahim Abouleish (10) was born into a typical, though well off, extended family in Egypt, with homes in both the city and countryside.

My grandfather listened to all my childlike questions and found comprehensive answers for me, which were deeply satisfying. He sat down beside the bright white flower with the dancing butterfly, and took me on his knee. I leaned back against him, enjoying his gentleness. The butterfly opened its colourful wings, and flew from the white blossom up into the sky. We both followed its flight for a long time.

Ibrahim's approach to education, given than all that come in his life before, inwardly and outwardly, was very different from his fellow students. He felt reminded, in revisiting his societal origins, of the golden era of Islam and the flourishing culture in Egypt, and this feeling never left him, originating, as it were, in his childhood, and returning to his consciousness, as we shall see, as he embarked on his university studies, inadvertantly to start with perhaps, to ultimately pursue his (10) childhood dream.

I carry a vision deep within myself: in the midst of sand and desert I see myself standing at a well drawing water. Carefully I plant trees, herbs and flowers and wet their roots with the precious drops. The cool well water attracts human beings and animals to refresh and quicken themselves. Trees give shade, the land turns green, fragrant flowers bloom, insects, birds and butterflies show their devotion to God, the creator, as if they were citing the first Sura of the Qu'ran. The humans, perceiving the hidden praise of God, care for and see all that is created as a reflection of paradise on earth. For me this idea of an oasis in the middle of a hostile environment is like an image of the resurrection at dawn, after a long journey through the nightly desert. I saw it in front of me like a model before the actual work in the desert started. And yet in reality I desired even more: I wanted the whole world to develop.

We can see then that, in his childhood Ibrahim was well grounded in his Muslim faith, in general, and in the relevant sura from the Qu'ran, specifically, culminating, as we saw for Bulgakov (see previous chapter) in a vision of resurrection (path of renewal) at dawn. In fact, as Ibrahim turned form his childhood to his youth, he reached out from Egypt to Austria, where he pursued his scientific studies, in both engineering and pharmacology. During his studies, moreover, Ibrahim noticed inner changes taking place within himself. He became thoroughly involved with European culture, getting to know its music, studying its poetry and philosophy. Somebody looking into his soul would have seen anything "Egyptian" left completely behind, so he could absorb everything new. Because of his childhood and adolescent grounding, though, in Egyptian culture, and in Islam, he could not leave such entirely behind.

Ibrahim then told his children the story of a man who decided to move to the desert with his children and who created a big garden there. Once he had painted the picture in great detail he suddenly asked: "And what would happen if we were that family? Spontaneously there were shouts of joy". His son was 16 and his daughter 14. His son would ride a motorbike across the desert and his daughter would ride horses. To his soul mate in Austria Martha Werth he (11) wrote a farewell letter:

> *For my soul Austria was like a spiritual childhood garden. Now I hope the souls of Egyptian people can be revitalised and renewed by a garden in the desert. After establishing a farm as a healthy physical basis for soul and spiritual development, I will set up further things, following the example of human development: a kindergarten, high school, vocational education, hospital and cultural institutions. My goal is the development of humans in a comprehensive sense. I want to pass on this richness of nature and spirit to Egypt, to sow the seeds I have been given.*

Sekem's fourfold commonwealth

SEKEM's model for sustainable development, as it stands today, some 40 years from when it was initially conceived, integrates different spheres of life, natural and social scientific disciplines, into a holistic whole where all parts are independent and interconnected.

As Sekem's natural and social, functional and structural vision stands:

- *we establish biodynamic agriculture as the competitive solution for the environmental, social and food security challenges of the 21st century.*
- *we build successful business models in accordance with ecological and ethical principles.*
- *we want to provide products and services of the highest standards to meet the needs of the consumer.*

The intertwined natural, social, cultural and economic realms of activity within Sekem's group of companies begins on a practical level by healing the soil through the application of biodynamic farming methods. Biodynamic agriculture stands for a self-containing and self-sustaining ecosystem without any unnatural additions. Soil, plants, animals and humans together create an image of a holistic living organism. SEKEM's approach of sustainable agriculture includes the regenerative powers of agriculture.

Sekem's socio-political vision, moreover, states:

- *we create workplaces reflecting human dignity and supporting employee development.*

- *we locally and globally advocate for a holistic approach to sustainable development*
- *we build a long-term, trusting and fair relationship with our partners*

Most recently, and with a view to such, Sekem has its established the Heliopolis University for Sustainable Development, in Cairo, possibly the only university in the world dedicated to sustainable development. We now turn to Ove Arup.

Arup engineering: key to sustainable partnership

Designing a pool for penguins may not sound like the most sustainable feat of engineering in the world or, indeed, a significant example of the needs economy. But, in fact, London Zoo's Penguin Pool represents several features of the pioneering work and philosophy of Ove Arup. He is often described as the most important engineer of the 20th century, for whom the practice of engineering design was distinctly purposive, even if he shunned the idea of being rooted in any specific ideology. Of course, it is engineers who bear much of the responsibility for cocreating a sustainable environment.

Creative with concrete

Sir Ove Arup (1895–1988) was not only a prolific engineer but an artist, creative designer, and social philosopher. His aim was to create a business that moulded together the best talent, in a partnership that could transform the world of engineering and, hence, engineer the world's transformation. The Penguin Pool, completed in 1934, was one of his early-career masterpieces, which came about when he was working for the Danish firm Christiani & Nielsen.

Arup had become increasingly interested in the possibilities for reinforced concrete. The pool's primary designer was Berthold Lubetkin, of the Tecton Group. He realised that Ove Arup was innovating with concrete in a way that could enable his futuristic designs to be precisely engineered for a long and sustainable life. Arup agreed to work on the project because of his particular interest in working with architects and designers.

Many features of the structure were applauded, but it was the two narrow curving ramps, created in single cast 14 m long slabs, that received most praise. They were supported by hidden columns but appeared to hover over the water of the pool, as if balanced in thin air. In fact, the inner engineering of the slabs, their construction and pattern of tortion reinforcements were wholly original and represented a leap forward in the use of reinforced concrete as a building material. Apart from their beauty and innovative design they closely mirrored ice features of the penguins' natural Antarctic environment. The entire structure, its aesthetic, functionality and overall concept reflected a philosophy of sustainability that Arup would take to the founding of his own company in 1938, fully established in 1946, after the Second World War.

The key speech

Arup's philosophy and principles, which are retained by the company to this day, are contained in a Key Speech (12) that he delivered to his partners meeting in Winchester, in 1970. It is required reading for anyone wishing to join the business, nearly fifty years after it was first conveyed. In order to provide for long-lasting careers Arup decried Fordism, with its mantra of 'unbearable work made bearable by technology'. Instead, he opted for a philosophy of making work 'interesting and rewarding so that you enjoy work and leisure equally'. His was a distinct otium of the people.

But, his second principle displayed the heart of his business, which was his version of the pursuit of happiness:

> . . . [we] recognise that no man is an island, that our lives are inextricably mixed up with those of our fellow human beings, and that there can be no real happiness in isolation. Which leads to an attitude which would accord to others the rights claimed for oneself, which would accept certain moral or humanitarian restraints.

What he termed his 'humanitarian attitude' included seeking the happiness of all, so that every person, whether inside or outside the business is seen as an end rather than as a means. The implications of this were that Arup saw his engineering partnership as based in use-value, not simply in profit-maximisation within the market. Indeed, generating an economic surplus was, simply, seen as a necessary function for sustaining the business. Honourable dealing and decision making based on ability and character, within the business, were to be balanced by expressing, in every task and commission, a social conscience, 'joining hands with all those who fight for the same values'. Whilst prosperity for all, in the partnership, was seen to be crucial, in order to sustain the business, it shouldn't be regarded as the primary aim.

To these principles he added a restless search for first-order quality, which he termed 'total architecture', as a crucial part of serving the needs of clients. This meant that, as an engineering company, Arup should expand their activities to encompass the adjoining fields of architecture, planning, ground engineering, environmental engineering, computer programming, etc. and the planning and organisation of the work on site – a type of engineering commonwealth. But, as his previous life and work had shown Arup would also expand into aesthetics, art, drama and a wide range of servicing cultural activities.

Flexible three-folding

Sir Ove Arup was, equally, a very pragmatic individual who remained suspicious of over-arching principles and ideologies. Nevertheless, he created a business that incorporated the idea of sustainable development two decades before it placed that principle on the global map. In addition, he sought to rigorously maintain individual equality of opportunity in the business, such that he valued loyalty to the aims and principles of the Partnership above loyalty to himself or the firm's other leaders, as a living three-folding, pace Steiner.

The current firm is composed of 13,000 people, many of whom are Partners, some employees, in more than 35 countries. It is owned as a Trust, for its members, guided by the aims, values and principles that were represented in Ove Arup's 1970 Key Speech. The Trust has no individual shareholders and no external investors. As such, it is able to act independently, developing its work entirely on the basis of reinvesting its surplus in the promotion of the business and society. It is careful to only choose work that aligns with its values, aiming to set new standards in every project it is engaged in. The Partners make common decisions about the work they take on, in collegial self-administration, with profit very much subservient to the needs of clients and the holistic growth of the enterprise.

Projects such as the engineering design of the Sydney Opera House, Singapore Sports Hub, Welsh Water Resilience, The Francis Crick Institute and the London 2012 Olympics overview, inter alia, illustrate the creative strength and vision of Arup's work. The fact that the first major retrospective of Ove Arup's creative output was shown at the Victoria & Albert Museum, London (V&A) in 2016, indicates the breadth of his artistic vision. But, overall, it is the humanitarian ethos of Arup, mirroring the lifetime work of its founder, which marks it out as a global leader in sustainable business. Arup has succeeded in creating iconic and long-lasting artefacts right across the globe, meeting the needs of people as well.

Conclusion: the greatest problem we face today

For Steiner, the struggle of the working poor and the gap between rich and poor nations, the greatest problem we face today, has arisen with the coming of industrialism. All of industrialism, Steiner said, insofar as it keeps developing continually through its means of production, works in relation to the economy as a whole with negative equity. What does he mean by that? *Through industrialism, productivity must be repeatedly renewed through new capital investments. By contrast the productivity of agriculture and forested land, with all its natural foundations, its plants and animals, does not decline in value but can in fact increase with good cultivation practices.* A tractor which I buy today comes to the end of its useful life after say 30 years. A horse or cow can produce a whole herd in the same period if the necessary pastureland is available.

Organic agriculture – the only form for Steiner which can be seen as truly sustainable – cultivates living processes without feeds and fertilisers brought from outside the farm. Here agriculture is engaged in *primary* production, whereas industry involves *refining production*. Therefore *organic agriculture makes our natural foundations (soil fertility) healthier, whereas industry depletes them and reduces their value.* Land production is therefore the foundation of all economic activity. Through organic farming, as such, year by year, this foundation needs to be upgraded so as to enhance a farm's "individuality".

We now turn to what is probably the leading proponent of such organic agriculture today, that is Sekem in Egypt, starting out with its originator, Ibrahim Abouleish. Standing at the historical crossroads of civilisations, moreover, he was well placed to bring together Africa, Europe and Asia, not to mention also the all pervasive influence of America.

Bibliography

1 Steiner, R. (2013) *Towards Social Renewal: Rethinking the Basis of Society*. Forest Row: Rudolph Steiner Press.
2 Abouleish, I. (2005) *Sekem: A Sustainable Community in the Egyptian Desert*. Edinburgh: Floris.
3 Downs, A. (1972) Up and Down with Ecology – The Issue-Attention Cycle. *Public Interest* 28(1): 38–50, Summer.
4 Stern, N. (2006) *Stern Review on the Economics of Climate Change*. Cambridge: Cambridge University Press.
5 CBI. (2012) *The Colour of Growth – Maximising the Potential of Green Business*. London: Confederation of British Industry.
6 Flavelle, C. (2017) Apple, Wal-Mart Stick with Climate Pledges Despite Trump's Pivot. *Bloomberg Politics*, 30 March.
7 The B Team. (2017) *The B Team Statement on U.S. Withdrawal from Paris Agreement*, 6 June. [Available at: http://bteam.org/press/the-b-team-statement-on-u-s-withdrawal-from-paris-agreement/. Last accessed: July 31, 2017].

8 Isler, R. (2013) *Sustainable Society: Making Business, Government and Money Work Again*. Edinburgh: Floris Books.
9 Steiner, R. (2013) *The Philosophy of Freedom*. Forest Row: Rudolf Steiner Press.
10 Abouleish, I. (2005) *op cit*.
11 Abouleish, I. (2005) Sekem: A Sustainable Community in the Egyptian Desert. Edinburgh. Floris Books.
12 Arup, O. (1970) *The Key Speech*. Winchester: Arup Engineering.

9 Sarvodaya

Dignified work to multiple capitals

GROUNDING HUMAN NATURE
AWAKENING SPIRIT
THREEFOLD NAVIGATION
EFFECT AWAKENING

Introduction: the awakening of all

As we reach the fourth section of our Eastern Pathway, in relation to evolving work, we consider the responses and innovations that are effected, as a result of awakening to the values of a world in need. In both "eastern" theory and practice we examine the remarkable movement of Sarvodaya, in Sri Lanka. Inspired by Buddhist philosophy and encompassing a constellation of village programmes – across a nation that has been wracked by civil society division and conflict, over several decades – Sarvodaya has sought to embody not only meaningful work but social reconciliation.

The movement has occupied a particular role in meeting the needs of landless poor in Sri Lanka. Consequently, we ask the Burning Question: is it the role of business to tackle inequality and poverty? We find that there is considerable debate about the nature of inequality in global society. But, there are a range of interventions that business can be involved in to make work meaningful and rewarding, not least those that emerge out of a Buddhist understanding of work.

From a spiritual, Judeo-Christian perspective at this point, we inquire, via Mark's gospel, into our relationship with the poor, and indeed, overall, our relationship with the world of work. Work is to be purposeful. But, it only becomes so as we align our values to the value of work and meeting needs that such a purpose is emancipated and embodied. Then, finally, in this chapter, our Window into Wisdom examines what Jesus really meant when he said "the poor are with you always". Once again, we see that work, as blessing, lies at the heart of identifying and responding to need, by effecting social innovation. The theory we thereafter pursue, via Sarvodaya, is that underlying "the awakening of all".

We finally turn, practically, from Sarvodaya specifically, to social movements engaged with eliminating poverty, generally. As such, we also consider the work of the NGO "On Purpose", which educates young professionals in such alignment, through internships and work experience in social enterprise, for our Illustrative Case.

Burning Question: what is the role of business in tackling poverty?

On spiralling levels of inequality

One of the most discussed issues at recent gatherings of the World Economic Forum, at Davos, has been spiralling levels of inequality around the world. Whilst a global forum of some of the richest and most powerful business leaders and plutocrats, in the splendour of a Swiss mountain ski resort, may not seem like the ideal venue to debate the futures of the poorest, Davos has, in recent years, expended considerable energy (and hot air) in considering the gap between the rich and poor worlds.

The core questions have been: is the gap getting wider or narrowing?; and, should it be the role of business, alongside the state and multilateral organisations, such as the UN, to seek to alleviate the worst excesses of inequality? As is so often the case in such debates, it comes down to values and the willingness of rich people to grasp an awareness of what life is like on the other side of the tracks. Empathy is a key resource for tackling poverty and inequality.

The inequality divide is widening

Not all commentators are in agreement surrounding the data. But a report produced by Oxfam (1) for the Davos Forum placed the emphasis firmly on the side of a worsening situation. Under the title "An Economy for the 1%" the global charity authors pointed to several features of what they term the extreme crisis in global inequality. They quote analysis by Credit Suisse (2) which indicates that the world's wealthiest 1% have accumulated more assets than the remaining 99%.

Oxfam's highly controversial statistic that just 62 individuals owned the same wealth as 3.7BN people (i.e. the bottom 50% of the global population), whilst much disputed, served to focus attention. Even if it was a slight exaggeration, which Oxfam challenges, the fundamental premise remains shocking to most people, who consider some value of equity or fairness of outcomes to be an economic good. What is less disputed is that since the turn of the millennium just 1% of the increase in global wealth has been secured by the bottom 50%, whilst 50% of increasing wealth has gone to the top 1%. This is a remarkable and alarming mirror image statistic for many.

Work drives income inequality

Whilst wealth returns to capital have significantly outstripped income distributions to labour, even within the world of work levels of inequality have become eyewatering. Since the financial crisis of 2008–2009 average wages have stagnated in most regions, even within the West, under so-called 'austerity measures'. At the same time the returns to top CEOs has sky-rocketed, with many business stakeholders expressing increasing concern about executive pay, often voiced at share- and stock-holder meetings.

The average wage growth for US corporate CEOs has risen by more than 50% since 2009, whilst the returns to women in two-thirds of world locations have barely moved in money terms and have, often, declined in real terms, against inflation. Women remain the poorest demographic across the globe, making up the largest proportion of workers in the lowest paid and most precarious jobs. At the same time, each industrial sector contributes to the inequality gap in different ways.

The financial services sector has burgeoned remarkably since the Crash, accounting for 20% of all billionaires. An OECD (3) survey has shown that countries with disproportionately large financial services sectors have the highest levels of income inequality at work. Within the extractive sectors, especially related to energy from oil and gas, increasing privatisation of these industries has resulted in huge windfall gains to individuals. In stark contrast, the wages of, mainly women, garment workers actually fell in money terms over 2001–2011.

The income inequality divide is narrowing?

The Oxfam report, which focused on inequalities in wealth, heralded a snowstorm of rebuttals. According to Branko Milanovic (4), one of the leading researchers on income inequality, his calculations indicate that between 1988–2008 the world had seen the first reduction in income inequality since the Industrial Revolution. This reduction in inequality is predominately explained by rising wage rates for lower middle-class earners in China, India and other rapidly emergent economies.

But Milanovic and Oxfam do converge in their estimates in respect of the question of mean averages and top pay. Milanovic offers the caveat that income inequality will only continue to decline if national average incomes continue to converge between nations and if returns to the wealthiest are held in check. It is debateable if this did, in fact, happen over the three years between his and Oxfam's assessments.

Many commentators hold that the economic theory pointing to within country incomes tending towards convergence over time has been contradicted by the evidence. Globalisation, the growth of tax havens, privatisation of utilities and liberalisation of state fiscal policies, over the past two decades, may have led to the Oxfam analysis proving more realistic, suggesting that the gap is widening and not narrowing. Even if there has been a slight reduction in levels of global inequality, which is certainly true in terms of rising life-expectancies and health inequalities, the overall picture, in respect of returns from work remains bleak, especially for women.

What can business do to curb excessive inequality?

There are a number of specific interventions that global business can make to reduce inequality and poverty levels. These include:

- Businesses can reduce tax avoidance measures and require executives to pay domestic taxes, alongside curbing illicit outflows of cash to tax havens. This will often require specific measures by shareholders at annual meetings, followed by close audit scrutiny.
- Companies should both lobby for and seek to pay a national living wage. This is not far-fetched as many business groups are advocating this in a number of global territories, not only Europe.
- Workers should require (not rely on being given) the right to organise. Many worker groups and Unions face intimidation, fear and reprisals when they seek to collectively organise, even within the United States. Equally, Unions should seek to protect and campaign for the rights of workers who are nonmembers, especially women, marginalised and disabled workers.
- As we saw in an earlier section, the precarious nature of the so-called 'sharing' or 'gig economy' has made the position of some workers very fragile, as they have had worker rights withheld. Businesses should seek to give employment benefits to all workers instead of reserving some for 'declassified' roles.

Finally, as Marjorie Wood, of the Institute for Policy Studies and Nick Galasso of Oxfam (5) note, quoting Fritz Schumacher's call for a Buddhist approach to economics: "we clearly need a new economics that works to improve the lives of everyone, not just those already well off." The point is that business, the economics profession and global leaders in work will only take the needs of the poor seriously when they align their values with the value of human life and dignity. We now turn to our Window into Wisdom, again drawing on the "eastern" Gospel of Mark, to consider one of the most abused verses in the New Testament.

Window into Wisdom: are the poor always with you? (Mark 14:1–9)

One of the most abused verses in the New Testament occurs in the context of Jesus being anointed for his death. He is having a meal at the house of a well-to-do but 'unclean' man, Simon the Leper, in

Bethany, where he sometimes stayed. Mark tells us that the religious leaders were already plotting about how to have Jesus arrested for blasphemy, tried and executed. This was the Tuesday–Wednesday of the week, two days before what would become "Good Friday".

In memory of her

A woman (unnamed by Mark) enters with an alabaster jar of incredibly expensive perfume. She breaks the jar open and pours the nard perfume over Jesus' head. Some of the assemblage complain that this was worth a year's average wage and could have been sold to raise money for feeding the poor.

Instead, Jesus rebukes them, praising the woman for her act of generosity, with the memorable words: "whenever the gospel is preached throughout the world, what she has done will also be told, in memory of her". Feminist and other Christians recognise that this celebrated act was a most remarkable response of faith and indicated Jesus' desire to have this woman's action, as a sign of female leadership, memorialised.

Evangelism vs social engagement?

But, it is the phrase that Jesus uses to rebuke the nay-sayers that has been repeatedly mis-interpreted and even used to make the reverse point of Jesus' clear meaning. Jesus remarks: "The poor you will always have with you, and you can help them any time you want. But you will not always have me". Does this mean that the poor are less significant than Jesus, in his own eyes?

In some circles this verse has been used to legitimise attacks on a 'social gospel', which is seen as politicising Jesus' words. The argument appears to run that if Jesus sees poverty as ubiquitous then there isn't much point in Christians focusing their efforts on meeting the needs of the poor and working to reduce inequality. Rather, the gospel requires conversions instead of 'social action', as if there is some contradictory dichotomy between the two.

Most probably Jesus is quoting Deuteronomy 15:10,11. In the Mosaic Law this is an injunction to give freely to the poor at all times. It is because the poor will always be present in your midst that the Lord commands: "you shall open wide your hand to your brother, to the needy and the poor in your land" (vs 11). In other words, although the specific circumstances of Jesus' imminent Passion meant that the woman's act was immensely valuable, the spending of these riches on Jesus didn't absolve the observers from their responsibilities to the poor. Quite the reverse! It was in this act that the woman revealed the direct connection between honouring Jesus and giving to the poor. Wealth is not to be held back. It is to be freely offered-up as a means of worship and giving to God. And, as verse 10 puts it, in so doing work will become a blessing, because it is a means for earning money to be given away and not hoarded. To have the poor in our midst means to always have a source of blessing at work, as we hand some of the fruit of our labour to those in real need.

Social Theory: underlying the awakening of all

Dharma and development

We now specifically turn to the theory and practice of employing self-and-community, from an *eastern*, in this case specifically Buddhist perspective, where the starting point is not the creation of employment per se, but the *awakening of all*, spiritually, with a view to economic development, materially. As such, and as we shall see, Sarvodaya serves to employ self and society, family and community. Moreover, and for our purposes, the *noetics of nature* provides suitable grounding, the *economics of the household* an emergent backdrop, and the *threefold commonwealth* a means of underlying navigation.

For Californian environmental activist, deep ecologist and systems theorist then, as well as a student of Buddhism generally and Sarvodaya specifically, Joanna Macy (6), her development efforts over the last two and a half decades have demonstrated that, however clever or generous the schemes, the local populace will not use or profit from them unless it is internally motivated to do so. *To enlist popular participation and commitment, development programmes require a value-base that is meaningful to the people, relevant to their perceived needs, and affirmative of their inherent strengths.* And where are such values to be found? They are present, as in the Sarvodaya case, in indigenous religious traditions, which over centuries have shaped the people's perception of reality and their notions of what is good and true. Principles for the improvement of their present lives can be culled from these traditions, and rearticulated in ways that mobilise people to take responsibility for social change.

How to harmonise economic theory with Sri Lanka's spiritual wealth

For A.T. Ariyaratne, the founder of Sarvodaya, some fifty years ago, Sri Lanka, like many other newly independent nations, was a victim of western colonialism for over four centuries. Except for a negligible fraction of the native population who learned the coloniser's language, embraced the latter's religion, and adopted an alien culture, the vast majority of the people in these countries were languishing in poverty, ignorance, disease and squalor.

During the period of industrialisation in Europe and the subsequent commercial expansion toward the East, *production of wealth was a material and mechanical affair, from which spiritual and humanistic considerations were totally absent and was the sole economic philosophy that interested the Western capitalists.* Aryiaratne came to the conclusion in the middle of last century that his country could not go on that way. The dilemma he faced was *how to harmonise economic theory with Sri Lanka's age-old spiritual wealth, its culture, if you like, and its consciousness.*

Sarvodaya: the awakening of all

The *Sarvodaya* philosophy – the "awakening of all" – that heevolved (7) was syncretic in ideology and a universal concept, indeed interweaving Marx and Rousseau in Europe, Gandhi and Ashoka in India, as well as most specifically Buddha's teachings. According to Lord Buddha, man's suffering is due is to his ignorance of the true nature of things. The three particular Buddhist principles to be realised are those of:

- *Change*: all phenomena are in a state of constant change
- *Suffering*: one who fails to understand such "grasps" at things
- *Egolessness*: the deceptive notion of "I" is at the roots of anger, hatred and greed.

Long before the socialist economic theories were formulated in the West as a reaction to extreme capitalist exploitation, people practised a socialist way of life based on Buddhist philosophy. The concept of "dana", or sharing, was purely based on the notion that overcoming "craving" is the sole means to happiness, and "shrama" (8), as we shall see, is the notion of "work". In fact such indigenous philosophies have been all too often ignored by the colonial powers.

Political institutions and traditional morality

Sri Lanka is a country, then, where there is a Buddhist tradition that goes back more than 2,500 years, to the third century BC, despite the vicissitudes the nation suffered throughout its history. At the macro level the traditional king was considered a Bodhisatva or Nascent Buddha. Such a king usually possessed four important characteristics: *sharing, pleasant speech, fruitful activities and equality.* The king was equal to his subjects, not above them. *Traditional morality, moreover, possessed a twofold basis, in outward action and inward feeling that serve as a spring of such action.*

A group of wise people advised the king, and it is in that spirit that one could conceive of the Buddhist monks in the villages today, as moral as well as spiritual advisers to the people. Historically, the monks' role was interwoven with the people's agricultural life, irrigational activities, education, health, economic, cultural as well as religious activities. They were therefore a considerable social and political force. They were in turn a repository of traditional morality.

With the advent of the colonial powers, in the 17th and 18th centuries however, beginning with the Portuguese followed by the Dutch and the British, the basis of traditional morality was eroded, as exogenous values were forcibly imposed. *The traditional morality was superseded. The hiatus then created provided a breeding ground for violence and enmity, endless acquisition of wealth and exploitation of others.*

Local leaders who took over when the British left, in fact, had no real appreciation of the political institutions they had been bequeathed, and so they had no significant sense of what is essential to them and what could be dispensed with. In fact the British left behind a local elite that was neither British nor Sri Lankan, thereby failing to appreciate the inner spirit of the indigenous institutions they inherited, instead paying great attention to external trappings. Modern Sri Lankan society, for Ariyaratne moreover, has borrowed the concept of government based on parliamentary democracy that was an organic growth in the West. But the democratic spirit of free inquiry, openness to criticism and absence of hierarchy, he says, does not exist in Sri Lanka.

The inner spirit is that of the traditional kingship, which has now become perverted by undigested Western notions of such. Instead, and for example, the "free press", bereft of Western traditions of the free exchange of ideas, has become a tool of raw political power. Moreover, for Aryiaratne, in the 1990s in Sri Lanka, through to the new millennium, there was the agony of civil war, class war, and economic deprivation.

The awakening process

Yet at the same time, the three principles of *Impermanence* or change, *Suffering* and *Egolessness* have conditioned the minds of people, according to Aryiaratne, in Sri Lanka for centuries. All other things in people's lives, whether individual behaviour, economic development programmes, or moral conduct, historically sprang from this central Buddhist thought. *Sarvodaya's task was to counter the erosion of all of such by bringing back into public consciousness the liberating sprit of traditional values and morality.* As a result the Movement has striven for "a no affluence as well as a no poverty society".

What Sarvodaya has been trying to do, for half a century, is to rebuild a community which will not give priority to economically sound development projects without taking into consideration their moral, social and ecological costs. Sarvadoya (9) attempts to promote community planning and participatory learning programmes which will once again promote shared values of traditional morality and community life. What the Movement has sought to do is to revive the indigenous, age-old perception of reality that people can organise themselves on the basis of their own resources.

From theory to practice: the Sarvodaya Shramadana movement

Starting with pupil-volunteers

Sarvodaya thought or philosophy, overall then, is put into concrete action by an integrated threefold program: *an educational program, through Shrama/dana* (work and sharing); *a community development program, through Gramodaya (village reawakening); a direct participation program (through village self government).*

The shramadana camp, which Ariyaratne first instigated in the 1950s with his students, at senior school where he was a physics teacher, had two objectives: *experiencing traditional social living based on the principles of sharing, pleasant language, constructive activity and equality; sharing labour to complete a physical task that satisfies a long felt community needs.* A youth leader who was assigned to conduct proceedings invited a village elder or a village child to inaugurate the camp by lighting the traditional coconut oil lamp and hoisting the Sarvadoya flag. This was done to the chanting of religious stanzas by monks or to the singing of a Sarvodaya song. This ceremonial opening was followed by a "family gathering".

The pupils-volunteers had come to learn and not to teach. At the same time, a mass education program was set in place, under Ariyaratne's instigation, where the history of the village, their habitual customs and beliefs, their problems and aspirations were discussed. Relevant questions from great religious teachers and other great men were read and explained. Song and dance items were intermixed with serious discussions regarding community, national and international problems. Family get togethers were held daily. Hence one saw the rare sight of a university professor seated on a mat with an illiterate villager.

Village level organisation

Through their direct participation, as such, in organised activities, the Sarvodaya movement in each village made an attempt to:

• bring about a *change in their ideas*, attitudes and objectives according to the Sarvadoya philosophy

- bring about *improvements in the methods* and techniques adopted by people in their day to day life specially in economic production, distribution and consumption
- bring about *change in their existing organisations* and institutions for the better.

The *first* activity of the children's group was to start *a children's library*. The children's organisation becomes the starting point for the formation of other groups. The *second* group organised in the villages was the *mother's group*. Some of its objectives are proper bringing up of children, home improvement, religious work, moral reawakening and activities to supplement the family income. The *third* group was *the youth group*. They began with what they can do in the village such as community development and education and sports projects. As you can see Sarvodaya employed the whole society.

The farmers' groups, *fourthly* had five clear objectives:

- ensure unity among farmers
- win freedom from exploitation and right of participation in framing policy and implementing programmes
- safeguard agricultural values
- make occupational recognition of farmers a reality.

For Sarvadoya, it was, overall, *an endeavour to achieve "dynamic harmony" through non-violent direct action by the threefold program of education, development and participation*. Calling a halt to exploitation or violence in all fields, economic, political, administrative or social by nonviolent direct action was the duty of all who believed in total freedom. The Movement today, some fifty years later, has its own Development Educational Institutes, Village Reawakening Centres, Co-operative Economic Enterprises and other such bodies, which we have examined elsewhere (10).

The awakening of all

Sarvodaya did not talk, from the outset, about employment or about welfare. Instead it talked about awakening. *Awakening of the individual to his highest potential; awakening of human groups to their total potential; awakening of the nation to its highest potential.* For rural people, such development had six components: firstly, a *political element*, in the sense of people having an opportunity to participate in decision-making; secondly, people look at development as a process where certain *social needs* could be fulfilled; thirdly comes the *economic* sector.

These three outer sectors then, political, social and economic needed to be combined with three others inner ones. Development is meaningless if it does not pay heed to *moral* principles. These are the *cultural* values that a society cherishes. These are also *spiritual* values which give meaning to people's lives. Therefore if we are to integrate any national development effort six factors are involved: moral, cultural, spiritual, political, social and economic. Ariyaratne then turns to science, both Western and Asian, as such.

Development as awakening

The word "Sarva" in Sanskrit means all embracing, integrating everything pertaining to man, society and nature. "Udaya" means well-being. Sarvodaya is a people-centred development process, involving a total awakening of the human personality, the family, and the community: local, national and international. The first three are micro, the second three macro-awakening. Without awakening of the individual personality there is no point in promoting economic growth or indeed in creating jobs. Outer, without inner, development, as Bulgakov has also stressed, is ultimately destructive. *No rational, spiritual, religious or sustainable development is possible, firstly, without the human personality itself being awakened to play a central role in rebuilding society.*

We now turn more specifically to each form of awakening, such being the ultimate keynote of our "eastern" path of renewal, thereby supplanting (self) employment.

Gram Swaraj: local awakening

Cultivating a critical mass of spiritual consciousness, Sarvodaya seeks to develop the other two elements that it regards as essential to social health: economics and power. *Gram swaraj* signifies the liberation of the village through the creation of grassroots economic and social programmes, and *deshodaya* signifies the national and political outcome of this village liberation process. Sarvodaya wants a dharmic citizenry that will generate a cultural-spiritual revolution to build up a dharmic civil society. Following Gandhi, this calls for a secularisation of religion as a basis for civil society, and a civil society as the locus for modernisation. Currently, and conversely, people at the grassroots are trapped between oppressive state and market forces. Sarvodaya seeks to liberate the grassroots from both.

For example, today there are 670 Sarvodaya village banks, run by the villagers themselves, and 3,000 villages with SEED support programmes, altogether providing for economic empowerment and self reliance. Moreover, Sarvodaya had recently set up its own Development bank, serving half a million people with loans and savings. It also has four regional telecentres, to service decentralised people centred development.

We now turn from the cultural and economic to the political.

Deshodaya: community awakening

Sarvodaya envisions a process of political liberation, a community-based participatory democracy, beginning from the grassroots, that parallels and builds upon the economic liberation that has begun with the village banks. Power is thus transferred from the elites to the lowest possible level, leading to village self-determination. Ariayatne points out that while Sarvodaya has initiated banking and educational programmes at the grassroots, the government has pursued a top-down policy of war, development and (attempts at) peace that have led to destruction.

Sarvodaya established a Deshodaya Organisation in 2001 to build up a consensual political culture, devoid of political parties, to enact a "new constitution" to establish such a system. Sarvodaya explains that deshodaya will result when a critical mass of villages reach the stage of gram swaraj and the people move to take charge of their own political destiny. Moreover, for Ariayate, when the present economic system collapses, as was the case with the Berlin wall, the way will be paved for deshodaya.

Vishodaya, world awakening

Perhaps the most important theme that Sarvadoya can contribute to the global dialogue today is that of development based on spirituality and spiritual consciousness. Although Sarvodaya has sought a balanced development that integrates social, economic, political and spiritual elements, the key to its "eastern" approach is the spiritual element. As such, Sarvoaya is a spiritual movement that seeks social justice and development, a total social revolution. Sarvodaya evokes Gandhian and Buddhist values to orient society towards spirituality, equality, simplicity and conservation. These are the alternatives they propose to the violent paradigm of global materialism and consumerism that threatened to undermine cultural values and bring social and environmental chaos to the world. Gandhi noted that people will never be able to live in peace in the world as long as some are living in palaces and others in slums. As such, we, finally, turn in this chapter to a young business that is seeking to place purpose at the heart of economic awakening "On Purpose".

Illustrative Case: the value of work – 'On Purpose'

The concept of 'triple bottom-line accounting' has been well-established for at least three decades, since Freer Spreckley coined the term in 1981[1] and John Elkington popularised it in *Cannibals with Forks* (11). It is a conviction of those who are involved in values-based business and corporate social responsibility (CSR) that profit-making should be balanced with concern for people and practices that sustain the planet. But, in recent years there has been a fourth 'p' added to people, planet and profit; that is 'purpose'. In other words, quadruple bottom-line accounting (QBLA) takes the values that people adhere to seriously, considering their implications and translating them into an accounting framework.

There is no consensus on the fourth leg of QBLA. Some commentators refer to 'ethical governance' as the fourth (cf Global Reporting Initiative), whilst others consider 'context-based sustainability' as of most significance (cf Henk Hadders). Equally, there is a growing movement examining multiple capitals (often, five or six, including 'human', 'social' and 'manufactured', as in the work of the *Forum for Futures*) that is being expressed in the terms of investment related to 'impact', for solving social problems. Each of these approaches considers *values* as a basis for establishing *value*. But, within our integral worlds model, viewed from the perspective of the East, we consider that all of these approaches can be subsumed under the principle of spirituality or 'Spirit'. As the Native American activist and film-actor Floyd 'Red Crow' Westerman (1936–2007), of the *Association for Sustainable Communities* (ASC), commented, "Everything is spiritual. Everything has a spirit . . . We have a common destiny with the tree. We are all from the earth. And when the earth, the water, the atmosphere is corrupted it will create its own reaction".

Although this may sound somewhat mystical it has considerable practical implications. When we consider fundamental human values we begin to drill down to the bedrock of what motivates people and, hence, to strip away some of the superficialities of modern life, to reach what really matters in communities, not least in respect of work and employment. This is the expressed aim of the consultancy "On Purpose" (OP), with centres in London, Paris and Berlin. Although OP doesn't specifically talk about spirituality, its CEO, Tom Rippon, has recently written about the power of values to motivate a movement of collective purpose:

> . . . some of the movements that shaped social progress in Victorian times (an age with startling similarities to the times we are living through now): the Quakers and the Salvation Army, for example, [were striking for] the fervour that they were infected with . . . maybe their moralistic (and often religious) enthusiasm is something we can learn from, in the way that it can bind communities together and galvanise support and action across large numbers of communities. The Salvation Army, for example, operates in well over 100 countries.

The OP community has an impressive array of partners and case studies to draw on for its work in mentoring CEOs, organisations and new social entrepreneurial communities in seeking to deliver QBL value, through harnessing their purposeful values. The primary objective of OP is to provide training, through placements, partnerships, internships and associate experiences, for European professionals who are seeking to enter or move jobs into more purposeful work. Although this might sound like a 'hipster' operation, the numbers are impressive. Its 300+ associates have delivered more than £10M of value to their placement organisations, according to those organisations themselves. In the process, they have created a marketplace where more than 85% of those who've attended their 1500 days of coaching have continued into and remain in businesses that are pursuing their work as a primary source for good.

Mireya Alvarez, who became an OP Fellow in 2013, has a classic story of moving from the world of commercial financial management into impact investing, a change that has led her into "a job that I would still do even if I won the lottery". Mireya had worked for a Global Private Equity real estate fund in Mexico City. But, her passion had been the volunteering that she did to support a charity that helped impoverished and excluded indigenous Mexican communities. Working as an investment officer for a UK social investment fund Mireya says that:

> The work I do now is more aligned with what matters most to me in life . . . Working in something that is closely connected to helping people achieve positive and sustainable long-term outcomes is the best thing that could happen to me.

Nor is Mireya's story unique. Figures from *UnLtd* and *Social Enterprise UK* indicate that about 27% of new start-ups in the UK are within the sphere of social entrepreneurship, many connected to impact investing. Increasingly, talented young professionals are developing their vocations by mobilising opportunities for purposive business, where the value of work is intimately connected to the values of social change, rather than an organisation's single bottom-line.

Conclusion

In this final chapter of Part III, considering the Eastern spirituality of work and employment, we have been centred on Buddhist and economics. A key principle has been that business and employment should be awake to the needs of the poor, at all times. As such, in our examination of the social theory and practice of Sarvodaya we saw how it bases its operations on social justice towards a social revolution in its Buddhist society. In a smaller way On Purpose has taken the practice of triple bottom-line accounting one stage further to include a fourth line of purposive business engagement, as social business transitions to societal entrepreneurship, or enterprise that changes society. In Part IV we turn North, to systems and technologies that look beyond employment to work as recreative.

Note

1 Spreckley's (1981) report on "Social Audit – a Management Tool for Co-operative Working" first introduced the term. But, it was John Elkington's work more than a decade later that popularised the concept of TBLA.

Bibliography

1 Credit Suisse. (2015) *Global Wealth Databook*, October. [Available at: https://ktwop.files.wordpress.com/2015/10/cs-global-wealth-databook-2015.pdf. Last accessed: October 2, 2017].
2 Galasso, N. and Wood, M. (2015) Eight Ways to Reduce Global Inequality. *Inequality.org*, 11 February. [Available at: http://inequality.org/great-divide/8-ways-reduce-global-inequality/. Last accessed: October 1, 2017].
3 Milanovic, B. (2013) Global Inequality in Numbers: In History and Now. *Global Policy* 4(2): 198–208.
4 OECD. (2012) OECD Employment Outlook 2012'. *OECD Publishing*. Chapter 3, 'Labour Losing to Capital: What Explains the Declining Labour Share?' [Available at: www.oecd.org/els/employmentoutlook-previouseditions.htm. Last accessed: October 2, 2017].
5 Oxfam. (2016) An Economy for the 1%. *Oxfam Briefing Paper*, 210, January. [Available at: www.scribd.com/document/355361615/bp210-economy-one-percent-tax-havens-180116-en?secret_password=gPeVPKSKCoSeOTBDFWmY#fullscreen&from_embed. Last accessed: October 2, 2017].
6 Macy, J. (1983) *Dharma and Development: Religion as a Resource in the Sarvadoya Self Help Movement*. West Hartfold, CT: Kumarian Press.
7 Aryiaratne, A.T. (1996) *Buddhism and Sarvodaya: Sri Lankan Experience*. NewDelhi: Sei Satguru Publications.
8 Kantowsky, D. (1980) *Sarvadoya: The Other Development*. New Delhi: Vikas.
9 Bond, G. (2004) *Buddhism at Work: Community Development, Social Empowerment and the Sarvadoya Movement*. Bloomfield, CT: Kumarian.
10 Scheiffer, A. and Lessem, R. (2013) *Integral Development: Realising the Transformative Potential of Individuals, Organizations and Societies*. Falmer: Gower Publishing.
11 Elkington, J. (1999) *Cannibals with Forks: The Triple Bottom-Line of 21st Century Business*. London: Capstone Books.

Part IV

North

Beyond employment: work
as recreation

10 The quest for meaning
Agape economics to rehoming work

GROUNDED IN LOVE
EMERGING ECOLOGY
NAVIGATING BEYOND EMPLOYMENT
EFFECTING EMANCIPATION

Introduction: living in truth to enhancing work and lifestyles

As we turn from the natural and communal *relational* 'south', subsequently through the cultural and spiritual 'east', on a path of *renewal*, we come onto the scientific and technological 'north', on the path of *reason*. In this chapter we ground our exploration of research-to-innovation in work, by considering what living in the truth of a meaningful economic life is like. To do this, we begin with looking at the history of economic thought through the eyes of Czech economist Tomas Sedlacek, adviser to former President Vaclav Havel. For Sedlacek, living in the truth of a meaningful economy requires developing civilising structures for reciprocity and love which, surprisingly to many, he finds in the writings of Adam Smith, the father of *homo economicus*.

In *the quest for meaning* we ask a first Burning Question: *is it possible to base economics on divine love?* 'Agape' is the Greek word for divine love, which is most used in the New Testament, especially in the writings of St John, "the beloved disciple" of Jesus. Through the experiences of Christian leaders in Latin America and the work of the World Council of Churches AGAPE Project, we see how an economy of love for the dispossessed is being developed in Panama and Brazil. Secondly, we open up a window on 'Northern wisdom', from the Gospel of John, as we discover the surprising meaning of his peerless Prologue. The opening of John's Gospel indicates that *God's plan is to embody love in the earthy realities of life*, including the meaning of what it is to *discover our vocation to work in the everyday*.

This theme is further taken up in our Social Theory, serving as navigation in this 'northern' instance, which is the question for meaning embodied, for the late Czech playwright, philosopher and president Vaclav Havel, in "living in truth". Finally, in our Illustrative Cases, we look at the work of two innovative sports trainer manufacturers, the French firm *Veja*, also working in Brazil and *Under Armour*, revitalising the rustbelt of Baltimore, Maryland, in the United States. Each of these companies is 'walking the walk' of a love economy, in enhancing the lifestyles, through their working practices, for their primary producers or high-tech workers. We now turn to our Burning Question, invoked here through grounding the search for meaning, by way of evolving work.

Burning Question: is agape economics based on divine love possible?

Dom Helder Camara, the former Roman Catholic Archbishop of Brazil famously commented that: "When I give food to the poor they call me a saint. When I ask 'why are they poor?' they call me a communist" [1]. One of the responses of the World Council of Churches (WCC) to the impoverishment of many communities in the global South – as a result of neo-liberal economics that derives from the North-West – was the formulation of a framework which was named AGAPE-Economics.

Agape is the Greek word for divine love that is used throughout the New Testament and especially in the Gospel of John, which we identify as the Northern Gospel, within our integral worlds model. In the Gospel of John the word agape (αγαπη) and its cognates is used. . . . In the Johannine Epistles 'love' is expressed exclusively by agape 21 times, by the verb agapao 31 times and the adjective ('beloved') 10 times. It is for St John one of the most important words in his lexicon. Indeed, the legend has it that when the aged Apostle, more than 90 years old, was brought out to address the crowds in Ephesus, at the end of his life, all he would say was "Beloved, love one another". Of course, his name "John" was the Hebrew word for "beloved". His story is one of growing into his name. His edict was a most lovely play on words, reminding himself, as much as others, of the heart of the gospel.

For the economy of life

It was in this sense that the WCC's Sao Paulo Declaration, of 2012, "International Financial Transformation for the Economy of Life" [2], was based on two framework principles:

*   Rejection of an economy that is organised around indebtedness and the financialisation of markets.
*   Affirming an economy of sufficiency for all, by rejecting an economy based on greed for a few, which generates levels of gross inequality (see Chapter 9, Burning Question Addressed).

The first principle develops the idea of an economy of *for-giveness*. In other words, the gift economy is not simply one that proceeds from sacred texts but is practically worked-out through the development of financial institutions that exist to give to the poor rather than create indebtedness. The multitude of microfinance and similar low-interest loan schemes across the South are cited as exemplars of such a forgiving economy. In addition, an economy of sufficiency is founded on the biblical principles of the manna ("what is it?") that the Israelites received each day on their sojourn with Moses towards the Promised Land, during the Exodus.

This is developed, by Jesus, in his explanation of the Feeding of the 5000, as redacted by John (6:30–42), when He describes himself as 'the bread of life', that comes down from God's heaven. Each day has enough food, so we can ask 'give us today our daily bread'. But, when the economy is revealed to store up bread for the rich leaving the poor with nothing we know this is built on financial structures that are antithetic to the gospel. As such, the sufficient economy is economic in that it has boundaries. But, these are not to be based on inflation-rigged prices but on the natural capacities of land, communities and the planet to sustain community-based living.

Sumak Kawsay – "good living", not living for goods

Bishop Julio Murray, Anglican Bishop of Panama, comments [3] that the indigenous *Quechua* people concept of *sumak kawsay* has been incorporated into the constitutions of Ecuador and Bolivia. The economy of love that is entailed in this concept emphasises that only a new economic order will deliver "good living" for poor and marginalised communities. This means going beyond enabling an economy in which the poor can gain better access to markets but, instead, reorganising the entire global system to meet the needs of the dispossessed, as the top priority of all economic policy-making.

Within Panama, Murray points to a series of examples that rest on four Christian principles for generating an economy of *sumak kawsay*. These are:

- Reconstruction from the margins, where justice and peace are being embodied.
- Grassroots movements for the transformative redistribution of power.
- Cocreation of an ecumenical economy (oikumene) that crosses divisions of Faiths and religious/spiritual traditions.
- The Church's call to action takes place in civil society, not simply within the Church.

One practical example of the economy of love-in-action

Official reviews of the Panama economy often describe the weakness of its agriculture, in terms of the contribution it makes to the overall export earnings of the country. Whilst 20% of people work in agriculture in that Central American country – which controls access to some of the world's major shipping routes – it generates only 5% of Gross Domestic Product (GDP). But, viewed from the perspective of sustainability, this is a success story. As Murray explains the use of innovative crop rotations, including tomatoes, onions, potatoes and green peppers has restored much infertile, waste land to productivity. The indigenous agriculture scheme within the *Cocle del Norte* watershed region, which is also noted for its ecological diversity, has utilised local knowledge to revitalise subsistence farming. Marginalised people have been able to draw on traditional knowledge to restore their "good living".

The effect of this activity was that landowners attempted enforced eviction of indigenous farmers, in order to gain access to newly fertile lands. As a result the local Church teamed-up with volunteer lawyers and the Ministry of Agriculture. They forced the owners to either lease or sell the land to the local people, who had legal rights, given that they had been faming the land for more than five years.

This was one example of the love economy of "good living" in action, whereby new land was brought into productive use, through the recovery of ancient farming knowledge, alongside local people, the Church and State acting in concert to protect the livelihoods of indigenous people, instead of simply supporting an export-based financialised economy. Although this is only one micro-example, it indicates that it is, indeed, possible to work towards a love-economy, deepening spirituality and transforming lives, through a local commitment to justice and valuing the land that God has given. This naturally leads on from such communal grounding in agape to spiritual up-lifting, through God's plan to elevate our earthly realities.

Window into Wisdom: God's plan is to embody love in the earthy realities of life

John's Gospel Prologue (1:1–18) – Beyond dualism

The work of Czech political economist Tomas Sedlacek, adviser to Vaclav Havel, which will follow from here, will seek to contrast the ways in which economic thought has been used to investigate both good and evil uses of myths and spiritualities. As many have turned to John's Gospel, which, we conceive as Northern, they see in his contrasts of light/ darkness, belief/ unbelief, spirit/ flesh an essential dualism between the material and spiritual worlds. In fact, this is precisely the reverse of what John's Gospel seeks to indicate. His entire emphasis on the incarnation of Jesus Christ, the Son of God, is to reveal that the material is created from the Spirit. Consequently, the call to vocation is one of how to bring the things of the spirit to bear in the world of material human affairs and agency.

The Word became flesh

This is nowhere more evident than in the majestic prologue with which John opens his Gospel, echoing the first words of the Hebrew scriptures: "In the beginning was the Word (logos), and the Word was with God, and the Word was God" (1:1). So much, so apparently ethereal. But, John continues in verse 14 "The Word became flesh and made his dwelling among us". Of course, to any right-thinking Greek philosophy-inspired person this would have been an utterly disgusting idea. The eternal Logos being made into flesh? But, that is the message of John, about Jesus Christ.

The point is that John is seeking to express the inexpressible and, yet, completely earthy reality of the embodiment of God-in-Christ. Jesus lived amongst his disciples. And when they saw Jesus they saw God. Nor was this a temporary visitation, as if Jesus, like ET, needed to go home to the "spirit world". At the conclusion of John's Gospel, after the crucifixion and resurrection, Jesus invites Thomas to put his fingers in the marks of the nails on his body, now resurrected (20:24–31). Then, a little later, He eats a fish breakfast with his disciples beside the Sea of Galilee (21:22–23). It is clear that material existence embodying the spirit – as a unity or, we might say, integrally whole – is the way that God seeks the Creation to be completed, in Christ.

The work of the Word

It is in this sense that John introduces the vocation of all believers. Although Jesus as the light coming into the world was not recognised as such, "to all who did receive Him, who believed in his name, he gave the right to become children of God . . . born of God" (1:12, 13). The work of those who are in Christ is to live out the life of God in the world, not separated from it.

In other words it is God's work to help people to work out His purposes in material existence, as much through work as through any other human activity. Nor is this to be some airy-fairy spiritual exercise. It is earthy, tough, back and heart-breaking work to bring love into situations such as the sort of agricultural, manufacturing and new industrial revolution work mentioned here and in the subsequent chapters of this section. The real 'theory of moral sentiment', pace Adam Smith, as quoted by Sedlacek, is that God became flesh, so that flesh might work out what it means to follow the way of love, in God. And, to work this out means, as much as anything, to do so in the world of 21st-century work.

The economy of truth and love that we've visited in this chapter is far from a purely spiritual ideal. As has been shown it is earthed and grounded in the social, political and cultural realities of diverse peoples. To see this in action we have travelled to the eastern fringes of the North, in the Czech Republic, to the impact of Northern principles from the WCC, as worked-out in Central America, and to Northern companies in France and the US. Even so, the predominate failure of Europe to pursue such an economy – via its richly varied constituent cultures and societies, rather than pursue the "western" American, economic dream – has, arguably, led to its current stasis. We now turn for our Social Theory, by way of northern "grounding", to Sedlacek.

Social Theory: *the quest for meaning: living in truth*

The economy of civilisation

For our "northern" European grounding, specifically then, via the quest for economic meaning, we turn initially, to the center of Europe, that is to the Czech Republic, noted in its post-communist era, for its renowned philosopher and playwright-President Vaclav Havel (4), *Living in Truth*. For him as such:

> The question about capitalism and socialism, in the context of modernization, seems to emerge from the depths of the last century. It seems that these highly ideological and semantically confused categories (isms) have long since been beside the point. The question is wholly other, deeper and equally relevant to all; whether we shall, by whatever means, succeed in reconstituting the natural world as the true terrain of politics, rehabilitating the personal experience of human beings as the initial measure of all things, placing morality above politics and responsibility above our desires, in making human community meaningful, in returning content to human speaking, in reconstituting, as the focus of all social action, the autonomous, integral and dignified human I, responsible for ourselves because we are bound to something higher.

Economics then as we know it today, for Tomas Sedlacek (5), who was economic advisor to Havel, and is now chief economist at CSOB Bank in the Czech Republic, and a member of *Narratives for Europe*, commissioned by former EU President Manuel Barosso, *is a product of our European civilisation.* It is not, however, a *product* in the sense that we have intentionally *produced* or invented it, like a jet engine or a watch. The difference lies in the fact that we understand a jet engine or watch – we know where they came from. We can almost deconstruct them into their individual parts and put them back together. This is not the case with economics.

Modern economics is generally considered to have begun in 1776 with the publication of Adam Smith's *Wealth of Nations*, though as we saw in Chapter 3, Italy's civil economists, and the monasteries ("work and prayer") in the middle ages, came well before. Our postmodern age though is more likely to look further back, as Sedlacek in fact does, and is aware of the power of history, mythology, religion, fables. *All of economics,* for him then, *is in the end the economics of good and evil. It is the telling of stories by people of people to people.*

As such, he goes on to show that mathematics, models, equations and statistics are just the tip of the iceberg of economics; that the biggest part of the iceberg of economic knowledge consists of everything else; and that *disputes in economics are rather a battle of stories and meta-narratives.* People today, as they have always, want to know from economists what is good and what is bad. *The Economics of Good and Evil* therefore, is in two parts: *in the first part looks for economics in myths, religion, theology, philosophy and science; the second looks for myths, religion, theology, philosophy and science in economics.* In that overall guise, as we would see it, the "northerner" Sedlacek stands firmly on social and economic ground that has been prepared for him by the "south" and the "east".

Meta-economics: development of the economic ethos

As such, Sedlacek seeks to chart the development of the *economic ethos* in the Middle East. He asks *primary* questions that came before any *secondary* economic thinking can begin – both philosophically, and, to a degree, historically. The area here lies at the very borders of economics – and often beyond. It may be referred to as *meta-economics.* In fact almost all the key concepts by which economics operates, both consciously and unconsciously, have a long history, and their roots – for us grounding – extend predominantly outside the range of economics, often completely beyond that of science. For Sedlacek then, there is at least as much wisdom to be learned from philosophy, myth, religion and poetry as from exact and strict mathematical models of economic behaviour.

The traces of our thinking are more readily understood when we look at their historical beginnings, when the thoughts were, so to speak, more naked. He argues then that economic questions were with mankind long before Adam Smith. He maintains that *the search for values in economics did not start with Smith but culminated with him. In fact Smith's most fundamental economic contribution,* according to Sedlacek, *was ethical.* Traces of "the invisible hand", moreover, appear in Judaism and Christianity. In other words, and for us, Sedlacek is engaged with the grounding and emergence of economics, prior to its navigation and effect, serving to release its full "northern" GENE-ius. He starts with the ancient world, most especially with the ancient Hebrews and Greeks.

Progress: a secularised religion

One of the seminal ideas the writers of the Old Testament gave to mankind is the idea and notion of progress. *The Old Testament stories have their development; they change the history of the Jewish nation and tie into each other. The Jewish understanding of time is linear – it has a beginning and an end.* The Jews believe in historical progress, and that progress is in *this world*.

Our European civilisation, for Sedlacek therefore, is especially indebted to the Hebrews for that idea of progress. In the course of history, however, this idea itself underwent major changes, and today we perceive it very differently. *As opposed to the original spiritual conceptions, today we perceive progress almost exclusively in an economic or scientific-technological sense.* What's more, economic progress has almost become an assumption of "modern" societies.

We expect growth. We expect employment. We expect jobs.

The desacralisation of heroes, nature and rulers

Aside from the idea of progress, the Hebrews brought another very fundamental contribution to our culture: the desacralisation of heroes, nature and rulers. *The land, the world, the body and material reality are for the Jews the paramount setting for divine history, the pinnacle of creation. Old Testament teachings rarely disdain wealth or sing the praises of poverty.* For the Hebrews, when a person does well in the (economic) world, it is frequently understood as the expression of God's favour. The Jewish heroes, moreover, as opposed to those in Greek fables and legends, are more real, three-dimensionally imaginable people.

The creation of the world, as it is explained in Jewish teachings, is described in the Book of Genesis. Here God creates (i), separates (ii) and names (iii):

> In the beginning God created the heavens and earth . . . he separated the light from the darkness. God called the light "day", and the darkness he called "night". . . . God made the expanse and separated the water under the expanse from that above it. He called the expanse "sky". . . . God called the dry ground "land". And the gathered waters he called the "seas".

Such *real*-isation (for us moving from grounding and emergence to "scientific" navigation) represents the creation of a construct, the imputation of sense of order (which is beautifully expressed by the biblical act of *naming*, sorting or ordering). *Our scientific models put the finishing touches on reality because they interpret (1), they give phenomena a name (2), they enable us to classify the world according to logical forms (4).* When man finds a new linguistic framework or analytical model, or stops using the old one, he moulds or remoulds reality. Models though are only in our heads, they are not "objective reality".

Moral accounting for good and evil

For the Hebrews then, morals represent the best investment one could make. Nothing could help an economy more than being very particular about justice. Adherence to rules and a moral life would pay off *very well materially*. In the Old Testament in fact, there is little mention of heaven or hell. It *speaks of justice. Moral accounting had to be carried out during life on earth; it could not be deferred into the preserve of life after death.*

The Jews moreover had not only to observe the law – perhaps the word covenant would be more appropriate – but they were to *love* it because it was good. Hebrews were to do good (outgoing) because goodness (incoming) has *already been done to them.* God expects a full internalisation of the commandments and their fulfilment with love. By no means was this on the basis of the cost-benefit analysis so widespread in economics today. The Hebrews moreover, originally a nomadic tribe, grew up in constant freedom of motion. *One of Moses' greatest deeds was that he managed to explain that it is better to remain hungry and liberated than to be a slave.*

Social welfare, the social net and debt forgiveness

A remarkable complex of socio-economic regulations was in fact developed in the Old Testament, something we hardly find in any other nation of the time. In Hebrew teachings, indications of the concept of maximising utility *society-wide* appear for the first time as embodied in the Talmudic principle of *Kofin al midaat S'dom*, which can be translated as "one is compelled not to act in the manner of Sodom" and to take care of the weaker members of society.

Every 49 years, moreover, there is a year of forgiveness, when land is returned to its original owners. In such a jubilee year debts were to be forgiven, and Israelites who fell into slavery were to be set free. The economic system even then had a tendency toward asset concentration, and therefore power as well. It would appear that these provisions were supposed to prevent the process over the long-term, without the need for a regulatory body. A period of fifty years roughly corresponded to the life span at the time, and at the same time was evidently supposed to act to remove the problem of general indebtedness. The generation following the indebted or poor farmer got their land back and had a chance to start farming again. All land and riches, as such, came from the Lord. Man was only a tenant on the land, and ownership is temporary.

Among the Israelites we can find not only the roots of the modern wide-spread redistribution of wealth for the benefit of the poorest but also the well-substantiated concept of economic regulation. In Judaism, charity is not perceived as a sign of goodness; it is more of a responsibility. Since the community has an obligation to provide food, shelter and basic economic goods for the needy, it has a moral right and duty to tax its members for this purpose. In line with this duty, it may have to regulate markets, prices and competition, to protect the interests of its weakest members.

Debt can be a good servant, but an enslaving master as well

In the process the Jews as well as later Aristotle, in fact, both behaved very guardedly towards loans. The issue of interest/usury became one of the first economic debates. Without having an inkling about the future role of economic policy (fiscal and monetary) *the ancient Hebrews may have unwittingly felt that they were discovering in interest a very powerful weapon, one that can be a good servant, but (literally) an enslaving master as well.* What then about the notions of labour and work?

As opposed to the negative connotation of work ascribed to labour (manual labour is suitable only for slaves) by ancient Greeks, labour was not considered degrading in the Old Testament. Work is now considered an honour, albeit alongside rest. The observance of the Sabbath bears the message that the purpose of creation was not just creating but it had an end, a goal. *The meaning of utility was not to increase work permanently but to rest among existing gains. This dimension has disappeared from today's economics.* Sedlacek then turns from the ancient Hebrews to ancient Greece.

The Bible and economics then, for Sedlacek, are much more closely tied together than one would think. Of Jesus' thirty parables in the New Testament, nineteen are set in an economic or social context. The Sermon on the Mount, Jesus' longest and probably most important speech, starts with the words: *Blessed are the poor in spirit, for theirs is the kingdom of heaven"*. Jesus is therefore turning the maximisation theorem inside out.

A mutual or reciprocal gift, meanwhile, is a much deeper and older method of transaction than purchase and sale with an explicit price. For many generations of human history, things simply did not have a price; people got by without pricing. People long ago gave things reciprocally or lived in communities, where things were also exchanged – even if the first was more common – a theme which has been recently picked up by the Italian civil economists (see Chapter 3). The first nonmonetary social systems were gift economies. When barter did occur, it was either usually between complete strangers or potential enemies.

So where do we go from there?

Living on the edge

It appears that *contemporary economics* (and also economic policy based on it) should leave some new ideas and – on the other hand – return to many of the old. It *should abandon the persistent dissatisfaction, artificially created social-economic shortcomings, while it should rediscover the role of self-sufficiency, resting, and gratitude for what we have*. The reason for this rethinking is that economic policy following the material goal only inherently runs into debts.

Those who constantly live on the edge should not be surprised when the edge cuts. Those who cut the (competitive) edge should not complain, Sedlacek argues, when the edge cuts them. Those who fly too high and too close to the sun, like the fabled Icarus cannot be surprised when their wings sometimes melt; the higher he flew, the further he fell. And we skated too long on an edge that was very sharp. Economic policy has been set loose, and a deficit psychosis in terms of gigantic debt is the result. Learning from the crisis appears to be our only hope. The debt crisis is much wider and deeper than an economic one. Our era lacks moderation. Sedlacek calls on us to be aware of our own satiation. *We have overcome nearly everything, and have long been able to do as we pleased. The fact that we did not do much good in recent years with our freedom is a sad realisation.*

All of such serves to put economic growth, the creation of full employment, and the like, in historical perspective. In fact we would argue that the EU's current crisis is not lodged in the UK's pursuit of Brexit, per se, but in Europe's failure to draw on the full historical perspective, or grounding, that Sedlacek has revealed, instead of attempting to become more competitive, economically, on the world stage. Indeed, for Sedlacek's mentor, Vaclav Havel (6):

> Living within the truth becomes articulate in a particular way, at the point at which something is born that might be called the independent, spiritual, social and political life of society . . . A new experience of being, a renewed rootedness in the universe, a newly grasped sense of higher responsibility, a new-found inner relationship to other people and to the human community, these factors clearly indicate the direction in which we must go.

We now turn to two Illustrative Cases, serving to effect, in practice, the quest for meaning to which Havel and Sedlacek have alluded.

Illustrative Cases: Veja/Under Armour – enhancing work-and-lifestyles

New generation 'traditional' working

Although they may not recognise the heading, the work of trainer manufacturers *Veja* and *Under Armour* are contemporary examples of a more loving and truthful economy in action. These state-of-the-art advanced manufacturers are seeking to revolutionise the production of high-tech trainers by bringing production, workers and consumers together in a range of local facilities. In doing so, they are equalising distributions along supply chains, creating environmentally friendly products, bringing work to areas of former deindustrialisation, decarbonising the manufacturing process, through a mix of reduced transport costs and the use of new technology and seeking a more integral pattern of team-working for their staff.

The fashion design and manufacturing industry is infamous for its antiquated processes, use of sweat-shop labour and dangerous working conditions. The tragedy of the *Rana Plaza* facility collapse in Dhaka, Bangladesh, in April, 2013, drew the world's attention to the conditions under which many clothing and textile workers operate and in which our clothes are manufactured. Eleven hundred workers died with hundreds more injured for life. It led to many Western retailers, such as *Primark*, assessing their trading practices. Four years after *Rana Plaza* a host of more ethical clothing manufacturers and retailers, such as *Matt & Nat, Gather and See, Nobody's Child* and *Birdsong* have sought to revolutionise the marketplace for fashion-wear.

But, it is in the arena of trainer design and manufacture, one of the world's most competitive markets, dominated by a few well-known global brands – which are always featured at major sporting events – that some of the most impressive transformations are taking place. *Veja* buys its organic cotton thread from 320 small cotton producers, under Fair Cotton Agreement terms, in Ceara, NE Brazil, the country's most impoverished state. The company sources wild rubber, for the soles of its trainers, from indigenous Seringueiros in the Amazon basin, purchased at almost two-and-a-half times the cost of synthetic rubber, produced from petrochemicals. *Veja* doesn't advertise so that, although its trainers costs more than three times that of other leading manufacturers, it can, nevertheless, retail them at competitive prices, with a far reduced carbon footprint.

The workers in *Veja*'s Porto Alegre factory, which is one of Brazil's most prosperous regions, are mainly descendant's of German in-migrants of the late 19th century. But, their work conditions are closely monitored by both the *Fairtrade Labelling Organisation* (FLO) and *EcoLabel*. Workers are paid 15% above the industry minimum, which is augmented by an annual fairtrade premium payment. They are encouraged to join Unions and form worker's committees, are drawn from local communities, within a maximum 30 mile radius of the factories and are able to take four weeks annual leave plus bank holidays. Veja is seeking to revolutionise the conditions for workers in one of the most traditional fashion industries.

Transforming manufacture

A very different approach is being taken by *Under Armour* at the *Baltimore Lighthouse Factory*, in Maryland, US. This area, which many would associate with the American 'Rustbelt', is undergoing a manufacturing revolution, led by the use of 3D printing design and manufacture technology, advanced robotics and the use of full-body scanning, to customise production for local customers. The Baltimore factory is seeking to minimise its carbon footprint by bringing manufacture as close to consumers as is humanly (or robotically) possible.

Their manta is 'making local for local'. The principle is that new technology is enabling the collapse of a lengthy supply chain, allowing for almost one-to-one personalisation. Such pioneering manufacture relies on the use of 3D printing for its state-of-the-art *Architech* mid-sole trainers (or 'sneakers' in US parlance). Additionally, the use of body-scanning imagery is being used to manufacture fully customised sportswear for local athletes and competitive sports teams.

Under Armour is also planning to take its local-for-local principle to factories in Europe and Latin America. Admittedly *UA* is a large global brand and may be seen as on the wrong side of the tracks, as far as many radical new companies are concerned. Even so, the principles behind *UA*'s initiative in Baltimore is about enabling advanced manufacture, robotics and new technology to create local jobs and transform work into an experience that brings makers much closer to customers and seeks a more locally-sourced circular economy (see Chapter 11).

In their very different ways *Veja* and *Under Armour* are seeking to recreate manufacturing economies for the soul, as well as for the sole. They are challenging received wisdom about the need to generate maximum profit by relying on the cheapest labour in the furthest locations. Instead, they are seeking to love the worker, the locality and the planet as they transform the fashion footwear industry – walking the walk.

Conclusion

It may seem strange that we have begun in the Northern realm of systems and technology with a focus on love, as the organising principle grounding "good living". But, in the South American context with which this chapter opened, the need for a *modus vivendi* beyond the exploitation of capitalist markets has been seen as a quite literal matter of life and death. Choosing life-in-employment has meant embracing an alternative system to the one which has led to so much repression and violence in Latin America.

Tomasz Sedlacek and his mentor Vaclav Havel take this principle to a further stage arguing that it needs to become the basis for a new independence in European society, impacting employment of the community, by transforming our self-relationships with one another. This is to rediscover the grounding of European culture in reciprocity and gift relationships, examined in Part I, but herein, systematised as a political economy that takes 'poverty of spirit' seriously (see Chapter 14). In France, as well as in the rustbelt of the USA, companies such as *Veja* and *Under Armour* are seeking to rework manufacturing with the human spirit in mind, within production processes and the supply chain. From here, we turn to the East of the North and, hence, to a political economy that takes planetary ecology seriously.

Bibliography

1 Zildo, R. (2000) *Helda, the Gift: A Life That Marked the Course of the Church in Brazil*. Sao Paulo: Editoro Vozes, p. 53.
2 World Council of Churches. (2012) *The São Paulo Statement: International Financial Transformation for the Economy of Life*. Geneva: WCC, October.
3 Murray, J.E. (2016) The AGAPE Economy: The Church's Call to Action. *Anglican Theological Review* 98(1): 125–35.
4 Havel, V. (1989) *Living in Truth*. London: Faber and Faber.
5 Sedlacek, T. (2011) *Economics of Good and Evil: The Quest for Economic Meaning*. Oxford: Oxford University Press.
6 Havel, V. (1989) *op cit.*

11 Critique of political economy

Sustainable employment to regenerative work

GROUNDED IN LOVE
EMERGING ECOLOGY
NAVIGATING BEYOND EMPLOYMENT
EFFECTING EMANCIPATION

Introduction: new industrial spirit to circular economy

As we continue to navigate through research and innovation in the world of work, we enter into a new critique of political economy. In much of the contemporary West the idea of a political economy has become subsumed under the mass of assumptions deriving from marginalist neo-classical economics. But, there is a reaction taking place in academies and on the streets. For many students, post the 2008–2009 Crash their textbooks no longer help them to navigate the real world. Equally, most of us despair of economic experts ever helping us to interpret what is actually happening.

As such, we turn, in this chapter, to the work of Bernard Stiegler, who has sought to reconceptualise political economy. He sees the current phase of capitalism as one in which the technical nature of consumption – as much as production – has sapped society of its creative spirit. But, he proposes some new directions to remotivate work, beyond employment. On this basis we ask the Burning Question: *what will a new industrial spirit tied to ecology look like?* Thereafter, we see through our Window into Wisdom how St John *presents a circularity between God's work in Creation and our own everyday working.*

Subsequently, while in his Social Theory, on the one hand, Stiegler sees capitalist production as having overtaken patterns of consumption, on the other hand there is, for him, *a new wave contained within the environmental movement, which signals a new mode of production developing.* In our Illustrative Case, for final emergent effect, we look to the work of Ellen McArthur and the circular economy to see how parts of the labour market are being restructured in the UK. But, first, we turn to the Burning Question underlying the new industrial spirit.

Burning Question: what will a new wave of environmentalist production look like?

Renewal of libidinal energy

In the Social Theory section, we see how French social philosopher Bernard Stiegler has called for a contemporary critique of political economy to include a new stage of libidinal ecology. What he means by this, is that we need to discover a 'renewable energy of the libido'. His argument is that the most recent phase of capitalism has involved an industrialisation of desire. In consequence, motivation itself, which is the essential fuel that drives capitalist consumerism, has been exhausted and created a pollution of the spirit. Stiegler's metaphor derives from our exploitation of natural resources, such as fossil fuels, where reserves are being exhausted and, at the same time, their use has created an ecological crisis of anthropogenic climate change, which poses an existential threat to the human species, let alone post-industrial (libidinal) capitalism.

But, there are signs of hope for a contemporary critique of political economy, which arise from the latest wave of the environmental movement. We can take Stiegler's metaphor and apply it directly to the material green movement, through which many workers are able to counteract both the 'pollution of spirit' and that of the physical world. In a classic paper, from the 1970s, the American political scientist Anthony Downs (1) considered the rise of ecological thinking as a case of what he termed 'the issue-attention cycle'. According to this theory of the way in which the media and policy-makers report on, pay attention to and, subsequently, discard social issues, ecological concern would peak in the late 1980s and be history's concern by the turn of the 21st century. Yet, that didn't happen. Why not?

Greening means business

The answer lies in the fact that environmental concerns took on new seriousness once the scale of 'global warming' became apparent in the latter years of the 20th century. As such, after a stage of 'declining public interest' failed to materialise, we can identify a new wave of the environmental movement emerging, from before the 2008–09 financial crisis, but gathering pace following it. The green movement represented a rediscovery of libidinal energy in ecological renewal, itself. This reflected a switch from environmentalism as, primarily, a defensive consumer reaction against 'problematic industrial production', to one where the green movement represented engagement in new forms of productive activity. Green had moved from the consumption sphere to the production sphere.

The 'post-problem phase' of a relationship between business and environmentalism had turned into an 'opportunity phase', as increasingly significant swathes of business sought greening solutions. In the most recent wave of the green movement, business has embraced the environmental agenda to the extent that it has become the dominant paradigm, at least in the sphere of global corporations. As we noted earlier, in Chapter 8, John Cridland, the UK CBI's former Chief Executive asserted that it was a false premise to distinguish between "greening business" and growing business (2). Again, as indicated in the earlier chapter, corporate America published a rebuttal to President Trump's White House decision to remove the US from the Paris Climate Accord, of December 2016 (3).

Richard Branson's B Team cited such giant corporations as General Motors, Wal-Mart, Apple, Microsoft, Bank of America, Morgan Stanley, Exxon Mobil, Conoco Phillips, together with the vast majority of Trump's own supporters. In other words, 'going green' is seen as offering a distinct edge in the marketplace. The further question is: how is corporate greening affecting the world of work?

GreenBiz 2016

The latest report on Green Business in the US (4) indicates that new, disruptive technologies and business models are starting to transform patterns of employment in the world's largest economy. In particular, the so-called sharing economy (see Chapter 4) – with its focus on the use of collaborative, web-based tools, for directly connecting producers, consumers and prosumers – is leading to major shifts in business and jobs. These operate in such diverse sectors as international shipping and haulage (e.g. Cargomatic, Shiphawk, Convoy and Uship), the logistics of business space usage (e.g. Flexe, Liquid Space and PivotDesk), waste processing (e.g. Rubicon Global, NCC Mobile) and, even, offering new ways for rural smallholders in Nigeria to access tractors (Hello Tractor).

But, it is the shift in ways in which employees benefit from participating in sustainability schemes that is, perhaps, showing the greatest potential for green practices to become drivers of a libidinal, motivational change in working practices that can renew capitalist employment practices. We have previously noted Paul Polman's drive to embed a 'Sustainable Living Plan' in the mentality of Unilever workers. Similarly, companies like Pepsico and Caterpillar have incorporated 'purpose-driven business' directives into employee relations. Rather more pointedly, Ceres, a non-profit that measures business sustainability progress, has concluded that one-quarter of US corporates offer executive compensation packages for demonstrating sustainability behaviours. But, chronically, only a paltry 3% highlight sustainability performance in investor communications or reward voluntary attempts, by executive leaders, to reduce their carbon footprint.

Clearly, a tipping-point hasn't been reached, yet, in corporations seeking to require executives to embed green practices as part of their employment. As such, it is unlikely that sustainability measures will be incorporated into employee contracts in the near future. That said, some companies are leading the way. Bank of America, for example, gives its employees a $500 discount on their investment in residential solar panels, bought through Solar City. By 2016, 7,200 employees had made such an investment.

This does not significantly counter Bernard Stiegler's proposition. Yet, some small acorn signs of a new ecological industrial spirit, to motivate employees towards greater sustainability practices at work and home, are coming down the logistical track. Nevertheless, there is a long way to go to counter the tendency of corporate capitalism to suck the libidinal energy out of everyday business practices and to reverse both the pollution of spirit and the destruction of natural capital.

We now turn to a Window into Wisdom, drawing on John's gospel in a way that will serve to interconnect Stiegler's critique of political economy with McArthur's circular economy, form his particular biblical perspective.

Window into Wisdom: circulating from God's creative work to our everyday work

John 5: The Pool of Bethesda

The controversy between the Pharisees and Jesus about 'healing, deliverance and work on the Sabbath' is familiar in each of the Gospels. But, John places his own distinctive perspective on it. His is one that aligns particularly well with both Stiegler's integration of technical and psychosocial individuation and McArthur's circular economy.

A crippled man was at the Pool of Bethesda, in Jerusalem. He had been waiting for the waters to be stirred 'supernaturally' for thirty-eight years. His problem was that every time the circular ripples appeared in the pool he wasn't quick enough to get in and be healed.

Jesus asks the man if he *really* wants to get well. There is an implication that the man has become 'institutionalised' and reliant on charity. Well, you would, after thirty-eight years! But, the man indicates that he does wish to be healed. At which, instead of Jesus commanding the healing, he simply says "Get up! Pick up your mat and walk". Instantly, the man receives his healing. This may have been a mixed blessing, as he would now have to rely on other ways of making a living than lying around at the poolside.

Spreading circular ripples

The Pharisees and lawyers were furious at what Jesus had done. This was no reflection on the healing. Rather, it was the fact that carrying a mat was regarded as a work activity, prohibited on the Sabbath. So, in one action, Jesus had brought personal healing, addressed the issue of the Sabbath and challenged the nature of work. The ripples spreading-out from the Pool were considerable.

In response to the criticism of the religious leaders Jesus makes the comment: "My Father is always at work to this very day and I, also, am working" (5:16). This only created stronger ripples on the surface of the religious pond, as Jesus was seen to be equating himself with God. What we see is Jesus instituting a type of integral and circular economy.

The point he is making is that God doesn't stop working to keep the Creation alive simply because it is the Sabbath. As such, it is not wrong for the Son of God to keep performing his work on the Sabbath. Nor, then, is it wrong for anyone else to cease being about God's work at any time. In so doing, we are sharing in the circular work of Creation, sustenance, work and service, integrally linking God, humanity, labour and the world's healing.

But, there is a further circulation which connects to the future of work, as conceived by Bernard Steigler. Through the healing at the Pool, Jesus is connecting together everyday work and the breaking-in of the future Age of the Kingdom. There is a new motivation in the man who has been healed. Gone is the routinised drudgery of his thirty-eight-year wait. Now, although there are fresh challenges, here is the opportunity to break out into a new 'libidinous spirit'. The ripples of that could spread far-and-wide throughout the economy and culture.

We are now ready, by way of 'northern' navigation, to engage fully with Stiegler's critique of political economy.

Social Theory: a new mode of production developing in the environmental movement

Toxic global consumerist model

For Bernard Stiegler (5), \Head of the Institute for Culture and Innovation at the Pompidou Centre in Paris, and following in Sedlacek's research footsteps, albeit with a different emerging emphasis, *the global consumerist model is now massively toxic, and has reached its limits.* Stiegler moreover, as we shall see, is more influenced by (though by no means dictated by) the thinking of Marx than was Sedlacek. He is also very much a "northern" European, lodged in science and technology, pursuing a path of *reason*.

When, for Stiegler, we talk then of "investment" today it is a pure and simple re-establishment of the state of things, trying to rebuild the industrial landscape without at all changing its structure or axioms, all in the hope of protecting the status quo. *Such a consumerism intrinsically destructive of genuine investment – investment in the future – involves short/termism which has been systematically translated into the decomposition of investment into speculation.*

From commerce to market

One hundred and fifty years ago, in January 1859, Marx (6) published his *Critique of Political Economy*, so that in arguing for a new critique Stiegler is commemorating this anniversary. At the same time he is paying homage to a communist party journal, *La Nouvelle Critique*, where as a young militant he first read about psychoanalysis, anthropology, linguistics and philosophy.

From the outset of his economic critique, Stiegler maintains that commerce is always an exchange of *savoir-faire* (knowledge of how to make or do) and *savoir-vivre* (knowledge of how to live). It is in this same sense that *"commerce" may in French refer more generally to all forms of fruitful social relation.* On the other hand the *consumerist* market presupposes the liquidation of both *savoir-faire* and *savoir-vivre*.

Philosophy, economy and ideology today

The philosophy of our time, for Stiegler, has abandoned the project of a critique of political economy, and this constitutes, for him, a disastrous turn of events. Because if it is true that economism has led to horrific outcomes, nevertheless the absence of a critique of today's economy prepares other horrors – and at the same time leaves the current generation tragically unprepared, often masked by an obsessive relation to philosophical texts devoted to the economies of the past.

To think and critique political economy as *commerce* that has become *exchange* under the conditions of an industrial society – that is, that has submitted to a *mutation of labour*, to a functionalisation of the processes of production and consumption, to a resultant *functionalisation of social relations*. As such it can no longer be envisaged without mechanical technology – requires aiming at the examination of both economics and politics, and speaking of them as though they are indissociable.

Revisiting the question of work

Today, as we emerge from our latest economic crisis, one that seems to constitute the end of a long cycle, can we keep posing *the question of work* in the same terms? The latter *was essentially conceived, over the previous century, in accordance with an industrial model resting on the coupling of production and consumption*, and it is precisely this functional pairing, Stiegler reckons today, which seems to have exhausted itself. In fact he says 150 years after Marx's *Critique of Political Economy*, the productivist and consumerist industrial model, having become global, is splitting at the seams. In the course of 2008, for example, Ford Motors lost three quarters of its value, while road networks of carbon-time were replaced by immaterial digital networks.

Marx and Engels predicted that capitalism, or what one calls the market economy, would rapidly reach its limit as the role of labour – that is variable capital – diminishes due to productivity gains. In the 1990s though it was widely believed by the followers of the "conservative revolution", as per Thatcher/Regan, that the capitalist dynamic had overcome the tendential fall in the rate of profit. Nothing, according to Stiegler, could be more false, and Marx was in fact far from mistaken. *What Marx though failed to predict was the role of a new energy, not the proletarianised producer, but rather the energy of the proletarianised consumer*, in our digital age.

Automation, digitalisation and grammatisation

The proletarian, as we read in contemporary French philosopher Gilbert Simondon (7), is a *disindividuated worker, who serves the machine-tool, and it is the latter that has become the technical individual* – in the sense that it is within the machine tool, and within the technical system to which it belongs, that an individuation is produced. This takes place through a process of concretisation through which the system of industrial objects become functionally integrated and thereby transformed – as does the socio/technical milieu. The proletarianised worker, or consumer, is literally excluded from this transformation – *dissociated* from it.

Conversely, in the milieu of associated work, the workers fashion an experience in which they cause their milieu to evolve. They *open up (ouvrent)* this milieu of which they are the workers (*ouvriers*). Proletarianisation is that which excludes this participation of the producer from the evolution of conditions of production, and through which he works. From a bearer of tools and a practitioner of instruments the worker has himself become a tool and an instrument in the service of tool-bearing machines. In fact, as Marx and Engels (8) indicated, this is the fate of all producers, whereby "the proletariat is recruited from all classes of the population". In other words, *the evolution of industry, through grammatisation, is affected not only by machines, but also apparatuses, expert system, services, networks, technological objects and systems.*

Reconstituting work

As then the number of consumers is enlarged, automation ceaselessly widening the field of proletarianisation while distinguishing the role of labour – that is of variable capital. *Trading* has itself been automated. Engineers have themselves been proletarianised. The engineer who conceived, developed, installed and managed a system has disappeared. Today there are ever more automated processes.

The *proletarians of the nervous system*, whose nervous energy must be placed in the service of "technical ensembles", for Stiegler then, are no less deprived of knowledge than are *the proletarians of the muscular system*. It is then the cognitive itself which has been proletarianised. Incorporated within such is "creative", "cognitive" or "immaterial" capitalism. In fact *those who are called "creative workers" today*, for him, *are merely creators of that kind of value which is capable of being evaluated by the marketplace*, like public relations officers or advertising executives who do not create any works or open up any work (as per *oeuvre*).

Towards an economy of contribution

What took place then during the course of the 19th and 20th centuries was the organisation of the capitalist transformation of the world, which consisted firstly in the legitimating powers and secularisation of beliefs: not in their destruction, but in their transformation into calculable beliefs, including the harnessing of scientific beliefs to devise ways of transforming matter, nature, technique, human beings, behaviour. *This transformation of beliefs was able to accomplish enormous gains in productivity throughout the 19th century, enabling new forms of membership and social cohesion within the social project, by the bourgeoisie.*

In the 20th century, the mobilisation of libidinal energies took place through the capturing, harnessing, and channelling of attention: causing the tensions accumulated in proclivities of consumers to reach out toward industrial products. In the recent financial crisis there was such a collapse of demand. *An economy of contribution, today and in contrast then, constitutes the sociotherapy proper to the contemporary stage of grammatisation – its system of care. Our epoch then is very singular: unlike any before it has made carelessness into the very principle of its organisation. Such is the urgency and the challenge – global and unprecedented – to conduct a grand overturning of tendencies in the face of generalised, drive based emptiness, and decadence of industrial democracies.*

The task of Europe in the division of the west and global individuation

Europe must still have expectations of, and learn from, a more sustained exchange with America – but America too must learn from others, rather than just drawing them in. *Just as Nietzsche thought the future of Germany by projecting it onto the level of Europe, thereby denationalising it, so too Europe can only think itself by thinking of the global future, and by thinking itself in becoming planetary*, in the sense that the process of European psychic and collective individuation can today only occur within a much vaster process of individuation, one that is now manifestly that of planetary humanity, not a new form of Eurocentrism.

Europe, for Stiegler, is obviously constituted by its "heritage", which is its force. But this is only a force as the power of the future – that is as the capacity to break with that decadent, exhausted and self-destructive state affairs to which the industrial model of the 20th century has led, shaped by the American way of life, and which became the model for every industrial democracy. The future of Europe, for him then, lies in its critique, as a model which is collapsing, and in the invention of another model. The project of conceiving a new industrial model requires a complete rethinking of the organisation of production and consumption. In such, Europe needs to engage deeply with China, another ancient civilisation.

This must be precisely the process of a new European *individuation*, itself inscribed in a planetary process, differentiating itself from what until now has been the industrial and democratic West in its totality. Localising itself in Europe, *it replays through the projection of a reinvented industrial future the individuation of its pre-individual European foundations which this continent, a geographical and historical entity, supports on its soil and through its inhabitants.*

The lure of the leisure society

The fable of "post-industrial society", which has in recent decades been dominant, has to a great extent seduced political and philosophical thought. According to this fable, which began to be told in 1968, we have entered into the age of "free time", that is leisure time. "Post-modern" philosophy inspired social democracies to assume that we had passed from an era of mass labour and consumption of the industrial age into the time of the middle classes and to presume the proletariat is disappearing.

But the proletariat remains very important, firstly because workers have been to a large extent proletarianised (enslaved to mechanised systems depriving them of initiative and professional knowledge) but also because such a proletariat now includes middle class consumers. The "leisures" they pursue control such consumers via hyper-massification. Produced and organised by the culture programming industries, these constitute mostly banal programmes. Such a culture and service based capitalism, via computer technology, standardises existence though marketing concepts. In "post-industrial society", purported to be a "society of leisure", culture in that context is represented by brands, and fashion.

Otium and negotium: towards care

Singularity then and that which sustains it as that which is raised, is to be able to see from the shoulders of giants and thereby achieve a longer and broader view, is what is deemed extraordinary. And for this reason it needs to be ceaselessly protected, affirmed and cultivated. All practice moreover, insofar as it is *otium*, is sustained by tertiary retention – secondary retentions objectified and materialised, expressed in some material form, and thus transmissible, inheritable and adaptable. This is the way in which, for example, the Church, before being the opium of the people was its otium, constituting a *salvation of souls: existence as elevation*.

In fact no society has ever existed that did not contain practices similar to what the Roman nobility called *otium*. No such society exists, except today in the Western industrial democracies which, taking themselves for post-industrial societies, are submitted to the "leisure" industries, industries that are in fact the very negation of *otium* as practice, because they are dominated by *negotium*. Such for Stiegler is their decadence.

This epoch of industrial populism, then, is the indispensable complement of consumer capitalism. Libidinal energy, which on the one hand underlies such, on the other hand destroys consumer capitalism, through diversions specific to our epoch. *Industrial populism has given the whole world the feeling of heading toward catastrophe, and it has seen the ruination of psychic and collective individuation, which is also to say of economics and politics.* Such then for Stiegler is the political question as therapeutic procedure, where this is understood as requiring a system of care, cura, care of self and others, in brief the *otium of the people*.

TV, cinema, video games, 3G phones, personal assistants and other communication devices are no more or less toxic than other temporal objects that brought about the transition from *mythos* to *logos*. Alongside such, however, are required ecological measures intended to *prevent the loss of attention* generated by the above. For such an industrialisation of the spirit, in the absence of such counter-measures, is like smoking or speeding, forming a new type of addiction. Such counter-measures require a new kind of *care*, a new type of *otium*. If it is true that at the heart of capitalism is a libidinal economy, and that this is leading to the destruction of sublimation and the superego, for Stieglitz, then we must enable this economy to move to a new stage of libidinal *ecology*. Society then for him is always diseased, but health consists in a horizon of consistencies.

We now turn, more specifically via Ellen MacArthur, to the world of work, set in the context of the circular economy.

Illustrative Case: the end of employment in the circular economy

Wrapping employment into the circular economy

Whilst Stiegler's conception of a struggle for the life of the spirit is recognisable, it is, equally, the case that, what he calls, a horizon of consistency is becoming more visible in parts of the world. The metaphor of a *circular economy* became apparent to the solo round-the-world yachtswoman Ellen McArthur, when she navigated towards the horizon. As she circumnavigated the globe, McArthur realised that the standard industrial model of "take, make, use, dispose" was at the root of the environmental crisis. Instead, a model of "recycle, design-in regeneration, use and further recycle" could transform processes of industrial production, from being linear to circular.

Fresh implications for employment, in circular economic processes, emerge by embedding ways of navigating from the old economy of production-for-waste to a new one of continuous recycling-by-design. Much of the work on restorative and regenerative processes, designed into manufacturing productive goods, focuses on the use of materials. But, increasing attention is being paid to the implications of the circular economy on employment levels and practices. A recent report by WRAP for the Green Alliance (9) looks at job creation in a more resource efficient Britain. The clear evidence that emerges from the report is that there are new business and employment opportunities emerging with an expanding circular economy sector.

Recycling reduces imbalances

Although Britain has been enjoying levels of almost full employment in the aftermath of the financial crisis, official statistics mask considerable regional disparities in levels of employment and, most particularly, rates of pay, employment benefits and job satisfaction. Equally, the 'enjoyment of employment' is a moot point, given the nature of the UK labour market. The most recent data from the OECD (10) indicates that Britain is a very job-rich but productivity-poor economy. Whilst living standards are above the OECD average, regional disparities mask considerable pockets of disadvantage, low skill and social inequalities across the country.

Each of these factors is addressed in the report on the impact of a circular economy on British working and employment. As is well understood, low skilled work and higher than average levels of unemployment are concentrated in areas of the North of Britain and the least affluent parts of London. Even so, there is evidence that some circular economy jobs, in waste reuse and recycling are disproportionately

concentrated in the North of England, near to areas of former manufacturing concentration. That said, there is little evidence that expansion of the circular economy will substantially affect differences in
regional employment.

By contrast, evidence is respect of wage rates and skill levels show
distinct benefits accruing from circular economy working. Pay rates in
circular economy jobs are currently 13% higher than the UK average.
At the same time, it is recognised that the waste and recycling sectors
will remain reliant on relatively low skilled workers. Even so, new
jobs in remanufacturing, closed-loop recycling, together with rental
and leasing of equipment will require mid-level skills, whilst some
work in the bio-refinery and servitisation sectors will need high-skilled
workers. Given that many of these new sectors will be located in less
advantaged and peripheral regions they could assist in rebalancing the
highly imbalanced UK regional economy.

New jobs beyond those for old

Expert panel analysis for the WRAP Report indicated that in some
regions, such as the North East of England, new circular economy jobs
would most likely be net job gains, rather than replacing existing ones.
The only regions where circular economy jobs would replace existing
work would be in the South East and South West, given that these are
close to full employment. But, in these regions job substitution would
only take place where low skilled work could be replaced by medium
or high-skilled jobs, leading to an overall and much-needed increase in
overall skill levels across the economy as a whole. Furthermore, it would
be likely that such transfer developments would feed-through to circular economy jobs in similar sectors, in average lower-skilled regions.

Three scenarios of circular economy developments in the UK, over
the next fifteen years (to beyond 2030), were calculated. These ranged
from 8,000 at the lowest end to 88,000 at the highest projection, with a
mid-range figure of c 50,000 new jobs. Although this is a modest contribution to the overall UK work complement it would signal an important
shift in patterns of sustainable employment moving towards the mid-
century. The circular economy will not entirely transform the 'libidinal
motivation' of work that Stiegler looks toward. But, it is, clearly, one
step along the navigational road towards a new style of capitalist.

Conclusion

The new wave of industrial production is taking environmentalism seriously.
Indeed, one of the highest growth sectors is green business, which is out-
stripping overall industrial growth by c33% annually, in the UK (11). The

challenge of climate change and ecological collapse are, after six decades of strident eco-activism, at last, impacting the production sphere, alongside popular civil society protest, largely as a result of changing consumer behaviour. But, as we saw, through the eyes of Bernard Stiegler, the employment activities of individual businesses are only part of a transforming political economy of energetic ecology.

Even so, the circular economy revolution that Ellen MacArthur has sought to stimulate remains in its infancy. Building regenerative design into initial production processes, with the implications this has for working practices, as well as the relationship of the self to production and consumption – increasingly as prosumers, through the 'internet of things' – remains in its infancy. The pace of change will, however, continue to redefine the liminal boundary between the self, employment, production and consumption, so that work and leisure, or, at least, non-work time, will shift rapidly. That is the core theme of the next chapter, as we reach the peak of the North.

Bibliography

1 Downs, A. (1972) Up and Down with Ecology – The Issue-Attention Cycle. *Public Interest* 28(2): 38–50, Summer.
2 Carrington, D. (2012) Choice Between Green or Growth Is a False One, CBI Chief Says. *The Guardian Online*, Green Economy, 5 July. [Available at: www.theguardian.com/environment/2012/jul/05/green-growth-false-choice-cbi. Last accessed: October 31, 2017].
3 B Team, The. (2017) *Statement on U.S. Withdrawal from Paris Agreement*, 6 June. [Available at: http://bteam.org/press/the-b-team-statement-on-u-s-withdrawal-from-paris-agreement/. Last accessed: July 31, 2017].
4 OECD. (2017) *Economic Surveys – United Kingdom Overview*, October. [Available at: www.oecd.org/eco/surveys/United-Kingdom-2017-OECD-economic-survey-overview.pdf. Last accessed: November 1, 2017].
5 Stiegler, B. (2010) *For a New Critique of Political Economy*. Cambridge: Polity Press.
6 Marx, K. (1990) *Capital: Critique of Political Economy*. London: Penguin Classics.
7 De Boever, A. and Murray, A. (2013) *Gilbert Simondon: Being and Technology*. Edinburgh: Edinburgh University Press.
8 Marx, K. and Engels, F. (2015) *The Communist Manifesto*. London: Penguin Little Black Classics.
9 Makower, J. et al. (2016) *State of Green Business 2016*. GreenBiz and Tru-Cost. [Available at: State of_ Green_Business_Report_2016.pdf. Last accessed: November 1, 2017].
10 Morgan, J. and Mitchell, P. (2015) *Employment and the Circular Economy: Job Creation in a More Resource Efficient Britain*. London: The Green Alliance Trust and WRAP.
11 Bradley, T. and Ziniel, C. (2017) Green Governance? Local Politics and Ethical Businesses in Great Britain. *Business Ethics: A European Review* 26(1): 18–30, January.

12 The *otium* of the people
Automated work to work as recreation

GROUNDED IN LOVE
EMERGING ECOLOGY
NAVIGATING BEYOND EMPLOYMENT
EFFECTING EMANCIPATION

Introduction: industrial populism and the otium of the people

Populism, if not specifically industrial populism, seems rampant today. For Stiegler (1) then, the hegemonic power of Google, Apple, Facebook and Amazon, referred to as the "four horsemen of the Apocalypse", are literally disintegrating our industrial societies. In Marx's day, it was not the social media, but formalised religion that he considered to be "the opium of the people". In a play on words, ending up with a phrase that we have chosen to be a main theme of this book, Bernard Stiegler has alluded to the *otium* of the people, drawing on the Latin original of "otium": leisure, care, culture.

Building on those political economists who have come historically before, from J.S. Mill to Maynard Keynes and onto Clifford Douglas (see Chapters 15 and 16) we pursue the implications of *the end of employment*, and, as our navigation Social Theory in this "northern" European context, *the rebirth of work-as-recreation*. In particular, we explore Stiegler's view of the automated society. We finish the section on Social Theory with the work of Stiegler's compatriot Andre Gorz and his understanding of how a more leisured society, within the context of technological change, can be funded.

The Burning Question we seek then to address here is: *Will a robot be taking over your job anytime soon?* As we see, the answer to that question is mostly predicated on the nature of work in an increasingly machine-focused phase of capitalism. We continue thereafter with a Window into Wisdom which reflects on one of the great passages in John's (Northern) *Gospel, expressing the sorts of interactions we are to have, which point to our flourishing in work.* In our final Illustrative Cases we examine some practical examples and *implications of increasing human-machine interactions in work and society.* But, we begin with our Burning Question.

Burning Question: the rest of the robots – will one take over your job?

The American scientist and science fiction writer Isaac Asimov is famous for his robot books, *I Robot* and *The Rest of the Robots*, which explore the dilemmas created by his 'three laws of robotics'. The first of these states that: "a robot may not injure a human being, or, through inaction, allow a human being to come to harm". But, if it takes away your job or capacity to work you might dispute whether any robot was capable of obeying the first law. After all, unlike the rest of us, robots have no need to rest.

The nature of automated work

Of course, it is quite impossible to accurately say what proportion of current jobs will be replaced by robots. Figures that are often quoted range from 10–50% of work roles. But, a recent authoritative study for Nesta (2) indicated that it is more the nature of work that defines its capacity for machine substitution, rather than the basic numbers. Put simply, the more creative the type of work the less likely it is to be automated. In the UK about one-quarter of jobs can be classified as 'creative', compared with about one-fifth in the US.

The Nesta researchers estimate that about 85% of creative jobs are immune to being performed by a robot. Overall, that means with approximately 32 million people employed in the UK, according to the Office for National Statistics (November, 2017, although not identical to the number of jobs, given multiple and cross-transfer work), 1.2M creatives and 24M other workers could be substituted by robots and machines over time. That is a massive 79% of all jobs.

Of course, the reality is that the vast majority of noncreative jobs will not be replaced by machine workers. That is because they are in small-scale service sectors, where it is uneconomic to utilise the latest technology, or in personal services where many functions require human care or would not be ethically acceptable, if performed by a robot. Perhaps 20% of work could be relatively easily be automated.

Even so, planners tend to overestimate what will happen in a single decade and underestimate what might happen in two. The adoption curve will accelerate but not substantially for the next decade after which the rate of change is likely to be more bewildering. As such, it is reasonable to suggest that up to 30% of current jobs will either not exist or will have been substituted by a machine in the mid-21st century.[1]

What are the likely impacts of emerging technologies?

Futurologist at the Brookings Institute, Darrell West, recounts a salutary story (3). He had asked his PA, Amy, to rearrange an appointment with a colleague. His colleague's PA, Hilary, was amazingly persistent in getting back with possible changed times, especially over the weekend. It was only the following Monday that they discovered that "Hilary" was a machine, a "virtual PA". West doesn't comment on how long it took him to replace Amy with "Amy".

He does indicate some of the main disruptive technologies that are most likely to further the process of generating what Stiegler calls "automatic society". The following is a brief inventory of the main categories and their likely impacts, based on West's estimates, from 2015:

1   *Industrial process robots.* There are approximately 2M process robots in operation around the world, in 2017, the largest proportion in Japan. The adoption curve suggests a five-fold increase in ten years, with this rate increasing dramatically, to, perhaps, 150M robots by 2050. Nor are these solely in facilities such as automotive manufacture. Robots have already revolutionised warehousing operations, with few people needed to transfer items. And they even exist in such functions as providing 'virtual pets and companions' for children with attachment difficulties, taking the role of assistant chefs and servicing booking and check-out functions in hotels. With the costs of new technologies falling sharply almost all repetitive and routinised tasks are likely to be substituted, at least in the major economies and wherever globalisation is having a significant impact.

2   *Computerised algorithms.* These have revolutionised the operation of stock markets, financial services and arbitrage trading. The movements of markets is already determined by these algorithms, making vast fortunes for those who control the maths behind them.

3   *Artificial Intelligence.* This is no longer the stuff of science fiction but is technological fact in areas such as transport, telecoms, finance and aviation. AI means the ability of a machine to respond to situations using critical reasoning judgement and iterative learning processes. AI is particularly helpful in areas of hazardous operation and where critical decision-making is required faster than a human agent can manage. It is being used in space exploration, experimental manufacturing, energy development, transport and healthcare.

4   *Augmented reality.* AR involves the supplementing of human sensing and knowledge systems with information sources, data, visualisations, graphics, video and geo-location apps. It is being used in such diverse areas as museum displays, transport navigational devices, gaming and military activities, associated, for example, with drone attacks.

5   *Autonomous vehicles.* This is one area that is being advanced at bewildering speed, such that the UK Government has set a target of 2021 to have significant numbers of driverless trucks and cars on British roads. There is ample research evidence to show that autonomous vehicles

cause fewer accidents, manage fuel and energy consumption far better and lead to better traffic flows. But, it remains to be seen what level of public acceptance there is for driverless vehicles, despite the fact that about 95% of all Road Traffic Accidents are the result of human error.

6   *Other automated technologies* include 3D printing, with its capacity to turn consumers into prosumers; medical sensing, with miniaturised drug and RTA intervention management; and machine-to-machine communications, such as managing "smart buildings" for minimising energy usage and maximising security.

The big picture for 'automatic society', as we shall see, suggests a mix of Gorz' and Stiegler's visions of the future. Some jobs will be substituted. Others will be augmented, offering the possibility of an 'otium of the people', whereby leisure, work, recreation and retirement are far more integrated. There will always be a place for culture and work to exist together. But, the question remains that if a robot does take, at least, part of my job, how will those aspects of life that make it worth living be resourced, perhaps outside the labour market and through other means? In order to examine this we turn to cases of human-machine interfacing. We now turn from the Burning Question, in relation to the end of work, into the Window into Wisdom that underlies such, drawing on John's Gospel.

Window into Wisdom: the gospel of how to flourish in work

John 15: "I am the vine, you are the branches'

One of the main issues drawn out in this section, on the automated society, is the extent to which human-machine interactions will result in liberating work, increasing leisure and emancipating people for their relationships and caring for one another. Whilst St John knew nothing of the automated society, the metaphor of the vine and the branches that John has Jesus expounding speaks directly to this issue. It is a picture of intimate interconnectedness that leads to a flourishing life.

In a carefully constructed message he utilises a metaphor that would have been powerfully evocative for his disciples, gathered in the Upper Room – probably of John Mark's mother's house in the backstreets of Old Jerusalem – on the night before Jesus was arrested and sent for trial and crucifixion. Recent research has shown that viticulture probably began in the Caucuses region about 9,000 years ago. But to

Jews of the first century CE the image of the vine would have been a familiar one from just about every single house and courtyard.

A grapevine has a very particular growth pattern, when properly trained and managed. There is a central stem from which spreads out a multitude of branches, each ready to produce a cluster of grape bunches, every one laden with fruit for pressing, prior to fermentation. But, Jesus begins with a blessing: "As the Father has loved me, I have loved you; abide in my love". God, the Father, is the root of the vine, Jesus is the stem and the disciples are the branches, who will bear much fruit if they abide in Him.

Clearly, the image of fruitfulness means more than telling other people about Jesus. This is an injunction to live a flourishing life. But, it is one that is deeply connected to work. Those who abide in Jesus will do the works that Jesus does and even greater works, as would have been echoing from Jesus' earlier comments (14:12). Abiding in Jesus, producing fruit and working effectively are intimately connected in this metaphor.

Staying connected

As such, this is an image of both prospering and of productivity. To stay connected to God means that the disciples wish to prosper, but they also will be able to produce more fruitful lives than they would have been able to do without abiding in their relationship with him. The nature of the work that the disciples are to do is not specified. Neither is it for us. What is more vital, though, is the quality of our relationships.

In this passage abiding in Jesus also leads to a deep connectedness to one another. And, it is out of that set of relationships and the productive work that they generate that the fruit are produced. In other words, whatever our work, it is to be as connected people and to act as those who love and serve others, just as we recognise that we are loved and served. This may not be about human-machine interfaces, but it is about the depth of integral connections that we have. Consequently, we may celebrate those aspects of the automatic society that connect us to one another, allow for greater productivity in more fulfilling work and that enable the sort of mutual abiding that John speaks of. But, where such interfaces lead simply to greater productivity that alienates us from one another or stops us doing 'greater work', they need to be sternly resisted. All that does is lead to branches that are fit for nothing except to be thrown in the fire and burned (15:6). This leads us back to Stiegler and his notion of "greater work" and recreation.

Social Theory: on the rebirth of work as recreation

Functional stupidity in driven-based capitalism

What Stiegler, for us a profound philosophical voice of the much neglected "north-and-south" as distinct from the much pursued "north-west", thereby terms "the automatic society", duly spearheaded by these "four horsemen", sets up a new mental context within which, for him at least, systematic stupidity proliferates. The overall result is a significant *increase in what he calls functional stupidity, that is drive-based capitalism and industrial populism.* The specific problem then for Stiegler is that this state of "proletarianisation" is inherently entropic (increasing disorder): it depletes the resources that it exploits – resources that in this case are psychic individuals and collective individuals, leading to their *dis-integration*. It in fact leads to a new form of *artificial crowd*, in the sense Freud gave to that expression, be that crowd based in the American rustbelt or in in deindustrialised Wales, where Trump and Brexit recently, respectively, prevailed.

But this extreme planetary disturbance, as illustrated in the US and the UK, if not in the EU as a whole, can also lead to a categorical invention. Such invention calls for therapies and therapeutics, as a new critique of political economy, as we have seen, where the challenge is to totally reshape an 'economy of spirit', whereby entropy is transformed into negentropy.

Negentropy and the rebirth of work

For Stiegler then we shall see in the future that the disappearance of the worker as a result of automation will lead to *a rebirth of work made possible by the disappearance of employment, employability and wage labour* according to the imperative of the increase in purchasing power – which since Keynes has been spurred on by economic growth.

It is *the industrial economy* itself overall for Stiegler, based on wage labour as the criterion for distributing purchasing power and the formation of mass markets capable of absorbing the ready-made commodities of the consumerist model, which *is in the course of disintegrating – becoming functionally insolvent*. This has huge implications for developed and developing economies alike, where the pursuit of employment, if not more especially self-employment, alongside economic growth, is the order of the day,

How then has this state of insolvency recently come to be?

Rewriting the goals of research and innovation

At the end of the 1960s, social movements arose with the aim of reclaiming the terrain of everyday life, which eventually led, in the 1980s, to a "counter-revolution", a conservative "revolution" in which the individual became redefined as a full-time economic agent, even in the context of "job-less capitalism".

For Stiegler, 24/7 capitalism as such,, is totally computational and it is, more precisely, capitalism conceived in terms of the power of totalisation. In other words it aims through its operations to impose an *automatic society,* in toto. The challenge then is to effect a *massive redistribution of thinking.* All this presupposes a fundamental reconceptualisation of political and eco-nomic rights and, for example in his home country France, a rewriting of the goals and practices of scientific research and innovation, education and training, in a new epistemological framework.

A transition between two industrial models

Stiegler maintains then that *there is still time to rethink* the contemporary world, *whereby automation will come to serve deautomisation.*

We're living through a transition, which can be understood on the basis of a metaphor of "metamorphosis" (see also Chapter 4), but this is not merely a technological transition but also a psychic and social one. The transition then is between two industrial models:

- *consumerism, founded on Taylorism, the culture industries and the wel-fare state designed to redistribute productivity gains of employees via purchasing power*
- *a fully automatised society where employment has disappeared and hence where wages are no longer the source of purchasing power,* in turn implying the disappearance of the producer/consumer, which requires *the institution of a new process of redistribution – not purchas-ing power but time,* including the time to constitute and purchase forms of knowledge.

What does the latter approach actually mean?

The need for fundamental epistemic change

We must then make an exit from Taylorism, Keynesianism, and consumerism by organising the economy and society differently, including the elaboration and transmission of knowledge itself. And achieving this requires a supple-mentary categorical invention, *a fundamental epistemic change leading to a reinvention of academic institutions as well as the knowledge industries.* In a society where knowledge becomes the primary productive function (and the first one to have seen that was Marx) *the new value that will be refound in the economy and politics will be no longer the time of employment, but the time of knowledge as negentropy* (order out of disorder).

To currently combat this current state of fact, that is to oppose this eco-nomic irrationality (the breaking of the production/consumption/ purchasing power redistributive cycle) requires a new integrated rationality, that is the invention in effect of a new epoch of CARE, for Stiegler, *a redefinition of rationality*, replacing calculability, with *taking care of all of the improbable.*

Towards a contributory economy: the need for social innovation

Innovation, in such a context, clearly has a real economic function: it evidently constitutes a production of negentropy. But what has now become obvious, is that this negentropy produced in the short term generates far higher entropy in the long-term. If then innovation is a negentropic factor that has become massively entropic, especially since the conservative revolution last century, how could a new industrial political economy lead to a new production of negentropy – and to new terms of thinking of innovation?

In the context of full and generalised automatisation, such must proceed, for Stiegler, from a *social innovation that reinvents the adjustments between the social and the technical systems, and does so according to a model where it is no longer the economic system, and the technological innovation it requires, that prescribe the social.* It must on the contrary be a model where social innovation, founded on a different economics – a contributory economy – and on a reinvention of politics, conceived as therapeutics, prescribes organological (the co-evolution of minds, bodies and social organisations) evolution, and does so by *interpreting* technical tendencies. Where then does this lead?

Work instead of employment

Since the appearance of the web in 1993, it has undergone, according to Stiegler, a process of levelling, through which it has been completely subjected to the imperative of calculability, itself fully configured by business models invented in California. This has led to *the logic of platforms* – just as the culture industry levelled the world in the 1980s (with the conservative revolution), *a steamroller subjecting all opinions to the law of audience ratings and subjecting all media to a competition for access to the advertising market.* Until now then there have been two main epochs in the history of the web: the first characterised by hypertext links and websites, the second by blogs, evaluated by search engines. *A third epoch must then arise, founded on what he terms a new organology, derived from a supplementary invention, conceived as a political technology.* The current mode of governmentality now appears even more alienating and addictive, and even less open to critique, than analogue media, because it is much less visible, and thus much more dangerous; it merges with the world it absorbs, flattens and annihilates by engulfing it.

So, Stiegler maintains, an ontological upheaval must be implemented to begin with in Europe, where the worldwide web was invented, involving a *new conception of social networks.* Such an organisation of automatic society, *founded on a contributory income in return for creativity, should receive preliminary testing in willing regions where younger people, catastrophically affected by unemployment inherited from an obsolete age, should be encouraged to seize the opportunities presented by an automatic society.* Employment, for Stiegler meanwhile, has disintegrated work, just as computational capitalism is now disintegrating collective individuation. Work then he goes on to say is definitely not employment. The ancient Greeks initially conceived their *politea* on the basis of a separation between those who work, that is slaves (now our "slaves" are our automatons), and nobles, who are thereby discharged from that need, thereby being structurally separate from the economic sphere, thus constituting the political sphere.

It was the industrial revolution that forever turned this upside-down, by integrating knowledge into the function of production.

Rethinking work in the epoch of automatons, which will eliminate a vast number of jobs in the next 20 years, is a key element in the new arrangement between politics, economics and *knowledge*. Stiegler now turns to Marx.

The reinvention of work

The computerisation of society, retracing steps, began in the 1960s. In 1993 the opening of the global public to the internet network via the protocols of the worldwide web set in place an infrastructure that would profoundly transform telecommunications and lead to the total reticulation of every territory, all of which became "digital territories". Humans and machines found themselves connected 24 hours a day, 7 days a week, with the entire planet, and with all the economic players in the world.

During the 1990s, more than 40 years after the first warnings of American futurist George Friedman (2), followed by those of social philosopher Andre Gorz (3) in France (*The Liberation of Work*) and social theorist (4) Jeremy Rifkin (*The End of Work*) in the US, a question arose, ever more pressing today, due to the immense productivity gains, and transformations, about the principle of *how to redistribute productivity gains in forms other than wage increases and purchasing power.* The issue is no longer reduction of the time of work but the very *reinvention of work* in itself. This new conception of work, for Stiegler, must be based on a new status of knowledge, and its elaboration, and the way it is implemented in economic life.

In the relationship between the hand and the machine it is in fact the latter that "works", and it does so blindly, that is automatically, in a way that cannot be described as craft-work, or in French *oeuvre* or *ouvrage*, given that this word also means opening: this form of serial production, on the contrary, is completely closed.

A new right to work, in that context, can no longer be conceived as a right to wage labour, but must be seen as a new age of *noesis* (see Chapter 6). Employment then is no longer the issue. The question then becomes that of *formation* or *bildung* (cultivation), that is the in-advance struggle for psychic individuals, forming them and immunising them as much as possible against the *deformation* that is the automaton. *Wealth will be in the future be evaluated and produced by and as the totality of society's new neganthropic capabilities.*

Contributory income through regional experimentation

We are then, in Stiegler's view, leaving the work-based society behind, but we are exiting backwards, though not yet capable of *civilising* liberated time or of founding a culture of available time. It is time then that is liberated, no longer work. This available time is not that of available work, and it must, for him, be civilised.

Faced with this situation Jeremy Rifkin advocated public support for a third sector (a civil economy as outlined in our earlier chapters) that would include, in addition to the social and solidarity economy, a vast network of regional authorities and businesses, including public utilities, which depend on it. For Stiegler though, it is not just a matter of creating a third sector, or of having a negative income tax, that is of a guaranteed minimum income (see Chapter 15), though he is not against either – quite the contrary. But he argues in addition that we must now *invent* another society founded on a *contributory income*.

This must be achieved firstly through regional experiments within the framework of action research protocols and supported by contributory technologies developed from this perspective – action research itself becoming contributory research. This implies the need to totally rethink, through these regional and experimental transitional practices, national policies, industrial policies, higher education and national educational policies, cultural and editorial policies, and financial policies – *reinventing work policies*. To reason in this way means revisiting the whole history of philosophy and onto-theology, starting from the question of work as transformation, and going beyond Marx, who never poses the question of deproletarianisation as such. Stiegler then turns to the relationship between energy and work in the 21st century.

The otium of the people

Towards a contributory economy

Liberated time, for Stiegler, must be liberated work. This presupposes *reinventing not only work but energy* – by reactivating its former meaning – *energeia* – as well as the meaning of *dunamis*, translated into Latin as *potential*, which is sometimes called such potential but also virtue, or in Latin *virtu*, which is also to say force, strength, what the Greeks called *arête*, also translated as excellence (see Chapter 14).

Moreover, as long as such a reinvention, or transformation, is not artic-ulated collectively, as a contributory economy, the far right (and its fun-damentalist defenders) will continue to advance throughout the world, to the degree that it reacts against a sociological transformation more colossal than any humanity has faced before. And now we come to the crux of the matter, as a central central theme of this book, related to work as recreation.

In a *contributory economy* founded on a *contributory income* then, *otium* (Latin for leisure, care, culture, recreation, freedom) must be cultivated, Stiegler maintains, at all stages of life, and such a culture is clearly a form of work – given that any activity, *Energeia* is a transformation of oneself. And because the psychic individuation in which such a transformation consists is effective only if it participates in collective trans-individuation, it is neces-sarily also a transformation of others, thereby leading to the employment of self and community.

The dual imperative arising involves specifically, for Stiegler, the reso-lution of the crisis of the idea of work, and more generally the way out of today's impasse, cannot be reduced to an energy transition as some purveyor of new jobs, or to the development of a third sector, or the adoption of a basic or guaranteed income – and not even to the combi-nation of these three measures. The dual imperative implies the *need to concretise a constitution of a contributory economy, founded on contrib-utory research and innovation, and taking account, at all levels of public action and the economy, of the consequences that follow when we reach the stage of full automation.* Before arguing, though, for a contributory income based on *contributory projects* founded on *contributory invest-ments* and on *contributory credit*, Stiegler wants to deepen the question of whether we can still talk about work while associating it with freedom that we otherwise call leisure.

Energia and dunamis

Indeed the war of words about the meaning of 'work', which continually resurfaces, will have been in vain if it does not reach down to the sedimen-tary layers that preceded this question. This includes the fact that for Stie-gler the issue of work has been over-determined by the market. Moreover, the market itself is constituted of a fiduciary space founded on a specific form of tertiary retention called money. Indeed, in the European mental-ity figures and numbers are the rational key to the reading of the world. The current notion of work, moreover, results from layers of organological arrangements and there is no longer an *essence* of work, though there are *social relations*. Free software, as we shall see in the next chapter, in as much as it is a challenge to the industrial division of labour, could constitute a model for the organisation of work. The widespread generalisation of such requires a *contributory organology* that remains entirely to be developed – in the first place with the free software communities that have been around for thirty years.

Behind the question of work, and beyond the word 'work', which has such an easy payoff, there is the question of *erga, ergon, energia*. Some two and a half millennia ago, *energia* and *dunamis* were at the heart of Aristotle's thinking.

Energy and transformation

Work as we conceive it then after a sedimentation of layers of meaning is a specific case of what the Greeks regarded as *energeia*. In the history of Western thought the meaning of the word *energeia* has evolved a great deal: in modern times it has been almost reversed as in the ancient Greek language, and especially *in the work of Aristotle, energeia meant the passage to act, the leap towards entelechy, that is, towards a particular end or purpose (telos). Nowadays we refer to fossil fuel as energy!*

Semantic transformations over the millennia have led to energy, activity, dynamic, power and potential. Work then in Newton's time (17th century) became a unit of *measurement of force*, which for Newton is a notion in physics while via Watt and his steam engine we come to the famous second law of thermodynamics, and to energy as *power and combustion*. The word *energia* always in some way involves a question of an activity of transformation, of a formation that is *taking a form*, a passage to the act as *individuation* and accomplishment of a potential that contemporary French philosopher Gilbert Simondon called pre-individual. With the appearance then of mechanical tertiary retention this retention is captured and displaced by the technical individual, at the expense of the psychic individual, who is thereby dis-individuated.

And these *machines have now no longer assumed "the passage to act", that is the leap into individuation, rather taking the form of combustible energy, muscular force, or the nervous energy of the brain*. The science of knowledge no longer exists in the worker's consciousness, but rather acts upon him through the machine as an alien power, as the power of the machine itself. This becomes a challenge to macroeconomic functioning where the process of production ceases to be the process of work.

The end of employment and de-proletarianisation of work

Energy refers to potential, that is, for Aristotle, to *dumasis*. Yet today the bipolarity *energia/dumasis* has been annulled. With it has imploded the transformation that Hegel had thought of in terms of work as *childbirth*. It is as if the work gave birth to itself by folding back on itself like a glove. Contrary then to what Marx would have us believe in *Capital*, it is not *proletarianisation* which is the bearer of transformation, but, as he envisaged in the *Grundrisse*, the end of employment. *The end of employment can and must lead to the de-proletarianisation of work, and in this sense its reinvention, whereby neganthropic knowledge becomes the source of value at once as life-knowledge, work-knowledge and conceptual-knowledge.*

Replaced by the machine he or she serves then, the worker becomes its employee as pure labour force in the service of an *energia* that the worker no longer embodies and in relation to which he has been disintegrated. For his own *energia* has been studied, formalised and standardised into some material form – template or algorithm – amounting to an industrially reproduced tertiary retention. The totality of social relations are dis-integrated in turn, and it is this Stiegler refers to as the hyper-industrial epoch.

The proletarian then, serving the machine that has replaced the worker, has been deprived of his *energia*. In this way *work becomes a concept of physics*. In the past, for Stiegler, it was striking and encouraging to see workplaces in which wage labourers, having been deprived of their *energia* through proletarianisation, nevertheless developed amateur practices such as choirs or bands, for example in mining communities. The industrialisation of culture now, he says, has prevented such. *To rebuild a libidinal economy, then, requires the installation of a new industrial model based on the economy of contribution, and process of de-proletarianisation.*

Libidinal energy and care: work as poesis

A true "creative economy", then, would be an economy of contribution, not the hyper-consumerist economy where a "creative class" governs a hyper-proletarianised global mass. *This economy of contribution therefore requires a complete change in industrial relations in order to create a new system of care – a technique of the government of self and others founded in a new way on what must no longer be the biopolitics of biopower, but the noopolitics of psychopower.* Like solar energy, libidinal energy is inexhaustible and renewable, but it is not a given: it is the fruit of social work.

"True" work, in such a context, is a *poesis* that responds to "the need the individual feels to appropriate the surrounding world, to impress his or her stamp on it, and, by the objective transformations he or she effects upon it, to acquire a sense of being an autonomous subject possessing practical freedom. What we call work then, before becoming a pure force of labour was par excellence, within for example a traditional community, was a participation in collective individuation. Specifically as such:

- *subsistence*, for Marx, was the *reproduction of the labour force*
- *existence*, which Durkheim called organic solidarity, related to the division of labour, was a signature case of *participation in collective individuation*

- *consistence* which incorporates subsistence and existence involves, over and above such, *participation in a collective dream* – what indigenous Australians call Dreaming and "westerners" call reason.

Beyond the anthropocene: otium of the people

Today humanity is confronted with the toxicity of its own development – to the point that we now have a term, the Anthropocene, to designate an age of the biosphere in which human activities have become the dominant strain above all other geological and natural forces that have hitherto prevailed: the action of the human species has become a true geological force acting on the planet. It is no longer a matter, then, of "making one's life into a work of art, but of *making organalogical life into a neganthropic work* – through the reinvention of work, restoring a global solvency differing from and deferring cosmic entropy.

The Anthopocene then is indeed the epoch of globalisation of the technical system and the destruction of the social systems through processes of uncaring, negligent financial capital producing negative externalities. With industrialisation, the relationship between the technical system and the social systems has had a massive and uniform impact, on a global scale, on biological systems. *A neganthropology, taking responsibility for the question of the Anthropocene, must constitute a new age of care that will also be a new age of economics, where economising will men taking care and where the economy will again become economical.*

It is as the specific challenge of the Anthropocene, moreover for Stiegler, that we must conceive and install the *otium* of the people, where the value of value is what is cultivated and remunerated through leisure, or indeed *recreation*.

Eliminating employment

Meanwhile, with the immense transformation occurring, which Stiegler describes as a metamorphosis, *public powers seem completely blind, impotent, negligent and stunned* – which is altogether, for him, nothing short of stupid. *The liberation of work then is not a question of "reducing work time" to share it out and reducing the rate of unemployment, but of eliminating employment as the key status* and function of a macroeconomic system that was conceived and implemented by Keynes and Roosevelt but whose effects have been reversed.

Maintaining the same discourse on wage labour and purchasing power allows those who extract profit to constantly exert downward pressure on the cost of labour in the employment market, in order to increase their profits still further. Proletarianisation is not disappearing altogether but, for Stiegler, it is ceasing to take the form of wage labour. Digital working is more like the 'Hollywood' model of organising work by projects. How did such historically arise, at least in the modern era? We now turn to the work of fellow French social philosopher, Andre Gorz.

Towards a binomial income

In the 1980s in fact Stiegler's French compatriot, and iconoclastic Marxist social philosopher, Andre Gorz (6), had proposed the establishment of a dual income:

> Since the economic apparatus produces more and better with less and less work, income levels can no longer depend on the evolution of the amount of work provided by each. The redistribution of production gains requires a comprehensive politics, appropriate for the time. This necessarily involves the introduction of a binomial income: income from work, on the one hand, which may decrease with the duration of work; and social income on the other.

Stiegler favoured this proposal, but taken in reverse (see also the *Social Creditors*, Chapter 16). Downward pressure on wages, he adds, inevitably leads to a fall in demand. And we know that the way this issue was resolved by the conservative revolution was through the introduction of sub-prime mortgages and credit default swaps, enabling the formation of an ultra-speculative and automated financial market, which was then bound to leave banks and states fundamentally insolvent.

In fact all industrial societies in the latter part of the 20th century, for Gorz, had been moving had been moving toward this "dualism: whereby a class of permanent workers was destined to play a conservative role in defence of the old order. On the other hand, the rest of "non-permanent" workers were engaged in some form of work-sharing (each of us have seen this while in hospital, amongst the overnight agency nursing staff invariably recruited from abroad), and generalised reduction of work time.

Revisiting preindustrial societies: a way out of capitalism

Gorz goes on to project into the future that socially useful work will no longer be anyone's full-time occupation, nor indeed the centre of their lives. *Life, like society itself, will become multi-centred. A wide range of forms of production and styles as well as rhythms of life will coexist, each person moving in different spheres and finding their own balance in the passage from one to the other.* Wages work will then shift from centre stage and be counter-balanced (see Chapter 15) by a guaranteed income for life provided for all.

However, this abolition of waged work as central to our lives, for Gorz, is a necessary but not a sufficient condition for liberating and enriching our lives. Beyond waged work, what is being challenged here is the primacy of the economic. Non-economic activities, for him in fact, as we ourselves saw in Chinyika (Chapter 2), are the fabric of life itself (for example dance, drama, and poetry and social relationships in the Chinyika case). They encompass everything that is done for love, friendship, compassion and concern – indeed for overall CARE – derived from the activities themselves rather than the end results. In all preindustrial societies these activities were, and are still in traditional rural communities, embedded into, and alongside, productive work. Work is given its rhythm by festivals and celebrations. A "popular art", as we witnessed in Chinyika, was and is woven into work and life.

Ultimately then for Gorz, *the solution to the unemployment generated by Stiegler's "automatic society" is for every professional, say, to work no more than four hours a day, and during the rest of the time they will be equal members in their local community*, just as is the case, for example in an Israeli kibbutz (7), urban or rural, today, doing the cooking, the gardening or the teaching like everyone else. We now turn to Illustrative Cases of automation and their implications.

Illustrative Cases: implications of increasing human-machine interactions in work

The augmented human – people and machines working together

The Deloitte–Oxford University study (8) of the future of automation at work, as used by the BBC, paints a gloomy picture of one-third of all jobs becoming fully automated by 2035. Other analysts are far more up-beat about the capacities of human-machine interaction at work. Chris Brauer, from Goldsmith's College, University of London, maintains (9) that the most productive work unit is the human-machine interface, offering a way through the chronic productivity lag in UK industry.

Brauer's core argument is that Taylorism and Fordism sought to turn people into machines, whereas the current fascination with autonomous machines risks a 'technological gold-rush', which is neither realistic nor desirable, towards usurping people at work. A much better path is to allow machines to do what they do best, releasing humans to become more humanised in the labour market. As he puts it: "We shouldn't be afraid to let machines do deterministic stuff as it's dehumanising and, hopefully, in the process, we'll learn how to rehumanise work and bring back activities that should have been the focus all along."

How augmented jobs will work

Indeed, the International Federation of Robotics (IFR) 2017 report (10) indicates ways in which such augmented jobs will work. In summary, the IFR's position is that:

1   *Robots increase competitiveness and productivity.* They see this as being particularly beneficial for SMEs rather than large scale, global corporations, enabling the reshoring of many, previously outsourced, jobs.
2   *Increased automation increases effective demand* and, hence, new job opportunities in, hitherto, undeveloped sectors.
3   *Historically, automation has led to increased labour demand* and higher wages. The main challenge will be to retrain workers in middle-skill work, which will become automated, for higher-level functions.
4   *The future will be more about robot-human augmented work*, rather than robot for human substitution. The IFR calculates that only 10% of work tasks can be fully automated, even in advanced labour markets.
5   *There is a need to provide intensified and co-ordinated public-private sector collaboration in up-skilling* and helping both companies and workers to capitalise on machine-human interfaces.

Of course, some of these 'ascent of the warm, sunny uplands' arguments reflect the IFR's lobbying against the introduction of robot taxes in the richest economies. Even so, their detailed evaluation of robot-human interfaces does suggest that the more dire warnings – about whole swathes of the economy being wiped-out, with no signs of replacement jobs being developed – are unlikely to be borne-out.

The case of Alexander Mann Solutions

Alexander Mann Solutions (AMS) is a HR talent management and recruitment business. It has installed AI robots into many of its global centres to manage routine admin tasks. For example, one bot can process more than 70,000 candidate application documents in 48 hours, which is 200 times faster than previous human admin assistants. But, no one has lost their job as a result. Instead, assistants have been retrained to perform much higher-level functions in managing relationships with candidates, clients and recruiters. The net effect has been to significantly increase the quality of the HR management service offered by AMS.

The case of smart farming

Agriculture may not be the first industry that springs to mind when we think about human-machine interfacing. But, in fact, it is developing more systems than, perhaps, any other industry. These range from sensors that track the conditions of soil and plants in an orchard, through bio-medical data from livestock, including animal activity, GPS positioning, tissue sensitivity and body temperature to systems that provide full life-cycle management for foresters and arboriculturalists.

Each of these systems not only gives farmers and growers better information, but the bots actually manage many of the systems, leaving farmers free to concentrate on higher-level activities, such as customer relationships and financial planning. One specific example is a system developed at the Catholic University of Conception, Chile. The use of wireless sensors in field irrigation for blueberries has reduced water usage by 70%. The point is that in each of these sectors the human-machine interfaces are, actually, allowing people to move away from drudge-jobs to higher-level skilled work, and also to be able to spend more time in work as recreation.

Conclusion

We began this chapter – navigating to the apex of the North – by asking if a robot will be taking away your job. More predictably, job substitution or augmentation will be the main implications of automation and this is likely to be more gradual than a sudden shock to the employment of selves and the community. Even so, many economies have experienced a swifter uptake in high-level automation, especially in such areas as warehousing, in the past 3–4 years. But, the advent of autonomous vehicles, in the early years of the 2020s, is set to have a very disruptive effect on the transportation and distribution sectors.

On that basis, we might celebrate those aspects of new technology which enable greater connectedness, whilst resisting automation that further alienates us from fulfilling and holistic working. This was the message of 'abiding' from John's Gospel. In assessing an increasingly automatic society, we looked towards a political economy in which non-working and leisure time is strongly financially rewarded, alongside the types of social welfare funding solutions introduced in Chapters 15 and 16. But, for the time being, there will be a tussle between conservative austerity and more socially liberal policies, seeking to smooth transitions in the labour market, alongside the otium of the people.

What is undeniable is the fact of automation. If our Illustrative Cases are normative the transition may be less traumatic than many commentators assert. We remain sceptical. It is in that vein that we turn, hence, to consider the liberating effects of new work patterns.

Note

1 To find out if yours is one of them you might wish to take the BBC test of robotic substitution (8). Incidentally, they are slightly more expectant about machine substitution, estimating that 35% of current work will be roboticised by 2035.

Bibliography

1 Stiegler, B. (2015) *Automatic Society: The Future of Work*. Cambridge: Polity Press.
2 Bakhshi, H., Frey, C.B. and Osborne, M. (2015) *Creativity vs Robots: The Creative Economy and Future of Employment*. London: Nesta.
3 Stylianou, N. et al. (2015) Will a Robot Take Your Job. *BBC Technology Online*. [Available at: www.bbc.com/news/technology-34066941. Last accessed: November 19, 2017].
4 Gorz, A. (1985) *Paths to Paradise: On the Liberation from Work*. London: Pluto Press.
5 Rifkin, J. (1997) *The End of Work*. New York: Tarcher.
6 Gorz, A. (1985) *op cit.*
7 Horrox, J. (2010) *The New Israeli Socialism*. Manchester: Manchester Metropolitan University, Unpublished Thesis.
8 Frey, C.B. and Osborne, M.A. (2013). *The Future of Employment: How Susceptible Are Jobs to Computerisation?* Oxford: Martin School.
9 Brauer, C. (2017) *FuturaCorp: Artificial Intelligence and the Freedom to Be Human*. London: Goldsmiths College.
10 IFR. (2017) *The Impact of Robots on Productivity, Employment and Jobs*. International Federation of Robotics. [Available at: https://ifr.org/img/office/IFR_The_Impact_of_Robots_on_Employment.pdf. Last accessed: November 19, 2017].

13 Open source

Immaterial labour to social networking

GROUNDED IN LOVE
EMERGING ECOLOGY
NAVIGATING BEYOND EMPLOYMENT
EFFECTING EMANCIPATION

Introduction: way of life to open source

In the current chapter, following in the footsteps of the "otium of the people", alias work as recreation, we ask the follow-up Burning Question: *can work shift from being a form of labour to becoming a way to life?* We consider the work of scholars Antonio Negri, Michael Hardt and Manuel Castells, who point to the immaterial nature of labour within an increasingly global, networked society. Then, we examine the principles behind Don Tapscott and Anthony Williams classic exploration of *Wikinomics* and the irrevocable changes that information technology has made to the nature of work. Thereafter, we look, in our Window into Wisdom at the final chapter of John's Gospel and the reworking of labour that Jesus instils in his disciples, after the account of the resurrection.

While Stiegler 'northern' orientation toward the *otium* of the people is hugely evocative, and his navigational orientation toward the "automatic society" is similarly indicative, the ultimate effect of such is less clear-cut. Indeed, even the work of his leading French compatriot, and social philosopher, Andre Gorz, has been more influential in theory that in practice. So, in this final 'northern' chapter we therefore turn to specific effect, of in fact *reconstituting work as life* (as opposed to work constituting life) beginning with that of Linus Torvalds, Linux and the "open source" movement, culminating in the "wealth of networks" cited by Israeli-American Harvard scholar, Yochai Benkler.

Finally, we consider, in our illustrative 'northern' case, exemplars of the way in which wikinomics is reshaping education, research and the media, *effecting new directions for work and society*. But, first, we turn to our Burning Question.

Burning Question: can work shift from being labour to becoming a way of life?

Can work be a way to life?

It is a vital principle of the approach adopted here – as well as the basis for the dynamic work of the present authors – that all Four Worlds need, integrally, connecting together. At this point we have identified that the technological break-through of the internet has reconstituted and deepened social relations, at the same time as freeing us to engage in a much more fluid and, potentially, sustaining range of material and immaterial communities. The internet is assisting in the navigation to novel forms of work and labour value. The big question that emerges, therefore, is whether or not, under these conditions, can work shift from being a way *of* life towards a way *to* life?

According to Italian political activist Antonio Negri and his American activist and academic colleague, Michael Hardt (1), in the final decades of the 20th century industrial labour lost its hegemony and emerged as "immaterial labour". Such "post-Fordist" labour created immaterial products, as knowledge, information, and communication. In fact, these can be conceived of in two principle forms. *The first form refers to labour that is primarily intellectual, involving problem solving, symbolic and analytical tasks*, producing ideas, codes, images. *The other form is "affective labour"*. For example, as represented in the work of those – such as legal assistants, flight attendants, fast food workers – who offer service with a smile.

Much immaterial labour combines both intellectual and affective work. Nor is it, in fact, more significant, in purely numerical terms, than agricultural or industrial work. But, Hardt and Negri argue that immaterial labour has become *hegemonic*, in aspirational and normative senses. It is the standard by which all other labour is judged, in the 21st century. In this way every farmer must, also, be a geneticist, soil scientist, meteorologist and financial analyst. And, in so doing, we see a shift from Capitalism functioning to organise labour of the hand-and-eye to being able to extract value from the brain-and-psyche.

The information revolution

For Spanish-French sociologist Manuel Castells (2), the final quarter of the 20th century paved the way for the shift from late-industrialism to 'informationalism,' in the 21st. Three movements coincided from the late 1960s which brought about the rapidity of this transition. These were the IT revolution, the fiscal crisis of the state (and monopoly Capitalism) and the rise of cultural movements, such as feminism, environmentalism and the dominance of media-focused libertarianism. What emerged were crucial changes to society, economy and culture. Mass society became *network society*.

Post-industrial economies became a single global-informational economy. And, cultures morphed into a cyber-space of 'real virtuality'.

The problem of network society lies in its interaction with the development of 'self-identities'. The lived spaces of most people's experiences become discrete locales, which are fragmented from one another, whilst global elites increasingly become 'nowhere people', flitting between spaces of representation that have no direct significance as communities of identity. In such a world, as Castells indicates, a new politics of cultural identity is required, allowing the solidarist values of communities to enable mutual support, alongside distinctive development paths.

It is part of the work of the current authors to support the emergence of such cultural indigeneity. Equally, we recognise that, if the global exogenous pursuit of ever-greater information networking is not integrated with the needs of localities, the effect is little more than the extraction of value from communities, to serve the wealth and power accumulation of elites. As such, it is vital that a diverse network of 'communiversities' is generated to capture the linkage between indigenous, communal knowledge and exogenous, global network society. The beginnings of these are being constructed out of what is coming to be understood as *wikinomics*.

A newly emergent form of business

According to Canadian management consultants Tapscott & Williams (3), wikinomics is based on four powerful new ideas: openness, peering, sharing, and acting globally. *Openness* is associated with candor, transparency, freedom, flexibility, expansiveness, engagement, and access. The quintessential example of peering, as we saw above, is Linux. The basic rules of operation, therein, are as different from corporate command-and-control as the latter was from feudal operations. Peering succeeds because it leverages self-organisation. Through *sharing* smart firms are treating intellectual property like a mutual fund – they manage a balanced portfolio of IP assets, some protected, some shared. *Acting globally* means specifically tapping into a global talent pool. These four principles – openness, peering, sharing and acting globally, increasingly define how 21st-century corporations compete and, also, collaborate.

Wikipedia is, obviously, the primary exemplar of this new way of working and value creation. It is a brilliant example of how the Web is helping to transform the realm of science into an increasingly open and collaborative endeavour characterised by:

- the rapid diffusion of best practice techniques and standards
- the stimulation of new technological hybrids
- the availability of increasingly powerful tools for conducting research
- faster positive feedback cycles from public knowledge to private enterprise, through industry-university collaboration
- increasingly horizontal distributed models of research and innovation.

The global collaborative environment

We are shifting, according to Tapscott therefore, from closed and hierarchical workplaces with rigid employment relationships to increasingly self-organised, distributed and collaborative human capital networks that draw knowledge and resources from inside and outside the firm.

Having travelled across the collaboration economy we have discovered that there are several new models that companies can harness for greater competitiveness and growth:

- peer producers apply open source principles to create products made of bits – from operating systems to encyclopedias
- ideagoras give companies access to a global marketplace of ideas
- prosumer communities can be an incredible source of innovation
- the New Alexandrians are ushering in a new model of collaborative science
- platforms for participation create a global stage where large communities of partners can create value
- global plant floors harness the power of human capital across borders
- Wiki workplaces increase innovation and improve morale.

Wikinomic design principles, for Tapscott and Williams as such:

- take cues from lead users
- build critical mass
- supply an infrastructure for collaboration
- take time out to get the structures and governance right
- make sure all participants can harvest some value
- abide by community norms
- let the process evolve
- hone the collaborative mind.

In this way we are beginning to see signs that work – under the conditions of navigating new technological possibilities – is shifting labour from a way *of* life towards a new kind of collaborative, communal and integral way *to* life. This is, further, reflected in recent work by the eminent anthropologist David Graeber (4). He comments that:

> "We could though easily arrange matters in such a way that pretty well everyone on earth lives in relative ease and comfort. In material terms this would not be difficult. Improvements in robotics combined with advances in materials science are ushering in an age where a very large proportion of the most dreary and tiresome mechanical tasks can indeed be eliminated. What this means is that work, as we know it, will less and less resemble what we think as "productive" labour, and more and more resemble "caring" labour – since, after all, productive labour consists mainly of the sorts of things most of us would least like to see done by a machine."

The challenge is to re-design work, along the lines that Tapscott and Williams suggest to make the connection between open, peering, shared and global work that is, in essence, "caring labour". We now turn to our Window on 'northern' Wisdom.

Window into Wisdom: how the immaterial materialises

Returning to vocation post-resurrection – living to work

There are a number of strange and, apparently, contradictory aspects about the final chapter of John's Gospel. The resurrected Lord eats a fish breakfast on the beach with his disciples, even though his material body seems able to appear and disappear at will. There is an immaterial basis to his labour. The disciple whom Jesus loved, presumably John (meaning 'beloved'), never names himself. His work is to simply 'be loved'. The three denials of Jesus by Peter – before the crucifixion – are replaced by three callings to 'feed My lambs' and 'take care of and feed My sheep'. Peter's labour is to be one in which he becomes the first person of a newly networked society, despite his obvious lack of capacity to do so.

Back to the future – of vocation

But, perhaps, the strangest anomaly of all is that in the light of Jesus' previous resurrection appearances the Galilean disciples have simply gone back to their old way of working life as fishermen. This will not, of course, be the end of the story. Even so, it is the nature of post-resurrection labour that we simply get on with the normal work of life, even though even the laws of the Universe have changed, in the light of Christ's resurrection.

Actually, the work is transformed, too. During the night Peter goes out to fish but catches nothing (21:3). At dawn, an unknown visitor appears on the beach and tells them to throw the net to the 'right side' (the side of friendship). The net almost breaks with the haul of fish; indeed it should, but it holds. They recognise that it is the Lord.

The immaterial materialises

The disciples are called to bring some of the fish to cook for breakfast. They do so but find that Jesus already has a fire lit with fish on the coals. He had fished before them, apparently. There is something about the whole event that turns them speechless with awe, apart from the fact that this is their Master, returned from the dead! The point is that immaterial work has become material food. There seems to be a wrapping together of work and love that is quite revolutionary.

Jesus doesn't ask them to give up their ordinary work. Instead, he shows them that its fruit is to be used to draw together a people who love one another, even in the midst of work. This is the labour of a mysterious networked society. In it they have been navigated, by the Lord's method of vocational reworking, to find Him at the centre of their labour. Much later, St Paul, who, also, never gave up his work as a tentmaker, despite the immensity of his missionary activity, would write to the church at Colossae: "And whatever you do, whether in word or deed, do it all in the name of the Lord Jesus, giving thanks to God the Father through him" (Colossians 3:17). In the networked society of the new economics of the Kingdom of God work is a source of thanksgiving, because it is a way *to* life, the life of the beloved. This brings us onto Linux, in Linus Torvalds' – Finnish founder of Linux – own words.

Social Theory: open source – work as liberation

Art and engineering: creating a world

I'm personally convinced that computer science has a lot in common with physics. Both are about how the world works at a fundamental level. The difference, of course, is that while in physics you are supposed to figure out how the world is made up, in computer science you create the world. If you're good enough you can be God, on a small scale. You get to create your own world. It is a combination of art and engineering, an exercise in creativity. You can do anything you want, but as you add complexity, you have to be careful not to create something that is inconsistent, within the world you have created. For it to be beautiful it can't contain flaws. In 1992 Linux graduated from being mostly a game to something that had become integral to people's lives, their livelihoods, commerce. A hacker named Orest Zborowski created a socket interface for Linux, which not only enabled us to have windows, but also to network with other computers. Networking, though, is a complicated business, and it ended up taking us two years to get it right. Yet, by the fall of 1992, tens of thousands of people were participating, voluntarily, in our news group, and I emerged as the leader (4).

I never planned to be a leader

Just as I never planned for Linux to have a life outside my own computer, I also never planned to be the leader. It just happened by default. At some point a core group of five developers started generating most of the ideas in the key areas of development. It made sense for them to serve as the filters and hold the responsibility for maintaining those areas. The best leaders, I discovered, enable others to make decisions for them. Otherwise the Linux development model would never have become an intricate web of hundreds of thousands of participants, with maybe 4,000 projects being undertaken at any one time. Hackers, in fact, working on Linux and other open source projects, forgo sleep because they love programming. And they love being part of a global collaborative effort – Linux was the world's largest collaborative project – dedicated to building the best and most beautiful technology that is available to anyone who wants it. And it is fun.

Letting go – open source is for free

If you try and make money by controlling a resource, you'll eventually find yourself out of business. This is a form of despotism, and history overflows with examples of its ill effects.

What was inspired by ideology has proved itself as technology and is working in the marketplace. The theory behind open source is simple. In the case of an operating system the source code – the programming instructions underlying the system – is free. Anyone can improve it, change it, and exploit it. But these improvements, changes, and exploitations have to be made freely available. The project belongs to no one and everyone. When a project is opened up there is rapid and continuous improvement. With teams of contributors working in parallel, the results can happen far more successfully than work being conducted behind closed doors. And when the money rolls in, as numerous value-added services are introduced, people get convinced. One of the least understood pieces of the open source puzzle is how many good programmers would deign to work for absolutely no money.

Open source driven by passion

Folks do their best work, at least in a society where survival is more or less assured, when they are driven by a passion, and having fun. This is as true for playwrights and sculptors (we would add here teachers and students) as it is for entrepreneurs and software engineers. The open source model gives people the opportunity to live their passion. Science was originally viewed as something dangerous, subversive and anti-establishment – basically how software companies sometimes view open source. And just as science wasn't born out of an effort to undermine the religious establishment, open source was not conceived in order to detonate the software establishment. It is there to produce the best technology and to see where it goes.

Science, on its own moreover, does not make money. It has been the secondary effects that create wealth. The same goes for open source.

It allows the creation of secondary industries that challenge established businesses. Like science itself, open source's secondary effects are endless. By not controlling the technology you are not limiting its uses. People use it as a launching pad for their own products and services. People don't quibble with the need for free speech. It is a liberty that people have defended with their lives. And the same is true of openness. It's a difficult stand to take, but it actually creates more stability in the end.

We now turn from information technology, most especially the case of Linux, specifically, to social science more generally, in this case drawing on both a legal and communications perspective, which, as we shall see, serves to interlink the 'north' and the 'south', through the *Wealth of Networks*.

The wealth of communications networks

An alter-modern networked information society

For legal scholar Yochai Benkler (5), Berkman Professor of Entrepreneurial Legal Studies at Harvard Law School, takes on from where Torvalds has left off.

what characterizes the newly emerging networked information economy is that decentralised individual action – carried out through radically distributed, nonmarket mechanisms, plays a much greater role than it did, or could have, in the industrial information economy.

The wealth of past-present-future networks, then, is offered as a challenge to contemporary liberal democracies, and autocracies, alike. *We are in the midst of a technological, economic and organisational transformation*, for Benkler, *that allow us to renegotiate the terms of freedom, justice and productivity in the past-future information society*. How we shall live in this new environment will in some significant measure depend on policy choices we make, in the 'north' and in the 'south', in the next decade or so.

An economic policy, allowing yesterday's winners, whether Microsoft in America or Anglo-American in Africa, to dictate the terms of tomorrow's economic competition, for Benkler, would be disastrous, in the U.S. as well as in Zimbabwe, though the policy choices are somewhat different in each case. So what does this imply for both parts of the world generally, 'north' and 'south', if not also, say, for Chinyika and Linux more specifically?

Information production and innovation

The potential break from the past 150 years, while simultaneously reaching back to millennia before, is masked by the somewhat liberal use of the term "information economy" in various permutations since the 1970s. While often evoked as parallel to the "post-industrial " age, in fact, the information economy, whether mediated by a Nokia in Finland or by Econet in Zimbabwe, was tightly linked throughout the 20th century with controlling the processes of the industrial economy. This is clearest in the case of accounting firms and financial markets, but is true of the industrial corporations, and of organising of cultural production as well. Hollywood in America, for example, and the American broadcast networks, like indeed the Zimbabwean one, as well as the recording industry, as a whole, were built around the physical production model.

Because of its focus around capital-intensive production and distribution techniques, this initial development stage may best be thought of as the "industrial information economy". *Radical decentralisation of intelligence in our communication networks and the centrality of information, knowledge, culture and ideas to advanced economic activity are leading to a new stage of this information economy, the networked information economy.* Whereas the former is structure building the latter veers toward structure changing. Indeed such a networked, though somewhat less information intensive, society and economy, was meanwhile characteristic of indigenous societies of old.

The low tech-high touch version

We maintain therefore, that *the Chinyika phenomenon we have witnessed* (see Chapter 2) *in Zimbabwe is a "low tech-high touch" version of the same network information economy as that we see in high-tech Silicon Valley.* Economic and social history, as such, is cyclical as well as linear, non-linear as well as progressive. Both American and Zimbabwean versions, ideally and ultimately in combination, hold out the possibility of reversing two trends, for Benkler: concentration and commercialisation. In the process we would be revisiting the preindustrial old as well as proclaiming the post-industrial, and ultimately, altogether and necessarily between them, advancing the "alter-modern" case. In other words, America cannot fully advance, in this networked informational sense, economically and socially, as it were, unless Zimbabwe does. In an alter-modern" world, modern needs traditional and vice versa.

More specifically, then, *in the "north" widespread co-operative networks of volunteers write the software and standards that run most of the Internet and enable what we do with it. In the "south" innumerable villagers, combined with selected extension workers, provide self sufficiency for tens of thousands, without any of them having jobs.* Potentially, moreover, the two could combine together to enhanced "high-tech, high touch" mutual effect, economically and socially, scientifically and economically, naturally and ultimately culturally.

When information production meets computer network

Take the example of music as an expression of culture, for example for Benkler, in the 19th century in America. Then it was largely a relational good, and still is in rural Zimbabwe today. It was, in the US, and is today in Chinyika, something people did in the physical presence of each other: in the folk way through hearing, repeating and improvising; in the middle-class way of buying sheet music for guest or attending public performances; or in the upperclass way by hiring musicians. Capital is and was widely distributed amongst musicians, for example in the form of marimba instruments in rural Zimbabwe, or geographically dispersed music scores amongst performing orchestras in urban America. With the introduction of the phonograph, a new, more passive relationship to music was made possible, in urban areas and in industrialised countries, together with a reliance on the high-capital requirements of recording, copying, and distributing recorded music.

As computers became more music-capable and digital networks became ubiquitously available, in the 'north' we saw the emergence of the present conflict between regulation of cultural production – the law of copyright – between the 20th-century industrial model recording industry and the emerging amateur distribution systems coupled, at least according to its supporters, to a reemergence of decentralised, relation-based markets for professional performance artists. In fact the latter case would be more analogous to rural Zimbabwe today, socially, and to the elite suburbs, technically. The question now remains as to how the two "a-industrial" models might be healthily combined?

Commons based peer production

At the heart of this new-old economic engine, of the world's most evolved (in the end, as per the American 20th-century poet T.S. Elliot, is the beginning) economies, we are beginning to notice a persistent and quite amazing phenomenon. A new model of production has taken root, not dissimilar to the very old; one that should not be there, at least according to our widely held, industrialised beliefs about economic behaviour. It should not – the intuitions of the late-20th-century Americans, as indeed the "modern" political or business cadres in Zimbabwe, would say – be the case that thousands of volunteers would come together to collaborate on a complex economic project. And yet this is precisely what is happening in the software world, on the one hand, and in Chinyika on the other. What then, we are asking here, if the two came together?

Free software as per Linux, like food security as per Chinyika,
does not rely on markets or on managerial hierarchies to organise
production

Programmers, like Chinyika villagers, do not generally participate in a project because someone who is their boss told them to, though some do.

Neither group generally participate in a project because someone offers them a price to do so, though some participants do focus on long-term appropriation through money-oriented activities, like consulting or service contracts in San Francisco, on the one hand, and rapoko for sale to food processors in Harare, on the other. What we have, then, is two kinds of related stories which have yet to be fully interwoven.

Free open-source software

The story of Chinyika (Chapter 2), on the one hand as we have seen, in Zimbabwe, started in the new millennium, instigated by Muchineripi and Kada, and continues to unfold. The story of free software began in America twenty years before then, in 1984, when Richard Stallman started work on a project of building a non-proprietary operating system which he called GNU. Stallman, then at MIT, operated out of political conviction, whereas Muchineripi, and Kada, through BTD (Business Training and Development), operated out of human conviction: *Uri Munhu Here.*

Stallman wanted a world in which software enabled people to use information freely; Muchineripi and Kada wanted a world in which their people respected their own culture, while being open to others, and thereby had food to eat. *These freedoms to share and make your own software, and foodstuffs, respectively, are fundamentally incompatible with a model of production that relied on property rights and markets.* In that respect, free software was at the more immaterial end of production, whereas agricultural produce is relatively – only relatively – more at the material end.

The next major step came in the 'north' when a person with a more practical, rather than prophetic, approach to his work began developing one central component of the operating system – the kernel. Linus Torvalds, as we have seen, began sharing the early implementations of his kernel, called Linux, with others, under GPL. These ultimately 60,000 others then modified, added, contributed and shared among themselves these pieces of the operating system. Building on top of Stallman's foundation, Torvalds crystallised a model of production that was fundamentally different from those that preceded it. Now we turn, with Benkler, specifically to the economics of social production.

The economics of social production

The increasing salience of non-market production in general, and peer production in particular, for him, raises three puzzles from an economics perspective. First, why do people participate? What is their motivation when they work for or contribute resources to a project for which they are not paid or directly rewarded? Second, why now? Third, for us then, what is special about the digitally networked environment, set against the backdrop of a rural community like Chinyika, that would lead Benkler and ourselves to believe that peer production is hear to stay as an important phenomenon, as opposed to am alter-modern fad that will pass, or pre-modern practice that will fade?

Of course, economically speaking, Smith and Marx still have their foundational part to play, albeit, always for us, building upon prior, particular origins. At the same time, we need to see that the material conditions of production in the networked information economy have been transformed, just as those in communal food production have maintained their relevance, both in ways that increase the relative salience of social sharing and exchange, as per 'uri munhu here", as a modality of economic production.

Social production in a digitally networked environment

There is a curious congruence, therefore, between what has happened, socially and economically before and what is occurring now. Both the Chinyika and the Linux phenomenon are still considered somewhat peripheral to software and food production, as per the market mainstream. A Microsoft on the one hand or a Monsanto on the other both remain better known to the business and economic mainstream. And yet, *sharing is everywhere around us in the old-new economy. Social production of goods and services, both public and private*, as illustrated in italics below, *is ubiquitous, though largely unnoticed*, as we often find when explaining the Chinyika phenomenon to potential sponsors. It sometimes substitutes for, and sometimes complements, market and state production everywhere.

The capital cost of effective economic action in the industrial economy shunted sharing to the economic peripheries – to households in the advanced economies, and to communities in pre-industrial ones. *The emerging restructuring of capital investment in communal and digital networks are at least partly reversing, and indeed simultaneously resurrecting, history.*

The political economy of property and commons

In this sense, for Benkler moreover, the emergence of this old-new set of technical, economic, social and institutional relations can increase the relative role that each individual is able to play in authoring his or her own life. At a more foundational level of collective understanding, *the shift from an industrial towards a simultaneously pre-industrial and post-industrial networked information economy increases the extent to which individuals can become active participants in producing their own cultural environment.* It opens the possibility, moreover, as pre and post-industrial societies meet, of a more critical and reflective indigenous and exogenous culture.

Better access to knowledge, then, and the emergence of less capital-dependent forms of productive social organisation offer the possibility that the emergence of the networked information economy will open up opportunities for improvement in economic justice, on scales both global and local. In these two great domains of life – production and consumption, work and play, the networked information economy, for Benkler, promises to enrich individual autonomy substantively by creating an environment built less around control and more around facilitating action, as we see in our rural Zimbabwean case. We now turn to our culminating 'northern' Illustrative Cases.

Illustrative Cases: effecting new directions for work and society

Wikinomics in practice

In the ten years since *Wikinomics* was first published a plethora of businesses have sought to capitalise on the 'power of We' in creatively destroying old business models through collaborative working. In 2010 Tapscott and Williams produced their sequel to the original book, *MacroWikinomics – rebooting business and the world*, in which they showed how the collaboration technologies that they outlined in the earlier volume were being accessed by educationists, research institutions and the media, together with government and social movements. Here are some examples from the sectors of education, research and the media of how *wikinomics* has evolved to 'reboot the world'.

Education: communities of practice (CoPs)

Communities of practice are as old as the tribe learning how to survive in a hostile world. But, collaborative web-based technologies have given the concept of co-operative enquiry a stimulus for a new era. As the Wenger-Trayners (6) put it:

> *Communities of practice are groups of people who share a concern or a passion for something they do and learn how to do it better as they interact regularly.*

Although some early examples of IT-based models of interactive professional learning domains were disappointing, the range of more recent synchronous and asynchronous collaboration tools have meant such CoPs have spread beyond conventional educational facilities to learning hubs in many organisations, policy fields and Government. At the same time, the internet is full of so-called forums which are empty of people. So, the technology doesn't guarantee a fruitful community, but it can enhance what is meant by 'community' to include distant participants, who may be as engaged in shared learning as those in the next door classroom.

Research institutions – mass scientific collaboration

Mass collaborations on science projects, which involve professional scientists, members of the public and, even, college and school-children began at the turn of the Millennium. Some of the earliest examples were projects such as SETI@home and Folding@home, both concerned to involve mass society in iconic space experiments. It was recognised that thousands of amateur scientists were motivated to lend not only their computing power but their intellectual capital to large-scale scientific studies as a way of participation beyond making a simple donation of money.

The power of networking tens of thousands of home computers together, alongside the intellectual abilities of their owners, has been transformative for many scientific enquiries. The FightAIDS@home project was revolutionary in both maximising the brain-power that could be utilised to tackle the health issue, but it, also, mobilised thousands more volunteers in public health awareness campaigns (7).

The Media – the irresistible rise of citizen journalism

There is an argument that states that journalism has come full circle with the rise of citizen reporting. Akbar held an assembly in the 16th-century Indian Mughal Court, where common people were allowed to put forward their views on how they should be governed. Indeed, it was only in the mid-19th-century that journalism came to be regarded as a Fourth Estate, a century after newspapers were first created.

Now, sites such as *HuffPost* and millions of personal blogposts attract far more viewing time than conventional newspapers. Crowd-sourced citizen journalism and the fact that most citizens have a smart phone in their pocket, capable of sending instantaneous images from every part of the globe to a media-hungry world of rolling news, means that standard media outlets rely on non-conventional sources for first-point coverage. This has not meant that professional journalism has died. Rather, it has transmuted from instantaneous news-gathering – except in the most dangerous and challenging circumstances – to second-order editorialising and a third-order commentariat.

This irresistible transition has also given way to an era of 'fake news', as indicated previously by Benkler. Indeed, leading politicians are not immune from either portraying opponents as purveyors of false-hoods at the very moment when they are, themselves, retweeting the most highly dubious material. The point is that the media has become an estate for democratic engagement at the same time as global corporations have been able to use their eye-watering resources to monopolise the distribution of 'official sources'. For some, new revenue streams have been created that give voice to intelligent citizens. But, far too often, the forces of global social media have been utilised to encourage a world of misinformation, non-news and crowd-surfing lies. What is clear is that the citizen journalism genie will not go back into the media mogul's lamp.

Conclusion

We have now completed our 'northern' journey, from grounding to effect, from the Czech Republic to Finland, through passing Zimbabwe and indeed America on the way. Our focus, as such, has been on social research-and-innovation, and on science and technology in relation to such, and on reconstituting work as life in the process. We now finally turn from 'north' to 'west', from liberating work to democratising it, starting in the UK, with *the economics and politics of "virtue"*.

Bibliography

1 Hardt, M. and Negri, A. (2005) *Multitude: War and Democracy in the Age of Empire*. London: Penguin Books.
2 Castells, M. (2000) *End of Millennium*. Oxford: Wiley-Blackwell.
3 Tapscott, D. and Williams, A. (2007) *Wikinomics – How Mass Collaboration Changes Everything*. New York: Portfolio Press.
4 Graeber, D. (2018) *Bullshit Jobs – A Theory*. London: Allen Lane.
5 Torvalds, L. and Diamond, D. (2011) *Just for Fun: Story of an Accidental Revolutionary*. New York: Harper Paperbacks.
6 Benkler, Y. (2006) *The Wealth of Networks: How Social Production Transforms Markets and Freedom*. London: Yale University Press.
7 Wenger-Trayner, E. and Wenger-Trayner, B. (2015) *Communities of Practice – A Brief Introduction*. [Available at: http://wenger-trayner.com/wp-content/uploads/2015/04/07-Brief-introduction-to-communities-of-practice.pdf. Last accessed: December 4, 2017].
8 Rinaldi, A.C. (2009) Science Wikinomics – Mass Networking Through the Web Creates New Forms of Scientific Collaboration. *European Molecular Biology Organization Reports* 10(5): 439–43, July.

Part V

West

Transforming employment: self,
enterprise and new community

14 Post-liberalism

Transformed workplaces to blockchain distribution

POST-LIBERAL GROUNDING
EMERGENT DIVIDEND
CITIZEN'S NAVIGATION
ULTIMATE EFFECT

Introduction: work, new technology and the proliferation of blockchains

The limitations of the two liberalisms

We finally turn from the technologically laden 'north' to a 'west' where economics and finance occupy pride of place, and where "self employment", and enterprise, today social as well as economic, are the prevailing order of our day. Indeed, one of the more recent champions of such, California's Tom Peters (1), renowned for going *in Search of Excellence*, in the 1980s, pointed out that such excellence is originally based on the ancient Greek, *arête*, meaning "virtue". For Peters, this especially involved, a bias for action and the pursuit of adhocracy. Little was he aware, then, that, for fellow westerners, Millbank and Pabst (2), over three decades later, the *Politics of Virtue* would take on a completely different meaning. As such, they serve to reground the "west", thereby following, rather than leading, the "west", this being a keynote of our approach to recognising and releasing GENE-ius.

John Millbank, an emeritus Research Professor of Religion, Politics and Ethics at Nottingham University, and Director of their Centre for Theology and Philosophy, and Adrian Pabst, Reader in Politics at the University of Kent, both based in in the UK, *propose a newly mutualist approach to both domestic and foreign affairs that substitutes for the dominance of market, state and technocracy the primacy of society, culture and interpersonal relationships*, in this chapter culminating with the potential offered by blockchains. Interestingly enough moreover, Pabst, himself originally German and a Catholic, is based in Canterbury, home ground to the Anglican Church, which will feature, in a manner of speaking, in this chapter's journey's end.

The metacrisis of liberalism

The triumph of liberalism today brings out more and more the "war of all against all" (Hobbes) and the idea of man as a self-owning animal (Locke). Just as liberal thought has redefined human nature as fundamentally individual existence abstracted from social embeddedness, so too *liberal practice has replaced the quest for reciprocal recognition and mutual flourishing with the pursuit of wealth, power and pleasure – leading to economic instability, social disorder and ecological devastation.* The only possible alternative, for Millbank and Prabst, is a post-liberal politics of virtue that seeks to fuse greater economic justice with social reciprocity.

To that extent (see Chapters 3 and 4), they are linking their 'west' back to our 'south', by way of grounding. So *faced with what they consider to be a double failure of post-war "embedded liberalism", which nationalised the economy and the neo-liberal model that privatised the state, they argue for a new settlement,* not unlike that of Rudolph Steiner (see Chapter 8), *both centred on association and mutualisation.*

Towards a post-liberal workplace and democracy

According to 18th-century Neapolitan "civil economist" Antonio Genovesi, as indicated in Chapter 3, virtue is not an invention of philosophers but instead a consequence of the nature of the world. By contrast, ever since the dawn of modernity, liberalism has privileged vice, egoism and selfishness, also then engendering an ever-spiralling ecological and social crisis. How then might what they term "post-liberalism" *transform our polity and the workplace?* This is our Burning Question. For our Window into Wisdom we turn "Westwards" to Matthew's gospel. Thereafter, we turn to the Social Theory of "post-liberalism", and finally, as illustrations of such in the workplace, we turn to the proliferation of blockchains.

Burning Question: how is technology transforming work-and-polity?

Given both the crises and contradictions of liberalism and capitalism indicated above, we ask whether or not the new technology of the blockchain might be able to able to rescue democracy, as a genuine popular, civil society movement? A key point of contemporary Liberalism, as Millbank and Prabst contend, is that, in its procedural logic and immateriality, it has lost both the values of a soul and, also, a direct connection to the human subject. In their call for cultural workers to be guided by a 'realisation of the good' they are looking for ways in which a broad politics of the common good can overcome the binaries that divide Western culture.

In a direct challenge to this polarisation of the West some are beginning to argue that the new technologies emerging in the financial world can be better diverted to engender a new politics of the connected worker. These are based in what is known as the blockchain and the potential for cyber-democracy. The point of considering the possibilities for new technology to transform democratic systems and, indeed, the extension of worker rights, is to address the sorts of centralising and authoritarian tendencies of liberalism, and its detractors, suggested above.

What is the blockchain and how does it work?

The pseudonymous technologist Satoshi Nakomoto created the blockchain protocol around 2007, at the start of the latest large-scale financial crisis affecting western economies. He developed the technology in order to found a new distributed currency that was not based-on or linked to the creation of money by central and wholesale banking. That was bitcoin. Since then a wide range of technologists have adopted the principles of the blockchain to generate other forms of unique, non-copyable distributed information that can be applied, for example, to ways of democratic voting and the organisation of collaborative political and economic structures.

The blockchain, according to Don Tapscott (3) (of *Wikinomics* fame), whose work we considered in the previous chapter, is "an incorruptible digital ledger of economic transactions that can be programmed to record not just financial transactions but virtually everything of value." If we use the analogy of Google.docs we get an idea of how blockchain protocols operate. Instead of the conventional iterative approach for updating documents, all parties can work on them at the same time, with full view of all changes being made. When these are shared with a large number of people, all with simultaneous viewing and editing rights, you create something that looks like a blockchain.

The process of the blockchain works by mutual verification of 'transactions', across a distributed network of computers, which are verified by algorithms within the network. If someone requests a transaction it is broadcast to a peer-to-peer (P2P) network of nodes (computers and domains). A known algorithmic identifier validates the user and the transaction is verified. This is added to the blocks of other such transactions, to create a ledger of blocks, in a chain – hence the blockchain. The record of the blocks in the chain is permanent and unalterable and, so, the transaction is completed. If this process is repeated thousands or, even, millions of times, a complex chain of distributed network transactions is created, whereby the chain of value is shared across the entire network, with no central regulation. Regulation is performed by algorithms within the network, as with bitcoin "mining", whereby new algorithms need to be found, in order to add to the transactions. The relative difficulty of this 'mining' process renders an increase in the value of the transactions, in this case for a crypto-currency.

Creating crypto-democracy

As Allen et al have recently shown (4) blockchains are being deployed beyond digital currencies to legal services, smart contracts and the operation of government. They are also being used to create distributed autonomous organisations and in industries such as agriculture, retail, media services and the energy sector, alongside financial services (as we see in the Illustrative Cases in this chapter). But, it is in the sphere of enabling citizen-level policy-making, addressing the crisis in liberal democracies, that these disruptive technologies hold greatest appeal for transforming the capacities of ordinary voters to participate in relevant, crypto-democracy institutions (5).

Within democratic systems there are equal and opposite threats to the orderly process of conducting elections and polls through 'disorder', such as electoral fraud, or 'dictatorship', such as vote-rigging or the failure of public bodies to maintain an accurate voter registry. Followmyvote.com claims to be the most efficient decentralised voting system, which reduces the potential for disorder whilst removing the voting system from centralised systems that could engage – wittingly or through accident – in dictatorship. This opens the field to a range of potential new democratic institutions to form, which may compete in establishing political programmes that avoid the problems of liberal, western statutory apparati.

Could 'quadratic voting' have avoided Brexit, Trump or the closure of many company facilities?

One such potential institutional solution lies in the development of 'quadratic voting' (QV). A major problem of the standard democratic model of 'one person, one vote' (opov) is that there can be a tyranny of an uncommitted majority. Opov does not account for differences in the degree to which voting preferences are held. The solution proposed by QV is that those who have a stronger preference regarding an issue can 'trade' votes on their issue against votes on other issues, using the blockchain.

Although early models, to combat problems of Pareto-optimisation inefficiency, relied on the use of actual currency transactions, thus disadvantaging poorer voters, more sophisticated models utilise the power of alternative preferencing. This could mean that multiple public policy votes could be co-ordinated together. For example, if I feel five times as strongly about Brexit I can trade against voting on an additional four other single issues. By using a blockchain algorithm, large numbers of preprogrammed preferences could be simultaneously traded, on the platform, to produce complex patterns of voter preference.

In this way it is possible, for example, that some of the 'left-behinds' issues that triggered support for Brexit in the UK, and Trump in the US, could have been traded against other policy support for the protection of local worker-based industries. This will not, of course, solve all the problems of liberal western democracies. But, it could, with imagination, lead to a revitalisation of flagging political institutions and a reversal of the democratic deficit, often witnessed amongst working-class communities, that has been so toxic in respect of the rise of the Far Right in many western societies. The use of non-copyable distributed information systems, as means to simultaneous multiple voting, could pave a new way for democracy in many regions, not simply the liberal west. We now turn to the gospel of Matthew, in fact the most overtly Jewish of all four Evangelists, for his Window into Wisdom on how to turn work around, in order to enter into the realm of the Messiah.

Window into Wisdom: turning work around with the advent of the Messiah

Blessings from the Money-Man – Matthew 5:1–12

As we entered the final section of this book, we moved into what we call the Western Realm, of politics, economics and the operation of markets. We, also, turn, to the New Testament Gospel that is most concerned with these issues, namely, the Gospel of Matthew. Matthew was written and edited by the Evangelist and Apostle named Matthew or Bartholemew, who was a tax-gatherer and financier. He knew a great deal about money and finances, which is why there are forty-four specific references to money in his Gospel (six in Mark and twenty-two in Luke).

Following Matthew's opening genealogy of Jesus, his account of the infancy narratives (familiar Epiphany story of the Journey of the Magi) and the preparation for Jesus' appearance, by John the Baptist, Matthew declares that 'the kingdom of heaven has come near to you, so repent' (4:17). In other words, his disciples (μαθητής – mathetes) are to expect to have their lives transformed and turned around as they enter into the Messiah's realm, should they choose to learn how to follow his way. Then, Jesus gives his first block of teaching, conventionally known as the Sermon on the Mount (Chapters 5–7).

The blessings of kingdom-based work

The opening blessings (or beatitudes) of the sermon address the nature of God's action in the lives of disciples, which focus on issues of life, work, power and politics. Importantly, they are not addressed to individuals but people groups and communities, especially those who are experiencing some kind of affliction. Matthew's Jesus is utterly realistic about what life is like. At the same time, he states, unconditionally, that each community is blessed by God when they come close to the kingdom, through Jesus.

The eight people groups addressed are: the spiritually bankrupt (will enter God's kingdom); the bereaved (will be comforted); the humble (will inherit God's power); those longing for rights (will receive justice); carers (will be looked after); those who live transparently (will see God); peace-makers (are God's offspring); and the unjustly persecuted (will taste God's rule). In other words, Jesus points to the ways in which God's kingdom reverses "western" materialism, with the implication that those who do not come close – because they already have money, wealth, power, good jobs and local justice – will not be blessed, because they think they've already received everything that life is about.

Much of the remainder of the sermon strips away the self-righteousness of the rich, powerful and well to do. The fundamental message is that God's people are more realistic and able to make an honest appraisal of themselves. They seek to limit the power of their own egos, don't seek over-promotion, 'pad their CVs' or present as something they aren't. At the same time, these blessings are an excellent basis for a new civic democracy, where power is given to the weakest and where politics is genuinely about service. These are the libertarian values of Millbank and Prabst. They turn upside-down the economic and values that have come to dominate in Western markets. They also point beyond our political institutions to an even more indelible ledger of "goodness" than is contained within any blockchain.

Social Theory: a post-liberal world – working towards a politics of virtue

We now turn more generally to the "post-liberal" social theory, of "the politics of virtue", developed by UK-based academic theologian (Andrew Millbank) and political scientist (Adrian Pabst), the latter born and bred in Germany.

The rise and crisis of ultra-liberalism

Over the last fifty years, for Millbank and Pabst, *the left has advanced a sociocultural liberalism that promotes individual rights and equality of opportunity for self-expression, while the right has advocated an economic-political liberalism that champions the free market* liberated from the constricting shackles of the bureaucratic state. And starting with Bill Clinton in America, followed by Tony Blair in the UK, both liberalisms converged in the "new centre", and with it left and right.

"Liberalism", historically then, as a theory and as a political practice then is based on the primacy of the individual which cannot be separated in England from *the whig settlement in the 17th century combining the alienation of agricultural labour, and economic primacy of financial speculation, the commercialisation of landed power* and the professionalisation of politics. Liberalism as such, moreover, has been doubly promoted from the outset by both secularising hedonists and Christian Puritans – both of those unashamed of egoism as the basis of economic order.

By contrast then with England's John Locke (6) and J.S. Mill (7), French liberal thought, and historically the Italian civic economists, accentuated the social nature of man, the centrality of civil society and the role of political participation in fostering human fulfilment through civil duty. However, dislodging individuals from their fixed social positions of the *ancien regime* provided greater individual freedom and opportunity. So in terms of a general liberal logic, corporatist versions of such, as in France, are always unstable, threatened with corrosion. In fact those 19th-century liberals in France, like Tocqueville (8), and in Britain, like Gladstone, who tried bravely to channel liberalism in a more organicist direction, tended to produce a hybrid which was no longer exclusively liberal.

Liberalism and capitalism

Unadulterated liberalism, then, exhibits in all its variants an individualistic consistency and is truly defining of the most influential, specifically modern, political outlook. Insofar as this has been constantly qualified, it has not been fundamentally challenged by "alternative secular modernisms", Marxism of course being the exception. Rather it has been mainly qualified by religious perpetuations of older outlooks whose creative mutations (as in the case of evangelicalism or Catholic personalism) can be seen to be just as contemporary as the dominant "modern" norms of liberalism and secularity.

In truth, for Millbank and Prabst however, it politically produces man as basically pursuant of *amour proper* (self love) and "trucking advantage" as per Adam Smith (9), trying through educative and cultural processes of "civil society" (in a new and specific sense) to create subjects who are negatively choosing and self governing. They are relatively disembedded from family, locality, tradition and artisanal formation (and so from civil society as we would now more widely understand it in a more generic, older sense). As such they are reflected in Adam Smith's *homo economicus* in terms of the "propensity to trick, barter and exchange one thing for another".

As the Anglo-Hungarian economic anthropologist Karl Polanyi (10) argued, in the early part of last century, when the economic sphere is sequestered by this neutralising sleight of hand, that is once the managing of our material needs for production and exchange is sequestered from other aspects of social life – the symbolic, the ritual, the ethical and political – then what is seemingly natural becomes culturally fundamental. Yet only by cultural illusion, as such, do we imagine that this primacy of the spuriously "natural" belongs to human nature. Only modern economics then treats the biological as foundational for our cultural existence. And this was greatly accentuated in the 19th century through the Malthusian (11) view that one requires the threat of poverty and the spur of hunger in order to force people to work in a world of lazy sinfulness and constitutive material scarcity.

Statism trumps individualism

What one can then anachronistically but validly describe, then, as the "liberalism" of Hobbes (12) and Locke was concerned mainly with the freedom of inequitable property ownership. In consequence the revolutionary traditions have tended to be fixated on property, while demanding more egalitarian access to it. Even for them Marx (13) remained fixated on the rights-property-revolution triangle. In this way, from early on, the rise of the "free market" and of "polite society" nonetheless involved an unprecedented growth in the power of the central sovereign state. Economy and the political order were radically tied together, ever more so in the 19th and 20th centuries.

So economism itself returns full circle. *In that guise the free market*, for Millbank and Pabst moreover, *was always linked to an authoritarian state, a model that Margaret Thatcher would revive and extend*. As such, historically, a legal framework to undermine older corporate and guild privileges, together with the institutionalisation of depersonalised contacts, had been implemented. So what, for Millbank and Pabst, is the alternative?

Post-liberalism and the common good

Post-liberalism suggests that a more universal flourishing for all can be obtained when we continuously seek to define the goals of human society as a whole and then to discern the variously different and in themselves worthwhile roles that are required for the mutual achievement of these shared aims. Indissolubly linked to such is a search for the "moral economy" of the entire social order, aligned with the vertical need for virtuous leadership, and to horizontal mutual obligation.

In Catholic Social Thought (see Chapter 3), *it is with respect to work that we see the personal origin of all human society and culture, the manifestation of individual and unique character*. It requires equally the patient relating and sympathetic cooperation with fellow workers and clients. The same consideration, for Millbank and Pabst, applies to notions of equality. How can we decide to own things in common and divide up other goods equally if we do not know what constitutes the good?

Virtue, gift and community

Rescuing a talented few, they go on to say, from an abject human morass is hardly a radical objective, even if lowly born talent should rightly be recognised and encouraged to succeed. Rather, for them, whole families and communities need to be nurtured. Against then the impersonalism of liberal institutions and policies, post-liberals shift the emphasis to the "whole person" – the unity of body, mind and soul, embedded in a social order that is more basic than state or market and to which these necessary realities may be referred.

Against the abstract universalism of liberal ideology and its preference for the global and the virtual, post-liberals argue for the honouring of place, Chinyika for example (see Chapter 2). With the advance of history, of course, diverse communities get evermore entangled with each other. Yet the circumstance only augments a need to newly construct a situated complex shared identity, which never altogether loses touch with its origins. Indeed *both the political and the economic, as such, spring from the social, embedded in relationships of mutual trust and collective endeavour.* We now turn more specifically to the economy.

Heralding the capitalist crisis

In the late modern capitalist system so much depends on creating abstract wealth, according to Millbank and Pabst, that it is increasingly unable to generate productive capital and genuine goods serving human needs. One indication for this is that global finance uses other people's money to trade almost exclusively with itself (see also Chapter 16): *only 3% of assets today on UK banks' balance sheets are accounted for by deposits and lending to industry, while international foreign exchange is nearly 100 times the volume of commerce in goods and services.*

Under such financialisation, at the grassroots moreover, those in debt are socially disempowered and financially weakened as they find themselves shut out from the formal banking system and driven into the arms of loan sharks, thereby reduced to the biopolitics of people to "bare life". Thus we are facing a meta-crisis of capitalism, to which Stiegler (Chapters 11 and 12) has already alluded, where *the simultaneous processes of abstraction and materialisation subjects the real economy of productive activities to combined speculation and exacerbation of commodification.*

In summary, for Millbank and Pabst, capitalism differs fundamentally from a market economy in that it rests on a permanent process of "primitive accumulation" and financial speculation that undergirds its appropriative production and exchange. This *abstraction leads to the destruction of private and communal property in favour of paper money and ever greater levels of national debt* via public credit creation through collusion between the sovereign state and the moneyed interests.

Capitalism, inequality and inertia

Inherited wealth, moreover, combined with newly excessive salaries today represent a kind of continuity with the debased aristocracies of the previous *ancient regimes* and with the moguls of 19th- and 20th-century industries. This altogether reveals just *how little, over the long term, either revolution or redistribution or social rights have been able to temper the inegalitarian tendencies of the capitalist market.* In our own day, moreover, ownership and inheritance of urban and rural land, as well as financial resources, is once more assuming a disproportionate economic, social and political role – and here we see one aspect of incessant capitalist "materialisation".

The more the right to make money by any means is ethically legitimated, the more one is unleashing speculation as a power of material as well as symbolic destruction. *The long-term tendency of capitalism may then be towards not just increased inequality but also economic stultification and devastation of both cultural and natural ecological systems of interconnected and reciprocal balance.* For Millbank and Pabst then contemporary late capitalism now manifests a kind of meta-crisis that seems more to do with the difficulties of sustaining abstract growth as such, a growth for which any sum, even one extracted from material destruction rather than production, counts as "gain". Unlike a normal economy that binds material value to symbolic meaning, *the capitalist double movement of abstraction and materialisation tends to separate matter form meaning and reduce materiality to calculable numbers representing "wealth"*, as indeed Stiegler has pointed out. Such a conception of wealth rests on the aggregation of abstract numbers that cuts all the relational goods (see Chapter 3) and the "commons" (see previous chapter) on which shared prosperity depends.

Capitalism's founding amorality then, thereby as per Adam Smith's "invisible hand" aiming to magically distil public benefits out of private vices, was indeed a Faustian gesture. For, in Millbank and Pabst's words, *this new elixir is proffered by a Mephistophelean sub-demon who whispers in the ears of financial magi that abstraction might perpetually be made merely from the already abstract – making yet more money out of money.* Meanwhile, greater state debt also further exacerbates inequality, since government debt is upheld by wealthy bond-purchasers and benefits them alone. And only this vicious triangle allows a vicious circle to be constantly reinscribed around it.

Restoring the primacy of the social

Over time, it is arguably the case that nature combined with human labour, ingenuity and creative production can generate an almost infinite flow of finite resources that help mankind meet real needs and provide universal basic goods – food, shelter, health, education, friendship. Scarcity as such, for Millbank and Pabst, is something artificially engineered, as Douglas will reiterate below, by both monopoly capital and the fabrication of fake desires. *Such a myth of scarce resources rests ultimately on the perverse moral philosophy that we owe to Thomas Malthus. Surveying the deprivation and struggle of the destitute in England in the late 18th century from the comfit of his vicarage he denounced the greed of a "reckless rabble".*

As such this prurient low church Anglican clergyman wished to promote a bourgeois version of heroic virtue in reaction to the spur of natural and moral evil. This spur was, above all, *that of scarcity of resources, which was supposed to teach by fearful example the puritanical need for thrift, self-discipline and sexual continence.* Adam Smith indeed embedded his market in networks of social sympathy, but his embedding was limited by a double distrust. First, in the human ability to extend virtue beyond the "thick ties" of family relations and friendship, and second, in association, which he believed inevitably leads to corruption. *For Smith, both markets and states need to be amoral and neutral because only the pursuit of self interest can produce social benefit.*

Digital technologies promoting association or manipulation

In fact for Millbank and Pabst, *the era of "de-industrialisation" is, in reality, just the opposite. It is an era of further industrialisation, rationalisation and routinisation* even of the consumer, family and leisure existence to the extent that all these aspects of our lives are now systemically subject to control, calculation and the extraction of profit. This occurs most especially in the "service industries" of the "tertiary sector" which enclose ever more the once freely living "commons" as packageable commodities, thereby depriving us of many craft and social skills, rendering also the middle class more as component operators of prescribed digital systems than the working classes were mere tools, they say, of their machines. Hence, for Stiegler as we have seen, the continued advance of *proletarianisation.*

Yet, despite their poisonous potential, the new digital technologies also have a curative and improving function, as we shall see next.

Illustrative Cases: the proliferation of blockchains

The blockchain in potential and practice

Although most people associate the blockchain with crypto-currencies such as bitcoin, etherium and litecoins, distributed algorithmic information systems are being used by a wide variety of businesses in sectors as diverse as retail, agriculture and energy. We use this Illustrative Case to profile a few of these speculative operators and operations.

The retail blockchain

One of the most important uses of blockchain in the retail sector surrounds issues of supply chain verification and authenticity. *Provenance* has created a business offering consumers a way of tracking raw materials and entire products from primary producers to finished goods. They utilise a real time data platform, which enables customers to see exactly where a product has come from and what its journey through manufacture to retailer has been. There is an obvious benefit to producers who are seeking to demonstrate the transparency of their products, in terms of, for example, Fair Trade benefits to initial growers or to show that fish were harvested from sustainable stocks.

The ungoverned open-ledger nature of the blockchain ensures that such data cannot be tampered with en-route. A similar use is deployed by *Everledger*, who assigns a unique identifier to each asset deployed in the jewellery industry, to combat the trade in so-called 'blood diamonds', reduce counterfeiting and insurance fraud. The permanent ledger for each asset means that there is a register of all transactions, which is almost tamper-proof. As a result the company estimates that it can substantially reduce the £45BN that is lost as a result of insurance fraud, every year, across the US and Europe. *BlockVerify* offers a similar service, which they have extended beyond luxury good to pharmaceuticals and electronics, again utilising the power of unique algorithmic identifiers.

Blockchain in agriculture

Looked at from the other end of the supply chain farmers and growers are increasingly turning to blockchain provenance. They can use the power of distributed algorithms to authenticate their products and generate smart contracts that are viewable by third party clients and customers, in relation to global giants such as *Starbucks* and *Coca-Cola*. *FarmShare* is a fascinating example of the potential use of blockchain to both reduce the power of multinationals and, also, to create local self-sufficient economies. Shares in harvested crops will be electronically distributed to members. Cryptographic tokens are exchanged for deliveries of locally-grown organic products.

This is a way to generate collaborative labour-relations, alternative local economies (see Chapter 15) and community property ownership. Based on the idea of community-supported agriculture and biodynamic systems, first proposed by Rudolf Steiner and implemented most powerfully by *Sekem*, in Egypt, *FarmShare* is bringing this into the distributed technology of the 21st century, in upstate New York, as a pilot project. Although in its infancy, such models as *FarmShare*

are set to become major forces in agricultural transactions. They can reduce the exploitation of small rural producers, by giving them instantaneous access to real-time information on global trades and creating locally sustainable economies. At the same time, workers in all connected industries can share in the benefits of community-supported agriculture (CSA), as the 'workshare' component of CSA can be expanded to include workers engaged in such tasks as delivery, machinery repair and working within the cooperative.

Energy in the blockchain

The integration of blockchain technologies and smart metering systems is already beginning to be used to restore trust between consumers and energy suppliers. The blockchain offers energy companies a more efficient, secure and accurate way to manage supply, distribution and bill-paying, on a global scale, using smart contracts that are almost impossible to hack into. Whilst there are a few companies, such as *InviroHub* and *LO3 Energy* that are integrating smart metering and crypto-technology together this has yet to take-off.

Even so, the potential for changing the working practices of the energy companies is truly staggering. One of the most obvious efficiencies that blockchain offers is in terms of smart-metering. Direct recording of energy usage, to a utility metre feed into a blockchain, would allow 100% accuracy in billing, with no need for metre readings and estimates. Furthermore, the bill could be paid on the blockchain, thus obviating the need for bank transfer charges. Such a function is likely to become a feature of bill paying in a wide range of industries.

It is fair to say that use of the blockchain is right at the start of its operational life. The potential is far greater than the practice at this current moment, in 2018. But, there is little doubt that the use of digital, algorithm-based, distributed information systems is going to transform the working world. Their utilisation within collaborative economies can work to the advantage of local workers and consumers. Use of the network has the capacity to place individuals in a new controlling relationship with governments and multi-national corporations, thus shifting the power dynamics of liberal democracies and economies back towards the citizen. How extensive the blockchain revolution will become, only time will tell.

Conclusion

We entered the Western realm by way of the ancient Greek philosophy of 'virtue'. In this sense, whilst the "old West" may have led in the past it is now required to follow, in the 21st century. As many other economic systems lead in virtue, the West desperately needs to catch-up, to avoid ecological, social and political crises, connected to employment, as we have seen, in previous chapters.

Even so, technological changes, which are integrating many global systems, are beginning to ground a new economy in distributed information networks. These are, surprisingly, a possible route to new public virtue, via civil democracies that reverse the distribution of power and restoring the primacy of the social, as advocated by Millbank and Prabst. As we turn to considerations of how to fund new patterns of employing self and community, even within the West, we, first, consider the value of our identities in the emergent age of distributed networks. That is where we begin in Chapter 15.

Bibliography

1　Peters, T. and Waterman, R. (2004) *In Search of Excellence: Lessons from America's Best Run Companies*. New York: Profile Books.
2　Millbank, J. and Pabst, A. (2016) *The Politics of Virtue: Post-Liberalism and the Human Future*. London: Rowan & Littlefield.
3　Tapscott, D. and Tapscott, A. (2016) *Blockchain Revolution: How the Technology Behind Bitcoin Is Changing Money, Business and the World*. New York: Portfolio Books.
4　Allen, D.W.E. et al. (2017) The Economics of Crypto-Democracy. *SSRN*. 24 May. [Available at: https://ssrn.com/abstract=2973050].
5　Berg, C. (2017) Populism and Democracy: A Transaction Cost Diagnosis and a Crypto-democracy Treatment. *SSRN*. 18 November. [Available at: https://papers.ssrn.com/sol3/papers.cfm?abstract_id=3071930].
6　Locke, J. (1988) *Two Treatises of Government*. Cambridge: Cambridge University Press.
7　Mill, J.S. (1989) *On Liberty*. Cambridge: Cambridge University Press.
8　De Tocqeville, A. (2003) *Democracy in America*. London: Penguin Classics.
9　Smith, A. (2010) *The Wealth of Nations*. Oxford: Capstone.
10　Polanyi, K. (2002) *The Great Transformation: The Political and Economic Origins of Our Time*. New York: Beacon.
11　Malthus, J. (2015) *An Essay on the Principle of Population*. London: Penguin Classics.
12　Hobbes, T. (2017) *Leviathan*. London: Penguin Classics.
13　Marx, K. (1990) *Capital: Critique of Political Economy*. London: Penguin Classics.

15 Basic income
Valuing identity to people's fund

POST-LIBERAL GROUNDING
EMERGENT DIVIDEND
CITIZEN'S NAVIGATION
ULTIMATE EFFECT

Introduction: emerging identities and universal basic income

Spiritual foundations to basic income

We now turn, by way of "western" local-global emergence, following our overall regrounding in "virtue", to emerging developments over the past two centuries, in Europe and America, that have a direct bearing on economics and finance, in general, and on alternatives to employment in particular. We start by asking a Burning Question surrounding the *emergence of universal income in contemporary identity*. Following this, our Window into Wisdom considers the way in which Matthew's Gospel addresses universal provision through the 'feeding of the 5000', illustrating that universal welfare is a biblical principle.

In our main Social Theory overview we consider the backdrop to what is now termed *Basic Income*, (hinted at in Chapters 11 and 12) *Guild Socialism* and *Economic Democracy*. Finally, we introduce the case of experiments in Universal Basic Income (UBI) taking place across the globe, particularly in Finland. But, we turn first to the question of income and identity.

Burning Question: the emergence of universal income in self identity

Can identity be a source for universal income?

In a previous chapter we commented on how the 'social economy' has become more of a buzz-phrase for a newly exploitative form of capitalism, rather than a model for genuine redistribution of value. But, in the light of the emergence of the blockchain and distributive information systems there is the potential to organise work, as employing the community, on a radical new basis. This takes Western markets fully into account, but recognises that their distributive mechanisms need to fundamentally alter, if there is to be the sort of transformative reordering of work, as self-to-community mobilisation, proposed in this volume. The basis of such a revaluing of persons-in-work rests on an exchange of income for identity.

There are many ways in which human capital has become commodified in postindustrial economies. The standard approach of industrial capital was to recognise that the essential labour power of workers was the source of value. This was the principle undergirding Marx's labour theory of value and, whilst vigorously disputed within liberal economics, remained the litmus test for accumulation by capitalists. As we have seen, with the advance of automation and knowledge-based economies, there has been a shift from labour per se to skills and, thence, the ability to manipulate and interpret information systems. But, the most recent valorisation of human capacity has been through the transmutation of identity itself into a valuable commodity.

Beyond social data minecraft

Several features of the current internet social interface revolution have changed the ways in which corporations interact with people-as-consumers. Social networks make billions of dollars out of using algorithms for data mining and turning such information into resources for marketing. Leading research institutes in the life sciences and pharmaceuticals industries hoard massive amounts of personal biometric data, including entire genomic sequences. Additionally, media and communications industry providers have increasing capacities to trawl data on consumer preferences, viewing habits, smart phone application usage and, even, daily movements in time. Phones are becoming person-trackers and homes act as 'smart spaces', controlled by voice-activation systems.

At the same time, the real threats of robotic automation and AI, taken together, as we've seen, threaten the employment-based livelihoods of, perhaps, 30% of workers, even in the West. Furthermore, the fiscal crisis of the contemporary state – which has been deepening for the past 40 years – relentlessly limits the redistributive capacities of central and local governments. Under these circumstances there is a new potential for 'identity markets' to open-up.

The identity marketplace

It is possible to envisage situations where citizens – as social network members, consumers and those with an identifiable identity – can be paid micro-currency transaction cash revenues, or as education credits, retail vouchers or other currency transfers, for sharing their data, in all the multifarious ways that we do. This would represent a shift in redistributive mechanisms from the state to corporations. Ours is an era when there is increasing concern over the abilities of national legislatures and treasuries to control either the activity behaviours or the taxable revenue streams of globalising multinationals. In such a time, new models for extracting value from corporations, to reward people for their data and, hence, provide a form of near universal benefit income, connected to global markets, is highly attractive.

How could such systems operate? In an infamous quote, Eric Schmidt and Jared Cohen of Google commented "we are what we tweet" (1). It is frequently recognised that the distinction between our online and offline selves is becoming ever more blurred. This isn't simply because online communication is a part of everyday life but, also, because in some senses we are never offline. Even when we are not directly using our devices, they are communicating from our pockets, homes, offices and factories about our status, presence or absence.

This may seem dystopian and, in many respects, it is. But, equally, as the platforms that we utilise and post to watch our browsing histories, shopping and entertainment preferences, map our 'friends', record our 'likes' and monitor our movements, each of these bytes of data represents valuable bits of identity. Indeed, David Birch (2) argues that our identities are the new money. For example, Spanish bank La Caixa already connects customers' bank and Facebook accounts, meaning that digital identity allows for the conduct and authentication of financial transactions.

But, how can payments for digital identity sharing be made? One potential solution lies in the possibilities surrounding 'self-sovereign identity management'. That is to say we own and control our digital identities, instead of merely renting them to platforms such as Facebook, Linked-In or credit control agencies, such as Experion or Equifax who, in 2016, were found to have insecure safeguards for handling personal financial information.

With the advent of the blockchain and other distributed ledger-based systems a 'permissioned' chain of trusted members can establish participation in a network of nodes, without the oversight of any intermediary. On that basis, members could loan their data to the multiplicity of online sites and servers competing for their identity information, in exchange for a micro-fee. Although such systems are in their infancy, with open-source platforms such as Evernym, based in Salt Lake City, working with the Finnish Government on their Universal Basic Income platform (see Case Study below), there is a glimpse into a possible, more sustainable future. Once there, everyone can be paid for their identities, in a genuine sharing economy, as a work-in-progress, rather than merely working to give away their identities to mega-corporate identity-raiders.

We now turn from our Burning Quesiton to the now Matthewan gospel that casts further light on such, specifically through "the feeding of the 5000".

Window into Wisdom – Universal Welfare is a Biblical Principle

The feeding of the 5000 (Matthew 14: 13–21)

The principle of universal basic provision, irrespective of particular circumstances and need is, equally demonstrated in the one and only miracle of Jesus that is important enough to be included in all four New Testament Gospels, namely, 'the feeding of the 5000' (Matthew 14:13–21; Mark 6:31–44; Luke 9:12–17; John 6:1–14).

In the feeding miracle, Jesus breaks and distributes five small loaves and two fishes to the crowd, via the apostles, so that all had more than enough to eat. Indeed, the disciples are able to collect twelve baskets of remnants from the meal. The number is significant, in reflecting the twelve tribes of Israel, indicating that even the leftovers of Christ's distribution are enough to universally supply all needs. As we (3) suggest, elsewhere:

> God-in-Christ meets the needs of all people, irrespective of which world they come from. That universalist principle, lying at the heart of the gospel, fundamentally opposes the principle of selectivism on the basis of social characteristics or just deserts.

Universal welfare is a biblical principle

This principle of universalism in welfare can, equally, be traced back to the Hebrew Scriptures. There is a clear emphasis on the positive right of subsistence in the laws governing gleaning (Leviticus 23:22), care for the foreigner (e.g. Lev 19:34) and support for the vulnerable (e.g. Deuteronomy 10:18) including women and children, where there is no 'bread-winner' in the household. But, as Graafland (4) points out, the principle of subsistence – in a society where almost all were close to living in poverty – is linked to that of community.

The point is that all those residing in the land are 'resident aliens', as they entered the land as foreigners, first through Abraham and, later, through Joshua. As such, all the Israelites are required to welcome others into their midst as those who share this status as 'strangers in a strange land'. Absolute poverty is an offence against God's standards, so that all those in such a state should be helped, whether by charity or out of an understanding of divine justice. As some theologians suggest, the original mythic provision of God in the Garden, prior to the Fall, is the state to which humankind should aspire under principles of the Kingdom of God. In such a state the needs of all should be universally provided.

From the above it is possible to see that the Judaeo-Christian texts and a modern perspective, drawn from the Bible, cannot simply be read off-the-page. It is clear that the Scriptures support a spiritual view that can be connected to the basis of wage-labour. But, perhaps, more significantly, the fundamental principles of distributive justice presented in the biblical tradition are those of building communal solidarity, where no-one is left in utter need. As such, it is quite plausible to argue that the universal basic income – within a defined community – has strong spiritual support. And what is true for the Judaeo-Christian community may, equally, be the case in other Faith traditions. We turn, now, to the underlying Social Theory that marks out this chapter.

Social Theory: backdrop to basic income: guild socialism and economic democracy

The Idea of basic income is not new

For Philippe Van Parijs (5), Professor of Economics and Social Ethics, and Yannick Vanderborght, Professor of Political Science, both based at the University of Louvain, in Belgium, the idea of a *Basic Income* is not new. Since the end of the 18th century it has occurred to a number of bold minds, as well as long before in a religious context. *Today however, the conjunction of growing inequality, a new wave of automation, and a more acute awareness of the ecological limits to growth has made it the object of unprecedented interest around the world.*

The claim of these two Flemish professors then is that, under 21st century conditions, there is a fundamental difference between an unconditional basic income and public assistance. The point of the former, they say, is not just to soothe misery but to liberate us all. It is not simply a way of making life on earth tolerable for the destitute but a key ingredient of a transformed society. In particular, *basic income is fully compatible with the view that recognition and esteem are not earned by self-employment, but by service to others.*

Utopian Dream to worldwide movement

Starting Out with Agrarian Justice: The year 1795 was when the magistrates of Speenhamland in England set up a mean-tested cash benefit scheme that started looking like a genuine minimum-income scheme, but soon led to a backlash. It was also when the book in which French philosopher Condorcet first formulated the general idea of social insurance, much later to become the main principle of our welfare states, was published. And it was the year when one of Condorcet's closest friends started writing a short piece that, while it was barely noticed at the time, would be rediscovered and recognised two centuries later as the first proposal of something quite close to a genuine unconditional basic income.

In a pamphlet entitled *Agrarian Justice* (1796), Thomas Paine, by then a prominent figure in the American and French revolutionary movements, put forward a scheme radically different from both public assistance and social insurance. In it he (6) proposed to "create a national fund out of which shall be paid every person, when arrived at 21 years, the sum of £15 as a compensation in part for the loss of his inheritance, by the introduction of the landed system of property'. This proposal, for Van Parijs and Vanderborght, is reminiscent of an idea that can be found in the Christian tradition, namely that the earth is the common property of mankind. But the world was not ready to hear it.

Then in 1848, the same year that Marx and Engels published their *Communist Manifesto*, John Stuart Mill (7) published his first edition of his *Principles of Political Economy*. The "social problem of the future", he maintained, was "how to unite the greatest individual liberty of action with a common ownership of the raw materials of the globe, and an equal participation of all in the benefits of combined labour".

Basic Income Debated – Roads to Freedom/Where Do We Go From Here: Something more akin to a real public debate took shape in Britain after World War 1. The first to open fire, in his (8) *Roads to Freedom*, was the philosopher, militant pacifist and Nobel laureate Bertrand Russell:

> the plan we are advocating amounts essentially to this: that a certain small income, sufficient for necessaries, should be secured to all, whether they work or not, and that a larger income should be given for those willing to engage in work which the community recognizes as useful.

Soon after Clifford Douglas (see below) came up with his notion of a "national dividend". The labor party Oxford economist, and guild socialist, G D H Cole (9) followed suit, in 1935, saying: "incomes should be distributed partly as rewards for work, and partly as direct payments from the State to every citizen as "social dividends", for each citizen's share of the common heritage of productive power". In fact another Oxford economist, James Meade (10), defended the "social dividend" with great tenacity.

Moreover, in the 1960s, it was in the US, at the peak of the civil rights movement, that a real debate on basic income picked up again. Firstly the economist Robert Theobold (11), in his *Free Men and Free Markets* argued for a "guaranteed income that would provide the individual with the ability to do what he considers important", based on the fundamental American belief in the individual. Ironically the two other main contributors to the debate were those champions of neoliberalism, Milton Friedman (12), in his *Capitalism and Freedom*, and Friedrich Hayek (13), in his *Road to Serfdom*. While Friedman in fact supported a negative income tax, Hayek unambiguously supported a minimum-income scheme as a condition of real liberty.

Also in the latter part of the 1960s the renowned Canadian economist, and author of *The Affluent Society*, John Kenneth Galbraith (14), together with the leading American economists James Tobin and Paul Samuelson signed a petition by over a thousand economists calling for the US Congress to adopt a system of income guarantees. And in his (15) last book *Where Do We Go From Here*, Martin Luther King wrote:

> I am now convinced that the simplest approach will be the most effective – the solution to poverty is to abolish it directly through a guaranteed income . . . The dignity of the individual will flourish when the decisions concerning his life are in his own hands . . . when he knows he has the means to seek self-improvement. We now want to bring the basic income story up to date, and turn to Rutger Bregman accordingly.

Utopia for realists and how we get there

Flurry of Interest in the Basic Income: When then the young Dutch social philosopher, Rutger Bregman (16) first began writing about basic income, in the second decade of the new millennium, most people had never heard of it. But now, just three years later, the idea, he says and as we have intimated, is everywhere. Finland and Canada have both announced large experiments. It's catching up in a big way, he says, in Silicon Valley. A major basic income study has been launched in Kenya, and in the Netherlands no fewer than 20 municipalities are putting basic income into action. The impetus for a sudden flurry of interest, moreover, was a referendum held in Switzerland in June, 2016, on a proposal for a basic income.

Though it was voted down let's not forget that as recently as 1959 Swiss men voted against their women's right to vote, which was overturned in a second referendum in 1971.

A Future Awash with Leisure: The notion of a basic income, though, should not be considered in isolation of the wider issues surrounding it. The notable English economist John Maynard Keynes (17), indeed, was neither the first nor the last to foresee, almost a century ago, a future awash with leisure (as per Stiegler's *otium* – see Chapter 7). A century and a half before him American founding father Benjamin Franklin had already predicted that four hours of work a day would eventually suffice. Beyond that life would be "all leisure and pleasure". And *Karl Marx* (18) similarly *looked forward to a day when everyone would have the time "to hunt in the morning, fish in the afternoon, raise cattle in the evening, criticize after dinner, without ever becoming hunter, fisherman, herdsman or critic"*.

At around the same time, the father of classical liberalism, British philosopher John Stewart Mill (19), was arguing that the best use of more wealth was more leisure. Mill opposed "the gospel of work", proclaimed by his great adversary Thomas Carlyle, with his "gospel of leisure". According to Mill, technology should be used to curb the workweek as far as possible. *There would be as much scope as ever for all kinds of mental culture, and moral and social progress, he wrote, as much room for Improving the Art of Living*. Yet the Industrial Revolution, which propelled the 19th century's explosive economic growth, brought about the exact opposite. Where an English farmer in 1300 had to work some 1,500 hours a year to make a living, a factory worker in Mill's time had to put in twice as much just to survive. Yet it was none other than Henry Ford – titan of industry, founder of Ford Motor Company and creator of the Model T – who became the first industrialist to implement a five day week. He had discovered that a shorter work week actually increased productivity.

Interestingly enough, during the miner's strike of 1974, when Prime Minister Heath reduced the country to a three-day week the lost of steel production, for example, was not the anticipated 50% but 6%. We now turn from the Basic Income, specifically, to Guild Socialism, generally, still in a "western" UK context, mediated by what was recently identified as "Big Society".

Guild socialism: Clifford Douglas and economic democracy

Reconnecting with the celtic past

In the second decade of the new millennium, the British Conservative government made an ill-fated attempt to inaugurate a *Big* Society movement, ostensibly to enhance the role that civil society would play in the UK, while diminishing the role of government. While there was also a philosophical impulse (20, 21) behind it, this seldom came to the surface. In fact, if you plumbed such depths, as we (22) did at the time, you would find that this movement was serving to bring together the country's Anglo-Saxon and Celtic heritages through *Guild Socialism*.

That particular English movement at the turn of the last century was that of *Guild Socialism*. The leading historical exponent, who we draw upon, is the working class, English engineer and cost accountant, who died in the 1950s, the late and great Clifford Douglas. In fact his close colleague, social philosopher and art critic in the early part of the twentieth century, Alfred Orage, called him "the Einstein of economics". As such, we will be drawing more extensively, and systematically by way of navigation on his work in the next Chapter 16 on *Social Credit Economics*, based on the seminal analytical work of Canadian philosopher and economist, Oliver Heydorn.

The ideas of Guild Socialism *reach back into the rich soil of Celtic Christianity, travelling forward through the protests of the common people at enclosure of the land* and the subordination of their culture to the encroaching value system of the successful raiders of the past. In fact Clifford Douglas was part of a working class based peace movement, in post-First World War Britain. At the same time so called "Guild Socialism" was making its influence felt. What then were its historic origins, as well as its current orientation?

The case for economic democracy

In contrast with communism and labourism, so called "guild socialism", in the early part of the last century, sought to overthrow neo-liberal capitalism by reclaiming the communality and utility of production. The implication is that wealth as money-making thereby conflated wealth and well-being. Rejecting the notion of individual profit such *guild socialists in Britain developed the notion of service to the community whereby producer and consumer could work in partnership for the common good.*

"Social credit", more specifically as such, represented the case for economic democracy on the grounds that wealth is produced by and through society in co-operation rather than competition. *Money should be a servant available to society, rather than its master. The question therefore of who has the rights to issue money becomes critical.* In fact the creation of meaningful political democracy awaits economic democracy. Debt-created money and banking stands in the way of such, and the right to livelihood becomes a sine qua non.

Cultural inheritance to money reform

The link between guild socialism and social credit arose out of the collaboration between guild socialist Alfred Richard Orage (1873–1934) and the originator of social credit theory Clifford Hugh Douglas (1879–1952), both based in the UK. Until the arrival of Douglas on the scene, Orage and the other guild socialists were at a loss to explain the role of money under guild socialism, or capitalism for that matter.

Douglas argued that the capitalist system was designed to lead to waste and warfare rather than peace, co-operation and self-sufficiency. Taken as a whole, Douglas' work provided the basis for development of a non-equilibrium economics in which sufficiency took precedence over economic growth, competition and the quest for profit. Production would cease to be dependent on wage labour, while a realistic balance between production and distribution would be maintained. There are five key ideas emphasised by social credit.

Firstly, *the contribution of each individual, whether as worker, capitalist or financier, pales into miniscule insignificance when evaluated alongside the cultural legacy of "the progress of the industrial arts"*, to use a phrase coined by Veblen, and often used by Douglas. Production, whether material or, intellectual or artistic, relies on the common cultural inheritance – Africans speak of "the spirits of the ancestors" – which forms the birthright of all citizens. Furthermore, co-operation in industry and other forms of collective activity gains an "unearned increment of association".

Such communally based craftsmen, secondly then, were originally both independent and interdependent, rather than being dependent, whether indeed in pre-industrial Britain or in precolonial Zimbabwe (see Chapter 2). They took pride in their work, as such, whether of iron-mongering, sculpting, weaving or baking, thereby producing commodities for everyday use.

The introduction of the profiteering money system, thereafter, enabled the financier to invest machinery and gain profit from the work of others. With the advent of the limited liability company, symbolised by the factory system around the world, more generally, strategy and policy formation was progressively separated from the worker, who for Douglas became a mere "wage-slave" in an increasingly centralised system. *The decentralisation of such power, therefore, becomes a prerequisite for economic democracy.*

Thirdly, for Douglas, it is possible to imagine a country, whether Britain or Zimbabwe, in which all inhabitants are regarded as shareholders in the birthright of the common property of real wealth, consisting of untapped and renewable natural resources and the cultural heritage of tools and processes. That is, *each citizen has a claim to a share in the potential to produce, rather than being forced to participate in a system of production, distribution and exchange. The circulation of purchasing power can be made to reflect this situation through payment of a "dividend" on the shared cultural inheritance.*

It is absurd, therefore, to stipulate that in order to obtain an income, every individual should seek employment regardless of demand for their services and no matter what their health, capacity for employment or better judgement might dictate. Nevertheless, the proposal that all should have a small basic unearned income as a right is greeted by waves of shock and horror by many who are themselves bound in a wage-slavery system.

Politicians and social reformers have long laboured under the misapprehension, fourthly, that the main problem of civilisation is to maintain an ever-increasing flow of production in order to meet unlimited demands for goods and services. However, *the abundance of nature combined with human ingenuity and invention can provide an ample sufficiency for all.* By eliminating built-in obsolescence, superfluous packaging, transportation and waste, a sufficiency of high-quality local food (as was the case for Chinyika) and other essentials could be provided locally. But instead, the money system dictates that production must be based upon profitability. In a world where millions suffer from malnutrition, billions of dollars are spent on slimming aids and products to overcome the effects of over-indulgence.

No matter, finally, whether it is wealth or waste that is being produced and consumed, producers and consumers must maintain a continuous stream of production and consumption so that debts can be repaid, and the process can start all over again. *An understanding of the mechanisms of the debt-based money system is a vital prerequisite for reform, but needs to be coupled with value-systems rooted in society and the natural environment.*

Releasing the individual

For Douglas though, *there is no virtue in taking ten hours to produce by hand a necessary which a machine will produce in ten seconds*, thereby releasing a human being to that extent for other means. In fact *it is essential that the individual should be released; that the freedom for other pursuits than mere maintenance of life should thereby be achieved*. How then are we to deal with this dilemma?

It is most important, to recognise that there are two distinct problems involved in this dilemma: one technical, the other psychological, *and it is just because the psychological aspect of industry has been confused with and subordinated to the technical aspect that we are confronted with so grave a situation at this time.* As we have seen, the development of the industrial activity has been very largely a practical application of the economic proposition in relation to the division of labour. This type of organisation carried out to its furthest limits, for Douglas, is pyramid control, whereby supreme power is reached and concentrated at its apex. Overall then, it needs to be admitted that a considerable amount of manufacturing will need to be done. These goods, of course, will not be furnished for nothing, and the money to pay for them will in the main be supplied by loans. So how do we resolve, or dissolve this dilemma?

Moving from efficiency to sufficiency

Guildsmen and social crediters, overall then, have sought to create an economics of sufficiency by replacing a financial system based on debt, speculation and the necessity for constant economic growth with one based on community control of the issue of credit. The credit scheme envisaged, as such, is a gradualist, decentralist reform of the financial system, thereby bringing under democratic control the credit-issuing agencies of the community. The scheme could be adopted across a whole economy, such as that of Britain or Zimbabwe or Nigeria or Sri Lanka, liberating the process of production distribution and exchange from the blight caused by the privatisation of investment.

The production and consumption of superfluous waste could be phased out, and access to "good work" made available to all. Guild socialists therefore adopted a reformist approach, seeking to unite all who work as producers of goods within a locality with each other, and with local consumers. *While the community as a whole created wealth, financial power was the key to the effective control of that wealth.* Home and childcare, knowledge and invention, education, the web of culture and the care of the soil are the responsibility of all members of the community. What is the overall purpose, or reason for being, of such a socio-economic system?

For Douglas (23), it must be clearly born in mind that *the object of industry is not work for its own sake; the industrial system exists primarily because society has need of goods and services.* After the fundamental requirements of humanity for food, clothing, housing and so on, have been met, any excess energy in the community must find an outlet.

Therefore, *once the maintenance of life has been shifted from the backs of men onto the backs of machines, it is all important to find a creative outlet for the human energy released.* Overall, there will be a fall in the man-hours required for routine operating work and a consequent rise in that required for design and research work. The industrial machine, as such, is a lever, continuously being lengthened by progress, which enables the burden of Atlas to be lifted with an ever-increasing ease. *As the number of men required to work the lever decreases, so the number set free to lengthen it increases.*

All credit-values, for Douglas, *are firstly derived from the community,* regarded as a permanent institution, not merely from the present genera-tion of workers "by hand and brain". *The rate of production, secondly, is dependent on the scientific and cultural inheritance of the community,* as well as its tools and plant, and its personnel. *Thirdly, the community does not control credit-issue, at present; rather the financial system does, misguidedly so. Fourthly,* for Douglas, nothing is to be gained by assuming that Capitalism has always been fundamentally bad. Rather, and *fifthly, the capitalistic system is doomed today* (he was writing in the 1920s) *because the world has ceased to have need of it, not because it is an invention of the devil.*

In fact, for Douglas, *the community dividend is the logical successor to the wage.* Whereas such a universal dividend is a payment of something due, to the community as a whole, for services rendered, and thereby is the primary step to economic emancipation, *the wage represents servitude,* or "make-work", however disguised. All purchasing power, in effect, comes out of community credit, and the economic life of the community is con-trolled by its distribution.

The draft mining scheme

Douglas then came up with a concrete example of a different kind of com-munal banking arrangement. In the Draft Mining Scheme that Douglas and Orage presented, for the North of England in 1922, as an exemplar, they argued for:

* the *vesting of control* over industrial credit to the community
* the *regulation of price* so as to secure distribution of purchasing power
* the establishment of a wide degree of *worker-as-producer control* of each "industry" as consistent with the common good
* the distribution of communal product by the mechanism of *a social dividend* rather than through hourly individual productivity.

In place of industrial disruption and strikes, the workers-as-producers in each industry could cooperate to take financial control. *Worker-producers would control the bank, and through that the industry. Furthermore, employees leaving the industry would retain their voting powers in the producer-bank, serving to create local industry-community links.* As producers' banks developed they would come to represent the community at large, rather than merely be employed in the various industries to which the bank was attached.

Towards people's banks

Douglas' (24) particular focus, in relation to guild socialism, was on people's banks: that is the creation of money at the local level through producer/consumer financial institutions. *The main point would be that a decision to invest would not be based on concept of profitability or the ability to return money, but on the needs of the community.* Production, distribution and exchange between freely associated producers, in relation to such, would need to be guaranteed and protected within a framework of law devised within a democratic process. *The essence of the social credit system was, therefore, the issue of a national dividend as a basic income and the organisation of provisioning through local co-operatives.* The key to their interaction would be the producer/consumer banks.

However, wealth is created by society as a whole: individuals and firms make very little contribution as *individuals*. Douglas, like Marx and Veblen, if not also Steiner, argued for the right of all members of society to share in the benefits of their shared heritage of knowledge, skills and resources. Overall then, Hutchinson and her colleagues are not advocating the implementation of the ideas of Douglas and his social credit solutions, wholesale. What they are exploring is his general theoretical framework and critique of debt-based money systems as the basis for *new forms of socio-economic theorising that will not confuse wealth creation with money-making, nor commodity production and exchange with the provisioning of human societies.*

One of the greatest difficulties in reclaiming democratic control over basic subsistence needs, however, is the confusion of needs and wants under capitalism. In its search for capital accumulation, the capitalist economy has incorporated both needs and wants. However, its ability to meet needs is not equitable or systematic. Meeting needs is not its prime function. Prioritisation of needs over wants can only be achieved if consumer demand and producer supply decisions are brought together. Putting supply and demand in the hands of people collectively as envisaged by social credit would address this problem.

The good ship TINA

Hutchinson and Olsen (25) liken the capitalist economy, in the final analysis and by way of a powerful metaphor, to an ancient galley ship. Designed and developed to meet the unsustainable aspirations of a bygone era, the ship draws its energy through monetary mechanisms which now require a thorough overhaul if social and environmental sustainability is to be achieved. *Economic analysts have spent their lives analysing the activity of the ship without looking at what lies beyond. In consequence, with unnerving speed, the ship/economy is heading toward a number of icebergs.* The American, and thereafter worldwide, 2008 debt crisis is the latest of these.

The ship today has grown so large that it has drained the land and its peoples of the ability to survive outside the ship. Notwithstanding the good ship TINA (There is No Alternative), the money economy of western capitalism, is an artificial construction, made entirely from non-ship materials and labour, it has been around so long it seems to be a natural construction. *Nobody, whether crew, passengers, slaves or non-ship labour, can imagine life without the ship.*

Radical socio-economic change, for Hutchinson, can only be achieved in the context of a clear understanding of the nature of the money society. Small-scale experiments will not overthrow the prevailing system, nor will isolated examples of small-scale localisation, indeed like Chinyika in local isolation of social and economic development in Zimbabwe as a nation, Southern Africa as a region, and indeed the global economy, as a whole. What is needed is a global commitment to everybody's local, in this case Chinyika-Zimbabwe, which would also embrace the habitat of non-human species. Exposing the real nature of monetary systems and their destructive role together with feasible proposals for new forms of socio-economic organisations, such as the producer banks outlined, can provide at least a pathway to that vision.

We now finally turn to practical experiments, specifically here with universal basic income (UBI), if not also generally with economic democracy.

Illustrative Cases: experiments in UBI

Ultimate praxis: backdrop to UBI

For many people – steeped as we are in the distinction between the 'deserving' and the 'undeserving', which has its English antecedents in the Elizabethan Poor Law – the idea of UBI sounds like "la la land", a sort of Hollywood fairytale. In fact, experiments with basic incomes founded on the universalist principle have emerged during the late 20th and early 21st centuries, even in the West.

Uniquely reaping the Alaskan dividend

Despite having such illustrious advocates, as Bertrand Russell and Martin Luther King Jnr, UBI has not actually, practically come to pass, in Europe and America, although there are a few exceptions. In the mid-1970s, Jay Hammond, the Republican governor of the state of Alaska between 1974 and 1982, secured ownership of the Prudoe Bay oilfield, the largest in North America, for the citizens of Alaska.

However he was concerned that the huge oil wealth would benefit only current generations, so he proposed setting up a fund to ensure wealth would be preserved for future generations. In 1976 the *Alaska Permanent Fund* was created and a dividend was paid from it to all Alaskan citizens, because for Hammond: "natural resources were owned by the Alaskan people themselves". There are now in fact fifty countries with similar sovereign wealth funds but the Alaskan dividend scheme remains unique.

Scotland's UBI experimentation

In the new millennium, experiments are taking place into the viability of introducing widespread basic income schemes. Some of the latest of these are soon to be launched in the Scottish communities of Glasgow and Fife (16). Whilst there was no easy or immediate policy decision to trial such schemes, the considered conclusion of local politicians was that a universal basic income was the most sensible way out of the poverty trap for their citizens.

Glasgow is an ideal location for a basic income scheme. It has some of the highest levels of health inequality and deprivation index scores of any city in the UK. Furthermore, the local and national political context, following the UK's Brexit vote, which was supported in Glasgow, in contrast to the vast majority of Scotland, makes it an important test case for radical fiscal policy reform.

Solidarity economics is important to policy-makers in Glasgow.

Whilst the concept may not be widely understood on the city's streets, the fundamental principle of a sharing, cohesive community is staunchly defended in Scotland's second city. At the same time, it is recognised that there will be considerable resistance to both the principle and the practice. The basis of most welfare policy in the UK – whether explicit or more occluded – is that of the 'deserving versus the undeserving poor', which was the foundation for Victorian welfare. Even the Beveridge Reforms, implemented after the Second World War, by Britain's reforming Labor Government, led by Clement Atlee, held a whiff of such moralising sentiment.

Overcoming the innate social conservatism of Scots, despite the tacit support of the ruling Scottish National Party (SNP), which heads the Scottish Government, will not be straightforward. But, under the conditions of Brexit and with the prospect of a second referendum on Scotland's devolution, once the UK has left the European Union, as is now looming, the time for radical anti-poverty action may never have been more germane.

The Finnish experiment

The inspiration behind the Glasgow and Fife experiments is the example of a Finnish scheme, which is being rolled-out in stages, as a national pilot, during 2017–18. The Finnish model involves diverting welfare payments to fund the universal basic income. One of the most fascinating aspects of the scheme is the approach being used. The experiment is being run by Kela, the Finnish federal economics agency. In late 2016 they selected 2000 unemployed persons, at random, to enter the scheme.

The hypothesis was that providing UBI to unemployed people would increase the employment rate, which was running at 92% (8% unemployment). In other words, UBI was not being used to test whether people would stop working if provided with a basic income. Nor was it addressing the issues of automation and 'robots taking jobs' (see Section 3). Rather, it was testing if people would start working when receiving UBI, in order to overcome previous problems disincentives to work, when social security benefits reduced as a result of entering the formal labour market.

Demos Finland – a leading, Left-leaning think-tank – was recruited to design a step-wise process for testing the Finnish hypothesis. This involved the national government passing laws to allow prototypes with UBI to be initiated. Whilst it is too early to say if the experiment has supported or refuted the hypothesis, global interest in Finland's bold model has been considerable, with many other schemes starting and being promoted. These are taking place in such diverse regions as rural Kenya, Oakland, California, Utrecht, in the Netherlands, Ontario, Canada, follow-ups to the 2010 Madhya Pradesh scheme in India, Livorno, Italy and the Fort Portal region of Uganda. Clearly, UBI is of global significance, to address the issue of employing the community, for the 21st century.

Conclusion

The pace of change in the workplace of the early decades of the 21st century is conditioning profound dislocations to previous patterns of labour and the marketplace, as Western societies have understood it for more than a century. But, as we have seen, the idea of a universal basic income is far from new. It is presumed within the Scriptures and is a principle within many spiritual traditions, which emphasise the employment of a community, which cares for the needs of all, materially as well as spiritually.

What is, nevertheless, creating a new series of fault-lines within national and global societies is the power of those who control data, knowledge and digital identities. As such, some of the most significant issues, affecting contemporary workers and citizens, surround the ownership, control and valuation of our identities. This raises further issues about the connections between ourselves, their value within work and the credit that we can access within society. It is to such issues of social credit that we, now, turn.

Bibliography

1 Schmidt, J. and Cohen, J. (2013) *The New Digital Age: Reshaping the Future of People, Nations and Businesses.* New York: Knopf-Borzoi Books.
2 Birch, D. (2014) *Identity Is the New Money.* London: Publishing Partnership.
3 Bradley, T. (In Preparation). *Songs in a Strange Land: Revealing the Biblical Quaternity Archetype GENE-Alogy for Renewed Cultural Enterprise Production in Liverpool.* Johannesburg: Da Vinci Institute and Trans4M, Unpublished Ph.D. thesis.
4 Graafland, J.J. (2010) *The Market, Happiness and Solidarity: A Christian Perspective.* Abingdon: Routledge.
5 Van Parijs, P. and Vanderborght, Y. (2017) *Basic Income: A Radical Proposal for a Free Society and Sane Economy.* Cambridge: Harvard University Press.
6 Paine, T. (1986) *Thomas Paine Reader.* London: Penguin Classics.
7 Mill, J.S. (2001) *Principles of Political Economy.* Boston: Adamant Media Corporation.
8 Russell, B. (1954) *Roads to Freedom.* London: George Allen and Unwin.
9 Wright, A. (1979) *G.D.H. Cole and Socialist Democracy.* Oxford: Oxford University Paperbacks.
10 Meade, J. (2013) *The Intelligent Radical's Guide to Economic Policy.* Abingdon: Routledge.
11 Theobold, R. (1965) *Free Men and Markets.* New York: Anchor Books.
12 Friedman, M. (2002) *Capitalism and Freedom: 40th Anniversary Edition.* Chicago: Chicago University Press.
13 Hayek, F. (2001) *The Road to Serfdom.* Abingdon: Routledge Classics.
14 Galbraith, J.K. (1989) *The Affluent Society: 3rd Edition.* London: Penguin Books.
15 Luther King, M. (2010) *Where Do We Go from Here?* New York: Beacon Press.
16 Bregman, R. (2017) *Utopia for Realists and How We Get There.* London: Bloomsbury.
17 Keynes, J.M. (2015) *The Essential Keynes.* London: Penguin Classics.
18 Marx, K. (1970) *Grundrisse: Foundations of the Critique of Political Economy.* London: Penguin Classics.

19 Mill, J.S. (2015) *On Liberty*. Oxford: Oxford World Classics.
20 Norman, J. (2010) *Big Society*. Buckingham: University of Buckingham Press.
21 Blond, P. (2010) *Red Tory: How Left and Right Have Broken Britain and How We Can Fix It*. London: Faber and Faber.
22 Lessem, R., Muchineripi, P. and Kada, S. (2014) *Integral Community: Political Economy to Social Commons*. Abingdon: Routledge.
23 Douglas, C.H. (1974) *Economic Democracy: The Delusion of Super-Production*. Sudbury, Suffolk: Bloomfield Books.
24 Douglas, C.H. (1974) *op cit*.
25 Hutchinson, F., Mellor, M. and Olsen, W. (2002) *op cit*.

16 Social credit

National balance to citizen's dividend

POST-LIBERAL GROUNDING
EMERGENT DIVIDEND
CITIZEN'S NAVIGATION
ULTIMATE EFFECT

Introduction: social credit as the payment for socialised working

We now turn from the our post-liberal local "western" regrounding in the politics of virtue and the local-global historic emergence of Basic Income, Guild Socialism and Economic Democracy, to *Social* Credit, as a means of global economic navigation. As such, in our Burning Question, we ask: can banking serve society? It is through transformed financial services, which operate in the interests of society as a whole, that work can become socially constructive, with leisure and well-being properly rewarded, as consequences of work based on social credit.

In this respect, our Window into Wisdom considers the intriguing Matthean parable of 'the workers in the vineyard'. For many people social credit – whereby the interests of society-at-work are placed above rewards of wealth to individuals, whilst avoiding the brutalising effects of Communism – may seem inequitable. Similarly, the cry of "it's not fair" rises from hearers of the parable. What may be missed is the reward accruing from serving the Kingdom as a whole.

The Social Theory section focuses on the principles of Social Credit, as elaborated by Oliver Heydorn (1). He is a Canadian philosopher, who graduated from the Pontifical Catholic University in Chile. As an author and activist, he is the founder of the *Clifford Hugh Douglas Institute for the Study and Promotion of Social Credit*, based in Canada. Douglas had his most significant influence in Canada, through writings on Social Credit, its implementation and implications for a produce working and leisure society.

Even so, as we see in our Illustrative Case, the actuality of Canadian implementation of Social Credit has been, largely, within the political, rather than the economic, sphere. By contrast, contemporary experiments in China have taken the ideological rhetoric of Social Credit but are using it as a means of social manipulation and behavioural control. To that extent, whilst Social Credit represents a major innovation for navigating work towards the employment of community, we conclude that it is yet to be effectively implemented. Even so, renewed global interest provides the real possibility of this theory becoming the seedbed for transformative practice, to fund the work society needs.

Burning Question: can the banks serve a working society?

The artifice of fractional reserve banking

Although the causes of the North Atlantic Financial Crisis (2008–2009) are complex – connected to the relationship of finance capital, the distribution of money credit on property and derivatives markets – the overall threat came from the banking system itself. As we will see in the Social Theory section of this chapter, Clifford Douglas' policy theory of 'social credit' acts to challenge the role of the banks. But, it is important to begin by asking the Burning Question: can the banks operate in the interests of society as a whole?

The fractional reserve banking system largely determines the nature of money which can serve as the life-blood of a nation's economy, the rate at which it can flow, and the conditions under which it can be issued. The first aspect of such a system is that, *under its rubrics, the banks have the power to create money out of nothing*. The new money that the banks create exists in the form of bank credit (intangible numbers formerly represented as numerals on paper and nowadays by electronic blips on computer screens). Nor is the money that banks create directly connected to the real supply and demand for goods, services and the products that condition the difference between starvation and plenty.

Banks create money *ex nihilo* in the form of bank credit. Equally, that money is almost always created in the form of interest-bearing debt. The creation and sale of debt-money is the *sine qua non* of the present banking business. The banks implicitly then claim the ownership of the credit they create and lend it to "make money" for themselves.

It is commonly the case that *well over 95% of the money supply of an industrialised country exists as bank-credit. And since bank-credit is typically created as interest-bearing debt, the present system is correctly described as a debt-based system*. In the UK about 3–5% of all money is held as tangible bank reserves, although the Basle III European protocols (which the UK will exit with Brexit) require more like 7%. Moreover, whenever debt-money is issued, it is on terms that maximise the financial advantages to those running the banking system *even at the expense of the community, with the effect that banks can claim ownership of entire countries, as was reflected in the banking bailouts of 2008–2009 following.*

Installing a national credit office or authority: NCO

The key to banks acting in the public interest lies in the development of a system of Distribution of Credit (DoC) rather than through their having a Monopoly of Credit (MoC). This could be facilitated through a National Credit Office (NCO), which would need to be introduced to assess, monitor and administer the foundations of that nation's life in line with such a DoC. Arguably, financial credit, belongs neither to the banking system, nor to government, but rather to the consuming public considered as individuals. The officials operating the NCO – akin to the UK's *Office for Budget Responsibility* (OBR) – would be subject to censure or removal by political representatives, should they fail to provide satisfactory results in the fulfilment of their duties.

The first task of the NCO would be to establish and maintain a proper set of *National Accounts consisting of a National Balance Sheet* and *Credit Account*. In the case of the former, an inventory of all items within the boundaries of a country would constitute its assets: *natural resources that are privately, communally or governmentally owned, capital equipment and infrastructure, intermediate goods and services, and human resources.* At any given time, the call made by productive agencies on these assets (on behalf of the consumer) would be recorded as drafts on the national Credit Account (the nation's productive potential), constituting the nation's liabilities.

The real basis of credit, then, is the consuming capacity of the community. On the credit side of the account, the officials at the NCO would tabulate the nation's production of both capital and consumer goods/services plus imports; this would be opposed by the figures representing the consumption of both capital and consumer good/services, as well as exports on the debit side of the nation's double-entry book-keeping.

A bank should envision the capacity of the community it serves

In a Distributed Credit Economy, moreover, there would be no favourable balances of trade, no excessive government debt, no redistribution of incomes, no bank created debt-money in the form of loans, mortgages or lines of credit for purposes of facilitating consumption and, perhaps most importantly, *no excessive production* (especially capital production). Indeed since real capital is a function, above all, of the cultural heritage of a civilisation, *a share of the real profit on the sale of goods and services belongs to each individual member of society, and should be distributed freely to them.*

The introduction of a National Balance Sheet and National Credit Account would allow us to be as rich in financial terms as we are in real terms. Accordingly, the money which is to be lent to producers would not be created out of nothing via the fractional reserve system of banking. Instead private banks would request the NCO to monetise the appropriate items in the national credit inventory and would proceed to borrow that money from the NCO interest-free. Their power to create money *ex nihilo* would completely disappear. In such circumstances the function of banking would be to envisage and support the capacity of the community it serves. To do so would be to finance real productive labour, enable increasing leisure and support community well-being. This is a far cry from the banking system that we have today. So what can a Matthewean window on wisdom have to offer?

Window into Wisdom: serving the kingdom as a whole

The labourers in the vineyard (Matthew 20: 1–16)

The parable of the labourers in the vineyard is unique to Matthew and demonstrates the theological mind of someone who is both used to handling money, as a banker, and, also, understands the upside-down nature of God's Kingdom. The story centres on a vineyard owner who explains to his workers that they will all receive the same day-wage money no matter when they are hired. Those hired early in the morning work the full twelve-hour day, standard in the Roman Empire. But, paradoxically to ancient and modern ears alike, those hired at 5 in the afternoon work only one hour and receive the full day's rate.

Those hired first complain. But, the owner explains that they all agreed to his terms, at the outset. That is the foundation for his understanding of fairness. It is based on a model of social credit. Payments are made according to the amount of work that is needed within this microeconomic society of the vineyard. The work that is required is all paid for, but the principle behind the pay is an egalitarian, rather than an equitable, one, so that social cohesion is developed on the basis of equality. Credit is available to all, with leisure time available for those who work less. But, the necessary work gets done and all are rewarded according to the social credit rules.

There is equal pay for all eternity

Of course, the Gospel message is that God doesn't discriminate according to when you entered the Kingdom. Those who accept God's grace as children are rewarded exactly the same as those who are death-bed converts. There is equal pay – the entirety of God's unmerited love and acceptance, for all eternity. This can seem unfair to some. Surely, our good and bad deeds should be weighed in the scales of a lifetime and 'eternal credits' awarded accordingly, it is argued. Not so, in Matthew's parable. The social credit of the Kingdom is more important than the individual's acts or point-of-decision. All that is needful is accomplished and the rewards are eternal for all those who enter. Only those who reject the vineyard owners terms, which are, in this case, submission to God's love and commands, are excluded from the social contract.

If the parable is simply about work it seems a recipe for industrial unrest and claims of discrimination. But, it is about more than work, under current conditions. It is about acceptance of society under God's rule. The parable emphasises the free gift of grace and the requirement for humility and graciousness in the face of 'natural justice'. That said, if the parable isn't at all about work it makes the Gospel unwordly, which is far from Matthew's ever-practical intentions. Perhaps, the real message comes in the pay-off line: "the first will be last and the last will be first" (20:16). If we seek status in work, wealth or kingdom we can expect to be excluded. But, if we accept God's kingdom gift of love then all these other things will be added – at the right time. We now turn to the underlying theory of social credit.

Theory of social credit: economic, social and environmental wellbeing

Stages of economic development

Clifford Douglas (2) begins his analysis of economic production with seven stages of economic development. For our purposes these pivot on the sixth and seventh stages, the introduction of *self-operating and, thereafter, intelligent machines*. A society which has given rise to such will find itself in the grips of a dichotomy. On the one hand, engineers, scientists, industrialists and others, by furthering the development of technology, will be *working incessantly on labour displacement*. On the other hand, politicians and the disadvantaged will be ever more *preoccupied with the elimination of the growing, consequent "unemployment problem"*.

In reality, for Douglas though, *the release of a certain percentage of the workforce from the necessity of toil is a definite component of true economic progress*, indicating as it does the capacity of the community to liberate at least some of its members from the economic duties imposed by nature. *But, being unemployed must cease to be synonymous with being poor or destitute*. Douglas' view, was that the real percentage of the available workforce necessary to produce the desired goods, with the least trouble to everyone, would be less than 20% of the employable population. Overall then, for Heydorn, we are rapidly progressing toward "the end of economic history". What does that more specifically mean for the nature and scope of a "social credit" economy, and enterprise?

Finance as the economic soul or otherwise

Nevertheless, as both Douglas and Heydorn recognise, the fundamental problem of poverty in the midst of plenty persists. None of the major economic systems of laissez-faire Capitalism, Marxist Socialism or the Mixed Economy has succeeded to eradicate the scourge of poverty and the threat of unemployment. If all conventional economic systems fail to facilitate adequately the true purpose of economic association, why, for Heydorn, do they fail? The answer lies in debt-based finance, to which the solution, for Douglas (3), is the power of social credit.

It is not in fact finance *per se*, but the *misdirection* of finance that artificially limits its economic "social credit". The financial system is, potentially, the soul of the economic body. For finance potentially mobilises and coordinates economic energies and distributes their physical output. But, Heydorn maintains, we need to distinguish between real credit and financial credit. Real credit is defined by Douglas as "the rate at which goods and services can be delivered, as, when, and where required", whereas financial credit is defined as "the rate at which money can be delivered as, when and where required". The two are related because the real credit serves as the basis for the financial credit. *It is the faith of a society in its real credit which is the ultimate source of "value" of its financial credit.*

Even so, under the conditions of monopoly Capitalism *real credit, which is substance, is subordinated to financial credit, which is its shadow, as numbers become more important than real things. The Biblical claim that "the love of money is the root of all evil" does not appear to be an exaggeration.* We are enslaved, according to Douglas, by a numerical abstraction. Not only does the financial system maintain financial credit in a state of artificial scarcity, the banks also claim *ownership* of all the financial credit which they create. According to Heydorn, *in claiming ownership of the financial credit they originate, the banks are in fact usurping the legitimate property rights of the individuals who compose society.*

Real credit is a function of *the labour and enterprise of individual human beings.* Equally, it depends on *natural resources* (gifts of God, to be shared), on the *unearned increment of economic association, on our specific cultural heritage, and on the individual desire to consume goods and services.* As such, every individual in the community has a legitimate claim to a personal share in the beneficial ownership of real credit. Thus, if financial credit derives its value from real credit, then the creation and use of financial credit should always be determined by the course of action that will most benefit the true owners of real credit, who are the individuals composing society.

By not automatically providing sufficient credit to mirror real credit, the financial system fails to fully catalyse useful production. As long as there is real demand, and, on the other side, a real capacity to satisfy that demand, there can be no legitimate economic reason, for refusing to issue money that is necessary to link the two by catalysing useful production. What is physically possible is financially possible. What is needed, according to Heydorn, is additional purchasing power, not more work.

Transfer of purchasing power from the poor to the rich

The charging of compound interest, moreover, on debt-money acts as a siphon that constantly redistributes purchasing power from the lower 90% of households to the top 10%, thus increasing the gap between rich and poor and reinforcing the hierarchy of wealth, power and privilege. Insofar as both producer and consumer credits are only advanced on the basis of some collateral, the present money system also ensures that large quantities of real property are actually under lien to the banks. By means of public debts, additionally, it is likewise possible for a whole city, region or country to be under lien to financial powers.

That said, the service for which banks should be able to make a financial profit, according to Heydorn, is the full actualisation of the real credit of the community. In other words their *financial profit should be dependent on facilitating the maximisation of the real profit of the community, on the production and distribution of the desired goods and services with the least amount of trouble to everyone.* The problem is that banks choose to loan to highly profitable industries, such as armaments, which have no realistic connection to ordinary workers.

The plague of consumer debt

One of the most important methods presently employed by the financial system to bridge the macroeconomic deficiency of consumer purchasing power, is the direct extension of debt-money to consumers for the purpose of facilitating consumption. Mortgages, car loans, educational, personal lines of credit, credit cards, instalment purchasing, are all necessary, not because invariably people are inclined to live beyond their means (though this often does apply), but because the production of the economy cannot be bought in its entirety without the increasing level of consumer purchasing power. *Increased quantities of debt-money for consumption are becoming more and more an essential adjunct of the economy without which it would collapse.* What then are the wider implications of such, according to both Douglas (4) and Heydorn?

The implications of monopoly credit

Failure to Distribute Communal Profit: The return for effort is much less than it should be because the capacity to produce is not *automatically* balanced by the financial capacity to consume. *There is,* instead, *a failure to freely distribute the communal profit, that is the proportion* *of production that cannot be purchased by the insufficient volume of consumer incomes.*

Unjust Taxation Systems: The prevailing structure of economic organisation moreover, for Douglas, involves a tax system that is fundamentally unjust, in that it completely inverts the idea that the population should have free access to the communal profit. In fact *a large proportion of the monies paid in taxes are actually employed in meeting the interest payments on government debts.*

Wage and Debt Slavery: Meanwhile the vast majority of economic agents are not in such a financially favourable position that they can opt out and "refuse to play the game". The contracting of debt-money is all too often needed. But once an economic association has collectively acquired debts, the necessity of having to work in perpetuity to pay off debt forcefully imposes itself. *The weaker individuals and nations in the economic pyramid*, according to Heydorn, *are in a condition of debt and wage-slavery.*

The Burden of Third World Debt: The international financial system moreover, consisting of the key Institutions of the World Bank, the Bank of International Settlements, the International Monetary Fund and the World Trade Organization, most of the world's central banks and multinational commercial banks, reproduces on an international scale the same type of social structure that characterises national economies. Many *third world countries* have paid back their original debts several times over. Nevertheless, these debts remain and often continue to grow due to the charging of compound interest, *instead of being able to use tax revenues for health, education and the development of infrastructure.*

A Loss of Wellbeing: *The choices which individuals and institutions make are very often at odds with the choices that would enable them to live well*, that is in harmony with their own best interests, with those of society, and with those of the natural world. For those who don't have enough money to meet their needs, moreover, the artificial scarcity of money is generally experienced as a burden, whereas those who occupy the upper echelons of the economic pyramid experience the artificial scarcity of money as something positive, since it is the source of their wealth, status and power.

Economies are Insolvent: The underlying deficiency in consumer incomes, overall then for Heydorn, means that the economic system is inherently insolvent. *The spectacle of the ordinary individual trying to make ends meet* is not therefore a natural or unavoidable component of economic life nor is necessarily due to the greed or incompetence of the individual; rather it *is a necessary implication of an economy operating from a position of gross insolvency.*

Intrusive Government Bureaucracy: On the side of the worker, meanwhile as such, *the lack of money that comes as a result of unemployment* *necessitates government bureaucracies to reduce the potential conflict by managing unemployment insurance, welfare, job creation and so on.* This growth of government bureaucracy is deemed "good", but if a country had a proper financial system, for Heydorn, none of this would be needed, and in fact, for him, it is a tremendous misdirection of collective effort.

Forced Economic Growth: In truth then, *much economic growth is undertaken not because the resultant goods and services are needed or wanted but because the lack of consumer purchasing power needs to be addressed if financial homeostasis is to be achieved.* Under the structures of the prevailing economic system almost everyone must either work in order to obtain an income to purchase the things they need for survival or be supported by those who do, in order to protect the necessity of forced growth.

The Production of "Illth" instead of Wealth: Because it is forced economic growth, *much of the resultant economic growth is actually productive of "illth"*, to use the term coined by John Ruskin, that is goods and services which actually constitute evils, destroying well-being, such as armaments for export, cigarettes, processed foods and pornography.

International Economic Conflict: To further exacerbate matters, exporting in exchange for money can lead to international conflict. *It is mathematically impossible for all countries of the world to have a favourable balance of trade. International trade in goods and services then is a mad scramble.* So the time, energy and economic resources expended in unnecessary competition is, for Heydorn, a senseless waste.

Individual, Societal and Environmental Wellbeing: Just as the formal economy involves the production, distribution and consumption of goods, *the social life of an association may also be thought of as involving economic activities, except that these are undertaken more on the basis of caring than with a desire to maximise profits.* The raising and education of children in the family, house work and voluntary work in the community are examples which hardly register in the formal economy. In effect, the "real economy" is nothing but a superstructure erected on the basis of social and environmental production-distribution-consumption cycles. *Without the caring done in society, the formal economy would not function, but that has, also, become subject to enormous stresses induced by burdens of debt on social care agencies.*

Spiritual Health: The corrosive effects of the domination of money, moreover, destroy genuine culture and prevent the individual from consolidating and enriching his own indemnity as a spiritual person. *The primary form of expression which is available to an individual who spends most of his days labouring as a corporate wage-slave is the unabashed consumption of ephemeral things.* Present economic arrangements also demoralise individuals by making it more difficult if not impossible for them to have the purchasing power and leisure necessary for the fulfilment of their creative desires.

Economic rehabilitation via a national dividend: beyond self employment

Society as a gigantic cooperative

So, what does Heydorn understand as the terms for economic rehabilitation? This brings us to the heart of the matter as far as *Social Credit* is concerned. *Just as companies that make a profit*, according to Heydorn, *in the form of dividends to their shareholders, a nation could maximise a certain portion of its profit as determined in the National Credit Account and distribute the money to its shareholders, its citizens.* The National Dividend would thus transform the whole of society into a gigantic cooperative in which each citizen would have an individual inherited, and equal claim to the real surplus of economic association, that is the unearned increment of production.

The dividend would be distributed at a flat rate and tax-free to all individual citizens who are permanent residents of their country as an inalienable right, whether they be richer or poorer, in recognition of the fact that, *in a modern, industrialised society, it is not necessary for all able-bodied adults to work in order for that society to produce the goods and services the individuals require.* In fact even if all such persons are not needed as workers in the economy needs them as consumers, and that every person has a right to consume just because he exists.

These features must be accommodated for a reformed financial system because a system by which purchasing power is distributed mainly through the agency of wages conflicts sharply with the physical reality involved. In other words a decreasing number of persons tend to be involved in the production of the necessary amount of goods and services. *Universal employment then is neither desirable nor possible.*

As there is a tendency for more and more workers to suffer displacement without being usefully reabsorbed by industry, the purchasing power of the dividend payments in relation to wages and salaries would increase as time goes on. Heydorn emphasises, moreover, that the Social Credit proposal of a National Dividend is quite distinct from the contemporary suggestions that are being advanced today from many quarters, as illustrated in the previous chapter, for the implementation of a basic income. *Unlike the basic income, which represents a guaranteed amount, the dividend depends on the nature and volume of real production.* If more and more production is being generated with less and less labour thanks to the increasing capitalisation of industry, then the dividend received by consumers will increase in terms of its relative purchasing power.

Ethical and pragmatic objections to the national dividend

One of the chief obstacles to the introduction of the National Dividend, in fact, is the ethical objection that it is somehow intrinsically wrong, that it is immoral for individuals to "get something for nothing" and that goods and services should only be distributed as a reward for working in the formal economy. If this objection were valid, for Heydorn, then the ultimate solution would be to ensure that all of the labour-saving technologies which have been proliferated since the dawn of civilisation were summarily destroyed! Moreover, for an advocate of *Social Credit*, John Hargrave (5):

> When the Sun shines upon the Earth there is no charge for the stream of Solar Energy that we receive. It is something for nothing. Yet without such there would be no life on this planet. Solar Energy is God's gift to man . . . the whole of Creation is, in fact, a something-for-nothing scheme.

Since each individual is rightly regarded as a beneficiary of the communal factors of production, each citizen can and should be regarded as a shareholder in the economy's real capital. For Douglas (6) then:

> The property that is common to the individuals who make up a nation is that which has its origins in the association of individuals to a common end. It is partly tangible, but to a great degree intangible, in the forms of scientific knowledge, character and habits.

A "consumer motivated" economic democracy

Yet instead of living under such an authentic economic democracy, Heydorn laments, *we live under what is, to a greater or lesser extent, a financially induced economic dictatorship that masquerades as an economic democracy.* The lack of consumer income, that is the artificial scarcity of consumer purchasing imposed on the market by the financial system, means that the choices that are made by consumers are very often reflective not of what they would really like, but merely what they are able to afford, or else are pressured into buying. *One cannot then speak in any reasonable sense of "economic democracy" when the vast majority of consumers cannot consistently obtain from the economic system, as a matter of course, those specific goods and services they have a right to expect from it.*

In contradistinction then to many of its ideological competitors, Social Credit does not sanction worker control of industry, or government control, or least of all banker control of industry, but rather consumer control. Social Credit envisions therefore a functionally aristocratic hierarchy of producers accredited by, and serving, a democracy of consumers. Only by combining the free market system of distribution through the mechanism of consumer choice with the allocation of sufficient purchasing power can the consumer be restored to his rightful place as the sole occupier of the commanding heights of the economy.

There is moreover, for Heydorn, yet a second meaning that might be attached to the concept of economic democracy. *Just as political democracy is deemed to imply universal suffrage, a nation cannot be considered as embodying a perfect economic democracy, if it does not distribute, by right, a sufficient volume of monetary votes to all of its citizens to ensure a basic level of participation in economic life.* By means of the National Dividend, such universal economic suffrage would be incorporated. Overall then, what sorts of specific economic improvements can be expected?

What economic improvements can be expected from economic democracy

Solving the paradox of poverty amidst plenty

In developed countries, for Heydorn, the paradox of poverty amidst plenty (the fact that real wealth cannot connect with real demand) is mainly caused by the deficiency of consumer purchasing power, not by a shortage of actually existing real wealth or the physical capacity to produce such. This is where the National Dividend comes in.

Resolving the paradox of servility in the place of freedom

By allowing technological improvements to advance at their own pace, secondly, without any fear of the labour displacement this may cause, Social Credit, according to Heydorn, *will also facilitate a continual reduction in the necessity of "natural" labour*, that is labour that is inherently necessary to operate society's productive machine. Indeed, for Douglas, the perfect industrial system would require no labour at all! Employers moreover would have to regard their workers more as co-operators, rather than as mere underlings. This means that the scope for the exploitation of labour alongside wage-slavery would be a thing of the past.

The curse of unemployment is turned into the blessing of leisure

Indeed, thirdly, the single greatest benefit which would follow from the introduction of the National Dividend is that it would *put an end*, according to Douglas and to Heydorn, *to the phenomenon of unemployment, and replace it with leisure*. No longer would those who, through no fault of their own, cannot find a decent job, be threatened with poverty, economic insecurity, and social exclusion. For Douglas (7) then:

> It is my own personal opinion that the undue acquisitiveness of a small section of society very largely arises out of fear, and that by far

the best way to reduce it to its normal proportion would be to remove the fear and insecurity in the existing state of affairs by making plain what is undoubtedly the truth, that the modern production system can meet every possible need of society without any stress or strain, if only it is freed from the fetters imposed upon it by the financial system.

It is the artificial pressure which conditions the nature and circumstances of work which tends to turn into an all-encompassing end in itself. By restoring a certain measure of security, independence and freedom, the National Dividend would make it far easier to view work as a mere means to an end, only engaged in to the extent that it serves the real purpose of the economic association. *Individuals would thereby be able to choose what field of work or leisure to pursue, allowing plenty scope for the pursuit of noble and constructive motives* through meaningful activities replacing mere pecuniary reward.

Securing increased efficiency in production

The elimination, fourthly then, of a servile labour force together with the removal of economic fear and insecurity is likely to greatly increase the efficiency of human effort. For Douglas (8) as such:

> The fear of poverty is the worst possible incentive to successful industry. I have no hesitation whatsoever in saying that the most important work, the hardest work, is done by men who have no fear whatever of poverty. Conversely, those sections of society which are constantly faced with the fear of poverty tend to become incapable of anything but the lowest grade of work.

The "psychological efficiency of voluntary work" is vastly superior to effort made under the threat of coercion. Indeed it is likely that in a Leisure State many people will, by being able to do freely those things that most interest them, work more effectively.

The transformation of civilisation

Fifthly by making leisure a practicable possibility for everyone, the dividend would also tend to release the tremendous potential contained in human associations for a faster rate of authentic progress. According to Douglas (9) again:

> It is hardly an exaggeration to say that 75% of the ideas and inventions to which mankind is indebted for its progress can be directly or indirectly traced to persons who were by some means freed from the necessity of regular employment.

Indeed perhaps the most startling effect, for Heydorn, that the National Dividend is likely to exercise on society is *the transformation of our civilisation from one which is centred on economic good and evil, rewards and punishments, to one which optimally facilitates the free expression of individuality*, what we term here "employment of the self". It will become possible for new and higher forms of living in society to emerge, for culture to yield the finest flower and for civilisation to reach its highest peak. For Douglas (10) as such:

> Production, and still more the activities which commonly referred to as "business", would of necessity cease to be the major interest of life.

Many of the earth's *natural resources*, in fact, its *cultural heritage*, the *increment of association* and the *real capital of a society* are economic assets to which each individual must have sufficient unfettered access if he is to procure in reasonable quantities the goods and services he needs to survive and flourish. Neither the collectivisation nor the privatisation of these types of resources through various forms of enclosure can be tolerated as both are attempts to monopolise elemental economic factors. As Douglas (11) concludes:

> I would commend to you a most serious consideration, whether you wish the economic system to be made a vehicle for an unseen government, over which you have no control; or whether, on the other hand, you are determined to free the forces of modern science, so that your needs for goods and services may be met with increasing facility and decreasing effort, thus, in turn, permitting humanity to expend its energy on altogether higher planes of effort than those involved in the mere provision of the means of subsistence.

We finally now come to the illustrative cases of applying at least some of the principles of social credit, in fact in Canada historically and China currently.

Illustrative Cases: social credit in Canada and China

Social credit stories

Indeed, and notwithstanding the inevitable and enduring obstacles (Social Credit has been part of Canada's social and economic history for eight decades) the story in that "western" country continues. Not only has Oliver Heydorn established his *Clifford Hugh Douglas Institute*, but social and economic activist Anielski (12), with his base in Alberta, amongst others, has not given up on the social credit cause.

Even so, *Socred* has had an unusual political history, in terms of its ideological deployment. In Canada it had been a movement for the democratic and religious Right. More recently, in China, it has become a tool of the totalitarian Left. As such it appears to transcend traditional political positions, although it has had little success, in Clifford Douglas' terms. The question is: whether or not it has failed or, as many argue, never actually been attempted?

The Canadian 'Socred' political movement

Somewhat surprisingly *Social Credit* was a politically Right-leaning, Conservative movement that governed a large part of Canada, including British Columbia and Alberta, through much of the 20th century. In this respect it is worth noting that conventional political ideologies do not always easily translate when considering alternatives to current models of Western liberal economic democracy. That said, it is, certainly, the case that the advocacy of *Social Credit*, in Alberta, by Christian evangelist William Aberhart, was instrumental in effecting the party's success, as a response to the Great Depression, which was particularly cruelly felt in rural Canada. Under Aberhart and his successor, Ernest C Manning, *Socred* governed Alberta until 1971.

In fact, the party moved away from the more radical aspects of Clifford Douglas' theory early on, both in Alberta and, later, in British Columbia, where it had major successes from the 1950s–1980s, including fielding two premier's in the 1970s and 1980s. *Socred* was, also, successful for a time in Saskatchewan, Manitoba and, even, francophone Quebec. But, by the 1990s it had dwindled as a political force with no state representatives. Throughout its time the party had eschewed Douglas' radical social philosophy. But, its inheritance has been to keep the idea alive, largely through name recognition.

In Britain, leading Labour Party figures of the 1930–1940s, including Hugh Gaitskill, who would be a later party leader, concluded that *Social Credit* was insufficiently radical, in terms of the Clause 4 commitment to taking 'the means of production, distribution and exchange' into public ownership. That said, viewed from the second decade of the 21st century *Social Credit* seems considerably more Left-leaning, especially in terms of banking reform. We now turn from Canada historically to China currently.

The current Chinese experiment

The most recent flirtation with *Social Credit* has come from the unlikely source of the Chinese Politburo. But, as with the Canadian experience, albeit from an almost opposite ideological perspective, *Socred* is being used for political purposes to which it has no obvious connections. That said, the current Chinese experiment does pick up the theme of the previous chapter, in exemplifying how the hoovering-up of mass digital data sets can be used, in this case by an authoritarian state, as a mechanism for attempting social control.

It appears that big data is being syphoned as a means of mass surveillance in China, to generate a new social distinction between the 'deserving' and 'undeserving'. On this basis, 'social credit' is being offered to those 'deserving', as model citizens, and withheld from those who are seen as "subversives". Of course, the latter include not only petty criminals and those who commit acts of 'anti-social behaviour' but, also, human rights lawyers, artists such as Ai Wewe and political dissidents.

The purpose of the Chinese 'social credit rating' system is to offer a few rewards but more penalties for either 'good' or 'bad behaviour', as sanctioned by the state. Socially constructive acts, such as demonstrating filial piety, morally correct purchasing and flawless online payments records can earn rewards such as fast-tracking at airports, rentals without deposits, especially with municipal bike and car-sharing schemes. By contrast, bad behaviour, such as jaywalking, non-payment of fines or attempting to dodge public transport fares incur credit rating penalties, imposed through *Sesame Credit*, an arm of the giant e-commerce corporation *Ali Baba*. These can result in the loss of jobs, the refusal of state bank loans and vilification on the local lists of 'bad citizens'.

This sounds Orwellian and, indeed, it is. Of course, this attempt at *Socred* is only being trialled in a few municipalities, currently, but is set to go nationwide. It is being opposed by many local citizens committees. But, it reflects the capacity of an ideologically appealing slogan, such as *Social Credit* to be adopted by the state for its own purposes. The fact that it is almost directly the reverse of what Clifford Douglas and, indeed, Oliver Heydorn had in mind, will probably not give President Xi Jinping many sleepless nights.

Conclusion: western research to southern transformative innovation

There is some work in progress, Social Credit-wise, in Canada and China, as elsewhere, however flawed, across our four worlds. Equally, while there is prolific and fundamental social research in the developed world ('north' and 'west'), it is in the developing world ('south' and 'east') that transformative action, on a large scale, is taking place. In fact, and in our penultimate chapter, prior to our final conclusions, we turn from the "north-west" to the "south-west", from Canada to Nigeria.

Therein we discover a variation on the Social Credit theme, via a unique combination of "Non-Interest" and "Integral" Banking, serving to employ, not just individuals, but also whole communities. In many ways, Ciser (Centre for Social and Economic Research) is taking up from where Chinyika in Zimbabwe (see Chapter 2) has left off. We now turn to the concluding chapter of our Western journey, which points us back to the South, where we began and from which a new circuit can be envisaged.

A note from Mark Anielski

That said, and to end this chapter on a sobering note, we add a recent e-mail exchange with our Canadian colleague, Mark Anielski (12), and author of *Does Money Grow Trees*, where he makes the following poignant comments, starting out with a reflection on American theologian Walter Brueggemann, who is well known to us:

> Walter Brueggemann is a very insightful man. He and I have been discussing his theme of 'coming out of modern Egypt' which is the slavery of debt money under the tyrannical rule of the money power (occult and esoteric). It is the same power who in my mind wanted Jesus Christ of Nazareth crucified for he upset their money changing enterprise who sullied the pure and direct relationship we could all have with God (ABBA, Father). James Buchan's brilliant book Frozen Desire: The Meaning of Money literally nails the subject how Jesus was crucified by the money power; they had the most to lose from their usury practices. As Buchan notes reflecting on a rare painting of Rembrandt of Judas returning the 30 pieces of silver 'in every money transaction, wholesale or retail, Christ is Re-crucified.' It sends chills down my spine.
>
> As for Social Credit I think this movement in Canada and the UK under Major C.H. Douglas was ultimately a monetary reform party unlike any party before or since. No other political party took on the issue of the money power. In Alberta it was led by the Protestant 'Bible Bill Aberhardt' who was smitten with Douglas's theorems about money reform yet did a poor job of executing his ideas. Recall that the bankers from Bay Street in Toronto and Bank of Canada destroyed Alberta's aspiration for creating our own sovereign money. We only have ATB Financial as his legacy; the largest public bank in North America. In principle a public bank can issue debt money without charging interest though it does not do so in fear that it would upset the current money powers.
>
> There is nothing left of the social credit movement and party that Aberhardt started which was guided by Judie-Christian values.

Some believe Aberhardt who died suddenly in office on his way to Vancouver was murdered.

Moreover CH Douglas was maligned in England as 'anti-Seminitic' and his ideas vanished drowned out by Hitler's blitzkrieg and rise to power.

My point is that even the far right Republicans do not go as far as the Social Credit movement in Alberta. Other than Ron Paul, few in the US understand the money system let alone propose alternatives to debt based money.

I would say any critic of Social Credit is a mis-representation, by strategic intention. The money power remains as our modern ruthless Pharaoh. As Walter and I have discussed, 'where is Moses who can call the bluff of the fertile fallacies of Pharaoh?'

Jesus gave us three lessons about money and it's future. But do we hear?

Best, Mark

And now we turn to our final chapter, now seeking a Window into Wisdom from Islam.

Bibliography

1 Heydorn, O. (2014) *Social Credit Economics*. 2nd Edition. Ancaster, ON, Canada: CreateSpace Independent Publishing.

2 Douglas, C.H. (1974) *Economic Democracy*. Sudbury, England: Bloomfield Books.

3 Douglas, C.H. (1973) *Social Credit*. New York: Gordon Press.

4 Douglas, C.H. (1979) *The Breakdown of the Employment System*. Vancouver: The Institute of Economic Democracy.

5 Hargrave, J. (1945) *Social Credit Theory Explained*. London: SCP Publishing House.

6 Douglas, C.H. (1935) *The Use of Social Credit*. Sydney: The Australian Social Crediter.

7 Douglas, C.H. (1978) *The Tragedy of Human Effort*. Vancouver: The Institute of Economic Democracy.

8 Douglas, C.H. (1935) *op cit.*

9 Douglas, C.H. (1936) *The Approach to Reality*. London: K.R.P. Publications.

10 Douglas, C.H. (1979) *op cit.*

11 Douglas, C.H. (1979) *op cit.*

12 Anielski, M. (2018) *Does Money Grow on Trees?* Vancouver: New Society Publishers.

17 Integral banking

Communitalism to communipreneurship

POST-LIBERAL GROUNDING
EMERGENT DIVIDEND
CITIZEN'S NAVIGATION
ULTIMATE EFFECT

Basheer Oshodi and Jubril Adeojo

Introduction

In this final chapter of section 5, primarily written by two Trans4M post-doctoral Fellows, Dr Basheer Oshodi and Dr Jubril Adeojo, we turn to Western effecting in that most Capitalist of sectors, banking and finance. Yet, here we discover, now again (see Chapter 5) in Nigeria, the employment of self-and-community, for the common good, through a process of *communipreneurship*. Equally, the "Eastern" wisdom focus turns from the New Testament, and Matthew's Gospel, focused in a 'new law', to the Islamic legal foundation of the *Maqasid al Shariah*.

This chapter connects the enriching of faith with and through enriching prosperity within the community. As such, it begins with the Burning Question of: can communipreneurship work within an Islamic framework? This leads directly into a Window into Wisdom, which focuses on a fourfold model of enriching, founded on Shariah. The Social Theory evolves Porter's five competitive forces of the market, to uncover the transpersonal, transdisciplinary, transcultural imbalances that require a new conceptualisation of communipreneurship. Finally, the Illustrative Case examines how the research academy and social innovation laboratory of CISER are being developed, to employ self-and-community within the Islamic banking sector of Nigeria, to build a social economy.

Burning Question: can communipreneurship work within an Islamic framework?

Understanding the being of communipreneurship (or isejoseneurship)

The word "Isejoseneurship" is rooted in a Yoruba cultural heritage and indigenous literacy, which connotes working towards a communal goal or aspiration. *Ise*, a Yoruba word means work (in the context of process or system), whilst *jose* indicates communal effort and aspiration, and **neur** originates from the Greek word meaning neuron, to connect as an actor. As such, *isejoseneurship* is defined as a process and system of starting and managing viable and sustainable businesses, in a communal manner, towards the common good of the society. This entirely elides with the goals of Sharia Law (see Window into Wisdom). At the same time, in reality, the Maqasid al Shariah genealogy of the 4Es (see below), with its dynamic balance, was rooted in the African culture long before Islam reached the region. Africans found themselves emerged in the culture of doing things together. They would cultivate family land collectively, engage in communal entrepreneurship, communal savings and investment which can be described as Isejoseneurship.

In order to enable local-to-global understanding of this new concept, we translated isejoseneurship to English, meaning "Communipreneurship". In our research-to-innovation centre, CISER (see Illustrative Case), we integrate the core values of the different forms of entrepreneurship from capitalistic, to social, and indigenous, to form the essence and embodiment of communipreneurship. From capitalist entrepreneurship we have built on the principles of viability and sustainability in terms of profitability and technology advancement. From social entrepreneurship we utilise the principles of conscience for the common good, together with societal impact. From indigenous entrepreneurship we activate collectivism and culturalism.

In Figure 17.1 we illustrate how we visually represented isejoseneurship/communipreneurship in line with the Yoruba cultural elements, towards the common good of the community. In this respect Isejoseneurship achieves a dynamic balance of enriching between the Four Realms, East, South, West and North.

Within the Eastern Realm enriching faith is closely associated with religion, tribal identity marks and drums. The Southern Realm grounds respect and being remorseful towards enriching prosperity. Expansion of wealth in old times is associated with the wars won and territories controlled thereby lodged in the Western Realm. Enriching intellect for the Yoruba is associated with the knowledge of the gods, of Orisha and Obatala. Those that consult the oracle were indeed the ones with divine intellect, who performed the rituals and directed the worship, according to the Northern Realm-.

The genealogy of the 4Es and communipreneurship

The genealogy of the 4Es (for Enriching) represents the ability of the human-self to catalyse its community, so that communipreneurship becomes firmly rooted in society. It then becomes necessary to scrutinise the practicability of the 4Es as they influence the community, sanctuary, research academy and the laboratory, as implemented in different parts of Nigeria.

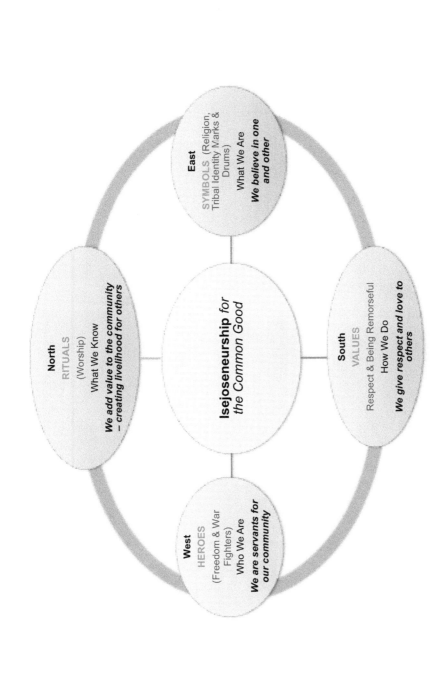

Figure 17.1 Isejoseneurship for the common good

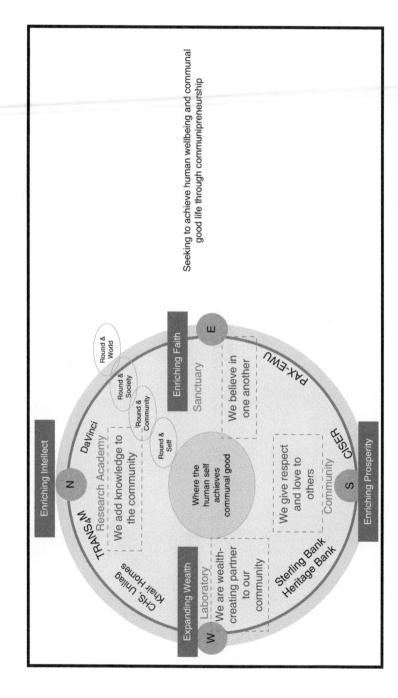

Figure 17.2 Integral banking for the common good of the community, society and the world

Source: Reproduced with kind permission of Drs Basheer Oshodi & Jubril Adeojo.

Enriching prosperity through the community ("southern")

This is the vital core of communipreneurship, where productivity of an eco-system is co-created and owned by the community for the common good. Communipreneurship and integral banking concepts are both grounded in the co-creation of sustainable livelihoods, in order to enrich prosperity in terms of jobs creation and wealth distribution in any given community. To make the enrichment of prosperity more prevalent across different communities in Nigeria for the common good, CISER decided to register as a microfinance institution, a social enterprise that will embark on the call to enrich prosperity across neglected rural communities in Nigeria.

CISER has adopted the concepts of integral banking and communipreneurship as its pivotal strategic propositions to improve the lives and well-being of the neglected communities via emancipation of the people to becoming communipreneurs, and co-creating communiprises and integrators that will continue to add value to, and safeguard the prosperity of the community. CISER also realises that the call must be ecosystem driven. On that basis, CISER works closely with local and international development agencies, which are active in Nigeria (and Africa), government ministries and agencies, and other private sector institutions such as development banks, commercial banks, microfinance banks and institutions, and Islamic banks.

Enriching faith through the sanctuary ('eastern')

Also in the spirit and GENE of integral banking and communipreneurship, enriching faith is critical. A real case example is the current transformative works in Ewu community, Nigeria, being spearheaded by *Pax Herbals* (see Chapter 16), where formerly idle women were socio-economically empowered and emancipated via the *Pax Herbal-Sterling Bank* Non-interest microfinance scheme. The shared spirituality and consciousness facilitated by the Ewu Monastery promotes the enrichment of not only faith, but also prosperity in Ewu community, towards a shared common good. The sanctuary sustains the moral core that is critical for the common good of the community.

Enriching intellect through research academy ('northern')

The practical research academy is founded in the symbiotic relationship between *DaVinci Institute for Technology Management*, South Africa and the *TRANS4M Centre for Integral Development*. These two institutions, through a mode 2 university approach pick up raw intellectual materials from communities and blend them with ingredients from the 4 Realms, the rounds, integral research method, methodology, critique and action (see Introductory chapter). This is further merged with social ontology, spirituality, enterprise and statehood *TRANS4M*-wise.

The *DaVinci* approach emphasises how enterprises can innovate through technology – intellectually, conceptually and material-wise. *TRANS4M* influences communities with by framing communal studies through its teaching. Equally, the *DaVinci Institute* helps to convert this knowledge-creation into embodied enterprises, and, indeed, through communipreneurship. In terms of Islamic formation, this type of Mode 2 (research-to-innovation) university or research academy is exactly what the Maqasid al Shariah seeks to achieve by truly enriching intellect through action research.

This was the style of university in the early Muslim world from the 7th century to the collapse of the Ottoman Empire (1). In the 14th century, Ibn Khaldun (1332–1406), from Tunis, was able to implement the theories he created by being an actor on the stage of governance, economics, militarily and academia. He showed how reducing government expenditure on mercenary armies could shift resources toward education and human development (2). The enrichment of intellect had always been given priority. But, what happened to the 'locus of control' and zeal of the Muslim world thereafter?

The maqasid, or purpose of Sharia, became limited to issues of faith, the five pillars of Islam and the articles of religion. But, now, the awakening of this reality for Africa, and indeed southern economies, is what has motivated the innovation described in this chapter. The action of building Islamic banking, through communipreneurship is, then, lodged in the sanctuary and academy, together, so that wealth is created, enhanced and expanded in such a manner that achieves communal well-being.

Expanding wealth through the laboratory ('western')

The aim of a community, within this Islamic programme, is to consistently expand social wealth by effectively and efficiently utilising factors of production, through the coordination of people (social reality), spiritual (value), state (action) and market (experience) (3). The *Centre for Integral Social and Economic Research* (CISER) aims to be an effective laboratory for this purpose. Acting through its agents, in financial and other social and action-research institutions it seeks to carry out this work of practical, hands-on implementation of the dividends of the community, sanctuary and research academy. This expansion of wealth is demonstrated in the activities of *Sterling Bank*, *Heritage Bank* and the emerging *Khair Homes* mortgage bank, each of which is based on integral and Islamic finance principles. Furthermore, CISER has expanded its activities to the *Centre for Housing Studies*, University of Lagos, Nigeria.

The trajectory of integral banking

The significance of this innovation and its utilisation of Islamic banking principles is vital at this time. Africa is witnessing economic growth without real development. More so, the financial institutions in African states show huge profitability without truly creating wealth. They accumulate and transfer massive funds into government securities, treasury bills and bonds.

But, this has the result of creating money scarcity (see previous chapter) and raises the high cost of funds to the real economy, while even more dividends are declared by financial institutions, for their shareholders.

This is an ever-repeating cycle. This increases social inequality. In Nigeria, almost 50% of the adult population are either without jobs or have undefined earnings (4). Moreover, as development indications have started to show improvements, since the turn of the Millennium, the number of the jobless has increased, while the banks failed to create more entrepreneurial opportunities. It is this failure of the Western neo-classical economic system that consistently dominates the African financial system.

Integral banking, based on Islamic banking principles, can, then, be seen as a financial model that seeks to solve some of these economic challenges. It is a system that promotes the common good of society through self-entrepreneurial activities, communally influencing society and, indeed, the entire world, positively. This is achieved by the power of the human self to mould destiny in the direction of man's happiness.

Of course, this raises the question as to the practicability of the integral banking model. There is a need to define integral banking as a force, an idea, a spiritual movement and a financial mechanism that influences financial intermediation or ventures towards the common good. This spiritual movement also influences the actors and participants striving to achieve human well-being. We are demonstrating that it can be embedded in a wide definition of capitalist, socialist, welfare, communal and Islamic commercial jurisprudence.

In so doing, the entrepreneur, as a state, corporation or person is, also, influenced by the spirit of communipreneurship which seeks to primarily achieve social happiness. Such a transformational agenda sits on the infrastructural base of the community, the sanctuary, the university and the laboratory, while being propelled by the power of the human self. On the other hand, integral banking and communipreneurship crystalises knowledge gained from social ontology to betterment of life for the populace. The vehicle to achieve this integral financial system lies with the human self. It is dependent on the ability of the human self to consistently transform itself, community, society and the world. Thus, any financial system that defines its operations within this context is indeed an integral financial institution, whether local or global.

We now turn from our Burning Question to our Window into Wisdom, in this case drawing on Islam rather than Judeo-Christianity.

Window into Wisdom: the Maqasid al Shariah and the genealogy of the 4Es

The works of Iman Al-Gazalli, around 1111, were elaborated by Professor Umer Chapra in relation to how human development and

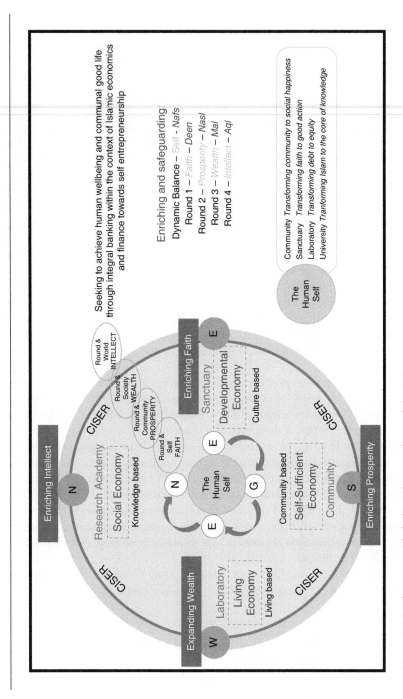

Figure 17.3 The Maqasid al Shariah Genealogy of the 4Es

well-being is interpreted within Islam. The Maqasid al Shariah is the primary purpose of Islam and it seeks to promnote communal good-life and human well-being. Furthermore, it promotes anything that safeguards and enriches the human self, faith, prosperity, wealth and intellect (5). Figure 17.3 illustrates the genealogy of the maqasid in relation to Lessem and Schieffer's 'process of holistic development' (6), starting with the human self.

The human self (nafs)

The human self is an important element of the five variables making up the maqasid. The human self (nafs) is the core of human activities. It is the spirit within the inner mind that produces, safeguards and enriches faith (deen), prosperity (nasl), wealth (mal) and intellect (aql). This human self, as human power, helps humanity to show dignity, self-respect, human brotherhood and societal equality.

The Self promotes justice, spiritual and moral uplift. It ignites the mind to give priority to the security of life, prosperity and honour. The human self envisages freedom and rights, from speech to economic emancipation. Equally, education, need fulfilment, employment and self-employment are integral to the human self. As such, the equitable distribution of income and wealth is vital. Such wealth may be conceived as that of the self, community, society or international. The importance of this human characteristic allows it to maintain a dynamic balance (7) in the Maqasid al Shariah/Genealogy 4Es, enriching faith, as the core of life for the faithful.

Enrichment of faith (deen)

Every religion establishes faith as prior. Of course, faith can seem independent of economics, politics, rule of law, health or education, although we have sought to emphasise its centrality to the employment of self and community, throughout this volume. Within the context of the maqasid, faith is associated with believe in one God, the Ever-Existing (al Daim), the Creator of the Creation (Khaliqi Makhluqat), the Sovereign (Malik), the Disposer of Affairs (Wakil), and the Source of Peace (Salam).

Faith in Islam is also associated with other articles, including reading of the books of God (Taurat (Torah), Injil (Gospel) and Holy Qu'ran), as members of the Ahl al Kitab (People of the Book, together with Jews and Christians), the Prophets, the Angels, the Day of Judgement, and predestination. The maqasid on the other hand places a stress on values and rules of behaviour, proper motivation, and moral as well as material education. It spells out the need for justice, freedom, security of life, property and honour while fulfilling socio-economic and political obligations, practices, tolerance and mutual care and trust.

Enriching faith is, also, associated with the removal of poverty and availability of entrepreneurial opportunities – self, communal, societal and global. Faith spells out equitable distribution, social solidarity and political stability and tolerance. Furthermore, enrichment of faith means humanity is expected to engage in acts of worship (ibadat). While some Islamic jurist have constrained worship to just the five pillars of Islam – faith (imam), prayers (salat), compulsory alms (zakat), fasting (siam) and pilgrimage (hajj), others agree that everything a man or woman does towards the pleasure of God is worship (ibadat). Worship, then, includes many other socio-economic and political activities for human good. Research, entrepreneurship, communipreneurship, political activities, charity activities and even smiles in the street become worship: on the Southern path of Relation.

Enriching of prosperity (nasl)

The enrichment of prosperity is associated with proper upbringing, morals and intellectual development. It promotes marriage, family and communal unity in a manner that fulfils human wants and needs. Prosperity, in this context, engenders an unpolluted human environment and eliminates freedom from fear, conflict and insecurity. The safeguarding and enrichment of prosperity has the goal of producing generations that are free from want, free from poverty, enabled to achieve self-hood, and able to transfer well-being to future generation.

It is not enough for the 'self' to be satisfied; or for one community to prosper whilst the neighbouring community struggles with basic survival. It is not prosperity when a society is unable to solve the challenge of poverty while the world looks on. The self, then, becomes important in the creation of communipreneurship, which is passed from one generation to the other. In the same vein, communal prosperity means members are able to create their own employment opportunities over time. Prosperity aligns with a self-sufficient economy, based on community efforts. It is the second layer of the genealogy of the maqasid leading to the third layer – the creation and preservation of wealth: on the Eastern path of Renewal.

Expanding and safe-guarding wealth (mal)

The wealth of self, of communities, of society and that of the entire world is motivated by the human-self. The ability to generate this wealth is a function of humanity's ability to direct the intellect, prosperity and faith into productive ventures. Wealth is further enriched through a sound educational background applied for man's common good rather than just self-interest.

It is on this basis that we have developed 'integral communipreneurship' through banking and finance. This wealth is directed towards the entire community and society, by providing employment and creating opportunities for self-employment. This action reduces real poverty and inequality rather than simply improving development indicators.

Attention has increasingly been placed – by the international community, academic elites and the political class – on the fact that GDP growth in an unequal society never reduces poverty, unemployment and income inequality. The 80:20 ratio pertains in many societies, as well as globally, although this seems to be concentrating to more like 1% of wealth controls 50% of all resources. It is the responsibility of communities to create their own wealth, such that community members become partners in business rather than working for one person or a group of the bourgeoisie.

We need to question why should the proletariat not assume the status of entrepreneurs? Can integral banking achieve this reality? Where will the start-up funds come from? What is the cost of funds? Enriching wealth calls for the perfection of co-ownership and partnership arrangements – the core elements in true integral banking and communipreneurship. How can integral banking address the concerns of Marx and Engels, in their narration of *The Communist Manifesto*, not for 1848 but for the 21st century?

> *It has drawn the most heavenly ecstasies of religious fervour, of chivalrous enthusiasm, of philistine sentimentalism, in the icy water of egotistical calculation. It has resolved personal worth into exchange value, and in place of the numberless indefeasible chartered freedoms, has set up that single, unconscionable freedom – Free Trade. In the word, for exploitation, veiled by religious and political illusions, it has substituted naked, shameless, direct, brutal exploitation.*

(8)

The Maqasid al Shariah seeks to achieve human well-being and communal good-life by safeguarding and enriching wealth. Thus it fits well into the communipreneurship ideology. But, can it shine effectively in a capitalistic world? Has integral banking genuinely avoided exploitation or is it simply masked as religious and political illusion? Has this laboratory of the living economy truly worked? Where in the world has it worked?

Again, Chapra is hopeful. He examines the enrichment of wealth as the optimum of development; as a means of saving and investment; of social solidarity and mutual trust; of equitable distribution of wealth; of freedom of enterprise backed by research and technological improvement leading to innovation (ibid). It is this innovation that shapes the development and expansion of wealth (mal), which is trust from God leading to a living economy – a laboratory of self, communal and societal exploration: on the Western path of Realisation.

Enrichment of Intellect (aql)

The intellect is the distinguishing characteristic of a human being and its continual enrichment is expected to lead to technological advancement and innovation. The intellect is the source of humanity's ability to hold its own fate and structure it to taste. The intellect is the power humanity has over every creation of God.

Humankind has utilised only a fraction of our intellect and wisdom. S/he has prioritised bodily pleasures over the potency of the intellect. Self, communities and societies with intellect have excelled in developmental matters far above nations that depend on natural resources. More so, the ability of integral banking and communipreneurship to be feasible and viable is dependent on the ability to reshape the future through a sustainable imagination of the intellect.

It is through this abstraction that man releases the faculty of reasoning to innovation, communal and self-employment, industrialisation and the creation of a transformational realm. Sound intellect is the reward for creative work. It is the reason for adaptive finance, one of integral banking and communipreneurship characteristics.

How would a community explain that its massive land area, excessive labour and entrepreneurial zeal has earned him nothing but poverty? Capital was created from co-operation of the people – from collective labour to collective savings, and then, to collective and mutual facility. Call it esusu or ajoo. It is the foundation of the African financial institution (3, ibid) at a time when the proletarians of Europe did not even have their land for cultivation.

So, what capacity can communipreneurship offer, in order to avoid the trajectory of Western industrial Capitalism? With wealth comes pride which breeds a different form of reasoning, a different intellect. The maqasid then seeks to promote, safeguard and enrich the type of knowledge-based reasoning which can transform society into the social economy – a unique form of university, the university of life, of societal happiness, and of sincere advancement: on the Northern path of Reason.

But, the Maqasid al Shariah remains as a theoretical exercise if it is unable to practically transform communities and societies. This communal good-life can be achieved when communities are able to collectively create wealth through communipreneurship. It is in this light that communipreneurship is discussed as a co-creation process and application of the new thoughts within the Nigerian context.

We now turn from our Burning Question, and Window into Wisdom to the Social Theory that underlies this penultimate chapter.

Social Theory: communipreneurship towards employing self-and-community: Nigeria's experience

In our calling to promote and achieve the employment of self-and-community over the promotion of (self) employment, we critiqued the prevalent Porter's five market competitive (external) forces (9) that commonly force businesses to fail. The critique was aimed at introducing the Integral 4 Community Cooperative Actions for employment of community.

The Integral 4 Community Cooperative Actions are:

• Contribution from the integrators
• Contribution from the people and community
• Contribution from the communiprises i.e. complementary businesses, alternative businesses, and technical support businesses
• Benefits for aspiring and new communipreneurs

Contribution from the integrators

Unlike the Porters' competitive forces, that are focused on the threats imposed by the bargaining power of the suppliers on businesses or enterprises, the integrators in this context are either suppliers or bigger businesses (commonly in the urban ecosystem) that aim to co-create sustainable business (or livelihood) opportunities for communipreneurs in the rural ecosystem (and even in their urban environment as well). A real case story is *Fruit and Veg City Limited* (trading as *Food Lover's Market*) in South Africa (across other African countries), that serves as an integrator by encouraging outgrowing of agricultural products, as well as providing guaranteed purchase prices or marketing of the products.

Another case story is of the collaboration between *Heritage Bank* (via our coresearcher, Olugbenga Awe at CISER) in Nigeria and the *Central Bank of*

Nigeria (the duo) to cocreate and implement the *Agriculture Anchor Borrower Programme*, which encourages smallholder farmers (as communipreneurs), in the rural communities, to form themselves into groups and cooperatives in order to outgrow agricultural products in bulk. The duo also engaged food processors (such as rice millers) in the urban ecosystem to serve as the anchor or off-taker (in this context, the integrators) to provide guaranteed purchase of the products at an agreed price for the common good of both parties. It is this practical approach to explaining the maqasid that leads to the contribution of the human self to communal good-will and prosperity.

Contribution from the people and community

In the case of Porter's forces, the bargaining power of the buyers and consumers also poses a threat to the growth and survival of the business, by driving down the prices of the products or services, due to low market demand, as well as the changing taste of the consumers. In the case of the integral community co-operative actions, consumers and buyers are perceived as the people and the community that consume or use the product or service of the communipreneurs for the common good of the community.

The people and community see the communipreneurs as an integral part of socio-economic development, for the community, purposefully in the areas of jobs creation, as well as wealth distribution, and as such, the people and community are committed to a continued relationship with the communipreneurs. They also provide resources needed by the communipreneurs such as labour, land, and innovative ideas to improve the quality of the products and services. An example of this (see Illustrative Case, this chapter) is the case of the Ewu community (anchored by Fr Dr Anselm Adodo (see Chapter 16), and Dr Basheer Oshodi of CISER), where the Monarch of the community contributed unused fertile farmlands to emancipate the new and existing communipreneurs in the community. This, effectively, boosted their productivity, creating socio-economic development and inclusiveness in the community.

Contribution from the communiprises

In the case of Porter's competitive forces we have threats from alternative or substitute businesses. In the realm of communipreneurship, there is an emphasis on the need to have complementary businesses (or enterprises) to provide for necessary missing support services and contribute to the growth and sustainability of the communipreneurs and the enlarged community. The development of communiprises assist in financial co-creation, providing support through technological capacity, innovation, financial services, infrastructures and overall systemic thinking, towards well-being.

In the case of financial services, the communiprise can be the formal bank that supports beyond basic financial services to the communipreneurs and the community. The financial institution will be close to the community and be part of the business, thereby providing supply-lending finance or partnership arrangement aimed at ensuring that communal ventures survive and grow. In this context, the communiprise supports the communipreneurs with proper business records-keeping, in terms of revenues and expenses in line with modern standards.

A co-researcher at CISER, Yusuf Adeojo employs this approach in his dealings with rural communities in Nigeria. One case story was in Ajegunle community in Lagos, Nigeria, where Yusuf via *Heritage Bank*, adopted existing enterprises to act as a communiprise (an agent of the bank) to render basic financial services to the Ajegunle communipreneurship and community. Where communipreneurs need access to markets via online presence, a communiprise can also be co-created to provide for the common good of the communipreneurs at an agreed settlement arrangement.

Benefits for aspiring and new communipreneurs

According to Porters' forces, there are barriers to entry for new entrants, but under the integral community cooperative, within the path of the maqasid, there are some benefits of being new and aspiring communipreneurs, in order to serve and add value to the community at large, as depicted in Figure 17.3.

A case example of this has been that of the *Young Entrepreneurs Business Training Programme* (YEBTP) scheme, anchored by one of us (Jubril, within CISER), via *Heritage Bank*. Within the Ajegunle community, aspiring new communipreneurs were empowered and mentored by existing and experienced communipreneurs, in the same line of businesses. The community and experienced communipreneurs encouraged the young individuals to venture into specific sustainable business lines, in order to develop self-sufficiency, for the common good of the people. They gained a variety of benefits relevant to starting their businesses, such as access to markets, information and financial advice, for business survival and growth.

Integral banking for the common good

Integral banking is a relatively new phenomenon, assimilating a neo-modern mix, within the model of the four worlds, of theory ("Northern"), through action research ("Western"), infused with the Maqasid al Shariah ("Eastern"), for community benefit ("Southern"). It is this communal togetherness that creates wealth through the material economic resources of the people, the community.

This composite *Integral Dynamics* model (10) manifests its constituent elements of nature and community, sanctuary, university (now research academy) and laboratory, where each one depends on the other to form an integral ecosystem. We (11) related the maqasid to the strength of the Islamic economic system to create wealth, achieve prosperity and reduce poverty. Again, Ronnie Lessem (12), in *Integral Advantage*, went even further to draw attention to the integral bond and dynamic balance that is achieved in societies, in economies and jurisdictions where the spiritual and material merge so perfectly well with nature and the social. It is when nature, culture, technology and the market fuse closely, under the organising principle of an internal polity, that a society truly releases its economic genius.

Achieving communal good-life through communipreneurship

We can compare learning from the Maqasid al Shariah and the genealogy of the 4Es, co-creation and conceptualisation process of communipreneurship with conventional entrepreneurship. We have cocreated a new concept of entrepreneurship rooted in the specifics of the African and Yoruba cultural heritage. Our goal was to produce an effective approach that integrates indigenous and exogenous knowledge in entrepreneurship (or livelihood co-creation), with innovations, in order to cocreate socio-economically inclusive communities. Hence, the process and system is initiated and driven by a community, rather than by an (heroic) individual, as is represented in many cases of conventional exogenous entrepreneurship found in capitalistic and social entrepreneurship.

The conundrums with entrepreneurship (and self-employment)

The practical interpretation of the maqasid, then, becomes our clear objective, which is made easy by learning from other school of thoughts. Schumpeter (13) repeatedly argued that any form of entrepreneurship is vitally productive for the economy, in terms of the business cycle, as innovation generates the employment of capital (both human and physical) and labour, to create and distribute wealth. He, also, placed strong emphasis on the importance of entrepreneurs remaining profitable in business.

We have realised, on the one hand, in contemporary Africa, that while entrepreneurs pursue profitability for their own prosperity the communal good-life of the people can suffer. On the other hand, we, also, recognised that the self-same end result can apply to social entrepreneurs, when they strive to achieve social impact, if they focus on making a profit for self and the enterprise. To further understanding this conundrum, we dissected the impact of entrepreneurship into two forces, the positive one, and the destructive force. At the end of the dichotomy of the forces, we realised that the effects of the destructive force can be more long lasting, and completely outweigh, that of the positive force.

We established that the effects of positive force of entrepreneurship on the community are as follows, but not limited to them:

- Livelihoods are created, and wealth distributed as a result of the jobs offered by the entrepreneur.
- Via the above, those employed and their households are able to afford access to basic amenities including healthcare and education.
- Women are empowered, when employed by the entrepreneur (who may be a woman).
- Cooperative society is formed and funded by those who are employed, to enable availability of credit supply for its members, for the common good of the community.

Yet, moving on to the destructive force of entrepreneurship, for entrepreneurs to remain profitable in business, they can sacrifice many of their resources to achieve profitability. Some of those resources are human (those employed in the community), physical assets, and financial. Such sacrifices result in some of the following consequences (but are not limited to them) for the community:

- Rising poverty levels in the community, as those employed become unemployed, sacrificing employment of the community.
- The economy of the community becomes static or even deteriorates, as a result of absences of the entrepreneur from the community, reducing its mobilisation.
- Disruption in the availability of basic amenities for the people.
- A survival mentality is generated in the community.

Following this introduction of the new concept of communipreneurship, we turn to its practical application in communities within Nigeria, via the co-researchers of CISER. We now, finally, turn to our Illustrative Case.

Illustrative Case: CISER: a laboratory enfolded in Sterling Bank

In a bid to achieve communipreneurship, one of us (Basheer), a cofounder of *CISER* and Group Head, Non-Interest Banking at *Sterling Bank*, has consistently transplanted the learnings of the *CISER* community and the *DaVinci-TRANS4M* action research methodology into the laboratory of Sterling Bank. As advocates of Islamic economics and banking, which finds its root in the maqasid, we realised that Nigeria and, indeed Africa, has abundant human and natural

---

resources, but lacks the communipreneurship abilities to effect timely socio-economic development.

Interest is not allowed in the Islamic banking principles but equity and debt transactions are allowed. Equity transactions include a variety of partnership and co-ownership contracts. Many Islamic banks avoid partnership transactions because of their huge exposures to moral hazard and performance risk. As such, Basheer has been able to introduce such co-ownership transactions in the areas of innovative technology, agricultural production and agro-commodity trading, micro and small businesses, and real-estate development for the common good of the society.

Communipreneurship enthusiasm has, then, been demonstrated in the bank, with the effect that over 500,000 people have been impacted positively from this action. Innovative transport payment solutions, through communipreneurship, have brought about convenience for hundreds of thousands of commuters in Lagos, on a daily basis. Farmers are, also, able to partners with the bank to buy commodities in bulk during harvest, sell on the futures market and share the profits/ losses when goods are sold. Additionally, the bank has engaged in developing e-learning materials for school pupils, through partnership with vendors.

Through partnership, the Islamic banking window of *Sterling Bank* engaged three property development firms to build over 600 units of affordable houses for middle income segments in Lagos and Abuja in 2016–2017 alone, while refinancing or replacing another 200 units of interest-bearing mortgages. The Islamic banking window used lease-to-own as a debt finance model, diminishing co-ownership structures, to create home finance mortgages in the most efficient manner. Prospective home-owners, seeking off-plan mortgages, contribute their equity or security deposit over the construction period, rather than being required to fund a deposit of 20–30% percent equity, which is a standard precondition for receiving a mortgage facility from a conventional for-profit bank, in Nigeria.

The bank has also created debt-based contracts for micro and small business owners, which are in single-digit profit mark-ups, at a time when conventional interest-based loans are charging 26–30% interest rates per annum. The *Sterling Bank* Islamic banking window, also, accepts only 10% equity contributions and two personal guarantors in lieu of collateral, which the bottom segment do not have. The bank has, equally, granted interest-free loans to the Ewu Community to promote communipreneurship. This fund is expected to increase over time.

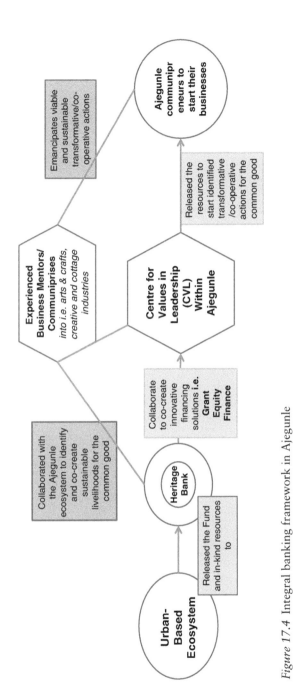

Figure 17.4 Integral banking framework in Ajegunle

Innovation from Heritage Bank

At *Heritage Bank* in 2016, Jubril and Yusuf Adeojo (brothers, located at *CISER*) embarked on a transformative journey in Ajegunle, Lagos. Via the duo, Heritage Bank partnered with the *Centre for Values in Leadership* (CVL) to collectively activate Ajegunle community, with the ultimate goal of empowering young men and women. The bank and CVL worked together on the implementation of the *Young Entrepreneurship Business Training Programme* (YEBTP) in Ajegunle to mentor and provide finance to help, young peoples' start-up businesses, as a sustainable livelihood for the common good of the community. Figure 17.4 shows the integral banking framework for the transformative work in Ajegunle.

The activation of Ajegunle was in response to burning societal imbalances, stemming from lack of livelihood (business or job) for the youths, to increasing crime rate amongst the male youths, and increasing level of prostitution amongst the female youths.

Embodiment of integral development – common good indicators

Individual level

- 100 young people trained, emancipated and empowered to become communipreneurs; 90 women; 10 men.
- Over 5,000 unbanked people helped to open accounts.

Organisational level

- 15 Experienced Business Mentors/Communiprises supported the young communipreneurs in their target business areas.
- Young communipreneurs started their enterprises in a variety of different sectors.
- Enterprise sectors: Shoemaking, bakery, hair dressing, mechanics, fashion design (and tailoring).
- Every emancipated communipreneur accessed grant-equity finance of *N80,000 ($200USD)*, to create an enterprise.

Community Level – transforming community to social happiness

- Formation of *Ajegunle Communipreneurs Cooperative Society* (ACCS) – consisting of the communipreneurs, *CISER, CVL* and the business mentors/communiprises.

- Reduced levels of crime and prostitution.
- Livelihood opportunities – each communipreneur has employed at least two staff members.

The emergence of khair homes

Khair is an Arabic word which means noble, admirable and praise-worthy. It's purpose is to fully enhance and expand socioeconomic wealth – thereby achieving communal good-will and human well-being. *Khair Homes* has emerged as a new property development and home finance provider. It is an innovative integral financial institution, aligning with the maqasid. *Khair* is a mortgage bank involved in equity-based finance, over a range of projects, including property development, Real Estate Investment Trusts (REITs), social housing, affordable housing, urban regeneration and renewal, utilising special purpose vehicles. *Khair* mobilises deposits through a variety of crowd-funding arrangements, sukuk, private equity, co-ownership, partnership and, mainly, long-term debt instruments – both local and foreign.

The objective of Khair is to close the almost 20 million housing gap deficit in Nigeria. There needs to be a close interplay of people, spirit, state and market in order to achieve true communipreneurship for the betterment of mankind. As such, *Khair* seeks to provide a minimum of 1,500 new housing unit per annum, which would be the largest number offered by any single institution in Nigeria. In this respect *Khair* aims to be a laboratory for communipreneurship, where the community are part owners of the *Khair Homes* business franchise.

Khair Homes will use the *Centre for Housing Studies*, University of Lagos as its research academy, alongside *Trans4M* and the *DaVinci Institute*. The *Center for Housing Studies* is presently developing a 10-year housing master plan for the largest state in Nigeria and already consulting to provide 5,000 affordable unit housing project in Lagos. In addition, Basheer Oshodi, as a Senior Research Fellow and Lecturer at the Centre, leads other coresearchers in identifying alternative finance sources for housing delivery in Nigeria.

Conclusion

The primary purpose of Islam is the Maqasid al Shariah, which is founded on five elements. The human-self acts as the custodian of the remaining four rounds in a manner that allows the community to enrich prosperity, by giving respect and love to others. Sanctuary transforms the enrichment of faith, thereby believing in others to achieve communipreneurship. The university or research academy enriches the intellect by adding knowledge to the community. The laboratory transforms debt financial instruments to equity while expanding communal wealth through partnership ventures.

In this way, an Islamic template is being developed to reproduce the integral 4 Worlds model in Nigeria. The unfolding narrative captured in this chapter starts with communipreneurship, alongside the new thinking of integral banking and finance. This chapter provides a clear example of the way in which the employment of community for the common good of society is being shaped in Africa, taking us back, in circular vein, to where we started, with Chinyika, in Chapter 2. As such, we have seen how work can practically evolve from grounding in community development, through emerging self-mobilisation, navigation using new systems of the circular economy and liberation, to the genuine employment of community. This circles onward to further rounds of the GENEalogy, through co-creation, enabling environments to foster employment of self-and-community. We finally, now, turn to our concluding chapter.

Bibliography

1 Morgan, M.H. (2007) *Lost History: The Enduring Legacy of Muslim Scientists, Thinkers, and Artists*. Washington, DC: National Geographic Society.
2 Khaldun, I. (2005) *The Muqaddimah: An Introduction to History – The Classic Islamic History of the World*. Oxford: Princeton University Press.
3 Oshodi, B.A. (2014) *An Integral Approach to Development Economics: Islamic Finance in an African Context*. Farnham: Gower Publishing.
4 Oshodi, B.A. (2015) *Measuring Inequalities in Africa's Largest Economy*. Social Science Research Network.
5 Chapra, M.U. (2008) The Islamic Vision of Development in the Light of Maqasid Al Shari'ah. *Occasional Paper Series 15*. International Institute of Islamic Thought. London: IIIT.
6 Lessem, R. and Schieffer, A. (2015) *Integral Renewal: A Relational and Renewal Perspective*. Farnham: Gower Publishing.
7 Lessem, R. and Schieffer, A. (2010) *Integral Research and Innovation: Transforming Enterprise and Society*. Farnham: Gower Publishing.
8 Marx, K. and Engels, F. (1848/1969) *Manifesto of the Communist Party*. Selected Works, Vol. 1. Moscow: Progress Publishers, pp. 98–137.
9 Porter, M. (1980) *Competitive Strategy: Techniques for Analysing Industries and Competitors*. New York: The Free Press.
10 Lessem, R., Schieffer, A., Tong, T.T. and Rima, S.D. (2013) *Integral Dynamics: Political Economy, Cultural Dynamics and the Future of the University*. Farnham: Gower Publishing.
11 Oshodi, B.A. (2014) *An Integral Approach to Development Economics: Islamic Finance in an African Context*. Farnham: Gower Publishing.
12 Lessem, R. (2015) *Integral Advantage: Revisiting Emerging Markets and Societies*. Farnham: Gower Publishing.
13 Schumpeter, J. (1949/1989) *Economic Theory and Entrepreneurial History*. Reprinted from Change and the Entrepreneur. Cambridge: Harvard University Press, 1949. In Clemence, R. (Ed.) *Essays on Entrepreneurs, Innovations, Business Cycles, and the Evolution of Capitalism*. New Brunswick: Transaction Publishers.

18 Evolving work

Employing community, self and enterprise

Final summary: GENE and gene

As we reach our final summary it is important to present a synoptic over-view of the entire story-line of the book. To this end, we set-out, below, a brief GENEalogy of each section and chapter. The book, as a whole, has cir-culated around the four worlds, so that each main Part covers one of these, from grounding in the South, through emergence in the East, navigating via the North and effecting in the West.

Just as the entire book is organised around the four integral realities/ worldviews, so is each section. In that respect, as below, we summarise the (larger) GENE process, from South around to West in each Part of the book. Furthermore, within each Chapter, we, also, followed the rhythm of the (smaller) gene, through grounding in *The Burning Question*, emerging in a *Window into Wisdom*, navigating according to some aspect of *Social Theory* and, to complete, effecting an *Illustrative Case*.

As has been seen, although the book is rooted in principles, philosophy and spirituality – which we have presented as a vital aspect of a 'fourth way' into economics, and will be explored much more completely in the next book in this series of four – we have been determined to provide real and extant cases, for each chapter theme, from across the globe, taking us to examples from Africa, Asia, Eastern and Western Europe, North and South America.

Thus, we started our story of employing self and community in the South and, for one of us, at least, (Ronnie/ Samanyanga) our homeland, in Zim-babwe, working our way, as per the integral rhythm of this book, through *Evolving Work* in each worldly case through the *gene*, with a particular focus on grounding and navigation in each instance.

South: employing community

Chinyika: communal identity to communal up-skilling: grounding community

Key Tenet

Opening in the South of the South we understand that community grounds what employment fundamentally means. It builds on COMMUNAL

IDENTITY (grounding) thereafter pooling vocations, in a REPRODUC-
TIVE ECONOMY (navigating) for communal up-skilling, so that all have a
livelihood together, beyond the self.

G: *COMMUNAL IDENTITY*: A fourfold interpretation of community
involves: *membership identity* (southern), *shared emotional or spiritual connection* (eastern), *social influence* (northern) and *fulfilment
of needs* (western).

E: *POOLING VOCATIONS*: The economy of the kingdom, in Luke's
gospel, is *built around table fellowship with people who are called
from the world of money, not to renounce it, but to see it in SOCIAL
perspective.*

N: *REPRODUCTIVE ECONOMY*: The large gatherings provide an
opportunity for VILLAGERS to sing and dramatise the social and
economic challenges facing the community. WOMEN *have awoken
to take up their traditional role – the home stands because of the
mother –* in the shona language of Zimbabwe *'Musha ndimai'*.

E: *COMMUNAL UP-SKILLING*: *Habitat has grown* worldwide *to
offer self-build housing options in communities across more than 100
countries, constructing 500,000 homes, during its 40 years of operation.* Local people and businesses donate building materials, volunteers are sought, home-owners up-skilled in self-building techniques.

Civil economy: gift relationship to emancipatory work: emergent reciprocity

Key Tenet

Emerging through the East of the South we see how employing the community is liberated, where self-interest in transformed into civic mutuality. It
establishes GIFT RELATIONSHIPS, which emerges reciprocity, in a CIVIL
ECONOMY, where work is emancipated, so that shared labour becomes
the organising principle of the economy.

G: *GIFT RELATIONSHIP*: Our parents passed on life to us. The sun
keeps shining. We connect economics and communality, from early
gift relationships to today's fantastically fast digital money circulation.
All are part of a reciprocal sacred economy.

E: *EMERGING RECIPROCITY*: Luke's parable emphasises the primacy of a gift relationship for emerging reciprocity. *If we give to we
will receive more. But, if we haven't given, we will lose even what we
had.*

N: *CIVIL ECONOMY*: This embodies a vision of commerce, in relationship to social well-being, which transforms self-interest into common

good. *In civil life individuals and self-directed passions become social, in order to employ and produce "civil happiness".*

E: *EMANCIPATORY WORK*: Through FECOFUN, Nepal, women forest workers experience higher levels of *community leadership, emancipation and self-determination, as a result of mobilisation, within civil society* organisations.

Relational sociology: collaborative platforms to humane working: navigating relationships

Key Tenet

Navigating via the North of the South, new technologies enable the development of a sharing economy, where patronage gives way to a relational society. COLLABORATIVE PLATFORMS open-up possibilities for mutual submission, under the conditions of a RELATIONAL PARADIGM, which effects an economy of humane working.

G: *COLLABORATIVE PLATFORMS:* present new opportunities for developments in a sharing economy. But, work based in these need to provide protection, fairness and real flexibility, to *move towards a relational understanding of community mobilised employment.*

E: *MUTUAL SUBMISSION*: The Last Supper offers *a model of mutual self-giving, submission and servant leadership*, which runs counter to practices of patronage in the 'gig economy'.

N: *RELATIONAL PARADIGM*: Former sociological models, based in structuralism, functionalism, social agency and interactionism are giving way to relationalism. Social interactions and the *elements that compose society need to be understood relationally*, developed out of the indigenous, 'bottom-up' experiences of communities.

E: *HUMANE WORKING*: *Co-operativo Mondragon* has established a relational economy of co-operatives, in the Basque Country, based on the principle of labour sovereignty. Even in times of economic crisis and 'Western austerity' *Mondragon has maintained communal employment for human flourishing and worker dignity.*

Employing community: confederal association to intentional community: mutual effect

Key Tenet

Effecting in the West of the South, evolving patterns of communal organisation are showing how the employment of community is being practically worked-out, through CONFEDERAL ASSOCIATION, based in the

Table 18.1 Employing the community

	South	East	North	West
GROUNDING	Communal Identity	Pooling Vocations	Reproductive Economy	Communal Up-Skilling
EMERGENCE	Gift Relationship	Emerging Reciprocity	Civil Economy	Emancipatory Work
NAVIGATION	Collaborative Platforms	Mutual Submission	Relational Paradigm	Humane Working
EFFECTING	Confederal Association	Common Ownership	Communitalism	Intentional Community

common ownership of property, generates COMMUNITALISM, visibly reflected in movements of intentional community.

> G: *CONFEDERAL ASSOCIATION:* represents a step-by-step process of dismantling former municipal state structures and private ownership, towards *communal organisation and local decision-making.*
>
> E: *COMMON OWNERSHIP*: The 'primitive communism' of the Acts economy, in Jerusalem, showed how *the pooling of property created the means of distribution*, on the basis of need, effected in the employment of a spiritual community.
>
> N: *COMMUNITALISM*: The work of Fr Dr Anselm Adodo and *Pax Herbals*, in Nigeria, reveals how *communitalism*, which integrates capitalist innovation with communal service, *navigates community healing and prosperity in the heart of Africa*, and beyond.
>
> E: *INTENTIONAL COMMUNITY*: The *Rojava Communes*, in West Kurdistan, demonstrate how *the democratic organisation of co-operatives can transform working*, from the employment of selves to communal organisation, even in war-torn regions.

Now, we turn from South to East, and the emphasis now, in *Evolving Work*, shifts from employing the Community to employing the Self.

East: employing the self

Noetics of nature: self-realisation to divine trade:
grounding human nature

Key Tenet

In the South of the East, ancient and contemporary spirituality reflect genuine vocation as the grounding for employment of the Self. SELF-REALISATION, founded in true calling, proceeds from turning the

HEART'S FACE towards the divine, reversing patterns of ownership and stimulating fair trade.

> G: *SELF-REALISATION*: Work that is based in a prior vocation – serving a greater purpose, by *engagement in the mystery of participation with the inner self, deeply with others and with the divine* – is more fulfilling. It reflects an emergence of the real Self.
>
> E: *TRUE CALLING*: The call of the first disciples illustrates that *true vocation is safer – even in the 'cloud of unknowing'*, as some mystics describe authentic self-life – than the unfulfilling secure work that, otherwise, we can let define us.
>
> N: *HEART'S FACE*: According to 13th-century Sufi philosopher Ibn al Arabi, the locus for the 'employment of the Self' is in *the heart, which is the centre of knowing/unkowing*, trans-rationally. Therein lies the Self's true face, employed as a reflection of the divine.
>
> E: *DIVINE TRADE*: Sophi Tranchell and *Divine Chocolate* have enabled a co-operative of cocoa farmers in rural Ghana to *own themselves, through an indigenous/exogenous confectionery company*, working integrally using the imagery of the Celtic cross.

Economics of the household: home working to partner with others: awakening spirit

Key Tenet

Emerging in the East of the East, it is recognised that home and work should be integrated. HOME WORKING emerges from wisdom, seeing the spiritual house as foundational for the HOUSEHOLD ECONOMY, providing for partnership with others.

> G: *HOME WORKING*: Contemporary labour markets increasingly reveal a *blurring of the divided self as per work and home*. New practices are a harbinger for transformed work patterns, which demonstrate a balance of wisdom in and through work.
>
> E: *SPIRITUAL HOUSE*: In the First Epistle of Peter, his readers – who are strangers in a strange land – are reminded that theirs is a home for the homeless. *The household of faith is a holy temple, built of living stones, in which every person is a needed part.*
>
> N: *HOUSEHOLD ECONOMY*: Russian political economist Sergey Bulgakov considers humanity to be both a spiritual and a material being. As such, *economic science and the study of labour and employment should be understood as part of a household economy*.
>
> E: *PARTNER WITH OTHERS*: Because its founder, Spedan Lewis, was realistic about inequalities created in a shareholder controlled,

profit-motivated businesses, the *John Lewis Partnership Constitution he established is based on the well-being of the Partners (workers), to provide satisfying, worthwhile employment.*

Commonwealth: ethical egoism to sustainable livelihood: threefold navigation

Key Tenet

Navigating from the North of the East ETHICAL EGOISM is placed at the heart of common wealth. The ASSOCIATIVE ENTERPRISE – founded in liberty, equality and, especially now, fraternity – is the basis for generating sustainable livelihoods.

> *G: ETHICAL EGOISM*: Green concerns – in consumption and production spheres – epitomise what Rudolf Steiner terms 'ethical egoism'. In order to live sustainably, as a civil society, each person (self) needs to live, work and act sustainably.
>
> *E: COMMON WEALTH: The message of Jesus is that personal wealth gets in the way of common wealth.* Riches restrict real human relationships, persuading us to get through the gate first. Once we're through, we often forget about those behind us.
>
> *N: ASSOCIATIVE ENTERPRISE: The economy is predicated on association, freedom and rights.* Employers need to find alternative work for those they lay off, in association with others, as part of the organisation of the whole economy.
>
> *E: SUSTAINABLE LIVELIHOOD*: Sekem, Egypt, has established biodynamic agriculture as a solution for the environmental, social and food security challenges of the 21st century. It is a successful business in accordance with ecological and ethical principles.

Sarvodaya: dignified livelihood to cultural capital: effect awakening

Key Tenet

Effecting in the West of the East, DIGNIFIED LIVELIHOOD aligns with other spiritual traditions to point-out how BLESSED WORK supports those in need and AWAKENING OF ALL individuals, groups and society, thereby drawing establishing cultural capital.

> *G: DIGNIFIED LIVELIHOOD*: In Small is Beautiful, Fritz Schumacher famously called for a Buddhist approach to economics. Business, economists and global leaders only take the needs of the poor seriously when they align with values of human life and dignity.

Table 18.2 Employing the self

	South	*East*	*North*	*West*
GROUNDING	Self-Realisation	True-Calling	Heart's Face	Divine Trade
EMERGENCE	Home-Working	Spiritual House	Household Economy	Partner with Others
NAVIGATION	Ethical Egoism	Common Wealth	Associative Enterprise	Sustainable Livelihood
EFFECTING	Dignified Livelihood	Blessed Work	Awakening Of All	Cultural Capital

E: *BLESSED WORK*: Wealth is not to be withheld. It is to be freely offered-up as a means of worship and giving to God. *To live in the midst of the poor means always having a source of blessing at work,* as we give to them some of the fruit of our labour.

N: *AWAKENING OF ALL: Sarvodaya,* in Sri Lanka, did not talk about employment or about welfare, but about awakening to six sets of values. To integrate any national development, the *moral, cultural, spiritual, political, social and economic* is involved.

E: *CULTURAL CAPITAL:* A growing movement is examining multiple – *including cultural inclusive of spiritual – capitals,* as being expressed in the terms of impact investment, for solving social problems. Each of these approaches establishes *value, subsumed under the principle of spirituality or 'Spirit'.*

We now turn from east to north, and from the employment of community and of self to work as recreation, as the end of employment, so to speak.

Turning north: beyond employment: work as recreation

The quest for meaning: agape economics to rehoming work: grounded in love

Key Tenet

In the South of the North, love provides the grounding for a new employment economics, not as a feeling but as a gritty response to global inequalities. AGAPE ECONOMICS offers a model for embodying love, as a 'third way' toward LIVING IN TRUTH, partly resulting in rehoming work.

G: *AGAPE ECONOMICS:* One response to the impoverishment of many communities in the Global South is the formulation of 'agape

Economics'. This gives rise to national debt for-giveness, towards *releasing creative communities from the burden of indebtedness.*

E: *EMBODYING LOVE:* Recreation is part of the divine plan for work. It is earthy, lively, heart and mind-stretching work, bringing love into agriculture, manufacturing and service activities, within the new industrial and communications revolution.

N: *LIVING IN TRUTH:* For Czech ex- President Vaclav Havel, capitalism and socialism have become redundant. The question is: *can we reconstitute the natural world as the true terrain of politics,* rehabilitating the personal experience of human beings?

E: *REHOMING WORK: Veja* and *Under Armour* challenge received wisdom about profit-maximisation, by not relying on the cheapest labour in distant locations. They 'walk the talk', *loving the worker, the locality and the planet,* in the footwear industry.

Critique of political economy: sustainable employment to regenerative work: emerging ecology

Key Tenet

From the East of the North there emerges a new political economy of employment, to look beyond standard industrial production to one based in ecological principles and recreation. SUSTAINABLE EMPLOYMENT is increasingly adopting circular working methods. These embody an ENERGETIC RECREATION, fostering an ethos of in-built, regenerative work.

G: *SUSTAINABLE EMPLOYMENT:* The latest wave of the green movement has seen a switch from defensive consumer action to green productive activity. This represents *a rediscovery of ecological industry, where the focus is on employment for sustainability.*

E: *CIRCULAR WORKING:* God doesn't stop working on the Sabbath, so why should we. *Through work we are sharing in the circular, four-fold task of creation, sustenance, work and service,* integrally linking God, humanity, labour and the world's healing.

N: *ENERGETIC RECREATION:* For Bernard Stiegler, *work-as-recreation is required to break the iron grip of slavery,* which represents an industrialisation of the spirit. Such counter-measures will lead to a new stage of libidinal/energetic ecology.

E: *REGENERATIVE WORK:* Ellen MacArthur's economic industrial model replaces the standard of "take, make, use, dispose" with one of *"recycle, design-in regeneration, use and further recycle",* to transform industrial production, from linear to circular.

The otium of the people: automated work to work as recreation:
navigating beyond employment

Key Tenet

The North of the North displays the rapidity of technological change, which is transforming work, so that navigation to recreative life is imminent and vital. AUTOMATED WORK is a reality within a connected society. REDISTRIBUTED TIME is inevitable with more work as recreation.

> G: *AUTOMATED WORK:* Automation, robotics and AI will mean that some jobs will be substituted, with others augmented. Culture and work should become far more integrated. The question is: *how will worthwhile life be paid for, outside of work?*
>
> E: *CONNECTED SOCIETY:* Work assists in connecting and integrating us as people. We may *celebrate those aspects of the automatic society that connect us to each other* and allow for more fulfilling work, enabling a greater quality of mutual abiding together.
>
> N: *REDISTRIBUTED TIME:* For Stiegler, we're living through the transition to automation, where *wages are no longer the source of purchasing power.* This requires a new process for redistributing time, to constitute and purchase forms of knowledge.
>
> E: WORK AS RECREATION: The increasing use of human-machine interfaces is allowing people to move away from drudge-jobs to higher-level skilled work, and, also, to spend more time in work as recreation, even in sectors such as agriculture.

Open source: immaterial labour to social networking:
effecting emancipation

Key Tenet

The West of the North is effecting liberating work that is taking unusual turns. IMMATERIAL LABOUR is creating much loving work. OPEN SOURCE is often unpaid, whilst socio-technical networking involves volunteers in economically valuable projects.

> G: *IMMATERIAL LABOUR:* Arguably, industrial labour is being replaced by "immaterial labour", through *the production of knowledge, information, and communication.* This takes two forms: intellectual and affective, respectively generating ideas and feelings.
>
> E: *LOVING WORK:* There are strange aspects to the final chapter of John's Gospel. The resurrected Lord eats fish, but his material body

Table 18.3 Beyond employment: work as recreation

	South	East	North	West
GROUNDING	Agape Economics	Embodying Love	Living in Truth	Rehoming Work
EMERGENCE	Sustainable Employment	Circular Working	Energetic Recreation	Regenerative Work
NAVIGATION	Automated Work	Connected Society	Redistributed Time	Work as Recreation
EFFECTING	Immaterial Labour	Loving Work	Open Source	Socio-Technical Networking

appears and disappears. *The disciples are called to take love to others, while and through continuing in their work.*

N: OPEN SOURCE: Programmers working on open source projects forgo sleep because they love programming and being part of a shared global effort. Linux was dedicated to collaboratively building the most beautiful technology for fun and for free.

E: SOCIO-TECHNICAL NETWORKING: The power of networking has been transform-ative for many scientific enquiries. The FightAids@ home project was revolutionary in both maximising brain-power and mobilising thousands in public health campaigns.

We now turn from "north" to "west", and from work, beyond employment, as recreation, to transforming employment through a newly integral self, enterprise and community.

West: transforming employment: new integral self, enterprise, community

Post-liberalism: transformed workplaces to blockchain distribution: post-liberal grounding

Key Tenet

In the South of the West we see the power of new institutions on the economy and politics, re-engaging communities. TRANSFORMED WORK-PLACES, linked to service values, can generate a MORAL ECONOMY, partly through blockchain distribution.

G: TRANSFORMED WORKPLACES: *Technology is transforming workplaces into potentially more democratic institutions.* It is in the sphere of enabling citizen-level policy-making that these disruptive technologies hold great appeal, with voters participating in crypto-democracy.

E: *SERVICE VALUES:* The fundamental message of Matthew's Gospel is that *real power is given to the weakest, so that politics becomes genuinely about service.* The kingdom of heaven turns economic values upside-down, with the last becoming first.

N: *MORAL ECONOMY:* The Post-Liberal World involves defining the goals of human society as a whole, so that each worthwhile role is deployed for the mutual achievement of these shared aims. This *requires both virtuous leadership and mutual obligation.*

E: *BLOCKCHAIN DISTRIBUTION:* Distributed information systems are going to transform the working world. *Use of the network has the capacity to shift the power dynamics* of liberal democracies and economies back towards the citizen.

Basic income: valuing identity to people's fund: emergent dividend

Key Tenet

The East of the West reflects the principles underpinning new, emergent forms of economic democracy. VALUING IDENTITY of each person is an important norm for universal welfare. Universal BASIC INCOME is a key policy goal towards a people's fund.

G: *VALUING IDENTITY:* Distributive information systems have the potential to organise work, as employing the community, on a radical new basis. This involves *revaluing persons-in-work, through an exchange of personal income for shared identity.*

E: *UNIVERSAL WELFARE:* The principle of universal basic provision is demonstrated in 'the feeding of the 5000'. In the feeding miracle, Jesus breaks and distributes five small loaves and two fishes to the crowd, so that all had more than enough to eat.

N: *BASIC INCOME:* Bertrand Russell advocated that a small income, sufficient for needs, should be secured to all, whether they work or not, with a larger income given to those willing to work. Clifford Douglas developed the idea of a "national dividend".

E: *PEOPLE'S FUND:* In Alaska, the state's oil wealth was used to create the *Alaska Permanent Fund,* so that a dividend was paid to all citizens. The principle behind this experiment in UBI was that *the Alaskan people owned their natural resources.*

Social credit: national balance to citizen's dividend: citizens' navigation

Key Tenet

In the North of the West we discover that some contemporary policies have old, even ancient, antecedents. NATIONAL BALANCE relies on principles of income equality and payments. SOCIAL CREDIT is experimental as a citizen's dividend.

G: *NATIONAL BALANCE:* A National Balance Sheet and Credit Account would balance financial and real wealth, augmented by full reserve banking, removing its power to create money *ex nihilo*. *Banking would support community well-being and leisure.*

E: *INCOME EQUALITY: Matthew's parable, the labourers in the vineyard*, presents kingdom wages based on equality rather than equity. *Everyone has their needs met.* Some consider universal provision to be unfair. But that is the social contract of the kingdom.

N: *SOCIAL CREDIT:* Every individual in the community has a legitimate claim to a personal share in the ownership of real credit. Financial credit should derive its value from real credit, so that *financial credit should always benefit the individuals of society.*

E: *CITIZEN'S DIVIDEND: Social Credit has been part of Canada's social and economic history for eight decades.* Despite political misrepresentations, the Socred story in that "western" Canada continues, with current economists not given up on social credit.

Integral banking: communal good to communipreneurship: ultimate effect

Key Tenet

As we conclude with our final example – turning from Canada to Nigeria – of effecting the employment of self and community, we see how innovative Islamic banking in Nigeria is transforming the lives of thousands. The COMMON GOOD is effected from a Godly purpose, in COOPERATIVE ACTION for communipreneurship.

G: *COMMON GOOD: Isejoseneurship is Yoruba meaning sustainable work for the common good.* It asserts that we are all servants of one

Table 18.4 Transforming employment: new integral self, enterprise, community

	South	*East*	*North*	*West*
GROUNDING	Transformed Workplaces	Service Values	Moral Economy	Blockchain Distribution
EMERGENCE	Valuing Identity	Universal Welfare	Basic Income	People's Fund
NAVIGATION	National Balance	Income Equality	Social Credit	Citizen's Dividend
EFFECTING	Common Good	Godly Purpose	Co-operative Action	Communipreneurship

another, so we return to the community, in Africa. It enriches faith and intellect, as well as wealth and prosperity.

E: *GODLY PURPOSE*: The *Maqasid al Sharia* is the goal of Islamic law. *Wealth is to be directed to the self, the community, social and world.* Integral communipreneur-ship is founded in the principle of developing the community through Godly intellect.

N: *COOPERATIVE ACTION*: Contributions from integrators, local people, communi-prises and communipreneurs establish co-operative actions towards communipreneur-ship. *Livelihoods are created and wealth distributed as a result of new community jobs.*

E: *COMMUNIPRENEURSHIP*: CISER (Centre for Integral Socio-Economic Research) is a laboratory for communipreneurship in Nigeria. Through principles of Islamic finance, youth entrepreneurship and community house-building, it serves the local community.

Final conclusions: transforming work in the age of integrality

And, so, we come to our final conclusions in relation to *Evolving Work*. A former colleague used to say that postmodernity was only the label we gave to our era "before we knew how to name the baby". Arguably, in the past decade, the baptism, bar or aqeeqah of contemporary "Western" society has occurred. We describe this as moving from postmodernity towards entering the *age of integrality*. If modernity asked the question "how do we manage?" and postmodernity was characterised by radical scepticism, asking the foundational question "who says?", the *age of integrality* is focused on asking "how do we connect" in the overall context of *working integrally*?

Of course, we see this in the rapid adoption of social media and the ubiquity of people – not only the young – tied to their mobiles, apps and browsers. But, equally, as we have seen in our explorations of the 'gig economy' and systems of sharing, profound new ways of working are emerging across the planet, not only in the west of the West, whereby connection is the *modus vivendi*, evolving and transforming working practices. It would have surprised many people a decade ago that some of the most innovative changes in financial management, at least for ordinary people in the retail banking sphere, would have emerged out-of-Africa. Even so, the spread of wireless connectivity across that continent, leap-frogging many former communications technologies, has meant that mobile peer-to-peer transactions are more frequent in Lagos and Nairobi than they are in London and New York. Connecting in the age of integrality is key to understanding how evolving work will proceed in the coming decades.

So, how to summarise the complexity of the story-line presented in this book? We have circulated around the Four Worlds – with their distinctive Realms – and have explored the fourfold GENEalogy in each World of the four themes of: the *EMPLOYMENT OF COMMUNITY* (G/ S); *EMPLOYING SELF* (E/ E); *BEYOND EMPLOYMENT* (N/ N); and

Table 18.5 Conclusion: the ultimate evolution of work

	South	East	North	West
EMPLOYMENT OF COMMUNITY	Communal Identity	Emerging Reciprocity	Relational Paradigm	Intentional Community
EMPLOYING THE SELF	Self-Realisation	Spiritual House	Associative Enterprise	Building Cultural Capital
BEYOND EMPLOYMENT	Agape Economics	Circular Working	Redistributed Time	Socio-Technical Networking
INTEGRAL TOGETHER	Transformed Workplaces	Universal Welfare	Social Credit	Communi-preneurship

TRANSFORMING EMPLOYMENT (E/ W) (you might wish to look again at Table 1.2. of *Work GENEalogies*, in the Introductory chapter). But, if we take a diagonal look through each Part, of the larger GENE, we see one aspect of this unfolding story. It doesn't contain the entire narrative, which is developed through all the chapters. But, it does give one way of summarising the transformative, integral dynamic of evolving work.

An oblique look at evolving work

In Table 18.5 we provide an oblique summary of the ultimate evolution of work. This can, of course, be read horizontally, along the rows, to consider how the *Employment of Community*, and so on, is evolving. Equally, it can be read vertically, down the columns, to appreciate how each of the Four Realms is contributing to this evolution. In what follows, space only allows us to suggest some ways of reading across the rows. You will need to read down the columns for yourself. But, hopefully, the preceding summaries will enable you to do that, in the integrality interactive way of today's world.

It is vital, nevertheless, to bear in mind, throughout, that the integral and dynamic model, upon which this entire book has been based, indicates that embodying integral development, or specifically integral work in this case, only occurs as all stages and points are connected. Fortunately, as we have attempted to show, in the enormously complex world about us, the surface of which can hardly be scratched in a multiple series of books, these connections *are* all being made – in this *age of integrality*.

The evolving storyline

Evolving the employment of community

The lamented loss of community in the second half of the 20th century spawned a plethora of community studies and romantic portraits of a lost world. These were, often, of either agriculture-based or working-class localities that were being torn apart by the forces that came to be understood as globalisation and industrial restructuring. But, in fact, many localities, tribal regions and economic eco-systems have proved to be far more resilient and solidary, and have been rediscovering their identities.

One of the most powerful drivers for such a reemergence of community – as reality rather than rhetorical idyll – has been patterns and systems of reciprocity and gift relationships. These stretch far beyond family and clan to encompass many complex patterns of sharing, as a Southern way of addressing evolving prosperity through work. Reciprocity is the Southern economic system that impacts the evolution of work, which emerges out of a relational paradigm. The effect is to generate intentional communities, such as *Chinyika, Fecofun, Co-operativo Mondragon* or the *Women's Communes of Rojava*. Each of these, together with many others, illustrate how the employment of community is evolving.

Evolving employing the self

The Self has been disintegrating under the conditions of postmodernity and, indeed, in the current age of integrality. Arguably, however, the connectedness of the hyper-digital age is enabling some new aspects of self-realisation, as vocation is understood in relation to service of others and, indeed, for some of a 'higher purpose' or God. The ways in which we connect, through work, can have a dark and fragmenting aspect. But, equally, they reveal new ways of discovering our place in a connected world, what might be termed a 'spiritual house', if spirituality is understood, outside religion and, even, Faith, to be that which sustains the human spirit in the midst of life's changes.

Connected Selves are more easily part of associative enterprises. As we write, news has been breaking of one of the UK's most iconic brands, now part of a global corporation, (*Colmans*, within *Unilever*) closing its factories, with 150 years' heritage, in Norwich, UK. But, one of the most intriguing features of the story, despite the tragedy of capital flight, is how pressure is mounting on Capital and employers to rehome workers and how employees, themselves, are refusing to simply accept the demise of work, because of their connectedness. *Colmans of Norwich* is not simply a mustard manufacturer but a repository of cultural capital. And it is the impact of work and employment on multiple capitals that is at the heart of evolving the employment of Self. *Spiritual economics* is the missing system in much theory, as the book following this one in our series will seek to demonstrate. But, cases such as *Divine Chocolate*, the *John Lewis Partnership* model of worker-ownership, *Sekem*, in the Egyptian desert, and *Sarvodaya*, in Sri Lanka each demonstrate that evolving the employment of Self is transformative for enterprise.

Evolving beyond employment

It might have appeared that discussing love within the context of economics and integral development was completely out of place. But, the experience of agape economics in Latin America, particularly, as a way of seeking liberation and defiance against repressive and, indeed, violent oppressive landowners has been transformative. Love is tough in the sphere of work. Equally, it points the way towards quite revolutionary ways of transforming modes of production, such as the circular working of Ellen MacArthur's economic model, in which reuse of materials and resources is built-in, by design. This is based on love of people, the planet and the purpose of prospering society beyond employment, even within a system of generating profit.

For very considerable numbers of people, however, former patterns of employment, under conditions of an 'automatic society', will simply disappear. This requires a redistribution of time and money. The otium of the people, wherein work and recreation, within knowledge-based economies, are interpenetrated, is fast becoming a reality and will be one of the most significant challenges and possibilities for the mid-21st century. Companies such as *Veja*, *Under Armour*, the *Ellen MacArthur Foundation*, *Wikipedia* and *Alexander Mann Solutions* are harbingers of this evolution beyond employment, through socio-technical networking.

Evolving integrality in the sphere of work

Even a decade ago the practices of crypto-currency and the blockchain were hardly known about. Now, they remain somewhat mysterious and shadowy, albeit having direct impact on the lives of many millions. In fact, the algorithms that underpin the technologies of distributive information systems are influencing the lives of billions, in both social media and financial markets. Even so, there are emergent and genuine possibilities that are predicated by the blockchain that are already beginning to alter political, market and enterprise systems, in every one of the Four Worlds. Some of the most obvious effects are in transformed patterns of working and workplaces, where the boundaries between workplace and life-place are dissolving.

Such changes and many others, as yet hardly enacted, will mean that one-third to one-half of all current jobs will disappear or be transformed beyond recognition. This will require society to consider new ways of resourcing everyday life. The numbers of state and municipal experiments with UBI (Universal Basic Income) and Social Credit are accelerating apace. But these are only the start of processes that will transform work, and our understanding of patterns of life through this century, especially as climate change and ecological threats mount. Even so, we concluded with a case of integral finance in Nigeria that pointed some ways ahead, in employing self and community, integrally. The authors of that practical case describe it as 'communi-preneurship', or the employment of self and community for the common virtue.

This is as good a place as any to conclude our story. We trust, also, that you may be able to produce your own commentaries on evolving work, from the previous chapters and cases. As we go forward further, evolving work in and through the age of integrality, in the south and the east, the north and the west, we feel sure that the principles of integral economics, development, research and innovation will further point to the evolution of Self and Community, impacting work and employment. Equally, we see that much of this evolution will occur through an ever-deepening recognition of the place of culture and spirituality in the reconstruction of economic systems. But, that is another story for another time.

Index

Note: Page numbers in *italic* indicate a figure and page numbers in **bold** indicate a table on the corresponding page.

263–266; on national dividend 244;
on social credit/finance 261–262
Downs, A. 126, 176
draft mining scheme 250–251
drama, for women's self-expression
30–31
Dreamstreets (Yallop) 111
driven-based capitalism 193
dunamis 197, 198–199
Durkheim, E. 62, 64, 201

"*Eastern" Holistic Reality*, overview
6, 10
economic democracy 247–248,
267–270
economic development, stages of 261
economic ethos 167–168
economic growth, forced 265
economic performance 130
economic rehabilitation 266–270
economics, gifts in **133**, 133–134
economics, of association 132
Economics of Good and Evil
(Sedlacek) 167
economy of contribution 182
edenic economy 116
education program, at Sarvodaya 151
effect, as transformative 8
egolessness, Buddhism and 149–150
Eisenstein, C. 36, 37–39, 49
Elkington, J. 154
emergent awakening consciousness 7–8
Employee Ownership Association
119–121
employing community: in Chinyika
28–32, 297–298; community
activation 19–20; confederal
association and 299–300, **300**;
evolving **10**, **310**, 310–311; *Habitat
for Humanity* and. *see Habitat for
Humanity*; meaning of community
20–22; overview of 9–10; St Luke's
Gospel and 22–24
employment: beyond 11, **310**, 312;
circular economy and 185–186;
of community. *see* employing
community; end of 199–202; of self.
see self-employment; transformation
of 11–12; work instead of 195–196
energy 197–201
Engels, F. 181, 285
enterprise, ancient scriptures and 13
entrepreneurship 290–291

environmental philosophy/movement
102–103, 178–184
ethical egoism 302, **303**
European individuation 183
Everledger 236
Evernym 241
evolving work **310**, 310–311

fair trade 103–106
faith: enrichment of *282, 283*–284;
through sanctuary *278, 279*
family benefits, work-based 112–113
farming, human-machine interface in
205
FarmShare 236–237
*Federation of Community Forestry
Users Nepal* (FECOFUN) 47–50
feeding of the 5000 gospel story
242–243
Feldman, D.C. 94
Filangieri, G. 43
finger millet 25, 28
Finland's UBI experiment 254
flexible working patterns 112–113
Florensky, P. 99
Foltz, B. 91, 97–103
food security, in Chinyika 30–31
Ford, H. 246
formalist approach, to relational
sociology 62–63
fractional reserve banking, artifice
of 258
Franklin, B. 245
Free Men and Free Markets (Theobold)
244
Friedman, G. 196
Friedman, M. 244
Fruit and Veg City Limited 287
Fuller, L. 32–33
Fuller, M. 32–33
functionalism, relational sociology
and 64
functional stupidity 193

Gaitskill, H. 271
Galasso, N. 146
Galbraith, J.K. 245
Gardner, K. 127
gender balance 50
GENE-ius (Grounding, Emergence,
Navigation & Effect), introduction
to 5, 7–8
Genovesi, A. 43, 226

*For Product Safety Concerns and Information please contact
our EU representative GPSR@taylorandfrancis.com Taylor & Francis
Verlag GmbH, Kaufingerstraße 24, 80331 München, Germany*

T - #0086 - 160425 - C0 - 234/156/18 - PB - 9780367517274 - Gloss Lamination